NEW SOUTH AFRICAN REVIEW **6**

THE CRISIS OF INEQUALITY

NEW SOUTH AFRICAN REVIEW 6

THE CRISIS OF INEQUALITY

EDITED BY GILBERT M KHADIAGALA, SARAH MOSOETSA, DEVAN PILLAY AND ROGER SOUTHALL

WITS UNIVERSITY PRESS

Published in South Africa by:

Wits University Press
1 Jan Smuts Avenue
Johannesburg 2001

www.witspress.co.za

Published edition © Wits University Press 2018
Compilation © Edition editors 2018
Chapters © Individual contributors 2018
Cover photograph: Bloubosrand Kya Sands © Johnny Miller

First published 2018

http://dx.doi.org.10.18772/22018010558

ISBN 978-1-77614-055-8 (Print)
ISBN 978-1-77614-098-5 (PDF)
ISBN 978-1-77614-099-2 (EPUB)

Edited by Monica Seeber
Project managed by Hazel Cuthbertson
Indexed by Mirié van Rooyen
Cover designed by Hothouse South Africa
Typeset by MPS

Contents

List of tables and figures

TABLES

FIGURES

The global crisis of inequality and its South African manifestations

Devan Pillay

We are, once again, in world history, approaching an age of extremes, as the global crisis of accumulation approaches its social and ecological limits, generating huge inequalities last seen in the nineteenth century (Piketty 2014). This has resulted in increasing crises of political legitimacy in various countries and regions; the rise of populist leaders such as Donald Trump, the new president of the USA; and the decision by British voters (by a small majority) to leave the European Union. To a large extent the Right had successfully blamed immigration for rising unemployment, eclipsing the Left's traditional focus on class inequality with a stronger emotional appeal of identity politics – in particular race, ethnicity and/or religion. The rise of religious fundamentalism – whether Christian, Hindu, Buddhist or Islamic – has reached alarming proportions in parts of the world. However, while recent elections in other major developed countries such as France and Germany reveal a rise in support for anti-immigration (and, indeed, neofascist) parties, a class politics seems to have resonance, particularly among younger voters. The Left has seen increased support in countries like Greece and Spain, and in the rise of Bernie Sanders in the USA, as well as Jeremy Corbyn as leader of the UK Labour Party.

South Africa is a microcosm, with its own unique features, of this global socio-economic and political crisis. Our colonial-apartheid past generated distinct racialised and gendered forms of inequality and poverty, but a rising black elite since 1994 reveals that at a fundamental level inequality is based on class conflict – namely, the determination of the rich and powerful to maintain their privileges, against the struggles of the poor and excluded to obtain a share of the social surplus. The characterisation of our political economy as one that is dominated by 'white monopoly capital' is analytically weak in that it directs social inquiry, politics and policy towards the *racial content* of capital and class domination, rather than class domination itself. Indeed, politically charged assertions about 'white monopoly capitalism' are inclined to exaggerate the extent of white control of the economy, and downplay increased black participation. President Jacob Zuma's assertion that only 3 per cent of the Johannesburg Stock Exchange (JSE) is owned by black people, contradicts research commissioned by the JSE in December 2013 that black people own 23 per cent of the Top 100 companies listed; white South Africans own 22 per cent; foreign investors hold about 39 per cent of shares on the JSE, with a further 16 per cent an unclear mix of shareholder demographics (Hogg 2015). While exact ownership figures remain an issue of dispute, few would disagree that ownership of shares does not necessarily translate into control of companies, and this requires further research. The '3 per cent' is nevertheless repeatedly cited on the ANN7 TV channel owned by the Gupta family, who have been waging a fight-back against charges that, through the president, they have been trying to capture the state.

In other words, if 'white monopoly capitalism' is the problem, is 'black monopoly capitalism' the solution, at least in the short to medium term? Certain elite interests might privately mutter 'yes', whereas those on the Left, like the National Union of Metalworkers of SA (Numsa) may find themselves serving a black elite agenda as they seek an 'authentic nationalism' in the short to medium term (or 'first stage' of the 'national democratic revolution').[1] The socialist 'second stage', of course, may never arrive, as new elites consolidate their power, both against the older white elites and against the working class and poor. It is the story of most national liberation movements throughout the postcolonial world.

A sociological analysis of class domination, following Miliband (1987), reveals a *combination* of private economic elites *and* state elites, including those at the helm of vast state-owned enterprises. In South Africa the former may be predominantly white, and the latter predominantly black, but they both constitute *one* power elite, even if they are often in fierce competition with each other (Southall 2013). As the core of the dominant class, they stand together in objective conflict with the rest of society, in particular the working class (broadly defined, including the unemployed).

While this class conflict manifests itself in a range of social struggles for resources within communities, as the poor struggle for basic amenities, it is most apparent in workplaces, as workers strive to increase their share of the surplus produced, while employers, in general, seek to pay as little as they can get away with. Business and state elites also have an objective interest in keeping corporate and personal taxes as low as possible, thus ensuring that they consume most of the social surplus. As social inequality (or relative deprivation) increases, so does conflict, leading to greater social and political instability. Declining political legitimacy of the ruling class often results in short-term concessions (such as increased taxation to fund an increased social wage and socially protective legislation) in an effort to maintain the hegemony of the social order. However, the inherent accumulation crises of capitalism arising out of both social and ecological barriers to growth generate further counter-movements from above against such concessions, which in turn generate counter-movements from below. And so the pendulum swings.

THE GLOBAL DIMENSIONS OF INEQUALITY

Global capitalism in the neoliberal era is characterised by rising inequality, precarious work, unemployment, rural dispossession and widespread poverty (including the 'slummification' of cities). There have been periods, though, when these excesses were mitigated. The protective counter-movement of the post-World War eras, which saw a massive societal reaction to the devastation wrought by the 'self-regulated' market, had predominantly two outcomes: social democratic welfare economies and state-socialist (or statist) economies. Both acted decisively to subordinate the market to social need and to redistribute the social surplus more equitably (with varying degree of success). The state, acting on behalf of society, played a critical role in taming or severely constraining private capital. In addition, many developing countries implemented various types of 'developmentalist' policies that also saw the state intervening significantly in the economy, also with varying degrees of success.

While the social democratic countries tried to achieve equity within the context of democratic rights and freedoms, the statist economies (as well as many developmental economies) were authoritarian and denied most rights and freedoms to their citizens. Many developing countries also succumbed to the rule of predatory elites, who skimmed off the social surplus for their private benefit, the state itself becoming largely dysfunctional.

Most of these nation-state-based socio-economic practices were gradually swept away after the 1979 election of Margaret Thatcher as the UK prime minister, followed by that of Ronald Reagan as the US president. These political leaders, in response to the accumulation crisis of capitalism, ushered in the era of globalised market liberalisation often called neoliberalism. With the crisis of the Keynesian compromise during the 1970s (stagflation, rising unemployment, declining economic growth) and the excesses of authoritarian statism in the commandist economies,[2] the discourse of free market fundamentalism moved from the margins to the centre of public consideration. The 'socialist' alternative was largely delegitimised, initially in Western Europe and North America, but more widely after the fall of the Berlin Wall in 1989.

All these different types of economies had one common objective – economic growth at virtually any cost. The natural or ecological barriers to growth, which began to be considered in the 1970s as the oil crisis grew, were ignored when oil was discovered in the West, and the urgency to achieve economic growth gathered pace. Since then declining resources, including fossil fuels, accelerated, along with climate change and other environmental impacts that threaten future growth prospects as well as the survival of the planet as a liveable place for humans (and other species).

Under neoliberal capitalism, future growth is likely to be accelerated net 'jobless' or unemployment-generating growth as a result of increased automation,[3] in particular artificial intelligence, which is oriented towards maximising profit, and not meeting social needs (Hughes 2016). This is partly due to global competition spurring on innovation, and the financialisation of capitalism since 1980, as manufacturing profit rates declined and firms became more invested in a wide range of financial instruments (or what some call 'fictitious capital'). While financialisation led to the crisis which began in 2007, resulting in mainstream economists and world leaders questioning the neoliberal orthodoxy and even the growth paradigm itself, this did not result in a return to Keynesian policies, let alone 'degrowth' and redistribution of existing wealth in 'over-developed' countries, as some have argued (see D'Alisa et al. 2014). Instead, it soon became business as usual, as the banks were deemed too big to fail and, after receiving taxpayer support, bankers proceeded to award themselves massive bonuses. This has provoked the populist backlashes referred to above, with uncertain outcomes.

Capitalism, as many argue (see Harvey 2014), is unable to employ all workers in decent jobs. The International Labour Organization (ILO)'s promotion of decent work, while a laudable ideal, is unattainable except for a few insiders under an economic system where the fruits of new technology – the social surplus – are appropriated by a few. Instead of leading to fewer working hours, a higher social wage and increased leisure time for all, new technology, through the market mechanism, is oriented towards profit maximisation. Unfettered capitalism creates what Marx identified as two poles of attraction, one of increased wealth and consumption for a tiny minority, and the other of increased misery for the vast majority, as people lose their means of livelihood and places to live (the land), to eke out a living either as the working poor, or as the unemployed begging in the streets (or engaged in the criminal economy). As Oxfam (2016) has shown, the richest 1 per cent receives 14 per cent of global income, while the poorest 20 per cent receives just over 1 per cent. Even more startling, the richest sixty-two people in the world own as much wealth as the poorest 3.2 billion people. Over the past five years the richest sixty-two saw their wealth increase by 45 per cent, while the poorest half of the world population saw their wealth decrease by 38 per cent.

Global capitalism, however, has not only benefited a tiny 1 per cent (or, more accurately, less than 0.1 per cent, as the Credit Suisse Research Institute (2016) shows), but also a substantial new middle class in East Asia and India, as recent research has shown (Milanovic 2016). The promise of US protectionism to return jobs to the country is also a potential threat to the rising middle classes in the East. Thus, at Davos in January 2017 we witnessed the irony of the leader of a so-called communist country, China, extolling the virtues of economic globalisation, whereas the new leader of the capitalist 'free world' warned of its dangers to the US working class.

SOUTH AFRICAN MANIFESTATIONS OF INEQUALITY

Without attempting to be comprehensive, this volume looks at different ways in which social inequality is manifested in South Africa. Part 1 looks at the contours of inequality in racial, gender and class terms, but homes in on the manner in which the poor and working class experience inequality. As Neva Makgetla (Chapter 1) shows, South Africa is a microcosm of the global trends, and remains the most unequal country in world, with a Gini coefficient of 0.66. While the richest have become more racially representative, and state social grants and services have alleviated poverty among low-income groups, joblessness, pay scales and asset ownership have maintained the inequality gap. This is the outcome of a failure to prioritise job creation, livelihood strategies, more equitable workplaces and quality general education for the majority.

Jana Mudronova and Gilad Isaacs (Chapter 2) show that in 2014 the top 10 per cent of workers earned eighty-two times more than the bottom 10 per cent. Within that top 10 per cent are a few individuals who earn way more. For example, the recently retired chief executive officer (CEO) of Shoprite Checkers, Whitey Basson, earned around R100 million in 2016, which is over seven hundred times that of an average Shoprite worker (Cameron 2016). At the state level, new elites seem keen to be paid 'market-related' salaries, and at the state electricity utility Eskom the CEO earned a total of around R14 million in 2016 (Peyper 2016). Like sports stars who compare their ostentatious salaries with each other, state elites probably complain that they are underpaid vis-à-vis private sector CEOs like Basson (who in turn measure their remuneration against that of global elites paid in dollars).

While average real wages in South Africa have risen, this is misleading, as the average combines the excessive earnings at the top end, with the low earnings at the bottom. The median wage, which is the midpoint, has remained stagnant, according to Mudronova and Isaacs. Real monthly wages declined for 80 per cent of wage earners between 1997 and 2008, but they rose for the top 10 per cent. Meanwhile, 54 per cent of full-time wage earners (5.5 million workers) are regarded by some researchers as the 'working poor', below R4 200 a month. These are mostly black African (59 per cent) but a significant 22 per cent are white. The newly announced national minimum wage is set at a low R20 per hour (approximately R3 500 per month for a full-time worker), but according to the Minimum Wage Task Team, 47 per cent of all those with jobs (or 6.2 million workers) earn below that (Valodia 2017). The proposed minimum wage could thus lift incomes for a substantial number of workers (with some exemptions), without having a net negative impact on employment.

Wage earners in poor households support an average of 2.75 dependents (but often go up to 5 or more), according to Sarah Bracking (Chapter 3). Wage poverty is accompanied by high unemployment (approximately 35 per cent of the working age population) and the informalisation of work (more than one-third of those employed). The poorest 40 per cent of South African citizens rely heavily on social grants to merely survive.

Bracking assesses the politics of poverty statistics, which plays a critical role in public policy. A common refrain, coming from the World Bank and repeated locally by lobbyists like the Free Market Foundation and mainstream media such as *Business Day*, is that poverty has declined significantly since 1996. According to this view a net 3.6 million people, or more than 7 per cent of the population, have been 'lifted out of poverty' (see Woolard et al. 2015; World Bank 2011, 2014, 2016). Bond (2016: 3) argues the opposite: 'In fact many millions have been pushed down into poverty since 1994' owing to the neoliberal policies pursued by government on the advice of the Bank. Bond notes that the last poverty census was in 2011, and used the Bank's South African poverty line of US\$2.5/day, or R473 per person per month. By contrast, noted Bond, 'StatsSA found that food plus survival essentials cost R779/month that year, and the percentage of South Africans below that line was 53 per cent. University of Cape Town economists led by Josh Budlender argue that Stats SA was too conservative and the ratio of poor South Africans is actually 63 per cent' (2016: 3).

Bracking, in this volume, concurs with Bond, arguing that based on a R1 036 per person per month upper bound poverty line (which includes basic food and non-food items) well over 50 per cent of citizens (or 29.8 million) live in poverty. The much lower food poverty line of R445 per month places 12 million people with not enough to eat (classified as extremely poor).

Whichever way one looks at it, these basic indicators reveal a global and national social crisis. As the chapter by David Neves (Chapter 4) shows, workers are becoming increasingly indebted to meet basic needs or to buy a few luxury goods (or, for some, to maintain housing bonds). Servicing debt to loans sharks is a major factor in rising wage demands in the mining sector, leading to the crisis on platinum mines and the demand for R12 500 per month. The response of the state and employers resulted in the police fatally shooting thirty-four mineworkers in what is now known as the Marikana massacre – unprecedented since the 1922 white mineworkers' strike, when the Smuts government mowed down white workers.

Marikana revealed the nature of the power elite in South Africa – how the economic and state elites act together against workers who threaten their interests. While private capital continues to monopolise key sectors of the economy (including the food chain that contributes to a food sovereignty threat), the state is seen as an instrument of accumulation by aspirant elites using a corrupted state tender system. The 'Zupta' phenomenon – collusion between President Zuma and the Gupta family – is the most brazen case of state capture, with the aid of a range of other actors, including the so-called 'premier league' (composed of premiers in Mpumalanga, Free State, North West and KwaZulu-Natal provinces), the African National Congress Youth League (ANCYL), the African National Congress Women's League (ANCWL) and the Umkhonto we Sizwe (MK) veterans' association.

The post-apartheid wave of state patronage began when the policy of black economic empowerment under the Mandela and Mbeki presidencies degenerated into what some have labelled 'black elite enrichment'. The apartheid state was a site of immense patronage for white people, particularly Afrikaners, and the liberation elite seemed to say 'if you cannot beat the system, then join it'. With the fall of the Berlin Wall, and the apparent demise of 'socialism' as an achievable ideal, the new elites, who came into the country from exile with little capital of their own, seemed to be saying 'accumulate as much as possible in the shortest space of time, to catch up with or displace the white elite'. The 'Zuptas', as the public protector's State of Capture report suggests, have just been more brazen, and have taken corruption to another level, in keeping with the behaviour of liberation elites in many postcolonial countries. Corruption and incompetence at the local level, where party 'deployment' is rife, have reached epidemic proportions, and have denied poor people their rights to decent housing and basic services. It is here that the deceptive focus on 'white monopoly capital' as the source of all the country's ills is sharply exposed.

It is now widely recognised that, more than absolute poverty, increasing inequality, or relative deprivation, breeds conflict, both in society (for example, community protests about service delivery) and within the workplace, as the working and middle classes demand a greater share of the social surplus. The responses of the state and management often contribute to the conflict, Marikana being a vivid example, leading to periodic cycles of conflict that could spiral out of control. While some left-wing revolutionaries may desire a twentieth-century-type socialist seizure of state power, social instability in this century is just as likely to see either an authoritarian state crackdown (as in Egypt) or the tearing apart of the social fabric (as in Syria or Libya). Indeed, anti-immigrant pogroms are morbid symptoms of this social malaise, as communities, unable to reach the well-policed urban suburbs, or unable to identify the real sources of social inequality, turn their anger against vulnerable foreign residents eking out a living in their midst, as happened in Johannesburg in 2008.

Part 2 deals with different political responses to inequality. Samuel Ojo Oloruntoba (Chapter 5) argues that the manner in which liberal democracy has been implemented in recent decades, often tied to loan conditionalities in developing countries, has made it inseparable from neoliberal economic prescriptions. Using Nigeria and South Africa as case studies, he argues that indigenous practices of democratic rule were discarded in favour of Western parliamentary democracy, and neoliberal policies widened inequalities. Hence, if liberal democracy is to have a future it will have to foster an inclusive society. This requires both effective states and active citizens.

While Oloruntoba leaves open the question of whether multiparty liberal democracy is the best system of government to achieve equitable growth, Daryl Glaser (Chapter 6) makes a strong argument *for* an egalitarian liberalism. In other words, the baby of liberal freedoms need not be thrown out with the bathwater of neoliberal economics. Instead, legitimate concerns about individual freedoms need to be addressed, and at the same time collective goals such as wealth redistribution for all need to be pursued. He warns against the reification of inter-group equalisation, which often courts the danger of increasing intra-group inequalities – as has occurred with the deracialising of the upper classes in South Africa.

In his contribution, Roger Southall (Chapter 7) picks up the theme of popular revolution, which can either usher in tyranny or be genuinely transforming. He is sceptical as to whether reparations by the beneficiaries of apartheid to compensate those who suffered under it are viable, except in specific cases where reparations target clearly identifiable perpetrators (such as mining companies whose employed workers contracted occupational lung disease). Instead, he favours redistributive measures that target the wealthy through higher taxes, and argues for a paradigm shift where hard questions are asked about current growth trajectories that do not spread the wealth. Indeed, these questions are being asked with greater urgency by workers going on strike for higher wages, and students demanding free (or 'decommodified') education for all.

Student protests for free higher education grabbed the centre stage during the latter months of 2015 and 2016, raising concerns about the state's spending priorities. While it is widely acknowledged that universities are underfunded, resulting in higher fees which mean financial hardships for many students, the key battleground is over education that is universally free or free only for those who are in financial need. A universal model funded partially by higher taxation for the rich, and shifting spending priorities, has the virtue of taking away the stigma attached to applying for financial assistance. However, should university students receive priority over other social needs or indeed other educational needs such as basic education – including the critically underfunded pre-primary schooling, which lays the foundation for a child's development? Other concerns include the danger of state interference in higher education if it is the only source of funding. These vexing questions – about what is likely to remain a hot issue for some time – are addressed in differing ways in Part 3 by Stephanie Allais (Chapter 8) and Enver Motala, Salim Vally and Rasigan Maharajh (Chapter 9).

Jacqui Ala and David Black (Chapter 10) make a strong argument for a neglected social group that is unable to assert its power as much as university students – the disabled. They argue that the 'social democratic' principles that seemingly undergird national policy are contradicted by neoliberal economic trajectories. The human rights and social justice development framework has been rendered ineffective, but Ala and Black take comfort in increased high-level signs that government wants to renew its commitment to greater equality for disabled people. Finally, Doreen Atkinson (Chapter 11) ends this section with a fascinating look into the changing patterns of social stratification in Karoo towns. She identifies four new social categories: local coloured and black political elites, young (mainly black) adult professionals, elderly (mainly white) investors starting niche cottage industries, and vulnerable people of all races falling into poverty traps.

In Part 4, the four papers explore how inequality shapes and is shaped by very different aspects pertaining to land and environment. Samuel Kariuki (Chapter 12) calls for the 'spatial defragmentation' of apartheid geography which has seen the overwhelming domination of land ownership by whites and of agriculture by vast corporate enterprises. Although 20 per cent of commercial farms produce as much as 80 per cent of the value of agricultural production, this is less a contribution to food security than a reflection of the sector's increasingly inequitable nature. If government policy is properly implemented, he argues, there would be effective development, participation and competition of small-holder producers.

The startling inequality found in South Africa's countryside is further explored by Sonwabile Mnwana (Chapter 13). That the overwhelming majority of the 14 million South Africans who live in 'communal areas' exist in desperate poverty is well known. Mnwana points out, however, that intra-rural inequality is less explored. His chapter offers a highly nuanced ethnographic study of how the expansion of the platinum industry in the north-west of the country is leading to new struggles over land and mining revenues.

The growth of resistance to inequality, in its guise as environmental injustice, is the focus of the chapter by Jacklyn Cock (Chapter 14). Environmental inequality and injustice have the most dramatic impact upon the poor, in the forms of toxic pollution and lack of access to critical resources – not only land, but also nutritious food, clean water and affordable energy. However, although environmental injustice and inequality are deepening in post-apartheid South Africa, we have yet to see the emergence of a strong, mass-based environmental movement. Cock's chapter explores a host of local initiatives which she is hopeful may yet cohere into a unified, mass-based environmental justice movement to drive an ecological transition.

In the final chapter, Jo-Ansie van Wyk (Chapter 15) shines a light on how South Africa's 'nuclear geographies' have contributed to class and racial inequalities. Although the African National Congress (ANC) has been historically opposed to it, the government is presently gearing up for its largest-ever expansion of nuclear energy. Van Wyk argues that this will not only add new nuclear sites to those existing at Koeberg, Pelindaba and Vaalputs, but will deepen inequalities across the five dimensions of nuclear geography.

The chapters in this volume contribute greatly to our understanding of social inequality in South Africa. While the country has its unique features, even allowing for debate about whether the depth of poverty has increased or decreased, in general it follows the pattern of increasing global inequality. The politicisation of race as a defining feature of inequality continues, and is likely to increase. Black nationalist assertions, prominent in the late 1960s and 1970s, but displaced by the nonracialism of the ANC and its allies, has re-emerged within the FeesMustFall student movement, as well as in offshoots of the ANC such as the Economic Freedom Fighters (EFF). The discourse around 'white monopoly capitalism', while used opportunistically by the 'Zuptas' to deflect attention away from allegations of state capture, is widespread. It is an attempt to capture the simultaneity of racial oppression and class exploitation, but for trade unions such as Numsa such a formulation gives greater weight to issues of race than its traditional emphasis on class domination.

While the 'intersectional' character of social inequality – the intertwined expressions of race, class, gender, sexuality, disability and culture (including religion) – is undeniable, and each manifestation of inequality requires its own policy responses, it is important to see the wood for the trees: that is, there is a profound distinction between the politically *dominant* contradiction under apartheid (which was racial oppression) and the *primary* contradiction under capitalism, which was (and remains) *class* exploitation (or as Miliband (1987) would have it, class domination). When South Africa's patterns of inequality are compared to those of global inequality, generated by unfettered global corporate power, the primacy of class domination becomes more apparent.

NOTES

1   See this extraordinary clause in the Declaration from Numsa's 2016 congress: 'If the aspirant native African industrial capitalist class takes leadership of the mass discontent, then South Africa is likely to adopt the same trajectory as India in the 1970s, and posit an *authentic* nationalist solution' [emphasis added].

2   The term 'commandist' is used to avoid the controversy around the meaning of 'socialist', and the character of the Soviet economies, which some describe as statist, state-capitalist or state-socialist. For democratic socialists the term 'socialism' is used to describe the subordination of both the state and market to society (or the people).

3   The term 'jobless growth' is in popular usage among critics of neoliberal globalisation, and refers to net job loss. While new technology creates new, often high tech jobs, it has generally not created as many formal jobs as it has replaced, and this trend is likely to accelerate with increased use of artificial intelligence, resulting in the trend towards increasing global unemployment (at least in terms of decent, full-time jobs) (ILO 2016).

REFERENCES

Bond, P (2016) The harsh realities about South Africa that the World Bank dare not speak. *The Conversation*, 16 February.

Cameron, J (2016) Whitey Basson's whopping bonus: Shoprite CEO scores quick R50m. http://www.biz-news.com/sa-investing/2016/10/03/whitey-bassons-whopping-bonusshoprite-ceo-scores-quick-r50m/.

Credit Suisse Research Institute (2016) *The global wealth pyramid 2016*. Zurich: Credit Suisse.

D'Alisa, G, Demaria, F and Kallis, G (eds) (2014) *Degrowth: A vocabulary for a new era*. London: Routledge.

Harvey, D (2014) *Seventeen contradictions and the end of capitalism*. Oxford: Oxford University Press.

Hogg, A (2015) Updated: JSE say blacks own at least 23% of SA equities – not 3% Mr Zuma. http://www.biznews.com/undictated/2015/02/20.

Hughes, B (2016) *The bleeding edge: Why technology turns toxic in an unequal world*. Oxford: New Internationalist Publications.

ILO (International Labour Organisation) (2016) Global unemployment projected to rise in both 2016 and 2017. http://www.ilo.org/global/about-theilo/newsroom/news/WCMS_443500/lang--en/index.htm.

Milanovic, B (2016) Why the global 1% and the Asian middle class have gained the most from globalization. *Harvard Business Review*, 13 May.

Miliband, R (1987) Class analysis. In A Giddens and J Turner (eds) *Social theory today*. Stanford: Stanford University Press.

Numsa (National Union of Metalworkers) (2016) *Congress declaration, Numsa 10th National Congress*, 12–15 December, Cape Town.

Oxfam (2016) An economy for the 1%: How privilege and power in the economy drive extreme inequality and how this can be stopped. *Oxfam Briefing Paper*, 18 January.

Peyper, L (2016) No raise on top of Eskom boss Brian Molefe's R9.4m salary. http://www.fin24.com/Economy/Eskom/no-raise-on-top-of-eskom-boss-brian-molefes-r94msalary-20161021.

Piketty, T (2014) *Capital in the twenty-first century*. Cambridge, MA: The Belknap Press.

Southall, R (2013) The power elite in democratic South Africa: Race and class in a fractured society. In J Daniel, P Naidoo, D Pillay and R Southall (eds) *New South African review 3: The second phase – tragedy or farce?* Johannesburg: Wits University Press. pp. 17–38.

Valodia, I (2017) Op-Ed: Sorry, wrong number! A reply to Dave Kaplan. *Daily Maverick*, 9 January.

Woolard, I., Metz, R, Inchauste, G, Lustig, N, Maboshe, M and Purfield, C (2015) How much is inequality reduced by progressive taxation and government spending? *Econ3x3*, 28 October.

World Bank (2011) *The changing wealth of nations*. Washington, DC: World Bank.

World Bank (2014) Fiscal policy and redistribution in an unequal society: South Africa. *Economic update 6*. Washington, DC: World Bank.

World Bank (2016) *South African poverty and inequality assessment*. Draft discussion note. Pretoria: World Bank.

INEQUALITY AND CLASS: POLARITIES AND POLICIES

1

Inequality in South Africa

Neva Makgetla

More than two decades after its transition to democracy, South Africa has remained one of the most unequal countries in the world.[1] The question is why this situation has persisted despite the elimination of apartheid laws and the establishment of one of the world's largest redistributive programmes.

To answer that question, this chapter first reviews measures of income inequality in South Africa overall and then by race, gender and location. The second section explores persistent inequalities in income from economic activity, while the third assesses the impact of state efforts to redress them.

High joblessness and unusual inequalities in earned incomes and asset ownership gave rise to South Africa's unusual inequality. State programmes focused on improving state services for the poor rather than restructuring the institutions that sustained exclusionary economic systems. In particular, economic programmes did not prioritise job creation, livelihood strategies for the jobless, more equitable workplaces or quality general education for the majority of children.

THE DISTRIBUTION OF INCOME

The core measure of inequality in any society centres on class differences, reflected in the distribution of income. In South Africa in 2016, economic inequality still largely tracked race, gender and location, although with the end of apartheid the first two gradually became less determinant.

The overall distribution of income

Most studies found that South Africa ranked poorly, often worst, among countries that reported on economic inequality. It had the highest Gini coefficient reported in the World Bank's World Development Indicators from 2006 to 2014 (the higher the Gini, the greater the income inequality).[2] Excluding South Africa, the average Gini coefficient for the reporting countries, weighted by population, was 39; for South Africa it was 63. Although the data on Gini coefficients were at best indicative, there is no question that in the 2010s inequality in South Africa ranked among the worst in the world. The poorest 10 per cent of households earned under R10 000 a year in 2015. The richest 10 per cent earned over R265 000 a year. According to tax data, in 2014 the richest 4 per cent of individuals earned over R750 000 a year (calculated from SARS 2016a).

Income tax data further underscored the extent of income inequality. In 2014, the richest 9 per cent of individuals accounted for 41 per cent of income tax payments (SARS 2016a). At the other end of the scale, as detailed below, only around 40 per cent of working age adults had any earned income at all, compared to the international norm of around 60 per cent.

South Africa achieved the dubious distinction of world-class inequality under apartheid. It was impossible to determine whether inequality improved or worsened after 1994 because data from the 1990s was highly unreliable.[3] But it is clear that the income distribution did not improve significantly in the first two decades of democracy.

Inequality by race and gender

Inequality under apartheid was virtually synonymous with race and gender. With the elimination of overtly racist and gendered laws in the 1990s, these divisions became less decisive, although by no means did they disappear.

Inequality by race

In 2015, the median household income still varied sharply with race. For Africans it was R2 900 a month, compared to R5 700 for coloureds and Asians and over R20 000 for whites. Just over a quarter of coloureds and Asians and fewer than one in ten white households lived on R2 900 a month, compared to half of Africans.

While economic inequality continued largely to track race, the richest group became somewhat more representative, although black people were still under-represented. According to the 2015 General Household Survey, almost 40 per cent of the richest 5 per cent of households were African, 14 per cent were coloured or Asian, and 48 per cent were white. In contrast, in the population as a whole, 82 per cent of households were African and only 9 per cent were white (Stats SA 2016a) The 2001 Census found that in the top 6 per cent of households, 26 per cent were African and 17 per cent were coloured or Asian, whereas 57 per cent were white.

These findings pointed to a significant improvement in representivity, although they were not fully comparable with the 2015 figures.[4] Reliable data is not available for the 1990s. The 1996 Census did not include income at all while the October Household Surveys had, at best, incomplete information.[5]

Gender inequality

Inequality by gender is difficult to measure at the household level because many women do not share equally in household prosperity. This section therefore analyses earnings for individuals by gender. It also assesses the position of 'woman-headed' households – essentially single-parent households. This type of household was far more common in South Africa than in other upper middle-income economies.

In 2015, women as a group were less likely to have paid employment than men, and to earn less than men if they did have paid employment. That said, African women faced the greatest disadvantage, while white women had more privileged positions than black men. In 2015, only one-third of black women were employed for pay, compared to two-fifths of black men and of white women, and two-thirds of white men. The median earnings for black women in paid employment were under R6 000 a month. For black men, they were close to R7 500 a month, while for white women, they were R20 000 a month and for white men, R28 000 (Stats SA 2016b).

Given low levels of paid employment and relatively poor pay, it was not surprising that black women were notably under-represented in the top decile of income earners. In 2015, African women made up 40 per cent of all working age people, but 33 per cent of

---

Figure 1.1: Working age population, employment and top earnings decile by race and gender, 2015

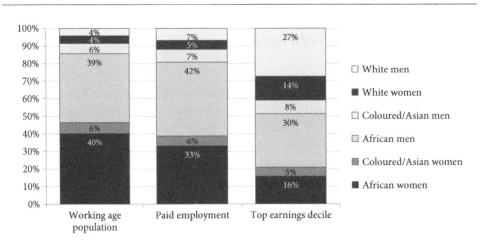

Source: Calculated from Stats SA (2016b).

all people with paid work and just 16 per cent of the top decile of wage earners. In contrast, African men also constituted around 40 per cent of the working age population, but 42 per cent of all those with paid work and 30 per cent of those in the top decile. White women and men constituted 4 per cent each of the working age population, but 14 per cent of earners in the top decile were white women, and 27 per cent were white men.

Although they earned less from economic activity, women were more likely than men to end up doing unpaid home and caring work. This was particularly visible in the case of single-parent households, which constituted the majority of households labelled 'woman-headed' in household surveys.[6]

South Africa had substantially more woman-headed families than is the norm for upper middle-income economies. For the seventy countries covered in the World Bank's Gender Statistics database, the average share in all households of woman-headed households, weighted by population size, was around 20 per cent, while it was 24 per cent for the African countries in the sample. In South Africa, the figure was over 40 per cent. That ranked it fifth among the sampled countries, after Ukraine, Swaziland, Zimbabwe and Namibia.

The relatively large share of single-parent households in South Africa arose primarily because of the persistence of circular migrant labour from the former so-called 'homelands', which in 2015 held around 28 per cent of all households. Some 54 per cent of all households in these regions were woman-headed. For the rest of the country the figure was 38 per cent.

In 2015, the median income for a woman-headed African household was under R2 500. For a 'man-headed' African household (a household managed either by a single father or heterosexual partnership), the median was almost R4 000; it was R17 000 for households headed by white women and over R35 000 for white men. The share of woman-headed households was largest from the third decile of households by income to the eighth decile. In this income group, the number of children per household was also relatively large.

Except in the best-off 20 per cent of households, woman-headed households typically had more children and elderly people than man-headed households, and fewer residents with paid employment. In 2015, half of African children, elderly people and working age women lived in woman-headed households, but only a third of men lived in woman-headed households. The figures for non-African households were closer to the international norm, with around a third of adult women living in woman-headed households.

Spatial inequality
The creation of labour reserves in the 'homelands' was central to apartheid. In 2015, these areas still held around a quarter of the population, down from over half in 1994, and were almost exclusively African. Continued deprivation in the 'homelands' was both a leading indication of economic inequality in South Africa and a cause of it.

The majority of people in the 'homelands' lived in Limpopo, KwaZulu-Natal, the Eastern Cape, the North West and Mpumalanga. Virtually none lived in the Western

Figure 1.2: Share of woman-headed households compared to share of employed and non-working age people by household income decile, 2015

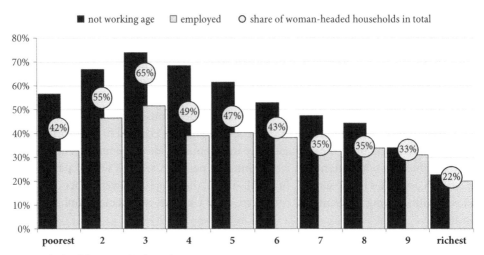

Source: Calculated from Stats SA (2016a).

Figure 1.3: Median household income in former 'homeland' and other regions, by province, 2015

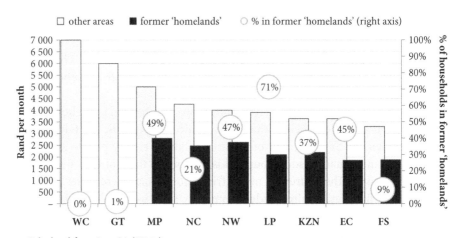

Source: Calculated from Stats SA (2016a).

Cape and Gauteng, the two richest provinces. In 2015, the median household income in the 'homelands' was R2 000 a month, compared to R4 050 in the rest of the country. Outside of the 'homelands', just over a quarter of households lived on R2 200 a month or less.

Figure 1.4: Share of households in former 'homeland' regions by decile, 2015

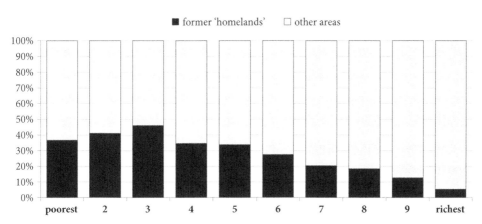

Source: Calculated from Stats SA (2016a).

The former 'homeland' regions held 28 per cent of all households, but only 5 per cent of those in the richest decile. They held 41 per cent of households in the poorest three deciles.

Overall, the situation in the former 'homelands' epitomised the congruity between class, race and gender inequality in South Africa, rooted in the fundamental deformation of the economy and society under apartheid. Being born in a former 'homeland' region in itself made a person much more likely to be African, to live in a single-parent household, to have very little in the way of assets, and to be poor. In contrast, by most measures of inequality the rest of South Africa came close to the norm for other upper middle-income economies.

Conclusions

The democratic state came to power with the expressed intention of establishing a more equitable and mobile society. Yet in 2016 South Africa remained one of the most unequal countries in the world. The available data indicated the following:
- Overall inequality in South Africa barely budged from 1994, although the data for the 1990s was too faulty to draw conclusions about minor changes either way.
- Representivity in the upper income group in terms of race and gender improved significantly from 1994 to 2015. Nonetheless, inequality still aligned largely with the apartheid categories.
- The population of the former 'homelands' fell from half to a quarter of the total population, but their deprivation remained a critical factor behind South Africa's unusually sharp inequalities.

Economists increasingly agree that inequality can itself initiate a vicious cycle by slowing growth, which in turn makes it harder to improve equality. In particular, it dampens demand for basic necessities, reduces productivity, and underpins unremitting contestation over policy and ownership, which in turn undermines economic stability (for instance, Ostry et al. 2014) In South Africa, unusually stark economic inequality had, by 2016, become an increasingly visible blockage to sustainable development.

INEQUALITY FROM THE ECONOMY

This section reviews the distribution of incomes from economic activity, before redistribution through the state. In South Africa, earned incomes were still unusually inequitable in 2017 because of the combination of extraordinarily high joblessness, especially in the former 'homelands', as well as highly differentiated pay scales and asset ownership.

Joblessness

From at least the 1980s, South Africa had low employment levels. The world norm for upper middle-income economies was that around 65 per cent of people of working age had paid employment of some kind.[7] In South Africa, the figure was far lower, hovering around 40 per cent. From 1994 to 2016 employment growth averaged around 2.3 per cent a year, generating some six million new jobs. That was sufficient to avoid an increase in the jobless rate, but not to overcome the historic gap in employment left by apartheid.

Unemployment was a central cause of inequality. Fewer than 40 per cent of all households in the poorest two quintiles earned any income at all from salaries or wages. If remittances and business income were to be included, around 70 per cent of these households had some kind of earned income, but it was typically precarious and low. In contrast, in the richest 20 per cent of households, over 95 per cent had some kind of earned income from employment or self-employment.

As the following graph shows, almost half of the poorest 40 per cent of households had no employed people at all, whether in wage work or self-employment. In contrast, the most prosperous 40 per cent of households had more than one income earner, and the richest decile had close to two. As a result, the poorest 40 per cent of households taken together had only slightly more jobs than the richest 10 per cent alone.

Joblessness aligned strongly with race and gender. In 2015, the employment ratio for African women was 35 per cent, for African men 44 per cent, for white women 55 per cent and for white men, 63 per cent. Joblessness was higher for Africans than for other groups at every education level.

Joblessness was substantially worse in the former 'homeland' regions, where only 24 per cent of working age people had employment, compared to 47 per cent in the rest of the country. Throughout the country, however, the richest 20 per cent of households averaged over 1.5 employed members.

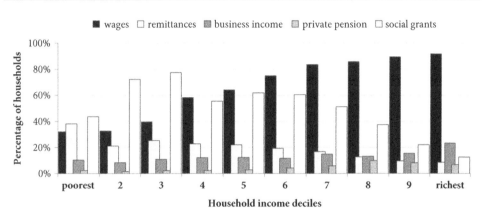

Figure 1.5: Household income sources by decile, 2015 (share of households reporting any income from each source)

Source: Calculated from Stats SA (2016a).

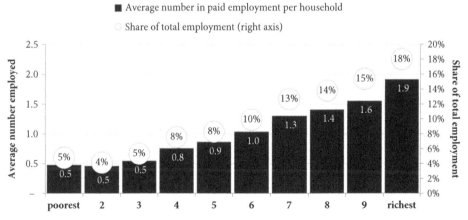

Figure 1.6: Average number of employed people per household and share of total employment by household income decile, 2015

Source: Calculated from Stats SA (2016a).

The employment data counts only resident income-earners, and may undercount migrant workers. Some 35 per cent of woman-headed households and 21 per cent of man-headed households in the former 'homelands' received remittances from non-resident family members. For the rest of the country, the figures were 24 per cent for woman-headed and 12 per cent for man-headed households. But remittances were typically far lower than earned incomes.

Figure 1.7: Share of working age adults employed, by sector, education, race and gender, 2015 (a)

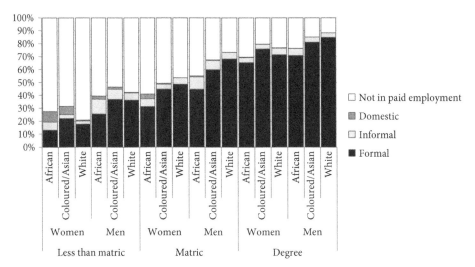

Note: (a) Includes any post-secondary diploma lasting longer than six months.
Source: Calculated from Stats SA (2016b).

In sum, the poorest households were disproportionately excluded from income-generating activity – whether employment or self-employment. That in itself constituted a critical factor behind unusually steep income inequality in South Africa.

Inequality in earned incomes

Even if they received some earned income, poor households typically had much lower and more precarious earnings. Unusually unequal earned incomes resulted from a combination of unequal wage scales and highly concentrated returns from assets.

Earnings from employment

By a variety of measures, the International Labour Organization (ILO) found that South Africa had among the most unequal systems of wages in the world (ILO 2016: 42). In the ILO's sample of large upper middle-income economies, the lowest-paid 50 per cent of workers earned around a quarter of all wage and salaries. In South Africa, they received around half of that. In other countries in the sample, the best-paid 1 per cent received less than 10 per cent of all wage income whereas in South Africa they received 20 per cent. Not surprisingly, the ILO's summary measure of inequality, the ratio of the tenth decile to the ninetieth decile of wage earners, was far higher in South Africa than in any of the comparator countries.

Figure 1.8: Median monthly wage or salary by race, gender, age group and education, 2015

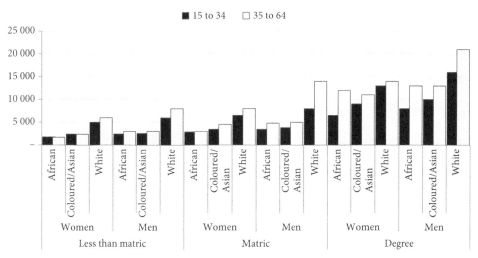

Source: Calculated from Stats SA (2016b).

Unequal pay scales translated into sharp differentiation in household earnings from work. In 2015, earned income for households with employed resident members ranged from R500 a month for the poorest decile to R5 000 a month for the seventh decile, then jumped to R40 000 for the richest 10 per cent of households. Income from remittances was R1 000 or less at every decile (Stats SA 2016a).

Median wages were highly unequal by race and gender. In 2015, the median wage for an African woman was R2 500, compared to R3 250 for an African man, R10 000 for a white woman and R13 000 for a white man. Inequalities in wages and salaries by race and gender appeared even for people of similar ages and education levels. For employed people, even taking age into account, the median pay for an African woman with a tertiary diploma or degree was lower than for a white man with matric only.

The median wage or salary in former 'homeland' areas was R2 000 a month, compared to R3 500 a month in other regions.

In short, poor households were not only less likely to find work but also more likely to earn very low pay if they did find it. In contrast, high-income households enjoyed both higher incomes from work and higher employment levels.

The distribution of assets
Unequal ownership of wealth is a key factor in sustaining economic inequality over generations. It provides a source of income to supplement wages; reduces the risk from job losses and other economic uncertainties; and enables families to invest more in education and healthcare. Unequal ownership of productive assets and household investments

Figure 1.9: Share of employers in total employment by decile, 2015

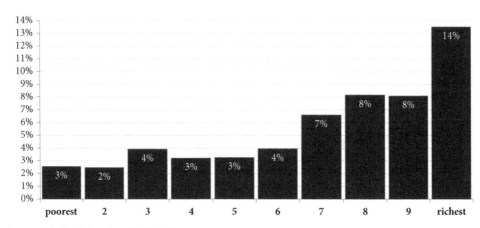

Source: Calculated from Stats SA (2016b).

was particularly pronounced in South Africa. The data on asset ownership was, however, uneven. The main available indicators were tax returns and survey data on income from assets and on business, home and land ownership.[8]

In 2014, over 550 000 companies were registered for tax. But 616 of those enterprises paid two-thirds of all company income tax (calculated from SARS 2016b: Table A3.3.1). Tax data also showed that the top 10 per cent of households controlled 95 per cent of personal assets (Orthofer 2016; also Mbewe and Woolard 2016).

Figures on employers – that is, business owners with at least one employee – from Statistics South Africa's Labour Market Dynamics survey provided some insight into the impact of unequal ownership. However, they were not comprehensive; above all, most productive assets were owned by listed companies, not individuals. Executives in these companies generally controlled their operations, but they would appear in surveys as employees, not employers. Furthermore, employers' income leaves out other income from asset ownership, especially from financial investments. In 2015, 780 000 people, or just over one in twenty of all employed people, were employers. In the richest decile, however, the figure rose to one in seven.

Income from business ownership was even more unequal than wages. The richest decile of employed people received just over half of all wages and salaries, but four-fifths of employers' income. In contrast, the poorest 40 per cent of employed people received almost no income from businesses.

Employers' earnings constituted almost one-fifth of all earnings for the top 10 per cent of income earners. For all other employed people, employers' earnings contributed just one-tenth of total earned income.

Figure 1.10: Share of different kinds of earned income by income groups for people with income-generating employment, 2015

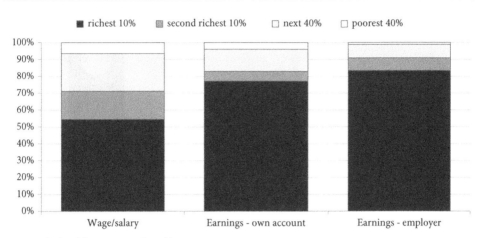

Source: Calculated from Stats SA (2016b).

Figure 1.11: Earnings by source and income group for people with paid employment, 2015

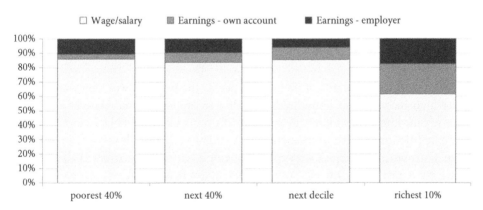

Source: Calculated from Stats SA (2016b).

The value of homes underscored the inequality in asset ownership. Two-thirds of South African households owned their homes in 2015, with a higher share of rentals in the richest quintile, in which the median home was worth R500 000 compared to a median value of around R50 000 for the poorest 80 per cent of homeowners.

Even at higher income levels, most black people, especially women, had less in the way of assets than whites, primarily because their families were unable to accumulate resources under apartheid. As a result, higher-income black households often struggled

Figure 1.12: Share of employers and working age population by race and median earnings of employers, 2015

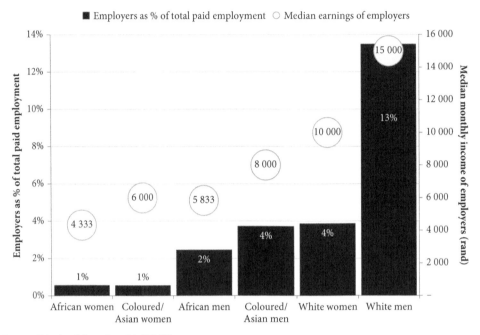

Source: Calculated from Stats SA (2016b).

to sustain the living standards of their white peers. The problem was aggravated by the fact that high-income black households often had to support poorer relatives.

At every income level whites were substantially more likely than blacks to be business owners. In 2015, one in five white men was an employer, as was almost one in ten white women. Only one in fifty black women was an employer. Three-quarters of all employed people were African, but only just over half of employers were African. Moreover, white business owners generally earned substantially more than black employers.

A similar pattern emerged for home ownership. In the top decile by income, nearly all white homeowners had a house worth over R500 000, compared to fewer than half of Africans. Only one in ten African homeowners in the richest decile owned a house worth over R1.5 million, compared to four out of ten white homeowners.

In terms of assets, the data on employers, housing and land underscore the continued disadvantages of residents in the former 'homelands'. The majority of employers in the 'homelands' were in the informal sector, with very limited assets. In 2015, 4.9 per cent of working age people were employers, compared with 5.3 per cent in the rest of the country – not a large difference, but the median income for all employers in the 'homelands' was R3 900 a month, less than half of the R8 000 median for those in the rest of the country. In other words, many of the employers in the 'homelands' clearly had only very limited productive assets.

This conclusion is underscored by limiting the analysis to formal employers. By this measure, the 'homelands' lagged well behind the rest of the country. In 2015, the former 'homelands' held 28 per cent of the working age population, 14 per cent of the formally employed, and just 6 per cent of formal employers. Outside of the former 'homelands', eighteen working age people out of a thousand were formal employers; inside them, the figure fell to just three, and the median income for formal employers was R8 000 a month, compared to R10 000 in other areas.

Housing showed similar disparities. In 2015 only around 10 per cent of homeowners in the former 'homelands' had houses worth over R250 000, compared to 40 per cent of homeowners in the rest of the country. At every income level, housing was worth less than in the rest of the country. That said, only around one household in seven at every income level rented; in the rest of the country, the figure rose from around half in the poorest 40 per cent of households to two-thirds in the richest decile.

Because the former 'homelands' regions were relatively rural, land ownership might be expected to contribute to asset ownership, but very few residents in these areas owned viable farms, although almost half of them did some gardening. In 2015, 45 per cent of households in these regions said they engaged in some agricultural activities, compared with 7 per cent in the rest of the country. Of households with agricultural activities, a mere 8 per cent saw farming as the main source of income or food – most simply did not have the land or other assets to do more. Around 800 000 households in the former 'homelands' owned the land they farmed, while another 435 000 worked communal land. But 90 per cent of landowners had plots of under 500 square metres.

Overall, inequality in business ownership was a key factor in high joblessness. The share of employers and self-employed people in the labour force in South Africa, at under 20 per cent, was around half of the norm for upper middle-income economies, excluding China. Among middle-income economies, although there were substantial fluctuations, countries with lower self-employment levels also tended to have lower employment ratios. Of the thirty-eight upper middle-income countries that provided data on self-employment levels (out of a total of fifty-seven), South Africa had the fifth lowest employment ratio and the third lowest level of self-employment (see World Bank Development Indicators, electronic database).

Historically, the shortfall in small business and self-employment in South Africa was a direct consequence of apartheid. To be brief and schematic, apartheid laws instituted the following:

- During apartheid, black people in general and Africans in particular were largely obstructed in conducting small-scale production and trade. They were prevented from owning most kinds of land (not only for farming but also for retail and industrial sites in economic centres); they had only limited access to credit; they often did not receive key infrastructure such as roads, electricity and piped water; and they faced myriad other state-run obstacles to economic activity.

- The suppression of small-scale black entrepreneurs was made possible in part by the strength of the mining sector. On the one hand, mining and (increasingly from 1994) the related financial sector tended to attract skilled people and to encourage contestation around the sharing of economic rents rather than investment in new kinds of production. On the other hand, mining laid the basis for a state industrialisation policy from the 1920s that generally focused support on large formal and energy-intensive ore and coal refineries and metals-based industries.
- Under apartheid, work organisation was broadly designed to generate incomes for owners and senior managers similar to those in Europe, in a pattern also visible in other highly unequal developing economies such as Brazil. Expectations of high incomes for owners and entrepreneurs have persisted into democracy. That leads to more risk aversion as well as lower investment and employment creation.

In effect, compared to other upper middle-income countries, democratic South Africa started out with a smaller class of established small-scale entrepreneurs who could build on long-standing family business assets, market connections and customers. The institutions to support small businesses (in general but especially for black South Africans) were variable and lacking in both the public and private sector. Large companies and government agencies often had procurement systems designed to acquire goods on a scale beyond the scope of small businesses; major providers of business services and credit focused on supporting existing and experienced clients; and emerging black entrepreneurs themselves rarely had social networks that could compensate for the lack of formal providers. In these circumstances, providing funds, land and mentorship without addressing the deficits in market institutions able to support small business often proved inadequate. In effect, a vicious cycle appeared: market institutions to serve small business did not emerge because there was no demand for their services – but small businesses could not emerge on a large scale in the absence of suitable systems for obtaining loans and training, access to inputs and outlets, and technological support and market information.

INEQUALITY AND THE STATE

After 1994, the democratic state initiated one of the largest redistributive programmes in the world. In 2011, according to estimates by Inchauste et al., these programmes reduced the Gini coefficient from around 0.77 before government taxes and spending to around 0.59, and cut the poverty rate from 46 per cent before state spending to 39 per cent after it – a substantially greater improvement in inequality and poverty than seen in peer economies (Inchauste et al. 2015: 31–2).

Nonetheless, the inequalities generated by South Africa's exclusive economy were far too steep to be overcome even by relatively large-scale government spending on services and social grants for poor households. The Gini coefficient for the primary distribution of income in South Africa, at 0.77, was around 40 per cent higher than that for the next most unequal country, Brazil. As a result, even after unusually extensive redistribution through the state, South Africa remained easily the most unequal country among a number of comparator countries (Inchauste et al. 2015: 31)

In contrast to the estimates of Inchauste et al., the figures usually used for international Gini comparisons do not capture the full effect of redistribution. Although they reflect cash transfers and taxes as part of income, they leave out transfers in kind through the provision of services.

This section outlines the impact on inequality of state programmes on education, social grants and household services, and the economy. It then assesses the fiscal constraints on further redistribution through state services.

Education

Education is critical for social mobility and equity. Apartheid educational restrictions essentially created a skills shortage so as to ensure higher pay for the few who could access a quality education. By extension, expanding quality education formed a critical step towards a more inclusive economy and a more equitable society.

In 2015, a good education, and in particular a tertiary degree or diploma, remained critical for getting a job and for higher pay. A person with post-secondary education was 25 per cent more likely to have a job than someone with matric only, and matric boosted the chance of employment by 18 per cent compared to those with less education. The median income for employed people with a tertiary diploma or degree was R11 000 a month, compared to R3 900 for someone with matric, and R2 000 for a worker with no more than primary education (Stats SA 2016b). Access to education remained highly unequal, however, which in itself reproduced inequality. In 2015, the best-off 15 per cent of schools – virtually all of them historically non-African although now mostly racially integrated – accounted for 30 per cent of university passes.[9] In contrast, the worst-off 25 per cent of schools, mostly located in former 'homelands', contributed just 15 per cent of all university passes. The richest 15 per cent of schools had an overall matric pass rate of over 90 per cent, with half getting university exemptions. In the poorest 25 per cent of schools, only 62 per cent of learners passed, and under one-fifth qualified for university (DBE 2016: 53).

The democratic state ended racial segregation and vastly improved resourcing and curricula in historically black schools. But it effectively allowed the semi-privatisation of quality schools and universities, which sustained inequalities in education. In particular:

- Students who lived near a school were assured places, which effectively guaranteed rich families access to quality suburban schools. Schools had the right to decide which students to admit from outside their catchment area, and in the process often relied on ability to pay as well as ethnic signifiers.

- Schools in richer communities were allowed to charge fees in exchange for lower state subsidies. Fee income was generally much higher than the foregone subsidies. As a result, schools in the suburbs remained far better resourced than no-fee schools, which made up around three-quarters of all schools. In themselves, the fees effectively excluded most low-income learners.
- Poor households ended up paying almost a year's income for each year of university – far more than many could afford.

This system led to persistent inequalities in school resourcing.

The average number of learners per educator in historically black schools, whether rural or urban, was thirty-two to one in the early 2010s. In historically white schools, most of which had been integrated by race, the figure was twenty-two to one (DBE 2016). Facilities showed similar inequalities. In 2011, almost half of schools did not meet national minimum standards, mostly because of inadequate classrooms. Around a tenth, virtually all of them in the former 'homelands', had no running water, with a similar figure for electricity. Four out of five formerly white schools had a library, compared with half of other urban schools and a fifth of schools in the former 'homelands' (DBE 2014: 21, Table 13; 45, Table 35). In addition to unequal access to quality education, relatively high fees for university limited access to tertiary education for poor students. Among all households with a university student, 40 per cent paid over R20 000 a year in fees, and 37 per cent paid over R8 000. Even the lower figure was equal to around a year's income for the poorest 10 per cent of households, although only about two weeks' pay for the top decile. Poor households paid for fees increasingly through loans, which added to their burden of stress and debt.

Figure 1.13: Fees paid by household income level and type of education, 2015

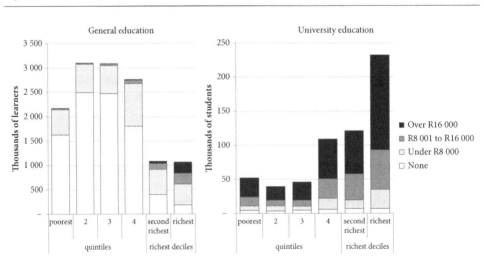

Source: Calculated from Stats SA (2016a).

Figure 1.14: Attendance by type of educational institution and income level, 2015

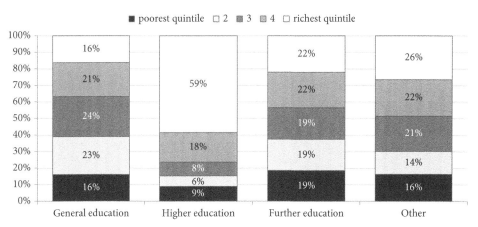

Source: Calculated from Stats SA (2016a).

The impact can be seen from the figures on university attendance by income level. For every thousand households in the poorest 60 per cent, only around forty-five people attended a tertiary institution in 2015. In the richest quintile, the figure climbed to 155 per thousand households, although these households had relatively few school-age members. Members of the richest quintile of households accounted for 59 per cent of all university students. In contrast, the richest quintile contributed just 16 per cent of learners in general education and 22 per cent of those in further education.

In short, education in South Africa continued to reproduce inequality after 1994, although with differences linked increasingly to class rather than race alone. Addressing this challenge would require far more rigorous efforts to ensure equitable access to a quality general education, as well as changes in the financing mechanisms for universities.

Social grants

In 2015, 16 million South Africans, or almost one in three, received some kind of social grant. People who could not physically work owing to age or disability and who earned less than R70 000 a year and had under a million rands in assets were entitled to a grant. The maximum old-age pension and disability pensions were pegged at just over R1 500 a month in 2015, while the child grant was R350. In 2015, child grants made up 70 per cent of all grants, old-age pensions 19 per cent, and disability grants 6 per cent.

In terms of the share of households affected, South Africa's income support programme was among the largest of upper middle-income economies. Almost 35 per cent of South African households received some kind of state transfer, compared to a weighted average of 15 per cent for peer economies (the other economies, of course, had a more equitable primary income distribution to start with).

Figure 1.15: Percentage of women and men who said they had received a cash transfer from the government in the preceding year in upper middle-income economies, 2014

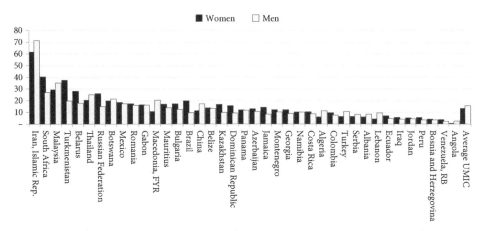

Source: Calculated from World Bank Gender Statistics database, series on received government transfer in the past year for women and men (www.worldbank.org, December 2016).

Figure 1.16: Number of people receiving grants per thousand households by household income quintile, 2015

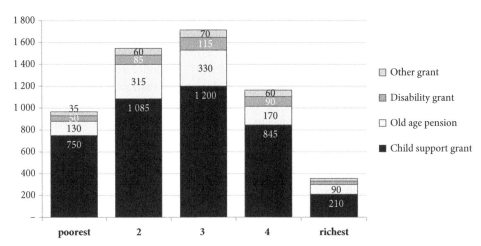

Source: Calculated from Stats SA (2015).

On average, South African households in the poorest 60 per cent received a child support grant, although the figure was lower for the poorest quintile. In contrast, the poorest quintile was much less likely to receive an old-age or disability pension than the next 40 per cent of households. In effect, the difference between destitution and ordinary poverty became access to paid work or to a social pension.

Figure 1.17: Estimated income from social grants per quintile, as percentage of median income per quintile and in rands, 2015

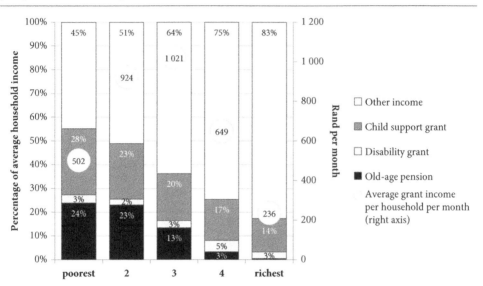

Source: Number of grants per household and median income calculated from Stats SA (2016a) electronic database. Average value of grant calculated from SASSA Annual Report 2015/16: 26, Tables 1 and 2.

Social grants accounted for around half of total income for the poorest 40 per cent of households. The impact per quintile in Figure 1.17 is estimated by comparing the average value of grants reported by the South African Social Security Agency (SASSA) with the findings from the General Household Survey on the median income per quintile and the average number of grant recipients.

Both the old-age and disability grants came close to the national and international poverty lines for a couple, while the child support grant would lift half a person out of poverty, using Statistics South Africa's food poverty line.[10] The World Bank's standard of US$1.90 a day leads to similar conclusions.

Housing and household services

The democratic state embarked on large-scale programmes to provide formal housing and municipal services to historically under-served communities. Still, despite considerable progress, poor households received services and housing far worse than rich households, in part because of massive rural-urban migration and in part because of fiscal constraints. The value of housing varied sharply by income group and location. Access to municipal infrastructure also varied by income group, with particularly sharp backlogs in water and sanitation in the former 'homelands', especially in the Eastern Cape.

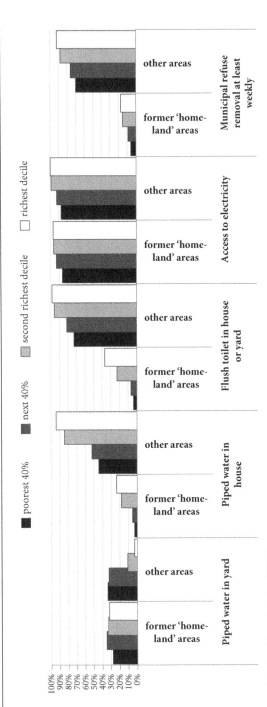

Figure 1.18: Municipal services by household income group, 2015

Source: Calculated from Stats SA (2016a).

Figure 1.19: Housing by type and by race, 1996, 2011, 2016

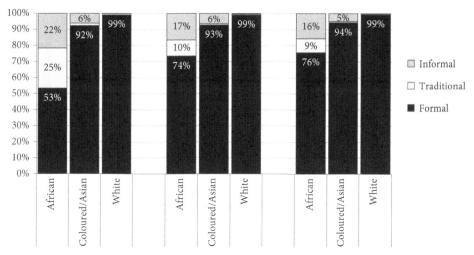

Source: Calculated from Stats SA (2016c).

The available data did not permit analysis of changes by income level after 1994. But figures by race demonstrated significant progress.

The share of Africans with formal housing climbed from 53 per cent in 1996 to 74 per cent in 2011 and the share of those living in traditional housing dropped sharply. In this period, the number of formal houses inhabited by Africans more than doubled, climbing from 3.4 million to 8.3 million, accounting for 90 per cent of the total increase in formal dwellings.

In 2015, more than two out of five families in the poorest 80 per cent who lived in a formal house built after 1996 had received a housing subsidy (Stats SA 2015). However, most new townships were still located far from economic centres, chiefly to take advantage of cheaper land, and the houses were typically even smaller than the traditional matchboxes built in the 1970s. In 2015, the median-sized formal house for the poorest 80 per cent of households consisted of four rooms, including the kitchen and sanitary facilities. In these conditions, the expansion in formal housing generally did not boost economic engagement as much as anticipated.

In terms of access to municipal infrastructure by race, substantial improvements also emerged from 1994.

A particular challenge in improving access to municipal services and formal housing arose from extraordinarily rapid rural-urban migration after 1994. From 1996 to 2016, the national population grew by 38 per cent – but the population of Gauteng climbed by over 70 per cent, and that of the Western Cape by almost 60 per cent. Other provinces, especially the Free State and the Eastern Cape, grew far more slowly than the national average.[11]

Figure 1.20: Access to municipal infrastructure by race, 1996 to 2016

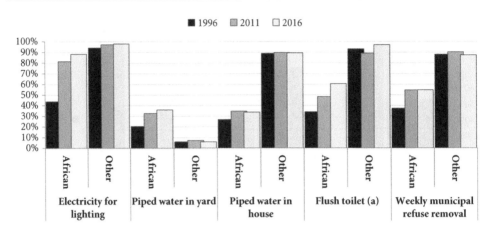

Note: (a) Census data does not indicate whether toilets were on site. In 2016, 3 per cent of African households used flush toilets outside their yard, but 42 per cent had toilets in their yards rather than in their houses. For non-Africans with flush toilets, 0.3 per cent were outside the yard and 6 per cent in the yard rather than the dwelling.
Source: Stats SA, Census 1996, 2001 and 2011 and Stats SA (2016c).

Figure 1.21: Estimated population growth by province, 1996 to 2016

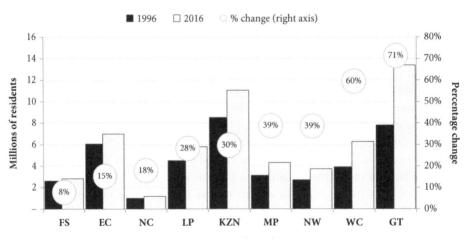

Source: Calculated from Stats SA 1996 Census and Stats SA (2016c).

Rapid migration and the small size of most new houses provided under state pro-grammes led to a marked fall in household size after 1994. In 1996, the average household had almost five members; in 2016, it had slightly over three. As a result, the number of households – and the related demand for housing and services – climbed by 90 per cent, while the population grew only by 37 per cent.

Economic transformation

In contrast to its extensive spending on social services and housing, the democratic state undertook only very limited programmes to promote employment and self-employment. State support for livelihood strategies based on self-employment remained particularly limited – in part because most unemployed people wanted better-paying and more secure employment. Land reform was the most obvious response to the dispossession imposed by apartheid on rural communities. It remained relatively small, however, and focused initially on restitution of groups explicitly pushed off land, rather than on the rural poor. Land reform also sought primarily to ensure a more representative class of commercial farmers rather than to improve incomes for the poorest rural people on a significant scale.

Most other programmes to support emerging enterprises focused on formal small and medium enterprise, generally seeking only to provide financial support and sometimes mentorship. Virtually none of these programmes sought to develop more robust institutions that could holistically address the myriad gaps facing micro-enterprise in terms of both institutional and infrastructural systems.

The alternative to expanding self-employment would be to expand paid employment in the formal sector much more rapidly. In the event, however, industrial policy measures focused primarily on enhancing technological capacity, diversification, export growth and black ownership of formal businesses, rather than on job creation. Industries producing mass consumer goods and services were generally not priorities, although they were key to rapid job creation in other industrialising economies.

Fiscal constraints

In theory, because key government programmes were highly redistributive, expanding them would do more to address inequality. Certainly there was some scope for improving the impact of social services and transfers on inequality and economic inclusion, and even for a limited increase in taxation. But benchmarking spending levels against peer economies pointed to the limits on further expansion.

In 1994, government purchases of goods and services as well as subsidies and transfers of all kinds (including to businesses and institutions as well as households) equalled 28 per cent of the gross domestic product (GDP) in South Africa. That compared to 32 per cent in Brazil but just 20 per cent for the twenty other upper middle-income economies (out of fifty-seven in total) that provided information for 1994. In 2014, the figure for South Africa had risen to 34 per cent. It was 30 per cent for Brazil and 27 per cent for the thirty-five other upper middle-income countries that provided the information.

A similar picture emerges from the assessment of tax revenues. Even before the transition to democracy, South Africa ranked high among developing economies in terms of central tax revenue as a percentage of GDP, with an unusually large share deriving from income and capital gains taxes. According to World Bank data, in 2014 central tax revenues in South Africa equalled 27 per cent of the GDP, up from 24 per cent in 1994. Taxes

Figure 1.22: Government spending as percentage of GDP, South Africa, Brazil and other upper middle-income economies (a)

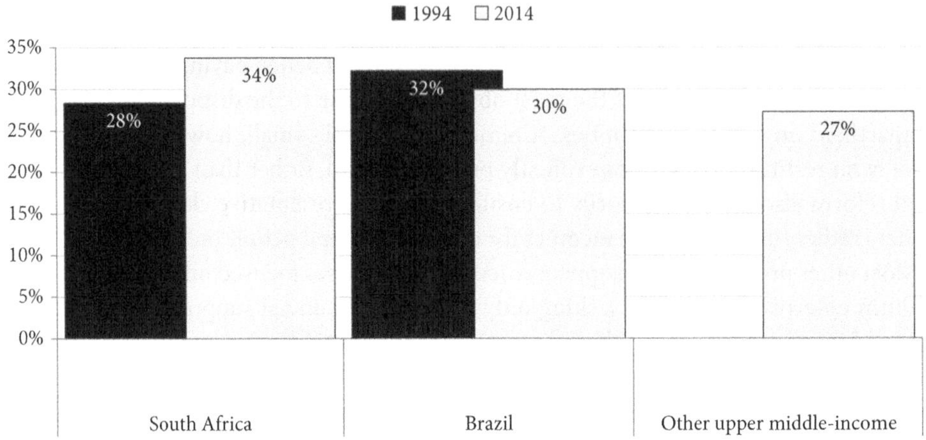

■ 1994   □ 2014

Note: (a) Figures for thirty-four out of fifty-seven UMIC reporting figures for 2014. China is not included.
Source: Calculated from World Bank. World Development Indicators electronic dataset, series on government expenses as percentage of GDP (December 2016).

on income contributed 48 per cent of the total, down from 54 per cent in 1994, largely due to growth in VAT revenues. For upper middle-income economies in aggregate, excluding China, taxes for the central government accounted for 15 per cent of the GDP in 2014, with only 22 per cent from income tax (World Bank, World Development Indicators).

Extending redistribution rather than addressing inequality in the economy entailed significant political-economic challenges. It required that a small rich minority continue to pay for programmes that largely benefited the majority. Sustaining this system required both high levels of tax compliance by a relatively small number of rich people, and continued commitment to redistribution from policy makers. Elected officials and senior management in the public service, from directors to the president, all belonged to the top 5 per cent of income earners in 2015, based on their salaries alone. Any move to raise taxes ran into a wall of criticism from international interests, expressed by both multilateral organisations and ratings agencies. In response to these pressures, the democratic state maintained a conservative fiscal strategy that tended to become pro-cyclical over time. Although it ran the deficit up to 6 per cent to counter the global financial crisis in 2008–2009, it sought strenuously to reduce it thereafter. After 2011, as the global commodity boom ended, declining revenues brought a renewed emphasis on fiscal consolidation.

As the following graph shows, state spending was expected to be substantially slower than GDP growth from 2016–2017 to 2018–2019. As a result, spending per person was predicted to fall over this period.

Figure 1.23: Fiscal trends, 2008/2009 to 2015/2016 and projected for 2016/2017 to 2018/2019

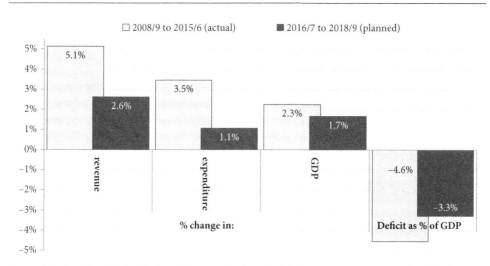

Source: Calculated from Budget Review (Relevant series downloaded from www.treasury.gov.za, June 2016).

Projections for spending by major functions indicated that in real terms housing and municipal services together would grow around 1 per cent faster than the population; social services would grow at about the same rate as the population; economic services would grow about half as fast; and public administration and security services would face real cuts.

CONCLUSIONS

Despite extensive state programmes aimed at redressing inequality, South Africa remains one of the most inequitable countries in the world. The fundamental reason is particularly great inequalities by global standards in three areas: joblessness, pay scales and asset ownership. The state has essentially focused on improving social grants and services for the poor, rather than reshaping the market and the government institutions that were established under apartheid to maintain an exclusive economy and state. The main outcomes are that:

- The richest group has become more representative in racial terms.
- State spending, especially for social grants and housing, has shifted toward low-income groups.
- The partial privatisation of social services means that they remain heavily unequal, despite improvements in state spending in low-income communities.

More effective programmes to address inequality would have to act on the underlying economic causes rather than focus on redistribution through state services. That, in turn, would require, above all:

- Development of market institutions able to support livelihood strategies for the unemployed, whether in the form of nonprofit companies, co-ops, marketing agencies, extension services or contracting-out schemes.
- Sustainable measures to make asset ownership and education more equitable, for instance through smallholder schemes in rural areas and on the urban periphery; merit-based access to existing quality schools; and a more focused emphasis on improving basic education to ensure more employable graduates as well as engaged citizens.
- An industrial strategy focused more strongly on the mass production of basic goods and services for South Africa and the region.

NOTES

1   South Africa is the most unequal country that reports on inequality in the World Development Indicators.
2   It should be noted that only 141 out of 195 countries reported a Gini; it is likely that some of those that did not provide one were relatively unequal.
3   The argument that inequality worsened in South Africa after 1993 is included in Inchauste et al. (2015), but without a clear reference. See also Leibbrandt et al. (2010). Bhorat et al. (2009) and Bhorat and Van der Westhuizen (2010) used the official Income and Expenditure Surveys for 1995 and 2005 to conclude that income distribution worsened from 1995 to 2005. While these surveys purport to form a series, they actually utilised very different methodologies, which makes comparability difficult. The main concern is that the 1995 survey may have failed to capture realities for Africans in particular. Van der Berg et al. (2006) use the All Media and Products (AMPS) survey to conclude that the overall income distribution remained essentially unchanged from 1994 to the mid-2000s.
4   The Census used income categories rather than actual incomes and did not probe responses. The General Household data, used for the 2015 findings, estimated income for households based on responses to separate income categories, including wages, profits and social grants.
5   In 1996, the October Household Survey reported incomes for only around 30 per cent of all employees.
6   The concept of 'man-headed' and 'woman-headed' is contested. The formal definition of household head in the General Household Survey is 'the main decision-maker, or the person who owns or rents the dwelling, or the person who is the main breadwinner'. This ignores equal partnerships in heterosexual marriages. In practice, in most household surveys if a household held a married couple the man would generally be considered the household head (Budlender 1997).
7   The ILO calls this figure the employment ratio; Stats South Africa calls it the absorption rate.
8   The National Income Dynamics Survey (NIDS) provided detailed information on income from assets, but reported a much lower income for the top decile than the larger Quarterly Labour Force Surveys (which form the basis of the annual Labour Market Dynamics Survey). That suggested under-sampling at the top, which in turn made it difficult to use the data to assess inequality. Analyses of the NIDS asset data are available in Mbewe and Woolard (2016); Hundenborn et al. (2016).

9   The Department of Basic Education divided schools into quintiles based primarily on the income of their communities and their facilities, but the quintiles were highly uneven, the top group holding only 15 per cent of schools and the lowest group 25 per cent.

10   In 2015, Stats SA (2015: 10) estimated a food poverty line of R501 per person per month in 2011. Reflating this figure using CPI, the poverty line would be around R620 a month per person in 2015. By this standard, the old-age pension could support around 2.2 people a month, and the child grant around half a person.

11   The 2016 Community Survey probably understates migration from 2011 because it is weighted by the mid-year population estimates. The 2011 Census found that Stats SA's mid-year population estimates substantially underestimated rural-urban migration. Nonetheless, the mid-year estimates since 2011 assume a falling migration rate. In interviews, Stats SA officials argued that the rate through 2011 was extraordinarily high by international standards and therefore could not persist – an argument that ignores the unique nature of South Africa's apartheid legacy.

REFERENCES

Bhorat, H and Van der Westhuizen, C (2010) Poverty, inequality and the nature of economic growth in South Africa. In N Misra-Dexter and J February (eds) *Testing democracy: Which way is South Africa going?* Cape Town: IDASA.

Bhorat, H, Van der Westhuizen, C and Jacobs, T (2009) *Income and non-income inequality in post-apartheid South Africa: What are the drivers and possible policy interventions?* Development Policy Research Unit Working Paper 09/138. Cape Town: DPRU.

Budlender, D (1997) *The debate about household headship. Discussion Document.* Johannesburg: Stats SA.

DBE (Department of Basic Education) (2014) Second detailed indicator report for basic education sector. http://www.education.gov.za.

DBE (Department of Basic Education) (2016) National ordinary schools master list, March 2016. http://www.education.gov.za.

Hundenborn, J, Leibbrandt, M and Woolard, I (2016) *Drivers of inequality in South Africa.* SALDRU Working Paper No. 194. Cape Town: SALDRU/UCT.

ILO (International Labour Organization) (2016) *Global wage report 2016/17: Wage inequality in the workplace.* Geneva: ILO.

Inchauste, G, Lustig, N, Maboshe, M, Purfield, C and Woolard, I (2015) *The distributional impact of fiscal policy in South Africa.* Policy Research Working Paper 7194. Washington, DC: World Bank.

Leibbrandt, M, Woolard, I, Finn, A and Argent, J (2010) *Trends in South African income distribution and poverty since the fall of apartheid.* OECD Social, Employment and Migration Working Papers No. 101. Paris: OECD.

Mbewe, S and Woolard, I (2016) *Cross-sectional features of wealth inequality in South Africa: Evidence from the National Income Dynamics Study.* NIDS Discussion Paper 2016/12. Cape Town: SALDRU/UCT.

Orthofer, A (2016) *Wealth inequality – Evidence from survey and tax data.* Redi3x3 Working Paper 15. http://www.redi3x3.org.

Ostry, JD, Berg, A and Tsangarides, CG (2014) *Redistribution, inequality, and growth.* International Monetary Fund Discussion Paper. Washington, DC: IMF.

SARS (South African Revenue Service) (2016a) Personal income tax 2012 to 2016. http://www.sars.gov.za.

SARS (South African Revenue Service) (2016b) Corporate income tax 2012 to 2016. http://www.sars.gov.za.

SASSA (South African Social Development Agency) (2015/16) *Annual report.* http://www.sassa.gov.za/index.php/knowledge-centre/annual-reports.

Stats SA (Statistics South Africa) (2015) *Methodological report on rebasing of national poverty lines and development of pilot provincial poverty lines.* Report No. 03–10–11. Pretoria: Stats SA.

Stats SA (Statistics South Africa) (2016a) General household survey (2015). http://www.statssa.gov.za.

Stats SA (Statistics South Africa) (2016b) Labour market dynamics 2015. http://www.statssa.gov.za.

Stats SA (Statistics South Africa) (2016c) Community profiles and community profiles survey 2016. http://www.statssa.gov.za.

Van der Berg, S, Burger, R, Burger, R, Louw, M and Yu, D (2006) *Trends in poverty and inequality since the political transition.* Development Policy Research Unit Working Paper 06/104. Cape Town: DPRU.

World Bank. *World development indicators.* http://www.worldbank.org.

CHAPTER 2

A national minimum wage in South Africa: A tool to reduce inequality?

Jana Mudronova and Gilad Isaacs

Rising inequality, in recent decades, has opened new spaces for research into its causes and consequences, drawing attention to new and established inequality-reducing policy measures, with inequality-enhancing labour market policies receiving renewed interest. Minimum wages are one such policy measure.

Current levels of global inequality are staggering. In 2016, Oxfam calculated that in the preceding five years the wealth of the sixty-two richest individuals rose by 45 per cent, whereas the wealth of the least wealthy half of the world's population dropped by 38 per cent (Oxfam 2016). The income shares of top earners are high in both developed and developing countries. In Colombia and Argentina the top 1 per cent take home approximately 20 per cent of total wage earnings (UNDP 2014); in South Africa this is a staggering 40 per cent (Finn 2015). Some developing countries have managed to reduce inequality – Brazil halved its top to bottom inequality in the 1990s and 2000s, the ratio between the top and bottom 10 per cent narrowing from around fourteen times to seven times (OECD 2011). It is increasingly recognised that extreme inequality is not only unethical but also destabilising and growth retarding, whereas long-run benefits accrue from reducing inequality (Berg and Ostry 2011; OECD 2014).

Changes in pay structure, paid employment and market flexibility, and a decline in trade union membership play important roles in explaining wage inequality (Dabla-Norris et al. 2015; OECD 2015). Where incomes have risen in emerging and developing economies, wage-income growth has played a leading role in inequality reduction. In Argentina and Brazil, wage compression accounted for 87 per cent and 72 per cent of the reduction of top-bottom inequality respectively. Similarly, wage compression, rather than changes in employment, drove inequality reduction in Peru and Russia (ILO 2015).

Over the past three decades, labour shares (the share of value added distributed as wages) have fallen globally (in both developed and developing countries), an important factor in determining overall trends in inequality. Between 1990 and 2006, the labour share in a group of sixteen developing countries declined from 62 per cent of gross domestic product (GDP) to 58 per cent (ILO 2013). A shift of income from capital to labour – a rising labour share – can be important with regard to boosting spending and reducing inequality. One policy measure to boost wage income and the labour share is the institution, or the increasing, of minimum wages.

Given the potential of minimum wages to play a role in reducing inequality, the proposed introduction of a national minimum wage has gained new impetus in South Africa. Currently, South Africa has a system of (often low) sectorally differentiated minima, determined either through collective bargaining or set via sectoral determinations (promulgated by the minister of labour on the recommendation of the Employment Conditions Commission).[1] A national minimum wage would cover all workers, be easier to enforce and would not set lower minima in sectors with more vulnerable workers (Konopelko 2016); it could also be set to take account of broader policy objectives and macroeconomic impacts, not only narrow sectoral considerations.

In this context, this chapter explores the potential of a national minimum wage to reduce inequality in South Africa (with some, but limited, attention given to poverty).[2] Section two outlines the nature of inequality in South Africa (with a strong statistical rather than sociological focus). This is followed, in section three, by an interrogation of whether minimum wages have been an effective tool to reduce inequality elsewhere in the world. Section four discusses minimum wages in South Africa and assesses the potential impact, based on recent statistical modelling, of a national minimum wage. The positive predictions of these modelling exercises match the reductions in inequality observed internationally as a consequence of minimum wages.

INEQUALITY IN SOUTH AFRICA

Despite some success in reducing poverty, inequality and unemployment have remained unprecedentedly and stubbornly high in post-apartheid South Africa. Inequality, measured by the Gini coefficient – 0 representing perfect equality and 1 perfect inequality – sits at 0.66, making South Africa the most unequal country in the world (see Chapter 1 in this volume). In 2014, the average income of the top 10 per cent of full-time workers in South Africa was eighty-two times higher than the average income for the bottom 10 per cent (own calculations from Stats SA 2015). Even though average real wages have risen, these increases have not been equally distributed. Real monthly wages between

Figure 2.1: Labour share in South Africa (1990–2016)

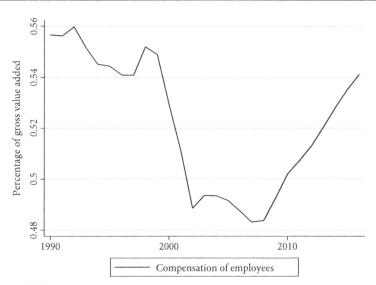

Source: Quantec (2017), own calculations.

1997 and 2008 declined for 80 per cent of earners, rising only for the top fifth (Leibbrandt et al. 2010). Average wages have therefore risen while median wages (the midpoint in the wage distribution at which 50 per cent of earners earning above and 50 per cent earning below) have largely stagnated. Importantly, disparities between income earners account for 62 per cent of inequality, while 'zero earners' (unemployment) are responsible for the remaining 38 per cent (Leibbrandt et al. 2010, 2012). Patterns of wage income therefore play the dominant role in persistent inequality (Finn 2015).

At the same time, a significant fall in the labour share occurred in the post-apartheid period, as seen in Figure 2.1. It occurred, by definition, because productivity growth outstripped growth in real labour compensation; the recent rise in the labour share is due to wage increases in a limited number of sectors (particularly mining) and a decrease in profits, not significant wage gains for the majority of workers. South Africa's labour share is approximately 5 percentage points lower than that of its emerging market peers (Strauss and Isaacs 2016).

Wages, as the main source of income for the majority of the population, also play a crucial role in poverty dynamics although the poorest 40 per cent rely heavily on social grants (Finn 2015). Poverty is lower in households with wage earners, but the presence of a wage earner does not guarantee that a household will escape from poverty – in fact, 50 per cent of households with at least one wage earner still remain under the poverty line.[3] Further, 54 per cent of *full-time* employees, or 5.5 million workers, qualify as the 'working poor' (Finn 2015). Working poverty remains heavily skewed; 59 per cent of full-time black employees are below the working poverty line compared with 22 per cent of white full-time employees. In addition, each wage earner in poor households supports a larger number of dependents than in non-poor households (Finn 2015). All of the above indicates that a more equal distribution of wage income is critical to overcoming poverty and inequality in South Africa.

MINIMUM WAGES AS A TOOL TO REDUCE INEQUALITY: INTERNATIONAL EVIDENCE

There are five interrelated dimensions to the assessment of whether minimum wages have been an effective inequality-reducing policy internationally. First, the minimum wage regime must raise wages for low-wage formal sector workers at a faster pace than the wages of higher-wage earners rise. Second, benefits from wage gains must not be undermined by negative impacts on employment. Third, wide coverage of low-wage earners by the minimum wage regime is important. Fourth, in countries with a significant informal sector, the minimum wage regime must not significantly increase informality. Fifth, a shift in income towards the labour share can be equity enhancing. Each of these is explored in turn below, with emphasis given to evidence from developing countries.

Minimum wage has an impact on the wage distribution

The wage distribution captures the level of wage income at different points along the earnings scale, often discussed in terms of percentiles.[4] Minimum wages have an equalising effect when wages of earners at the bottom end of the wage distribution increase faster than the wages of those in the middle and/or at the top of the distribution. This is usually expressed as a ratio between middle- and low-income earners (or the p50/p10) or a ratio between high-income and low-income earners (p90/p10).

Since the late 1990s, Latin America, the most unequal region in the world, has experienced a notable decline in its Gini coefficient, falling from 0.546 in 2002 to 0.475 in 2014 (SEDLAC 2016); the largest contributing factor has been wage growth. Most importantly, income growth was strongest among lower-wage and low-skilled earners (Tsounta and Osueke 2014). A critical intervention (although not the only one) has been significant increases to minimum wages. A positive redistributive impact from minimum wages was found in ten out of nineteen countries in the region between 1997 and 2001, where a 10 per cent increase in the minimum wage led to a 1 to 6 per cent increase in average wages (Kristensen and Cunningham 2006) with higher wage growth at the bottom end.

A more recent analysis, between 2003 and 2012, of four countries in the region – Argentina, Brazil, Chile and Uruguay – found significant reductions in wage inequality due to increases in minimum wages. In Figure 2.2 we see that the ratios of earnings between low-income and middle-income wage earners (p50/p10) fell dramatically, as did the Gini coefficients, in tandem with large increases to minimum wages. In Brazil and

Figure 2.2: National minimum wages and inequality in four Latin American countries (2000–2012)

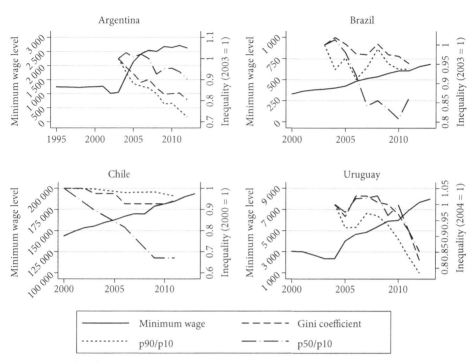

Source: Maurizio (2016).

Argentina, where minimum wages rose by 130 per cent and 200 per cent respectively, minimum wages explain 85 per cent and 32 per cent of the decline in the Gini coefficients (Maurizio 2016).[5]

The opposite trend is also observed. In Mexico a fall in the real value of the minimum wage between 1989 and 2001 accounted for 'essentially all of the growth in inequality at the bottom end of income distribution' (Bosch and Manacorda 2010: 129). In the USA the decline in minimum wage in the 1980s and 1990s explained up to a half of the growth of inequality at the lower end of the wage distribution (Autor et al. 2016). The compression of the lower half of the wage distribution through increases in minimum wages can also be observed in Russia, Indonesia, India, China, the UK and Ireland. In a number of cases minimum wages also contributed to closing gender wage gaps (Lukiyanova 2011; Dickens et al. 2012; Lu 2015; Rani and Ranjbar 2015; Bargain et al. 2016; Lin and Yun 2016).

In Indonesia, the real wages of formal-sector workers at the tenth percentile grew by almost 50 per cent between 1993 and 2007, a period during which the level of minimum wages doubled in real terms, while the real average wages of the earners at the ninetieth percentile grew by only 10 per cent (Chun and Khor 2010). Minimum wages also increased the wages for those who remained below the stipulated (minimum wages) level (due to noncompliance). The biggest beneficiaries are often the most vulnerable workers. In Germany, the newly introduced national minimum wage has been particularly important for workers in marginal part-time employment,[6] who represent almost 60 per cent of workers earning below the new national minimum wage level (Amlinger et al. 2016). The impact on inequality is therefore differentiated across sectors. In Costa Rica, for instance, minimum wages have had a greater impact on wages of workers in rural and small enterprises (generally low-wage sectors) than of those employed in the urban formal sector (Gindling and Terrell 2005).

In sum, the evidence from around the world confirms the ability of minimum wages to raise lower-end wages at a growth rate above that of middle- and higher-end wages. In contrast, in some instances where the real value of a minimum wage has fallen, inequality has increased. Minimum wages have also been effective in narrowing other wage disparities, such as gender wage gaps and rural-urban divides.

Minimum wages and employment

For the minimum wage to be effective it must not have significantly negative effects on employment levels. Until the 1990s, employment losses were assumed to result from minimum wages, justified theoretically by the 'competitive market' paradigm in which an increase in prices (the price of labour) would inevitably lead to a fall in demand (the demand for labour). However, in the last two decades an exhaustive body of evidence – the larger part of which comes from developed countries – has concluded that moderate increases in minimum wages, on average, have very small disemployment effects or none at all.

This has been confirmed by recent meta-analyses – research which combines a large number of individual studies. These meta-analyses show, on average, that a 10 per cent minimum wage increases results in between a 0 and 0.7 per cent fall in employment, a very small impact (for teen employment in the USA see Doucouliagos and Stanley 2009; for fifteen industrial countries see Boockmann 2010; for twenty-three developed countries see Belman and Wolfson 2014; for the UK see Leonard et al. 2014; for six emerging markets see Broecke et al. 2015; for eighteen developed and developing countries see Chletsos and Giotis 2015, reviewed in Isaacs 2016).[7] Schmitt (2013: 2) summarises these findings by noting: 'The weight of that evidence points to little or no employment response to modest increases in the minimum wage'; as Freeman (1996: 642) notes: the 'debate over the employment effects of the minimum wage is a debate of values around zero'. The findings are, to an extent, differentiated when disaggregated by population, sector and study type, but with contradictory results – for instance, gender is found to have no impact in three of the studies cited but a significant impact in one of them. It appears that the hospitality/food and home-care sectors may be harder hit, but the only consistent finding is that more recent studies point to lower disemployment effects and that the methodology employed in the individual studies matters a great deal.

The volume of studies in developing countries has grown recently but is still limited; on aggregate they show slightly negative or neutral impacts, with significant differentiation according to country, population group, region, sector, time period and methodology.

Developing countries are often thought to be more at risk of employment losses, given a higher proportion of low-skilled workers and the presence of large informal sectors – however, this has generally been shown not to be the case (Broecke et al. 2015; Chletsos and Giotis 2015). Where there is an impact, it tends to be negative but small. For the most vulnerable groups, such as women and youth, the impact has been more significant in some countries than others, and tends to be small either way.

There is limited research on the impact of minimum wages in South Africa with six sectoral determinations studied; the results are summarised in Table 2.1. In five of the six sectors (retail, domestic work, forestry, taxi and private security) the institution of a minimum wage had no statistically significant effect on employment.[8] In agriculture there was a statistically significant decline in employment. This may indicate that tradable sectors are more vulnerable. However, the meta-analyses which investigated sectoral decomposition internationally did not, in the main, find this, and it was the hospitality/food, retail, and home-care sectors – all non-tradable sectors – that were slightly worse off in some of the studies (Belman and Wolfson 2014; Leonard et al. 2014; Chletsos and Giotis 2015).[9] Further investigation would be required to distinguish meaningfully between tradable and non-tradable sectors in South Africa.

Table 2.1: Summary of South African studies

	Retail	Domestic work	Forestry	Taxi	Security	Agriculture
Employment elasticity[*]	−0.0002	−0.0005	−0.0001	−0.00005	−0.0001	−0.0418
Statistically significant	No	No	No	No	No	Yes
Hourly wage elasticity[**]	0.0568	0.0698	−0.0079	0.0152	0.272	0.1751
Statistically significant	Yes	Yes	No	Yes	Yes	Yes
Hours worked elasticity[***]	−1.203	−0.325	0.0757	−0.789	−1.741	0.106
Statistically significant	Yes	No	No	No	Yes	No
Better overall based on monthly income[****]	Yes	Yes	No change	No change	Yes	

Notes:
[*] Wage gap Post – Specification I
[**] Wage gap Post – Specification III
[***] Sector Post – Specification I
[****] As reported in study
Source: Bhorat et al. (2013a); Bhorat et al. (2013b).

The minimal aggregate effects on employment are explained on the basis that both firms and the economy have multiple channels of adjustment with multiple cost factors, country context and demand conditions – not wage costs predominately – explaining employment levels. Internationally, reductions in employment, hours worked, non-wage benefits (such as health insurance) and training, as well as shifts in the composition of employment (away from low-wage workers) have not been strong reactions to higher minimum wages. On the other hand, the most important channels of adjustment have been reductions in labour turnover, improvements in productivity through greater organisational and employee efficiency, reductions in the wages of higher earners ('wage compression'), trimming of profit margins, and small price increases (Schmitt 2013; Isaacs 2016). Demand stimulus from higher consumption spending from low-wage workers has also positively contributed towards growth and employment (Herr et al. 2009; Rani et al. 2013).

This evidence does not mean that increasing minimum wages cannot have negative employment effects, but rather that moderate increases, and at times regular increases resulting in large real wage gains, have not been found to have such effects on aggregate. A threshold above which wage increase may induce employment losses or slow employment growth is likely but this will depend on a range of economic factors and conditions; this is discussed briefly in Isaacs (2016) and seen in the statistical modelling below. This said, the lack of significant employment effects is important as these would erode aggregate real-wage gains for low-wage workers and potentially reduce the inequality-reducing impact of a national minimum wage; this has not been the case.

Coverage

Minimum wage coverage is important for minimum wages to effectively serve as redistributive mechanisms. This has three dimensions. First, ensuring adequate compliance with minimum wages is critical. In India, for example, greater compliance with minimum wage legislation gradually increased its marginal effect. In 2004–2005, when the rate of compliance was about 32 per cent, a 1 per cent increase in the effective minimum wage led to a 0.33 per cent increase in wages at the twentieth percentile, five years later, when compliance increased to 61 per cent, the twentieth percentile experienced a 0.47 per cent increase in wages from a 1 per cent increase in the minimum wage. At the same time the wage increase for the eightieth percentile diminished, combined resulting in a reduction of inequality (Rani and Ranjbar 2015: 16).

Noncompliance has been a significant problem in many developing countries, including in South Africa where, in 2007, 45 per cent of workers covered by sectoral determinations were found to be earning below the legal minima (Bhorat et al. 2011a, 2011b). Ensuring compliance relies on strong monitoring and enforcement, widespread knowledge of minimum wage legislation, vibrant worker organisations, accessible complaint mechanisms for workers and strong sanctions (see Murahwa 2016).

Figure 2.3: Compliance rate in selected developing countries

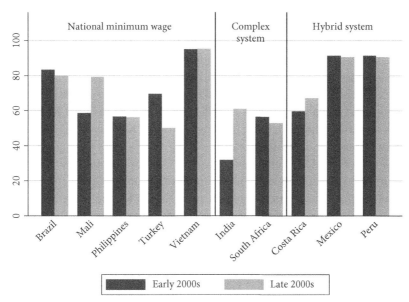

Source: Rani et al. (2013).

The second of the three dimensions is that the minimum wage regime matters a great deal.

Figure 2.3 shows clearly that countries with national or regional minimum wages enjoy higher rates of compliance. This is a strong argument in favour of South Africa moving from a sectorally differentiated system to a national minimum wage.

The third dimension is that minimum wages have also been shown to raise wages that are already above the minimum wage level, particularly in developing countries, indicating an impact beyond those who are 'covered' by the minimum wage in a strict sense. For example, in Colombia, the minimum wage increased wages for workers earning up to four times the minimum wage level (Maloney and Mendez 2003).

Minimum wages and the informal sector

Concern has been expressed that minimum wage increases in the formal sector may lead to a displacement of employment into the informal sector, and that inequality-reducing effects would be limited to the formal sector (see Khamis 2008). Both of these concerns are, in general, not borne out. Regarding the first, Broecke et al. (2015), in the case of ten emerging markets covering seventy-four studies, found 'very little evidence that increases in minimum wages lead to more informality'. This finding differs from that of Nataraj et al. (2014), but the Nataraj et al. finding uses only nine studies from six low-income countries. Further, if linked with incentives, minimum wage legislation can be used to formalise businesses, such as was the case in Brazil (Berg 2010).

Regarding the second concern, a large body of evidence highlights how increases in minimum wages for formal-sector workers lead to increases in informal-sector wages. This is because the two sectors are connected, both through the demand for goods and services (Maloney and Mendez 2003) and in terms of wage levels. First, rising spending among low-income earners increases demand for products (and thus labour) within the informal sector, which in turn creates upward pressure on wages in the informal sector. Second, a minimum wage can serve as an indicator of a fair wage in the economy, as well as a tool for increasing the bargaining power of workers (Khamis 2008). This phenomenon has been termed the 'lighthouse effect'.

In their study of nineteen Latin American and Caribbean countries, Kristensen and Cunningham (2006) demonstrated that minimum wages positively affected the wage distribution in the informal sectors in fourteen countries. In fact, in some instances, minimum wages have had a stronger equalising effect in the informal sector than in the formal sector (Amadeo et al. 2000; Fajnzylber 2001; Maloney and Mendez 2003; Keifman and Maurizio 2012). Belser and Rani (2015) calculated that average wages in informal sectors increased between 0.33 per cent and 18 per cent as a result of minimum wage increases in seven out of ten developing countries studied. In South Africa they calculated that minimum wage increases spurred an 18 per cent rise in informal sector wages between the mid-2000s and the late 2000s. The inequality-reducing effect of minimum wages therefore extends beyond formal sector employment.

The labour share

Shifting income from profits towards wages (increasing the labour share) has also been tied to reducing overall inequality (Checchi and Garcia-Peñalosa 2005; Daudey and Garcia-Peñalosa 2007; Schlenker and Schmid 2013) whereas eroding labour shares have been strongly tied to rising inequality (ILO and OECD 2015) including in South Africa.[10] At the macroeconomic level, the global contraction in labour shares appears to have harmed global aggregate demand (ILO 2013, 2014); this affects employment levels and incomes. Workers generally consume more out of wage income than capitalists do out of profits, and so a shift in favour of the labour share can spur consumption and hence output and growth.[11]

At the micro level there is generally a far higher concentration of property income (for example, net dividends, interest, rental income, undistributed corporate profits and so on) than wage income. This is strongly the case in South Africa. A higher labour share is, therefore, often associated with less overall income inequality as income is reallocated from (more unequally distributed) property income towards (somewhat more equally distributed) wages. Although it is not guaranteed, a national minimum wage, set at a meaningful level, may contribute towards such a shift.

Summary

Overall, the international experience shows that minimum wages have the potential to reduce inequality by increasing wages for low-income earners without causing greater unemployment. This is more effective the wider the coverage, and includes positive effects in the informal sector. The minimum wage also has the potential to shift income within the economy from capital towards labour, thereby reducing inequality and contributing positively to the macroeconomy. In the light of these conclusions, we now consider the potential for a national minimum wage to reduce inequality in South Africa.

THE POTENTIAL OF A NATIONAL MINIMUM WAGE IN SOUTH AFRICA

A limited number of studies have tried to estimate the impacts of the institution of minimum wages in South Africa. Like elsewhere in the world, the studies fall into two categories: statistical modelling exercises which – using models containing a host of mathematical equations that attempt to mimic the interactions within the economy – estimate what the future impact of minimum wages might be; and ex-post studies that analyse the impact of changes to minimum wages that have already occurred. The ex-post studies in South Africa, described above with regard to employment impacts, have not directly considered inequality. However, hourly wages rose in five of the six sectors (only forestry shows no statistically significant rise) while hours worked fell marginally in retail and private security. Overall, workers were better off in the majority of sectors and no worse off in any of them (see Table 2.1).

Despite increases to sectorally set minimum wages, inequality has remained persistently high. Figure 2.4 shows the real increase, between 2002 and 2015, in minimum wages under the eight sectoral determinations in which minimum wages are set (each series beginning in the first year in which the minimum wage was established).[12] We see a gradual rise in all sectors, with the largest increases in agriculture and forestry, mostly due to the 50 per cent increase in March 2013. In years where no increases were mandated, inflation eroded the real value of the wage. The overall percentage increases can be seen in Figure 2.5. The impact of these increases on inequality is unknown, but high levels of minimum wage violations and the overall relatively low level of minimum wages may be undermining any inequality-reducing effect.[13] A higher national minimum wage (with full coverage and better enforcement) is likely to have a more significant impact.

In statistical modelling exercises, the second manner of assessing the impact of minimum wages, the modeller creates 'scenarios' – in this case focusing on the level of the national minimum wage and which workers are covered – and then 'shocks' (alters) the appropriate variable, in this case the wage for those earning below the stipulated level. The effect of this shock then ripples through the equations (the economy) until the consequences are given as specific outputs for different variables, for example, average income,

Figure 2.4: Real wage growth for sectoral determinations (2002–2015)

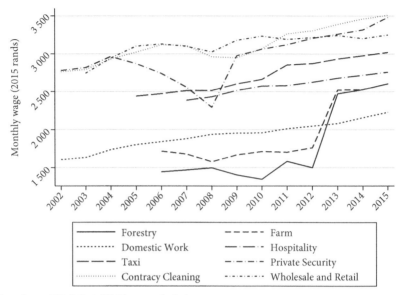

Source: From Isaacs (2016), DoL (2015), own calculations.

Figure 2.5: Percentage increase in hourly sectoral determinations between institutions, 2015

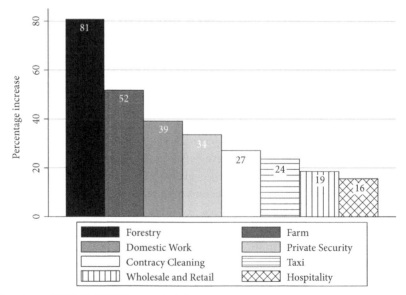

Source: From Isaacs (2016), DoL (2015), own calculations.

domestic demand and output, GDP growth and employment levels. Such exercises are useful but should be approached with caution.

To date, the majority of such exercises undertaken in South Africa predict dire job losses and economic deterioration, including at very low national minimum wage levels (Pauw 2009; DPRU 2010, 2016; Pauw and Leibbrandt 2012; MacLeod 2015). The National Treasury (MacLeod 2015), for instance, estimated that a national minimum wage of R1 258 in 2015 would lead to a loss of 96 000 jobs. This is surprising, given that a national minimum wage of R1 258 would represent an average increase of only R31 per month for 16 per cent of workers and lies far below the lowest sectoral determination (at the time the study was undertaken, R1 993 for domestic workers outside major urban centres). The other studies cited use similar models, with similar assumptions, and persistently show up to half a million jobs losses following the institution of a national minimum wage.

If accurate, this could, depending on the level and distribution of job losses, have negative distributional consequences. Unfortunately, these neoclassical 'computable general equilibrium' models, and the assumptions made, are inappropriate for modelling wage increases. By design these models will predict job losses and macroeconomic deterioration with the possibility of non-negative employment results precluded before the model is run; this is comprehensively detailed in Storm and Isaacs (2016) and explains why similar catastrophic predictions made elsewhere in the world are consistently at odds with the actual employment impacts assessed after the fact (see Minford 1998 for the UK; Schmöller 2014; Amlinger et al. 2016 for Germany).

Two other modelling exercises have been undertaken. First, Strauss and Isaacs (2016), using the United Nations Global Policy Model (GPM), analyse the macroeconomic consequences of redistribution via a rising labour share in South Africa, the first exercise of this kind and a considerable advance over other more simplistic approaches (see Onaran and Galanis 2012).[14] Essentially they ask: what happens to the South African economy when workers receive a larger slice of the pie? The increase in the labour share is achieved through real wages rising faster than labour productivity over the period analysed. As discussed above, this could result from the implementation of a national minimum wage set at a meaningful level.

The authors model three scenarios in which the labour share is increased by varying percentage points and compare these with a 'baseline' or 'business as usual' scenario in which the economy is left to continue along its existing growth path. The projections are made over a ten-year period and summarised in Table 2.2, which shows the percentage point increase or decrease in key variables in comparison with the baseline scenario. The level of impact differs by scenario but the direction is the same.

The model predicts an immediate positive impact on private consumption owing to increased disposable income, and the higher likelihood of workers spending out of wage income than capitalists out of profits (a well-established economic phenomenon). This spurs higher growth rates – which dissipate over time but leave the level of GDP permanently higher. The positive demand stimulus could potentially be outweighed by negative

Table 2.2: Percentage point increase in key variables relative to baseline by 2025

	Labour share	GDP	Private consumption	Government net lending to GDP
Scenario 1	Up 2%	↑1.1%	Up 0.5%	Down 0.22%
Scenario 2	Up 4%	↑2.3%	Up 1%	Down 0.46%
Scenario 3	Up 5%	↑2.9%	Up 1.2%	Down 0.59%
	Employment rate	Private investment to GDP	Current account deficit to GDP	
Scenario 1	≈	≈	Up 0.2%	
Scenario 2	≈	Down 0.1%	Up 0.4%	
Scenario 3	≈	Down 0.1%	Up 0.5%	

Scenarios:
Scenario 1: economy set on a path to increase the labour share by 2 per cent by 2025.
Scenario 2: economy set on a path to increase the labour share by 4 per cent by 2025 together with increased infrastructure investment in line with the National Development Plan.
Scenario 3: economy set on a path to increase the labour share by 5 per cent by 2025 together with a similar increase in the rest of the world.
Source: Strauss and Isaacs (2016), GPM model.

countervailing forces; indeed, imports increase, contributing to a worsening of the country's current account, and private investment as a share of GDP falls marginally (although aggregate investment is higher). These effects are, however, insufficient to outweigh the positive demand stimulus. Inflation remains contained and falls slightly due to productivity growth, increases in imports and a reduction in the profit mark-up; the employment rate is largely unchanged. When increases to the labour share are complemented by an increase in government spending, or similar redistributive policies elsewhere in the world, the positive impact strengthens. This redistribution of income in the South African economy, while predominantly beneficial from an economic perspective, cannot alone radically alter the economy's trajectory.

The second modelling exercise considered here, by Adelzadeh and Alvillar (2016), directly estimates the impact of raising wages, rather than an increase to the labour share. It uses the Applied Development Research Solutions (ADRS) Dynamically Integrated Macro-Micro Simulation Model for South Africa. The ADRS model is also an econometric model meaning the relationships assumed within the 3 200 equations, and more than 400 behavioural equations, between the 41 different sectors, are established on the basis of past historical South Africa data (see Adelzadeh and Alvillar 2016 for a technical discussion of the model). The model estimates the impact of four different levels at which a national minimum wage could be set, ranging from the 'minimalist' scenario of R2 250 to the 'maximalist' scenario of R6 000.[15] We focus here on the distributional consequences while mentioning

Figure 2.6: Average real wages (2025) and average annual growth rate of household income (2016–2025)

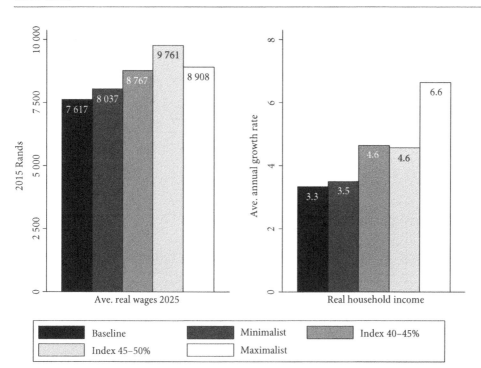

Scenarios:
- 'Minimalist' scenario: set the national minimum wage at R2 250 per month in the first year, thereafter increasing it by inflation.
- The intermediate 'indexation' scenarios link the national minimum wage to a gradually increasing percentage of the average wage. In both, very low-wage sectors – domestic work, agricultural and expanded public works – are set at a lower level.
- 'Indexation 40–45 per cent': begins at approximately R3 500 and reaches approximately R3 900 five years later (both in 2015 rands); thereafter it increases by inflation.
- 'Indexation 45–50 per cent': begins at approximately R4 600 and reaches approximately R5 500 five years later (both in 2015 rands); thereafter it increases by inflation.
- 'Maximalist' scenario: set the national minimum wage at R6 000 per month in the first year, thereafter increasing it by inflation plus 2 per cent.

Source: Adelzadeh and Alvillar (2016).

other impacts. As with the United Nations' GPM, these scenarios are compared with a baseline business as usual scenario.

Most relevant here is that real average wages and real household incomes rise, as shown in Figure 2.6. Without a national minimum wage real average wages would be R7 617 in 2025, but with a national minimum wage they go up to R9 761. The average annual growth rate of household income would be only 3.3 per cent over the ten years modelled, but with a national minimum wage it rises to between 3.5 and 6.6 per cent.

Figure 2.7: Macroeconomic impacts

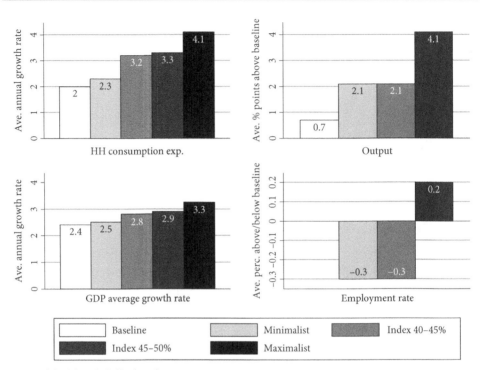

Source: Adelzadeh and Alvillar (2016).

The boost in household income is more pronounced at the lower end of the wage distribution, precisely the impact necessary to reduce poverty and inequality.

At a macroeconomic level, the higher incomes translate into higher household consumption, greater output and higher GDP growth rates, as shown in Figure 2.7. The
magnitude of these effects differs with each scenario, and different sectors are differently
affected.[16] The employment rate falls marginally, by at most 0.3 per cent (concentrated
in the service sector), in line with the existing local and international ex-post evidence.
Other benefits include increased investment in real terms (albeit lower as a percentage of
GDP), higher exports and imports, a fall in the demand for social grants and a rise in tax
revenue; inflation and government debt remain within sustainable bounds. Various macroeconomic indicators become unstable at the R6 000 level (see Adelzadeh and Alvillar
2016) indicating that there is a 'threshold point' above which the immediate institution of
a national minimum wage is projected to become destabilising.

Most relevant here is that real wage growth is concentrated at the bottom half of the
wage distribution, signalling that lower-wage earners would be the biggest beneficiaries and inequality and poverty would be reduced. The Gini coefficient is projected to
fall modestly below the baseline scenario in all the national minimum wage scenarios,

Figure 2.8: Impact on poverty and inequality

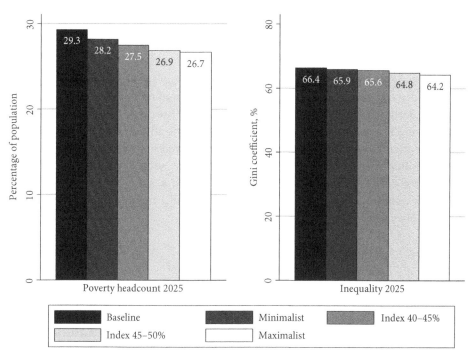

Source: Adelzadeh and Alvillar (2016).

as shown in Figure 2.8. Positive impacts are even more profound on poverty, with the poverty headcount falling by up to three percentage points. The poverty-reducing effect is greater for rural areas, women and those earning in the bottom 20 per cent. National minimum wages levels of between R3 500 and R5 500 are therefore shown to have significant positive impacts without introducing instability into the economy.

The predictions from these modelling exercises chime with the international evidence outlined above: a national minimum wage could therefore play an important role in raising incomes for low-wage workers and assist in reducing inequality. Such redistributional measures are shown to be of benefit to the South African economy and could therefore be one mechanism (among others) of bringing the economy out of its current malaise.

CONCLUSION

The most recent initiative to implement a national minimum wage in South Africa is, at the time of writing, being negotiated between the 'social partners' in the National Economic Development and Labour Council (Nedlac). The Ekurhuleni Declaration, which kicked off this process, emphasised the national minimum wage as a means of 'addressing wage inequality' (Nedlac 2014). The international evidence clearly indicates that minimum wages have the potential to close wage gaps in both the formal and informal sectors without significant harm to employment. These benefits are stronger the more comprehensive the minimum wage coverage, and moving from a sectoral system to a national minimum wage should increase coverage and compliance. The statistical modelling predicts that a national minimum wage set between R3 500 and R5 500 can directly raise wages of low-income workers and reduce poverty and inequality without destabilising effects on the macroeconomy. The deleterious consequences of inequality, and the moral indefensibility of huge income and wealth differentials, have entered the mainstream. With this has come a renewed appreciation for inequality-reducing policy measures. Minimum wages are one such measure. The evidence outlined here indicates that the movement towards to a national minimum wage in South Africa could contribute to reducing poverty and inequality and advancing a pro-poor policy agenda.

NOTES

1   The median and mean minimum wage for sectoral determinations was approximately R2 700 in 2015 (Isaacs 2016). This is in the bottom half when compared to comparative middle-income countries in purchasing power and as a percentage of the average wage, and well below the line of working poverty.

2   The interested reader is referred to the research of the National Minimum Wage Research Initiative (NMW-RI) at the University of the Witwatersrand at www.nationalminimumwage.co.za, from which this paper draws.

3   These poverty estimates use the most recent cost of basic needs poverty line developed by Budlender et al. (2015) which sat at R1 319 in April 2015 rands (Finn 2015).

4   Percentiles are points on the wage distribution above which a certain percentage of workers earn (for example, the fiftieth percentile – or the median – is the point above which 50 per cent of earners earn).

5   By contrast, minimum wages in South Africa have risen far more modestly. As shown in Figure 2.4, the real increase in sectoral determination ranged from 16 to 81 per cent with three-quarters of them below 40 per cent.

6   Marginal part-time employment is non-standard employment with very short hours of work (15–20 hours/week).

7   In the South African debate this research has often been ignored. Seekings and Nattrass (2016), for instance, in their discussion of the employment effects of minimum wages, avoid these studies in favour of reference to Neumark and Wascher (widely discredited for methodological biases, see Doucouliagos and Stanley 2009; Dube 2011) and a few cherry-picked studies.

8   Dinkelman and Ranchhod (2010) likewise show no negative impact on employment or hours worked for domestic workers and strong evidence of an increase in wages; Hertz (2005) finds a small disemployment effect. On aggregate, employment in the sectors studied rose over the period (DPRU 2010).

9   In Chletsos and Giotis (2015) certain manufacturing sectors were also shown to be more significantly affected but which subsectors drove this is not clear.

10   See Strauss and Isaacs (2016) for a lengthier discussion on the labour share and minimum wages.

11   A large body of theoretical and empirical literature supports the proposition of wage-led growth (for example Setterfield 2002; Stockhammer and Onaran 2013; Dabla-Norris et al. 2015); see Adelzadeh and Alvillar (2016: 40) on the link between minimum wages and growth.

12   There are multiple minima in certain sectors. In Figure 2.4, large urban areas (Area A) were selected, grade D security guards used, hospitality businesses with less than ten employees, taxi drivers and shop assistants in the wholesale and retail sector. The exact level is less important than the trends.

13   Alternatively, minimum wages may simply be ineffective at reducing inequality in South Africa, an unlikely conclusion given the international evidence.

14   The GPM is a globally consistent macroeconomic econometric model used for medium-term fore-casting by the G20 and the United Nations (see Strauss and Isaacs 2016 for a discussion of the model's specifications).

15   The issue of how to set a national minimum wage is thorny. The ILO and most experts place impor-tance on benchmarks against prevailing wage levels, the basic needs of workers, and economic sustainability/employers' ability to pay. This is the approach adopted by the NMW-RI (see Isaacs 2016; Konopelko 2016) and informs the modelling scenarios. (A critique of the approaches taken by Seekings and Nattrass (2016) is forthcoming.)

16   An implication of both models is that wage-led growth (via increases to low-income earners) is likely in the South African case. This proposition is dismissed (by implication) by all the CGE mod-elling exercises cited above and in Seekings and Nattrass (2016: 23–7), neglecting the theoretical and empirical support for this generally (cited above) and that the GPM is the most sophisticated attempt to directly tackle this question. However, the growth impacts are modest and must be complemented by other sources of demand- and supply-side interventions. Our chief concern here, and the point of a national minimum wage, is its impact on wages, household income, poverty and inequality.

REFERENCES

Adelzadeh, A and Alvillar, C (2016) *The impact of a national minimum wage on the South Africa econ-omy*. University of the Witwatersrand Working Paper Series No. 2. Johannesburg: University of the Witwatersrand.

Amadeo, EJ, Gill, IS and Neri, M (2000) *Brazil: The pressure points in labor legislation*. FGV/EPGE Escola Brasileira de Economia e Finanças, Getulio Vargas Foundation (Brazil). Economics Working Papers (Ensaios Economicos da EPGE) No. 395. Rio de Janeiro: Getulio Vargas Foundation.

Amlinger, M, Bispinck, R and Schulten, T (2016) *The German minimum wage: Experiences and perspec-tives after one year*. WSI Report No. 28e, 1/2016. Dusseldorf: WSI Institute of Economic and Social Research.

Autor, DH, Manning, A and Smith, CL (2016) The contribution of the minimum wage to US wage inequality over three decades: A reassessment. *American Economic Journal: Applied Economics*, 8 (1), 58–99.

Bargain, O, Doorley, K and Van Kerm, P (2016) *Minimum wages and the gender gap in pay: Evidence from the UK and Ireland*. Luxembourg, No. 2016–02. Esch-sur-Alzette: LISER.

Belman, D and Wolfson, P (2014) *What does the minimum wage do?* Kalamazoo: W. E. Upjohn Institute.

Belser, P and Rani, U (2015) Minimum wages and inequality. In J Berg (ed) *Labour markets, institutions and inequality: Building just societies in the 21st century*. Cheltenham: Edward Elgar.

Berg, A and Ostry, J (2011) *Inequality and unsustainable growth: Two sides of the same coin?* International Monetary Fund Staff Discussion Note No. SDN/11/08. Washington, DC: IMF.

Berg, J (2010) *Laws or luck? Understanding rising formality in Brazil in the 2000s*. University Library of Munich, Germany, MPRA Paper No. 43608. Brasilia: ILO.

Bhorat, H, Kanbur, R and Mayet, N (2011a) *Minimum wage violation in South Africa*. Cornell University, Department of Applied Economics and Management, Working Paper No. 126534. Ithaca: Cornell University.

Bhorat, H, Kanbur, R and Mayet, N (2011b) *The determinants of minimum wage violation in South Africa*. Cornell University, Department of Applied Economics and Management, Working Paper No. 126535. Ithaca: Cornell University.

Bhorat, H, Kanbur, R and Mayet, N (2013a) *The impact of sectoral minimum wage laws on employment, wages, and hours of work in South Africa*. Cornell University, Department of Applied Economics and Management, Working Paper No. 180096. Ithaca: Cornell University.

Bhorat, H, Kanbur, R and Stanwix, B (2013b) *Estimating the impact of minimum wages on employment, wages and non-wage benefits: The case of agriculture in South Africa*. Cornell University, Department of Applied Economics and Management, Working Paper No. 180095. Ithaca: Cornell University.

Boockmann, B (2010) *The combined employment effects of minimum wages and labor market regulation: A meta-analysis*. Institut für Angewandte Wirtschaftsforschung (IAW), IAW Discussion Paper No. 65. Tübingen: IAW.

Bosch, M and Manacorda, M (2010) Minimum wages and earnings inequality in urban Mexico. *American Economic Journal: Applied Economics*, 2 (4), 128–149.

Broecke, S, Vandeweyer, M and Forti, A (2015) *The effect of minimum wage on employment in emerging economies: A literature review*. Organisation for Economic Co-operation and Development (OECD) Social, Employment and Migration Working Papers. Paris: OECD.

Budlender, J, Leibbrandt, M and Woolard, I (2015) *South African poverty lines: A review and two new money-metric thresholds*. Southern Africa Labour and Development Research Unit, University of Cape Town, Working Paper Series No. 151. Cape Town: University of Cape Town.

Checchi, D and Garcia-Peñalosa, C (2005) *Labour market institutions and the personal distribution of income in the OECD*. CESifo Working Paper Series No. 1608. Munich: CESifo Group.

Chletsos, M and Giotis, GP (2015) *The employment effect of minimum wage using 77 international studies since 1992: A meta-analysis*. Munich Personal RePE Archive, No. 61321. Munich: MPRA.

Chun, N and Khor, N (2010) *Minimum wages and changing wage inequality in Indonesia*. Manila: Asian Development Bank.

Dabla-Norris, E, Kochhar, K, Suphaphiphat, N, Ricka, F and Tsounta, E (2015) *Causes and consequences of income inequality: A global perspective*. International Monetary Fund, No. DSN/15/13. Washington, DC: IMF.

Daudey, E and Garcia-Peñalosa, C (2007) The personal and the factor distributions of income in a cross-section of countries. *Journal of Development Studies*, 43 (5), 812–829.

Dickens, R, Manning, A and Butcher, T (2012) *Minimum wages and wage inequality: Some theory and an application to the UK*. University of Sussex, Working Paper No. 45–2012. Brighton: University of Sussex.

Dinkelman, T and Ranchhod, V (2010) *Evidence on the impact of minimum wage laws in an informal sector: Domestic workers in South Africa*. Southern Africa Labour and Development Research Unit, University of Cape Town, Working Paper No. 44. Cape Town: SALDRU.

DoL (Department of Labour) (2015) *Sectoral determinations (multiple agreements)*. Pretoria: Government of the Republic of South Africa.

Doucouliagos, H and Stanley, TD (2009) Publication selection bias in minimum-wage research? A meta-regression analysis. *British Journal of Industrial Relations*, 47 (2), 406–428.

DPRU (Development Policy Research Unit) (2010) *Addressing the plight of vulnerable workers: The role of sectoral determinations*. University of Cape Town. Cape Town: DPRU.

DPRU (Development Policy Research Unit) (2016) *Investigating the feasibility of a national minimum wage for South Africa*. University of Cape Town. Cape Town: DPRU.

Dube, A (2011) Minimum wages. *Journal of Economic Literature*, 49 (3), 762–766.

Fajnzylber, P (2001) *Minimum wage effects throughout the wage distribution: Evidence from Brazil's formal and informal sectors*. Social Science Research Network, Scholarly Paper No. ID 269622. Rochester: SSRN.

Finn, A (2015) *A national minimum wage in the context of the South African labour market*. Johannesburg: National Minimum Wage Research Initiative, University of the Witwatersrand.

Freeman, RB (1996) The minimum wage as a redistributive tool. *The Economic Journal*, 106 (436), 639–649.

Gindling, TH and Terrell, K (2005) The effect of minimum wages on actual wages in formal and informal sectors in Costa Rica. *World Development*, 33 (11), 1905–1921.

Herr, H, Kazandziska, M and Mahnkopf-Praprotnik, S (2009) *The theoretical debate about minimum wages*. Global Labour University, Working Papers No. 6. GLU.

Hertz, T (2005) *The effect of minimum wages on the employment and earnings of South Africa's domestic service workers*. University of Cape Town, Development Policy Research Unit, Working Paper No. 05099. Cape Town: DPRU.

ILO (International Labour Organization) (2013) *Global wage report 2012/13: Wages and equitable growth*. Geneva: ILO.

ILO (International Labour Organization) (2014) *World of work report 2014*. Geneva: ILO.

ILO (International Labour Organization) (2015) *Global wage report 2014/15: Wages and income inequality*. Geneva: ILO.

ILO (International Labour Organization) and OECD (Organisation for Economic Co-operation and Development) (2015) *The labour share in G20 economies*. Geneva: ILO, OECD.

Isaacs, G (2016) *A national minimum wage for South Africa*. University of the Witwatersrand, Summary Report No. 1. Johannesburg: University of the Witwatersrand.

Keifman, SN and Maurizio, R (2012) *Changes in labour market conditions and policies*. UNU-WIDER Working Paper Series. No. 2012/14. Helsinki: UNU-WIDER.

Khamis, M (2008) *Does the minimum wage have a higher impact on the informal than on the formal labour market? Evidence from quasi-experiments*. IZA Discussion Paper No. 3911. Bonn: IZA.

Konopelko, E (2016) *Indexing, setting and adjusting a national minimum wage*. University of the Witwatersrand, Policy Brief No. 7. Johannesburg: University of the Witwatersrand.

Kristensen, N and Cunningham, WL (2006) *Do minimum wages in Latin America and the Caribbean matter? Evidence from 19 countries*. Washington, DC: World Bank.

Leibbrandt, M, Finn, A and Woolard, I (2012) Describing and decomposing post-apartheid income inequality in South Africa. *Development Southern Africa*, 29 (1), 19–34.

Leibbrandt, M, Woolard, I, McEwen, H and Koep, C (2010) *Employment and inequality outcomes in South Africa*. Southern Africa Labour and Development Research Unit (SALDRU) and School of Economics, University of Cape Town. Cape Town: SALDRU. pp. 1–54.

Leonard, M de L, Stanley, TD and Doucouliagos, H (2014) Does the UK minimum wage reduce employment? A meta-regression analysis. *British Journal of Industrial Relations*, 52 (3), 499–520.

Lin, C and Yun, M (2016) *The effects of the minimum wage on earnings inequality: Evidence from China*. IZA Discussion Paper No. 9715. Bonn: IZA.

Lu, R (2015) *The minimum wage, inequality and employment in China*. Ph.D. thesis, University of Birmingham.

Lukiyanova, A (2011) Effects of minimum wages on the Russian wage distribution. *SSRN Electronic Journal*, 34.

MacLeod, C (2015) *Measuring the impact of a National Minimum Wage*. Presentation to Nedlac (Johannesburg South Africa) on 19 October 2015, updated version of 23 October 2015.

Maloney, WF and Mendez, JN (2003) *Measuring the impact of minimum wages: Evidence from Latin America*. National Bureau of Economic Research, Working Paper No. 9800. Cambridge, MA: NBER.

Maurizio, R (2016) *The consequences of minimum wages on inequality. Evidence for Latin America.* National Minimum Wage Symposium and Policy Round Table. Johannesburg: University of the Witwatersrand.

Minford, P (1998) *Markets not stakes.* London: Orion Business.

Murahwa, B (2016) *Monitoring and enforcement: Strategies to ensure an effective national minimum wage in South Africa.* National Minimum Wage Research Initiative, Working Paper No. 5. Johannesburg: University of the Witwatersrand.

Nataraj, S, Perez-Arce, F, Kumar, KB and Srinivasan, SV (2014) The impact of labor market regulation on employment in low-income countries: A meta-analysis. *Journal of Economic Surveys*, 28 (3), 551–572.

Nedlac (National Economic Development and Labour Council) (2014) *Ekurhuleni declaration.* Johannesburg: Nedlac.

OECD (Organisation for Economic Co-operation and Development) (2011) *Divided we stand: Why inequality keeps rising.* Paris: OECD.

OECD (Organisation for Economic Co-operation and Development) (2014) *Focus on inequality and growth.* Paris: OECD.

OECD (Organisation for Economic Co-operation and Development) (2015) *Why is income inequality increasing?:Income inequality the gap between rich and poor.* Paris: OECD. pp. 41–61.

Onaran, Ö and Galanis, G (2012) *Is aggregate demand wage-led or profit-led?* International Labour Organization, Conditions of Work and Employment Series No. 40. Geneva: ILO.

Oxfam (2016) *An economy for the 1%: How privilege and power in the economy drive extreme inequality and how this can be stopped.* Oxfam Briefing Paper No. 210. Oxford: Oxfam.

Pauw, K (2009) *Labour market policy and poverty: Exploring the macro-micro linkages of minimum wages and wage subsidies.* PhD thesis, School of Economics, University of Cape Town.

Pauw, K and Leibbrandt, M (2012) Minimum wages and household poverty: General equilibrium macro-micro simulations for South Africa. *World Development*, 40 (4), 771–783.

Quantec (2017) Timeseries Data. Statistical data portal, accessed in 2017.

Rani, U, Belser, P and Ranjbar, S (2013) Role of minimum wages in rebalancing the economy. *World of Work Report*, 2013 (1), 45–74.

Rani, U and Ranjbar, S (2015) Impact of minimum wages on wage quantiles: Evidence from developing countries. Available from www.rdw2015.org/uploads/submission/full_paper/376/wagedist_uma.pdf.

Schlenker, E and Schmid, KD (2013) *Capital income shares and income inequality in the European Union.* IMK at the Hans Boeckler Foundation, Macroeconomic Policy Institute, IMK Working Paper No. 119-2013.

Schmitt, J (2013) *Why does the minimum wage have no discernible effect on employment?* Center for Economic and Policy Research, Washington, DC.

Schmöller, M (2014) *The introduction of a minimum wage in Germany: Background and potential employment effects.* Bank of Finland, BoF Online No. 11.

SEDLAC (Socio-Economic Database for Latin America and the Caribbean) (2016) Socio-economic database for Latin America and the Caribbean. Data portal, accessed 2016.

Seekings, J and Nattrass, N (2016) Setting the level of a national minimum wage: what can South Africa learn from other countries' experiences? *Transformation: Critical Perspectives on Southern Africa*, 92, 1–36.

Setterfield, M (2002) *The economics of demand-led growth: Challenging the supply-side vision of the long run.* Cheltenham: Edward Elgar.

Stats SA (2015) *Labour market dynamics in South Africa 2014.* DataFirst data portal, accessed 2015.

Stockhammer, E and Onaran, Ö (2013) Wage-led growth: theory, evidence, policy. *Review of Keynesian Economics*, 1 (1), 61–78.

Storm, S and Isaacs, G (2016) *Modelling the impact of a national minimum wage in South Africa: Are general equilibrium models fit for purpose?* University of the Witwatersrand, Johannesburg: CSID, Research Brief No. 1.

Strauss, I and Isaacs, G (2016) *Labour compensation growth in the South African economy: Assessing its impact through the labour share using the Global Policy Model.* University of the Witwatersrand, Working Paper Series No. 4.

Tsounta, E and Osueke, A (2014) *What is behind Latin America's declining income inequality?* International Monetary Fund, IMF Working Paper No. 14/124.

UNDP (United Nations Development Programme) (2014) Income inequality. In: *Humanity divided: Confronting inequality in developing countries.* Geneva: UNDP. pp. 64–117.

CHAPTER 3

The politics of poverty and inequality in South Africa: Connectivity, abjections and the problem of measurement

Sarah Bracking

In this chapter I will add to chapters 1 and 2 by discussing what is knowable about poverty and inequality in South Africa and some characteristics of what it means to measure.[1] The importance of measurement is to try and catalyse social change by giving citizens and policy makers the knowledge they need to act and spend wisely for a better South Africa. However, there are problems in the calculation of economic statistics everywhere which are related to the production of 'bad statistics' (Andreas and Greenhill 2010: 7); and more generically to the discipline-based problems in the epistemology of economics. Mainstream economics assumes a number of relationships before it even attempts to count, and frames out issues of market imperfections, informality, criminality and extra-economic factors which affect distributional outcomes, such as power. For limits of time and space this article will not cover this discipline-based debate, but will focus instead on the more recent literature on the reactivity of measurement, where the act of measurement partly or wholly produces the thing in question (Espeland and Sauder 2007; MacKenzie 2011: 1784). This reactivity of measurement was described by Engle Merry (2011) as where the 'production and usage' of an indicator has both a knowledge effect and a governance effect: the former is generated as the gathering and organisation of information creates the impression of a standardised and rule-based thing, while the latter is produced as the numbers are used in the management of people. Moreover, it is 'often the imperative to govern that provides the rationale and the resources for producing the indicator in the first place' (Jerven 2013: 5). The domain of poverty measurement displays these attributes of reactivity and is the subject of this chapter.

As Jerven (2013) noted recently in a timely book on 'poor numbers', the accuracy of numbers is not a problem specific to Africa or exclusive to debates on economic development. However, 'a surprisingly small number of studies examine the role, power, and quality of the numbers applied to issues concerning African economic development' (Jerven 2013: 1). Although it is a personal conjecture – since motivation is notoriously difficult to examine – it may be that professional economists, technocrats and policy makers are so embedded in the expectations of paradigms of advanced liberal government (see Dean 2003; Oels 2006: 191–2; inspired by Foucault 2004), such as 'evidence-based policy', the 'what works debate' and 'value for money' that a collusive silence has emerged on the underlying inadequacy of the evidence on which policy can be based. Although it is countered slightly by some systematic review studies which review and explicitly judge the quality of argument and evidence in respect of a particular policy, economic development statistics overall appear to have been largely reserved from critique – or, at least, the long appendix of assumptions made to enable calculations is mostly unread. Numbers are 'cleaned', assumptions are reported and then hidden in appendices, while the short executive summary reads in a much more definitive and certain style.

These general observations apply to the case of South Africa: the discipline-based problems of measurement are readily apparent in a society where poverty is informalised and sometimes criminalised and where the elite enjoy exceptions to regulation and the ability to hide their full wealth. The measurement-related problem of reactivity is also readily apparent as analysts rely on only a few panel data sets and yet generate a highly contested concept of poverty in public policy. In effect, the measurement of poverty and inequality in South Africa is an effort in approximation, and in relation to inequality it is arguably both under- and over-measured. It is under-measured because of the probable effects of illicit financial flows (IFFs) on aggregate data, owing to the offshore economy of the wealthy, where South Africa topped the league in 2015 of African source countries for capital and wealth secreted illegally offshore, with a cumulative figure of US$209 billion disappearing between 2004 and 2013 (Kar and Spanjers 2015: 8). The volume of IFFs is mostly contributed by trade mis-invoicing, but the personal wealth holdings of the rich are also undercounted onshore owing to the hiding of their assets and share income offshore, often facilitated through these mis-invoicing activities. The extent of hidden wealth enjoyed by the rich is also inflated by the simple disappearance of persons from the databases of revenue officers, rather than their income being undercounted. It has been estimated that between 28 000 and 114 000 'high net worth individuals' (HNWIs) have disappeared from the South African Revenue Services database, losing South Africa an estimated US$10.9 billion annually in tax (Christian Aid and TJN 2014: 7, citing AIDC). The resulting undercounting of wealth in the top decile would have the effect of making inequality appear as less than it actually is. Even the World Bank and its chief economists note the problems of informational inadequacy on the income of the households at the top of the income distribution (World Bank 2014: 26; Inchauste et al. 2015: 15).

This lessening effect for inequality is then probably exacerbated by the undercounting of poor people, at the other end of the income scale. With between 500 000 to 1 million undocumented migrants, many hide, or are excluded, from the state's accounting processes (figures from Stats SA, quoted in Mwiti 2015).

Poverty and inequality may be overcounted because the formal categories of statistics fail to capture incomes and wealth in the informal economy and because certain poor people may have an incentive to under-report their income in order to maintain eligibility for social welfare grants. However, it is unclear how this undercounting of earnings would affect the poor or the rich differentially. In other words, because of the ubiquity of informal economic transactions it may be impossible to know the 'real' levels of poverty and inequality for either group. This is compounded by politics and power relations which contribute to these measurement problems, in that certain politicians and public sector power holders have an incentive to make measurement difficult, because they themselves enjoy monetary and other resources (such as gifts and favours) transacted in opaque political networks traversing the state, political party and private domains. Moreover, abjections which cause poverty and inequality are often authored in the politics of connectivity to the state and ruling party at the same time as others are rewarded within the same networks (Bracking 2016). Thus, because of the political economy derived from office-holding, and the wealth this generates, it might also be that we are not measuring sources of wealth that reduce the levels of poverty and (potentially) inequality for those who enjoy political connectivity, while we simultaneously fail to appreciate that 'poverty traps' (Woolcock 2007) are often also authored politically. One amelioration of measurement problems, and the poverty behind them, would in the first instance be in increased transparency of the economy generated through public policy and office holding.

Even if figures were deemed more accurate than at present, however, there remain two further problems attendant to measurement as a step to public advocacy, whatever its accuracy. First, that measurement in itself tells us very little about the causes of poverty; and second, that measurement and facts also do not enter public debate in a predictable way (Du Toit 2011, 2012; Seekings 2008; Ferguson 2007). The actual numbers tell us little about what policy makers may in fact do after they have been released, particularly when expenditure on reducing poverty competes with other spending priorities, as it inevitably does. To proceed, I will review the controversies over the measurement of poverty that have emerged in public debate in South Africa recently. Then, in the concluding section, I will briefly examine what the category of poverty means in public policy discourse, arguing that 'poverty' currently has little policy traction or ability to prevent poor people sitting at the bottom of a social order marked by spatial and relational exclusion.

POVERTY AND POVERTY MEASUREMENT IN SOUTH AFRICA

There are three poverty lines in South Africa, generated from a cost of basic needs approach: the food poverty line (FPL), the lower bound poverty line (LBPL) and the upper bound poverty line (UBPL). The first (FPL) is the rand value below which individuals are unable to purchase or consume enough food to supply them with minimum per capita per day energy requirements (set at a very low 2 100 kilocalories). The second and third poverty lines include non-food items, where individuals at the LBPL are not able to consume both adequate food and non-food items and thus miss meals to buy non-food essentials. Individuals at the UBPL are deemed able to purchase both adequate food and non-food items. The official poverty lines adopted in the National Development Plan of 2014 are R321, R443 and R620 per person per month (Stats SA 2015). Using these poverty lines, Statistics South Africa commented in April 2014:

> … poverty levels in the country have dropped since 2006, reaching a low of 45.5 per cent in 2011, when applying the upper bound poverty line (R620 per capita per month in 2011 prices). This translates into roughly 23 million people living below the upper bound poverty line (UBPL).

This was reported in a press statement under the headline 'South Africa winning war on poverty', although it is hard to see how a 'war' is being won when 23 million people are still afflicted (number from Stats SA 2014a). That point notwithstanding, the statement did not say anything further about what had happened from the point of the 2011 survey to the date of the 2014 news release. This is partly due to the time it takes to analyse data from national statistical surveys, but it also points to the problem of how one is to measure poverty at a point some time after a nationally representative survey, when the collection of statistics is expensive and has resource implications. National household surveys are conducted periodically to generate new data, which can be compared to 2011 prices in order to determine whether poverty has fallen or risen (at the time of writing, the 2015 exercise is still unavailable). But with statistical weightings applied to variables, not least the more than 2 million new persons in the official population statistics added since 2011, the data from the Consumer Price Index can be used to inflate the poverty line of 2011 to the present.

In fact, Statistics South Africa provides poverty estimates every 2.5 years or so from either its Living Conditions Survey or its Income and Expenditure Survey. Statistics South Africa also provides inflation adjusted poverty lines covering the period 2000 to 2014 using the Consumer Price Index. A series for the old poverty lines and the new 're-based' poverty lines is available, although it is not published as a report but only made available to users (mainly government departments) on request (see Simelane 2015: slide 7).[2] However, in terms of public discourse, there is, in effect, an advisory poverty line that exists up to five years after the data is first collected – thus in 2016 the advisory poverty line was based on data collected in 2011 and adopted in the National Development Plan of 2011. The poverty line was not officially updated subsequently, owing to an effort to widely disseminate the index linked adjustments. This has the effect of setting escape from poverty at an impossibly low level (if inflation is taken into account) and a potentially generous reading of government efforts to reduce poverty. The time lag attached to when poverty data is officially adopted and made useful to other related public policy processes has adverse consequences for the poor, even though departments do not appear to use poverty data to generate performance targets and benchmarks for social service delivery. This is because when the fixed lines are officially adopted (say, in the 2014 National Development Plan) poor people are represented in a price world that has passed (2011) when they are trying to live in another time (2016). In short, the price inflation which has occurred in the interim is effectively discounted as unimportant in policy terms, even though it still represents a cost to the poor.

The time lag effect between the measurement and use of official poverty lines could imply that government expects the poor to miraculously become immune to inflation. Strange as that may sound, there are many precedents in economic policy that make this assumption. Culturally, there are commensurabilities to this in the way poor people are treated in labour markets, with the established wage for a cleaner or security guard rarely rising according to inflation. The rises in the child grant in February and October 2015 again looked generous, but were not index-linked and actually represented a cut in the grant, if inflation were to be taken into account (Bond 2016a). These time lags between price inflation and income adjustment often result in increases in inequality – and this problem is compounded because there is much evidence to suggest that inflation itself does not have uniformly distributed consequences and often discriminates against the poor. That inflation is anti-poor, not least because the poor have little power to insist on timely adaptation of their incomes to adjust for it, has been established theoretically for some time (Yaffe 1973). Recent dense analysis of differential price movements across the income distribution from South African data show that both the poverty and inequality price decompositions 'characterise the 2005–10 period as one during which price changes were anti-poor' (Leibbrandt et al. 2016: 409). In this period, inflation rates for poor households typically exceeded those of rich households. The policy process in South Africa adversely contributes to this more foundational aspect of the working of price mechanisms in markets, rather than taking a pro-poor position – which would be to plan in anticipation of anti-poor inflationary price movements.

In addition, poverty measurement may underestimate the depth of poverty in a number of fundamental ways. For example, the calculation of the non-food component of the second and third poverty lines is not modelled from a basket of goods defined as needed (as in the calorific benchmark for the food) but on deviations from the food line based on actual households' expenditures. In other words, the non-food component is generated from the notional opportunity cost approach (Ravallion 1998), where the expenditures of households at the poverty line are analysed for how they start to swap a food item to spend on something else. The logic runs that since they only have the bare minimum quantity of food in any case, if they choose to forego any part of it the non-food item must be essential. This generates poverty lines where (as is often the case as members of households do not consume equally) a mother might forego her own food in order to avoid the shame of her child going to school without shoes. Budlender et al. (2015a) also recently applied the same 'cost of basic needs' approach to generate a food poverty line very similar to Statistics South Africa's (at R337 against Statistics South Africa's R335), but argue that the upper bound poverty line is too low: in 2011 Statistics South Africa calculated this at R779, whereas Budlender et al. (2015a) produce a figure of R1 042 per person per month as a level of total expenditure where households tend to buy sufficient food and non-food items. A more pro-poor methodology would be to benchmark 'essential' items against scientific evidence of need, for example, in nutrition, health and educational policy research.

However, both can be viewed as insufficient, particularly if the poor are suffering a different level of inflation from the aggregate figure (Leibbrandt et al. 2016: 410–12). Although the inflation rate per decile and region is not regularly or systematically counted, the Pietermaritzburg Agency for Christian Social Awareness (South Africa) (Pacsa) food price barometer does monitor the prices of foods typically bought by the poorest in shops where they are most likely to buy. Shockingly, the 2015–2016 drought pushed food inflation for the poorest to 14.6 per cent year on year from January 2015 to January 2016, with the three months to year-end showing a 9 per cent increase on an upward trajectory. Pacsa researchers claim that poor households prioritise a number of other expenditures before food, underspending by 55.6 per cent and taking on debt to cover food shortfalls (Pacsa 2016). Meanwhile, Statistics South Africa, in their initial upper bound poverty line, assumed that households spent 43 per cent of their expenditure on food, whereas Budlender et al. (2015b) estimate this as closer to 35 per cent. With Pacsa estimating the cost of the monthly food basket for seven people at R1 797 in January 2016 (based on actual expenditure preferences of poor households), we know enough to know that malnutrition is common. Pacsa summarise that the sharp price hikes in basic foods from 2015 means that 'the gap between what households are buying and what they would like to and indeed should be buying for basic nutrition is widening' (2016: 5).

As it stands, the difference between the current official food poverty line and the lower bound poverty line is just R122 per month – around the price of some good school shoes; or ten minibus fares; or one bar of soap, one tube of toothpaste, a clothes' washing bar or monthly feminine hygiene, which would together clear the whole monthly non-food budget (prices as of early 2016). The list of items illustrates another problem that serves to underestimate the depth of poverty: that, as Statistics South Africa acknowledge, the food basket they model is based on data from the consumptions and expenditures of actual households, with all their irrational foibles included. With clear beer excluded (since 'not everyone in the household will drink it' (Stats SA 2015: 7)), one large expenditure in some poor households has been removed and an undercounting of household members' poverty occurs. Non-nutritious items (polony and fizzy drinks) are included, even though the statisticians know that these, typically consumed to achieve the kilocalorie benchmark, do not meet the full range of food needs such as vitamins and nutrients.[3] In this sense an expenditure-based poverty line under-represents food hunger and malnutrition. Cultural preferences, inter-household inequalities in consumption and the need for people to demonstrate their identity through what they consume problematise rational calculative assumptions behind how people will behave when they have very little money. The money spent on non-food items would also reflect cultural preferences (such as the purchase of roughly three packets of cigarettes) which would exhaust the monthly non-food budget in 2016 – or the difference between the food poverty line and lower bound poverty line.

During 2015, a number of arguments over the poverty and inequality data arose between a group of economists (including those of the World Bank) who believed that inequality is declining and social and fiscal policy are progressive, and another group who claimed the opposite, notably with Bond (2015) arguing that social welfare was 'tokenistic'. For example, using the 2010–2011 Income and Expenditure Survey data, World Bank-based economists argued that social spending results in sizeable income rises for the poor and that fiscal policy acts to reduce income inequality and poverty, making fiscal policy 'equalising and poverty-reducing' even though levels of poverty and inequality still rank South Africa among the highest in middle-income countries (Inchauste et al. 2015). This World Bank report cites Statistics South Africa to the effect that between 2006 and 2011 the proportion of the population living in poverty fell from 57.2 to 45.5 per cent between 2006 and 2011, while the Gini coefficient fell from 0.67 to 0.65 (Inchauste et al. 2015: 1; citing Stats SA 2014a). In an article in *Econx3x* the same group of economists claim that the Gini coefficient:

> using *market income* is estimated to be around 0.77. However, for *final income* – i.e. when all taxes (indirect and direct, excluding corporate taxes) as well as key categories of government spending are taken into account – the Gini coefficient is estimated to be around 0.59 – a reduction of 0.18 Gini points (Woolard et al. 2015; see also Inchauste et al. 2015; World Bank 2014).

This data was then widely cited by key government figures and the business press to depict government generosity and then, in the face of downgrades from rating agencies, to suggest reckless generosity and the need for austerity (see also Bond 2015, 2016b and 2016c). For example, *Business Day* associate editor Joffe (2015) claimed that 'South Africa can claim to have one of the world's most redistributive public purses'.

Bond replied with a feisty rebuttal, pointing out quite cogently that the economists who claimed a drop in the Gini coefficient were not factoring in the quality of state services, the omissions in access to services or the distributional effects of state subsidies to capital and wealth holders which would then skew the Gini back toward inequality. He concluded that while the economists 'have meticulously measured something … what they have measured is not the whole picture' (Bond 2016b). The problem is perhaps, however, more foundational, in that with the statistical series available, all commentators are limited when assessing the movement of poverty data. Some people are more prepared to make a positive case for redistributive and progressive policy despite this, perhaps because of the responsibilities attached to their positions. Certainly, in a robust analysis by Leibbrandt et al., any drops in overall poverty or inequality were deemed very minor, from a poverty rate of 56 per cent in 1993 to 54 per cent in 2010, with inequality remaining 'stubbornly persistent' (2016: 397–400).

In sum, the poverty lines have weaknesses, as do current attempts to measure poverty and inequality, although some overall trends can be asserted with a degree of certainty. We should not forget that benchmarks for measurement and the establishment of statistical panel data resources were an achievement. Before the late 1990s, the poor were not important enough to attract statistical efforts at all. And here, perhaps, is the main point: that what a government chooses to measure, which poverty line it then chooses, and how far it has legal traction, are all fundamentally a matter of politics. After all, the national constitutional right to food and freedom from destitution in South Africa are already established *de jure*, owing to South Africa's signing and accession to the International Covenant on Economic, Social and Cultural Rights and the Universal Declaration of Human Rights. But they are everywhere breached de facto by the absence of a basic income grant. For a working age adult with no registered disability there is no income assistance from the government, regardless of whether and how a poverty line is set by a distant bureaucracy.

REACTIVITY OF POVERTY MEASUREMENT AND POVERTY RE-BENCHING

That issues of measurement involve political choices was illustrated in 2015 by the 'rebasing' exercise, which resets the underlying, notional basket of goods used in the calculations of poverty, and thus the rand value at which the poverty line is set. For 'accuracy and relevance' this basket must be as typical of current household expenditure patterns as possible, and thus adjusted using consumption data (Stats SA 2015: 2). A methodological adjustment was also made in relation to data collection for household income and expenditure, from a recall method survey to a diary method survey between 2000 and 2010–2011 (Stats SA 2015: 2, 15). Statistics South Africa suggested, and conducted, a rebasing exercise in 2015, although this was not because of a normative decision that the three poverty lines – officially R321, R443 and R620 – were too low. Rather, rebasing took place because the lines were outdated (based on 2000 Income and Expenditure Survey (IES) data) in terms of spending and consumption patterns. As Dr Sandile Simelane of Statistics South Africa explains (by e-mail, 17 November 2015), in 2000 expenditures on items such as cell phones and airtime did not feature prominently, but have been growing significantly over time, '[so] in a nutshell, the motive behind the rebasing exercise was to ensure that the lines remain relevant and in sync with current consumption patterns and levels'.

In the Statistics South Africa technical report it was recommended that these poverty lines (established using data collected in the Income and Expenditure Survey 2010–2011) be 're-based' against evidence of what people were actually buying in 2011 – patterns, like cell phone use, that would have become exaggerated subsequently.

The poverty line figures were all amended upwards, to R335, R501 and R779. The re-based 2011 upper bound poverty line then generated a poverty headcount of 53.8 per cent, or a total of over 27.1 million individuals who were poor in South Africa in 2011 (pegged at the need to spend R779 per person per month on food and non-food items). This is the most generous, re-based, poverty line on offer. At the food poverty line (or what could be called the bare life index, where people are assumed to spend on nothing but food) there was a high 21.7 per cent, or just under 11 million South Africans classified as extremely poor (pegged at consuming the readjusted R335 per month per person, or less).

There are three aspects of this technical document that are particularly interesting. First, this is a re-basing exercise, so in 2011, using the officially adopted upper bound poverty line, 45.5 per cent of people were measured to be poor. Once it was re-based, this was 53.8 per cent. It shows the power of changing the methodology of measurement in creating a condition and also the power to create emotive categories and to generate disturbances in the media and in public policy spheres. For example, when the report was presented, News24 misunderstood, and screamed the headline 'More South Africans living in poverty' (City Press 2015). This claim does not correspond to anything actually changing, apart from the form of measurement, but such headlines illustrate a powerful aspect of the act of measuring something. Measurement has the property, variously called performativity or reactivity, to conjure into existence the thing it claims to be measuring, or at least to change the way that thing acts in the world. The way reactivity works, in the language of social science, is to change the agency of the thing being measured. For example, a person earning R750 per month could have woken up on 3 February 2015 and noticed that yesterday they had not been poor in 2011, and today they are, and redefined themselves accordingly. The point is that when something (the underlying poverty) is measured it need not change but, equally, measuring it can help to conjure that poverty into existence in the public mind. The act of measurement can change the way the social category, or socially constructed idea of poverty is managed, understood and performs to change social and economic relationships. In fact, historically, one of the first results of absolute poverty measurement data in the 1990s, particularly through household surveying, was to convince people that they were poor, whereas before the surveying they might have termed themselves as living frugally, or coping with scarcity. More people thought that they were poor because it was being measured for the first time whereas others were offended that they were classified as poor. Fortunately, many saw the opportunity for strategic political action, and began to own and use the category to put pressure on government for economic change. In this respect, poverty data is useful.

To complicate the performativity aspect of poverty data, it changes depending on the institutional sites in which it is used. Since the poverty lines are advisory, and highly political, a South African can be deemed differently to be 'in need' (or not) by different parts of the state. For example, the 2015 eligibility for the child support grant was set at less than R6 600 for the monthly income of two adults together (or R3 300 per month for a single person), who were then eligible to receive R330 per month. If a person met those criteria, the social development department termed them 'a caregiver in need' – and yet, without a child, an adult falls a long way down in measurable income before being officially poor. In 2011 the child support grant eligibility was R2 600 per month for a single person, and R5 200 per month for a couple. Without a child they would be officially poor at R1 240 (twice the R620 official upper bound poverty line), at only 23.8 per cent of the income of the 'caregivers in need'. The state can act in contradictory and inconsistent ways to different categories of its population – in this case seemingly better to adults with children.

However, because of the history of South Africa, and the use of spatial geography and planning tools to exclude some persons, a person may not be 'seen' at all. The South African Research Chairs Initiative household survey in Clairwood in Durban found that those able to claim grants from government or social assistance was only 43.4 per cent in an area where 57.3 per cent of entire households existed on less than R3 000 per month. Moreover, only 87.8 per cent of this assistance came from the government. With an average of four or five persons per household, and a claimant income level for a child support grant for two people at R6 600, there were significant numbers of people unable to claim what was due to them (Diga and Bracking 2015: 18–9). In the survey, 18.1 per cent were successfully claiming child support, and 17.2 per cent were receiving an old age pension (Diga and Bracking 2015: 20). It has also been noted that the very structure of social grants can lead to exclusions and abjections from communities, as in the case of many men from rural villages such as Glendale, in Lower Tugela, KwaZulu-Natal, as they become a burden on women who, at least, have child grants (Dubbeld n.d.). The inability of an unemployed man of working age to access any form of government income support appears to be changing the nature of community, family and the likelihood of marriage (see Posel et al. 2011) as many fall into a 'permanent condition of nomadic being' (Murray 2008: 123), leaving households without men for much of the time (see Hunter 2010). It has been contended that rising *ilobolo* payments were deterring marriage in the context of widespread unemployment (Posel et al. 2011). However, Dubbeld (n.d.: 11) also argues convincingly that this may be conditioned by the structure of social grants where the government is the 'new husband' in a situation where grants also, counter-intuitively, expressed social insecurity 'expressing people's incapacity to imagine a future through them. In this sense, the social grant has paradoxically become visible as a sign of lack: an indication of the distance between the promise of social change and its realisation' (Dubbeld n.d.: 20).

RESIDUAL OR STRUCTURAL POVERTY?

The official World Bank narrative suggests that poverty in South Africa is declining, a small residual problem of cleaning up conditions for a small group who have somehow been left behind. The policy position appears to be that growth will eventually 'trickle down' to everyone. However, the poor themselves, as in the ethnographic account above, often view poverty as structural and innate to the macroeconomy of South Africa, with global financialisation reproducing the same conditions that will continue to cause poverty in the future. This poverty in the present is being co-produced by, first, the regulatory choices made by government to privilege mining and extractive industries over other policy priorities; and, second, the investment and project finance structures that emanate from the global economy, which can be conceptualised as financialisation (Bracking 2016).

So let us answer the question of whether poverty is residual in South Africa. Economic theory can be broadly characterised into two competing narratives or schools: neoliberalism and heterodox, critical or structuralist economics. In the former, poverty is largely seen as residual. As Milanovic (2003: 667) rather sarcastically summarised in the journal *World Development*:

> The only thing that a country needs to do is to open up its borders, reduce tariff rates, attract foreign capital, and in a few generations if not less, the poor will become rich, the illiterate will learn how to read and write, and inequality will vanish as the poor countries catch up with the rich.

In other words, growth will generate jobs eventually, and we need only wait a while for all boats to be lifted by the tide – but it is intuitive that if over half the population is considered poor, and one-fifth of the population is food hungry 'residual' is not a good descriptor. Instead, as Armah (1968: 118–9) summarised in *The Beautyful Ones Are Not Yet Born*:

> It would be the same for the children. They would grow up accustomed to senseless cycles … to efforts that could only end up placing them at other people's starting points, to the damning knowledge that the race would always be won by men on stilts, and they had not even been given crutches to help them.

Although a deeper theoretical debate on the meaning of 'structural' is not possible here, poverty in South Africa is indeed persistent, racialised and intergenerationally transmitted, and structural in the sense that it is reproduced by the particular political economy of South Africa.

POVERTY AND PUBLIC POLICY

One use of poverty data is to advocate for economic justice. For example, according to the official poverty line (not the recommended re-based line), 20.2 per cent of the South African population lived below this poverty line in 2011 (Stats SA 2014b). It is possible to calculate how much it would cost, at the food basket prices cited in the technical paper (Stats SA 2015), using the poverty line and the poverty gap, to remove the 10.2 million out of poverty. The poverty gap is 6.2 per cent, so it would take R19.90 per month (R238.82 per year) per individual to eliminate food poverty. Multiplying the yearly figure (R238.82) by the total population of poor people (10 185 450) gives a figure of R2.43 billion per annum to remove people from food poverty in 2011.[4] Or, we could use the lower bound poverty line, which was selected in the National Development Plan of 2012, when the government promised to eliminate poverty by 2030. The lower bound poverty line was R443 at 2011 prices and the poverty head count was 32.3 per cent, or 16.3 million poor individuals; the poverty gap was 11.8 per cent, so it would cost R52.27 per month or R627.29 per year to eliminate poverty per head. For the whole population, it would cost R10.2 billion per annum to remove all South Africans from poverty, using the official poverty line chosen by government. These figures for eliminating food poverty (R2.43 billion per annum) and lower bound poverty (R10.2 billion) can be compared to some other items of government expenditure. The cost of no fee increases in higher education, by comparison, has been estimated in 2016 at R4 billion per year, and free university education for those who cannot afford to pay at around R30–40 billion per year. In 2011, when these figures were calculated, R77 billion was spent on debt service – a full 8.7 per cent of the total National Revenue Fund. After contingency, this left R808 billion in the National Revenue Fund to be allocated between national, provincial and local government in 2011–2012 – just 0.3 per cent of the government's budget could have eliminated all extreme poverty.

In comparison, the cost of the Durban back-of-port infrastructure expansion (the second most important infrastructure project on the government's Special Infrastructure Project (SIP) list) is projected to cost R250 billion, although not all of this is strictly government money as much as it is projected sovereign debt. Whereas an orthodox economist might argue that it is nonsensical to compare the costs of eliminating the poverty gap (which represents an annual flow of income) with capital investments (which would then carry ongoing economic benefits), the future costs of chronic illness, disease and welfare associated with poverty must also be compared to the expected productivity gains of a healthy, educated populace. The point is that poverty is not a spending priority, and nor have these calculations been systematically attempted in relation to the current emphasis in macroeconomic policy on infrastructure, mining and the minerals-energy complex. Both these expenditure preferences can be explained by the nature of power and political economy in South Africa, co-produced by global financialisation processes. In fact, the two are synergistic: financialisation processes globally have the effect of privileging big projects, gigantism, infrastructure, minerals extraction and the energy complex nationally (Bracking 2016; Desai 2015, 2016). With an impressively expensive list of SIP projects and additional coal-fired power stations planned nationally, the gas shale fracking promised for KwaZulu-Natal, along with offshore oil exploration and a larger refinery, we stand at a critical moment in deciding the human and structural futures of the South African economy.

In this debate, it is notable that few of the infrastructure projects are justified by traditional types of economic impact assessment. As Desai (2015) recently summarised, the economics of investing R250 billion in a container port in Durban, where costs are already the highest in the world, do not make standard economic sense:

> Once more, like King Shaka airport, Moses Mabhida stadium, and the International Convention Centre, ratepayers will have to make up the shortfall for massively under-utilised infrastructure whose chief benefit is to those who get the contracts to build them and the political class who serve as the 'business partners' (Desai 2015: 25).

Desai terms this 'Faustian development' (2015: 27, 32), powerful because to oppose it is to be seen as 'go[ing] against the national interest'.

Why are financialisation and gigantism synergistic? There are three basic schools of theory on financialisation, where the term variously refers to the financialisation of capitalism itself; to the role of finance in increasingly shaping everyday life and other domains; and to the importance of greater shareholder influence in corporate decision making (Christophers 2012; Bracking 2016). We can discard the second- and third-named here. Within the first school, the greater influence of finance over other types of productive capital is stressed, with increased volumes of money capital relative to productive capital circulating and with greater shares of profits globally attached to derivatives markets as opposed to returns to corporates. The empirical evidence for these trends is ambiguous (Christophers 2012), although the overall relationship is empirically provable (Bracking 2016: 30–6). What is also clear is that the way in which holders of money capital can shape the design of investments and project finance in Africa, to privilege themselves over other types of shareholders and communities, is strengthening in the countries which believe themselves to be desperate for 'much-needed' foreign direct investment. Holders of finance can make sure that the derivative income stream from a fixed asset is secure, as risk free as possible, and extracted to an offshore special purpose vehicle (a type of private equity fund) by the way that they design financial products to privilege themselves over other investors and governments – for example, in many infrastructure public-private partnerships (Hildyard 2016). The financialisation of capitalism literature describes how finance works to constantly bring in new frontiers of people, animals and nature into marketised relationships. Moore (2012) recently wrote of this process as profit making from the four 'cheaps' of labour power, food, energy and raw materials. Key to capitalist accumulation are expropriation of the 'outside', the unpaid work of animals and humans from 'frontiers of uncapitalised natures' which lie 'outside the circuit of capital but within reach of capitalist power' (Moore 2014: 36). Finance working to extract value up and out to global money holders, and finance working to extract value from the four 'cheaps' are both prevalent in the political economy of South Africa. For example, mining licences are increasingly given at great ecological and human expense. The Petmin-owned Somkhele coalmine in northern KwaZulu-Natal extracts multiples of an Olympic-sized swimming pool every day from the iMfolozi watershed, using a 40 000 TPM coal washing plant, despite perennial water shortages in neighbouring Mpukunyoni communities and the needs of wildlife in the adjacent Hluhluwe-iMfolozi national park. Even when South Africa is ostensibly promoting carbon reduction and a green economy, expenditures show a preference for minerals and energy corporates. The public grants distributed through the Clean Development Mechanism of the United Nations Framework Convention on Climate Change largely went to national mining and fossil fuel corporates (Bracking 2015). Infrastructure is similarly privileged in expenditures. It is ubiquitously tagged as 'much-needed', with the World Bank promoting the view that there is a 'gap' or 'financing deficit' worth seemingly gigantic sums of money (World Bank 2016). Infrastructural builds with protected derivative income streams grow finance and reward financiers. For example, Torrance's (2009) work on a new Thames Water desalination plant in the UK showed the reordering of priorities to provide finance to investors rather than water to customers: '[a] more profound motivation seems to be the need for new infrastructural forms within which to ensure speculative gains' (Loftus and March 2015: 175, summarising Torrance 2009). Apparently, this plant may not produce water and may only be used in a drought, but it has inflation-protected returns for institutional investors.

President Zuma proposed a 'fast-track' for the environmental assessments of SIPs, which are now managed from the executive arm of government in the Presidential Infrastructure Coordinating Commission, following the passing of the controversial Infrastructure Development Act into law in 2014. This promoted a new realm in the politics of exceptionalism owing to a thinning of parliamentary oversight (Democratic Alliance 2014). In terms of financialisation processes overall there is a synergistic relationship between building infrastructure, concentrating power within party-states and the greater extractivism made possible for international financiers from African economies. The whole infrastructure exercise is then popularised through a language of 'mega-projects', the 'Madiba magic' of global inclusion and modernity (Desai 2015, 2016). For example, the operational plans for the Durban port expansion will require the removal of a large number – contested but in the tens of thousands – of settled families in Clairwood and surrounding neighbourhoods. This US$25 billion 'back of port' expansion plan (which includes petrochemical expansion) was named the second highest national priority in the National Development Plan 2012 (after the Waterberg-Richards Bay coal infrastructure expansion) and will take capacity at the Durban port from around 2 million to 20 million containers annually. Drawn up by consultants, the impact assessments read more like promotional literature. The key impact assessment already 'zones' out the people, and the names of the affected communities, in the title: 'A Local Area Plan and Land Use Management Scheme for the Back of Port Interface Zone'. In an alternative assessment of income, assets and actual employment already existing in the area, nearly 500 (mostly informal) jobs were found in the 1 000 representative households surveyed (Diga and Bracking 2015: 16). With disingenuous methodology, the impact consultants did not offset job losses caused by forced resettlement as a deduction to the widely advertised jobs to be 'created' – and as 23.4 per cent of the households were living on less than R1 000 per month any job losses would be critical to survival (Diga and Bracking 2015: 8). Further, it was discovered that over 11.5 per cent of the residents sampled were in informal (or 'illegal') settlements, which were not counted for the resettlement considerations (Diga and Bracking 2015: 9). The point here is that the models of developmental benefit, based on abstract multipliers of gross domestic product (GDP) and employment growth, had little reference to the affected persons or poverty reduction that could be attributed to their future lives.

The people and their environment have been historically neglected, and are not currently 'seen' by the state elite. Instead, financialisation spawns big projects to the benefit of consultants, members of the political elite and connected companies in construction. The poverty of the community was used against them in an impact measurement narrative that suggested that what would be lost by the port expansion was not worth saving – despite the huge cultural, social and historical infrastructure and social capital present in the neighbourhood (Bracking et al. 2015).

CONCLUSION

In South Africa, a post-apartheid legacy of zoning and criminalising informal settlements allows a spatial geography to distance the rich from the poor so that the latter are able to see affluence but not experience it. Mbembe's depiction of economic deprivation fits this situation well: 'an economy of desired goods that are known, that may sometimes be seen, that one wants to enjoy, but to which one will never have material access (Mbembe 2002: 271 cited in Ferguson 2006: 192).

In an economy struggling to generate employment a divide thus emerges socially and culturally between the rich and the poor. The measurement of poverty and the data generated by measurement describe this inequality – and in some senses (as seen above) create poverty as a category, but do not explain or appreciate it as a structural relationship between people and the overall political economy. Ferguson says it is this divide and cultural distance which is then performative of further inequality, such that 'the most challenging political demands go beyond the claims of political independence [in the context of African development] and instead involve demands for connection, and for relationship, even under conditions of inequality and dependence' (Ferguson 2006: 22).

The challenge in the future is to make a public policy for poverty reduction that can reduce the social distance and increase the elective affinity between citizens; which can foreclose on the planning and zoning norms which assign and abject persons to poverty through spatial differentiation; and which can critically engage with national and global decisions and processes that privilege international money-holders in a synergistic relationship with national elites at the expense of the poor. Unless and until this greater debate can be engaged, arguing about poverty measurement would appear to have little traction. The differences between those measured as poor are miniscule in practice as a lived experience of masses enduring deprivation – and the narrative of worsening poverty or incremental improvement lacks a persuasive evidence base on which to draw. The intellectual cogency of debates about poverty and inequality have, in effect, degenerated into engagements between those expressing a standpoint on behalf of power holders, banks or political parties ranged against the suspended disbelief of the citizenry and their increasingly violent efforts to attract elite attention in a spatial geography of exclusion.

NOTES

1   I am very grateful to Dr Sandile Simelane from Statistics South Africa (Stats SA) for commenting and correcting a draft, to Kathleen Diga for her extensive assistance with the calculations, and to Cathy Sutherland for comments and photographs when an earlier draft was aired as my inaugural lecture at the University of KwaZulu-Natal in November 2015.
2   E-mail from Dr Sandile Simelane, Stats SA.
3   Comment by Dr Sandile Simelane: Stats SA does not interpret the reference food basket used in the development of the three poverty lines as a healthy/nutritious or recommended basket. It simply represents a nationally 'representative basket of food' based on food expenditures reported in IES 2010/11. This point is highlighted on page 7 of the *methodological report on rebasing of national poverty lines and development of pilot provincial lines.*'
4   I am indebted to Kathleen Diga for these figures.

REFERENCES

Andreas, P and Greenhill, KM (eds) (2010) *Sex, drugs, and body counts: The politics of numbers in global crime and conflict*. Ithaca: Cornell University Press.

Armah, A K (1968) *The beautyful ones are not yet born*. Boston: Houghton Mifflin.

Bond, P (2015) Bretton Woods Institution narratives about inequality and economic vulnerability on the eve of South African austerity. *International Journal of Health Services*, 45 (3), 415–442.

Bond, P (2016a) The poor face double-digit inflation, *Mail & Guardian*, 26 February, available from https://mg.co.za/article/2016-02-25-the-poor-face-double-digit-inflation.

Bond, P (2016b) Do government spending and taxation really reduce inequality, or do we need more thorough measurements? A response to the World Bank researchers, *Econ3x3*, February. Available from http://www.econ3x3.org/article/do-government-spending-and-taxation-really-reduce-inequality-or-do-we-need-more-thorough.

Bond, P (2016c) The harsh realities about South Africa that the World Bank dare not speak. *The Conversation*, 10 February.

Bracking, S (2015) Performativity in the green economy: How far does climate finance create a fictive economy? *Third World Quarterly*, 36 (12), 2337–2357.

Bracking, S (2016) *Financialisation of power in Africa*. London: Routledge.

Bracking, S and Diga, K with Falschebner, P, Lombo, M, Rushambwa, T and Tshabalala, A (2015) *Clairwood survey: Community views of the value of Clairwood in the context of current development plans for Durban port expansion*. Research Report 2015 No. 1, https://appliedpovertyreduction.files.wordpress.com/2015/01/emailing-clairwood_qual_report-finished-minus-frequency-table1.pdf.

Budlender, J, Leibbrandt, M and Woolard, I (2015a) *South African poverty lines: A review and two new money-metric thresholds*. South Africa Labour and Development Research Unit, Working Paper Series no. 151, University of Cape Town.

Budlender, J, Leibbrandt, M and Woolard, I (2015b) How current measures underestimate the level of poverty in South Africa. *The Conversation*, 3 September.

Christian Aid and TJN (Tax Justice Network) (2014) *Africa rising? Inequalities and the essential role of fair taxation*. Available from http://www.christianaid.org.uk/images/Africa-tax-and-inequality-report-Feb2014.pdf.

Christophers, B (2012) Anaemic geographies of financialisation. *New Political Economy*, 17 (3), 271–291.

City Press (2015) *More South Africans living in poverty*, 3 February. http://www.news24.com/Archives/City-Press/More-South-Africans-living-in-poverty-Stats-SA-20150429.

Dean, M (2003 [1999]) *Governmentality: Power and rule in modern society*. London: SAGE Publications.

Democratic Alliance (2014) No parliamentary oversight over infrastructure spend could lead to corruption and undermine growth, Democratic Alliance, Cape Town, 25 February. Available from https://www.da.org.za/2014/02/no-parliamentary-oversight-over-infrastructure-spend-could-lead-to-corruption-and-undermine-growth/.

Desai, A (2015) Of Faustian pacts and mega-projects: The politics and economics of the port expansion in the South Basin of Durban, South Africa. *Capitalism Nature Socialism*, 26 (1), 18–34.

Desai, A (2016) Between Madiba magic and spectacular capitalism: The FIFA World Cup in South Africa. In R Gruneau and J Horne (eds) *Mega-events and globalization: Capital and spectacle in a changing world order*. Routledge: Abingdon, pp. 81–94.

Diga, K and Bracking, S (2015) *Descriptive statistics – The developmental value of the Durban port expansion project*. Research Report 2015 No. 2. https://appliedpovertyreduction.files.wordpress.com/2015/01/technical-paper-2-final.pdf.

Du Toit, A (2011) *Nasruddin's key: Poverty measurement and the government of marginal populations*, Working Paper 20. PLAAS, University of the Western Cape, available from http://repository.uwc.ac.za/xmlui/bitstream/handle/10566/580/WP20.pdf?sequence=1&isAllowed=y.

Du Toit, A (2012) *The trouble with poverty: Reflections on South Africa's post-apartheid anti-poverty consensus*, Working Paper 22. PLAAS, University of the Western Cape. Available from http://repository.uwc.ac.za/xmlui/bitstream/handle/10566/642/PLAAS_WorkingPaper22dutoit.pdf?sequence=1&isAllowed=y.

Dubbeld, B (n.d.) *How social security becomes social insecurity: Fluid households, crisis talk and the value of grants in a KwaZulu-Natal village*, mimeo. Stellenbosch University.

Engle Merry, S (2011), Measuring the world: Indicators, human rights, and global governance. *Current Anthropology*, 52 (3), S84.

Espeland, WN and Sauder, M (2007). Rankings and reactivity: How public measures recreate social worlds. *American Journal of Sociology*, 113 (1), 1–40.

Ferguson, J (2006) *Global shadows: Africa in the neoliberal world order*. Durham, North Carolina: Duke University Press.

Ferguson, J (2007) Formalities of poverty: Thinking about social assistance in neoliberal South Africa, *African Studies Review*, 50 (2), 71–86.

Foucault, M (2004 [1979]) In M Sennelart (ed.) *Geschichte der Gouvernementalität II: Die Geburt der Biopolitik, Vorlesung am College de France 1978–1979*. Frankfurt a. M.: Suhrkamp Verlag.

Hildyard, N (2016) *Licensed larceny: Infrastructure, financial extraction and the Global South*. Manchester, UK: Manchester University Press.

Hunter, M (2010) *Love in a time of Aids: Inequality, gender, and rights in South Africa*. Bloomington, Indiana: Indiana University Press.

Inchauste, G, Lustig, N, Maboshe, M, Purfield, C and Woolard, I (2015) *The distributional impact of fiscal policy in South Africa*. Policy Research Working Paper no. WPS 7194. Washington, DC: World Bank Group. http://documents.worldbank.org/curated/en/2015/02/23984236/distributional-impact-fiscal-policy-south-africa.

Jerven, M (2013) *Poor numbers: How we are misled by African development statistics and what to do about it*. Ithaca and Cape Town: Cornell University and UCT Press.

Joffe, H (2015) Piketty's wealth tax fails to solve SA's inequality riddle. *Business Day*, 7 October.

Kar, D and Spanjers, J (2015) *Illicit financial flows from developing countries: 2004–2013*. Global Financial Integrity, Washington, DC, 8th December. Available from http://www.gfintegrity.org/wp-content/uploads/2015/12/IFF-Update_2015-Final-1.pdf.

Leibbrandt, M, Finn, A and Oosthuizen, M (2016) Poverty, inequality, and prices in post-apartheid South Africa. In C Arndt, A McKay and F Tarp (eds) *Growth and poverty in sub-Saharan Africa, UNU-WIDER*. Oxford: Oxford University Press.

Loftus, A and March, H (2015) Financialising nature? *Geoforum*, 60, 172–175.

MacKenzie, D (2011) The credit crisis as a problem in the sociology of knowledge. *American Journal of Sociology*, 116 (6), 1778–1841.

Mbembe, A (2002) African modes of self-writing. *Public Culture*, 14 (1), 239–273, trans. Steven Rendall.

Milanovic, B (2003) The two faces of globalization: Against globalization as we know it. *World Development*, 31 (4), 667–683.

Moore, JW (2012) Cheap food & bad money: Food, frontiers, and financialization in the rise and demise of neoliberalism. *Review*, 33 (2–3), 125–161.

Moore, JW (2014) The end of cheap nature, or, how I learned to stop worrying about 'the' environment and love the crisis of capitalism. In C. Suter and C. Chase-Dunn (eds.) *Structures of the world political economy and the future of global conflict and cooperation*, 285–314, Berlin: LIT.

Murray, M (2008) *Taming the disorderly city: The spatial landscape of Johannesburg after apartheid.* Ithaca: Cornell University Press.

Mwiti, L (2015) Seven of the biggest myths about South Africa and xenophobia – and how they drive attacks. *Mail & Guardian*, 22 April.

Oels, A (2006) Rendering climate change governable: From biopower to advanced liberal government? *Journal of Environmental Policy and Planning*, 7 (3), 185–207.

Pacsa (Pietermaritzburg Agency for Christian Social Awareness) (2016) *Pacsa monthly food price barometer*, January. Media Statement.

Posel, D, Rudwick, S and Casale, D (2011) Is marriage a dying institution in South Africa? Exploring changes in marriage in the context of iLobolo payments. *Agenda*, 25 (1), 102–111.

Ravallion, M (1998) *Poverty lines in theory and practice*. LSMS Working Paper No. 133. World Bank.

Seekings, J (2008) Deserving individuals and groups: The post-apartheid state's justification of the shape of South Africa's system of social assistance. *Transformation: Critical Perspectives on Southern Africa*, 68 (1), 28–52.

Simelane, S (2015) Presentation Statistics South Africa, by Sandile Simelane. *Rebasing national poverty lines and development of pilot provincial poverty lines for South Africa*, 9th June 2015, p. 7. Available from http://www.assaf.org.za/ASSAf per cent20news/Events per cent202015/1 per cent20-per cent20The per cent20South per cent20African per cent20National per cent20Poverty per cent20Lines per cent20_per cent20Simelane.pdf.

Stats SA (Statistics South Africa) (2014a) Press statement: Poverty trends in South Africa – South Africa winning war on poverty. 3 April. http://www.statssa.gov.za/?p=2591.

Stats SA (Statistics South Africa) (2014b) *Poverty trends in South Africa: An examination of absolute poverty between 2006 and 2011*. Pretoria: Statistics South Africa. Available from http://beta2.statssa. gov.za/publications/Report-03-10-06/Report-03-10-06March2014.pdf.

Stats SA (Statistics South Africa) (2015) *Methodological report on rebasing of national poverty lines and development of pilot provincial poverty lines*. Technical Report, Report No. 03–10–11. Available from http://beta2.statssa.gov.za/publications/Report-03–10–11/Report-03–10–11.pdf.

Torrance, M (2009) The rise of a global infrastructure market through relational investing. *Economic Geography*, 85 (1), 75–97.

Woolard, I, Metz, R, Inchauste, G, Lustig, N, Maboshe, M and Purfield, C (2015) How much is inequality reduced by progressive taxation and government spending? *Econ3x3*, 28 October.

Woolcock, M (2007) *Toward an economic sociology of chronic poverty: Enhancing the rigor and relevance of social theory*. Working Paper 104. Manchester: IDPM/Chronic Poverty Research Centre (CPRC).

World Bank (2014) Fiscal policy and redistribution in an unequal society. *South Africa economic update 6*. Washington, DC: World Bank.

World Bank (2016) *Spending more and better: Essential to tackling the infrastructure gap*. 16 April. Available from http://www.worldbank.org/en/news/feature/2016/04/16/spending-more-and-better-essential-to-tackling-the-infrastructure-gap.

Yaffe, DS (1973) The Marxian theory of crisis, capital and the state. *Economy and Society*, 2 (2), 186–232.

CHAPTER 4

The financialisation of the poor and the reproduction of inequality

David Neves

This chapter examines 'financialisation' and inequality in contemporary South Africa. An expansive and inconsistently used concept (Lee et al. 2009; Bracking 2015), 'financialisation' refers to 'accumulation in which profits accrue primarily through financial channels rather than through trade and commodity production' (Krippner 2005: 174). In the last three decades, the global ascendency of the financial sector has seen the proliferation of various finance-related motives, markets, actors and institutions (Epstein 2005), the emergence of highly speculative instruments (derivatives, futures and so on) and an expansion of debt and debt financing. The dynamics of financialisation are furthermore intertwined with larger trajectories of economic growth and their unequal distribution. In South Africa, processes of financialisation are inseparable from long-standing patterns of economic growth, integration into the global economy and the racially skewed distribution of assets, ownership and opportunity. The precise ways in which financialisation comes to articulate with inequality is the focus in this chapter.

The chapter begins by explicating the concept of financialisation and its relationship to inequality, which is discussed in relation to the historical development of the South African economy. The chapter argues that intensifying processes of financialisation serve to undercut the potential for broad-based and inclusive (that is, inequality reducing) growth. Processes of financialisation therefore not only reflect historical patterns of radicalised inequality – they simultaneously reproduce it. Drawing on this analysis, the chapter then examines financialisation in terms of its effects on households and individuals, particularly through the mechanism of indebtedness. Discussing the adverse developmental outcomes and inequality that indebtedness engenders, the chapter concludes with reflection on how financialisation resonates with contemporary policy imperatives, notably the development discourse of 'financial inclusion'.

THE ANTECEDENTS OF FINANCIALISATION

Explanations of the process of financialisation conventionally locate it in the collapse of the post-war reconstruction boom, amid the global energy, currency and economic crises of the early 1970s. By this account, financialisation, market deregulation and privatisation are all adjuncts to the rise of neoliberalism, occurring in parallel with worldwide tendencies towards stagnating real wages, rising income inequality and declines in public provisioning and services. In turn, 'financialisation' has been used to describe an even wider range of phenomena, across an array of contexts, ranging from the imperative of maximising 'shareholder value' within contemporary regimes of corporate governance to the expanding role of finance in shaping identities and subjectivities, social and cultural life – even ecological decisions and priorities (Bracking 2015). Harvey (2005: 24) describes this as the 'financialisation of everything'. However, for the purposes of the current chapter these manifold meanings of 'financialisation' are less salient than a narrow 'political economy' informed reading of it.

A materialist political economy perspective emphasises trends towards structural stagnation within capitalism, and explains financialisation as a response to overproduction and overcapacity within capitalism (Fine 2010). Drawing on Marx, Ashman et al. (2011) suggest two processes of accumulation within the post-war expansion of capitalism. The first is the transfer of capital accumulated from conventional processes of production and exchange into the realm of interest-bearing capital, making for forms of 'systematic financialised accumulation'. The second is the subordination of patterns of real accumulation (that is, accumulated via the conventional extraction of value) to 'fictitious capital', of claims to as yet unrealised surplus value, through various instruments traded within financial systems (Ashman et al. 2011: 176). The first is the absorbing of capital drawn from the productive economy into finance, the second the expansion of finance over the 'productive' or 'real' economy. These twin movements see financial and financialised capital capture larger proportions of value from the realm of production (Fine 2013).

While the above account offers grounding for the concept of finacialisation, its precise status as mechanism, cause or consequence remains indistinct and unspecified. Sweeping accounts of financialisation also frequently fail to consider its differential impacts across various sectors of the economy, and its variegated effects at firm level and on individuals or households (Teles 2012). Finally, it is also necessary to account for the dynamics and effects of financialisation within specific national contexts. Here, the focus is on middle-income South Africa with its small open economy, highly sophisticated financial system and noxious bequest of persistent poverty and structural inequality.

INEQUALITY AND FINANCIALISATION

The relationship between financialisation and inequality demands attention to both con-
cepts. Inequality in the South African context has often been cast in dualistic terms, as
'disconnection' or underdevelopment of the so-called 'second' or informal economy from
the economic mainstream. Such conceptualisation is rejected in this chapter. Instead, the
argument here is predicated on a view of structural inequality generated within a uni-
tary and singular South African economy (Du Toit and Neves 2007). Inequality in South
Africa is therefore neither residual nor a matter of disconnection or 'exclusion'; it is the
inexorable outcome of a long trajectory of skewed and uneven development.

Four structural legacies buttress inequality in contemporary South Africa (Philip 2010).
The first is the history of spatial segregation, which has made for dysfunctional settlement patterns, locating impoverished Africans far from economic opportunity, thereby
exacting high transport, social, opportunity and other costs. The second legacy is massive,
trans-generational, racial asymmetries in patterns of human development and capacities
(health, education, skills). The third is the racially skewed pattern of asset ownership and
holdings (and subsequent returns and rents on these assets). The fourth and final pillar
of structural inequality in South Africa is the centralised, concentrated, capital intensive
nature of the economy, which 'crowds out' the potential for informal or labour intensive
employment, thereby locking the poor and unskilled out of the benefits of economic
growth. These legacies pattern the unequal access to and gains from employment and have
been aggravated by processes of financialisation in the last three decades.

FINANCIALISATION AND THE SOUTH AFRICA ECONOMY

Financialisation and rising inequality need to be located in both the historical development and the present-day structure of the economy. South Africa's industrial economy has its origins in the nineteenth-century discoveries of diamonds and gold. The
capital-intensive nature of mining saw an early concentration of firms, first in the hands
of Anglo-dominated capital, extending to Afrikaner capital around the mid-twentieth
century. Mining conglomerates reinvested and diversified their holdings domestically,
including into banks and financial services firms. This inward-directedness of investment was intensified by the political and economic isolation of apartheid, reaching its
apogee during the foreign disinvestment in the 1980s. Cumulatively, the mining, energy
and subsectors of manufacturing make up the minerals-energy complex (MEC) that
has 'constituted and continue[s] to constitute the core site of accumulation in the South
Africa economy' (Fine and Rustomjee 1996: 71). The concept of the MEC highlights not
only century-long patterns of accumulation but also the alliance it entailed between capital and the South African state. State support included decades of tariff protection, tax
concessions, the funding of heavy industrial infrastructure and subsidised inputs (such
as cheap steel and electricity). Continuities in public policy have served to sustain these

capital-intensive industrial and fiscal policy biases in the post-apartheid era (Black and Gerwel 2014). Finally, state support for the MEC also infamously included the segregationist laws that extracted, ordered and disciplined the cheap African labour on which the modern South African economy was built. In these ways, the development and workings of the MEC are deeply imbricated with underdevelopment and racialised inequality in South Africa.

Historic configurations of accumulation and economic concentration therefore fed into South Africa's patterns of 'uneven and combined' development. However, the legacy of structural inequality is not simply manifest among the (African) majority, historically estranged from economic opportunity. Its imprint is evident throughout the entire economy, including among the (still, effectively, racially defined) minority that historically benefited from it.

By the early 1990s demise of apartheid, the overarching trajectory of economic growth made for three salient structural characteristics. First, it made for a highly concentrated and oligopolistic economy, dominated by powerful economic conglomerates and extensive profit mark-ups. Anti-competitive practices were (and remain) widespread, inhibiting growth, productivity and employment creation (Aghion et al. 2008; Roberts 2010). The concentrated, monopoly structure of the economy has endured into the post-apartheid period, and concentration persists at industry and sectoral levels (Mohamed and Roberts 2006) despite the unbundling of conglomerates post-1994. Even the growth of new sectors (for example, private hospital groups, mobile telecommunications) has been contoured by prevailing patterns, and is similarly concentrated (Roberts 2010). South Africa's concentrated core economy continues to 'crowd out' opportunities for new, informal sector, or small-scale market entrants (Devey et al. 2005).

Second, patterns of economic growth contributed to a fundamentally lopsided, unbalanced and deindustrialising South African economy. Weak consumer demand from the impoverished African majority meant the consumer goods sector was comparatively small. Consumer goods production (for example, clothes, furniture, cars) was largely marketed to the minority white middle class (who never were more than a fifth of the population under apartheid) and was highly reliant on tariff protectionism. The intermediate goods sector was equally small and globally uncompetitive (Ashman et al. 2011). Then, post-1994 economic liberalisation saw many of these sectors – and, crucially, the low-skilled jobs within them – dramatically swept away by waves of cheaper imports.

Third, South Africa's growth path spawned a small economy with a large and sophisticated financial services sector. The concentrated economy was one where profits had for decades been channelled into financial rather than productive assets, resulting in a middle-income country with a disproportionately complex and advanced financial services sector. Reflecting extreme patterns of skewed development, this world-class financial sector managed to exist in a society where, even as late as 1993, three-quarters of adults were 'unbanked' (Porteous 2003).

In sum, the concentrated, unbalanced and proto-financialised South African economy that emerged by the end of apartheid was the terrain on which processes of financialisation would subsequently unfold. The persistence of these economic relations even after the advent of democracy partially reflects the compromise of the political transition. Although democracy ushered in political equality and a new constitutional order, existing property rights and ownership patterns endured. Despite its historic affinity to nationalisation, the ruling African National Congress (ANC) largely embraced the neoliberal orthodoxy of free market capitalism and its macroeconomic policy axioms of fiscal constraint, inflation targeting, real positive interest rates, a floating currency and relaxation of capital restrictions (Marais 2011). Patterns of apartheid era-inequality have therefore stubbornly persisted because the structure of the South African economy has remained fundamentally unchanged.

FINANCIALISATION AND POST-APARTHEID ECONOMIC LIBERALISATION

South Africa's post-1994 embrace of market liberalisation resulted in the reduction of key tariff barriers and restrictions. Loosening exchange controls saw domestic conglomerates unbundle their diverse interests, and 'externalise' overseas. Many (SAB, Glencor, Anglo American Corporation, Remgro, Didata) became transnational corporations and listed abroad. Others harnessed improved political relations and geographical proximity to expand elsewhere on the African continent (for example, MTN, Shoprite). Many drew on corporate South Africa's long-honed comparative advantage: the extraction of profit from low-income consumers (for example, SAB-Miller, Shoprite). Others (such as Sasol) leveraged their inheritance of substantial public investment and innovation under apartheid isolation, while the post-apartheid government acceded to the privatisation of state-owned or -created firms (for example, Telkom, Iscor).

The 'externalisation' of South Africa's largest conglomerates enabled them to access foreign markets, arbitrage gains from offshore operations, and diversify out of local currency and political risk (Ashman et al. 2011). These impulses are consistent with firm-level practices associated with financialisation globally, such as the proclivity for raising funding on open (non-bank) capital markets, and increasing proportions of profits derived from finance-related activities. Internationally, corporate capital is animated by shorter investment time horizons, tighter alignment to financial markets and larger transfers of value to shareholders and top executives – often to the detriment of other imperatives or groups (such as employees). Corporate externalisation and the restructuring of South African conglomerates in the 1990s opened them to international finance and deepened processes of financialisation. This legalised flight of capital out of South Africa (quite apart from substantial illicit outflows) had important consequences that included the weakening of domestic political and regulatory control over corporate behemoths and the hobbling of the state's ability to facilitate forms of labour intensive or pro-poor growth (Ashman et al. 2011).

Corporate capital flight also exacerbated the skewedness of South Africa's growth described earlier, by further 'hollowing out' the local productive and industrial economy.[1]

This led to job losses in virtually all the traditional bastions of low-skilled, labour-intensive industrial employment (for example, mining, light manufacturing, garments, textiles and footwear), which invariably occurred to detriment of the poor and low-skilled. These sectors (along with similarly job-shedding agriculture) are the lower rungs on the ladder of economic development. Their demise not only undercuts entry-level jobs, but also forecloses on prospective skills development, economic mobility, accumulation and future growth.

Finally, these adverse structural patterns have been bolstered rather than undone by redistributive efforts such as BEE (black economic empowerment). The political compact of BEE increased elite African ownership of the white-dominated economy, yet the existence of a small new elite, with debt-financed stakes in existing oligopolistic firms, has largely served to conserve the economic status quo. It has made the emergence of new competitors, enterprises or changed economic structure more difficult (Ashman et al. 2011).

There remain sharp continuities between pre- and post-apartheid economic structures and patterns of accumulation. Despite the relative decline of mining's contribution to the economy, the basic economic structure, pathways of accumulation and the configurations of public policy that enabled it remain influential. These contribute to an economy that continues to be capital intensive and employment 'un-intensive' (viz. 'jobless growth'), engendering a working population bifurcated into formally employed labour market 'insiders', and a vast army of chronically unemployed and underemployed 'outsiders' (Seekings and Nattrass 2006). The net outcome is enduring mass poverty for the African majority, alongside rising standards of living for a small (and increasingly deracialised) elite.

FINANCIALISATION AND THE POST-APARTHEID FINANCIAL SERVICE SECTOR

While post-1994 opening of the insular apartheid economy led to the 'externalisation' of South's Africa's lead firms, it also reconfigured the domestic financial services sector. The 'big four' banks (Absa, FNB, Standard and Nedbank) and financial services firms (Old Mutual, Liberty and so on) were historically linked to the MEC conglomerates through elaborate cross holdings. Liberalisation saw financial firms unbundled, and the entry of foreign capital into the domestic banking sector (buying stakes in Standard Bank and Absa). In common with much of the rest of the economy, South Africa's banks and financial services industry is concentrated and oligopolistic (FinMark Trust 2009), reflecting the nature of a highly regulated sector with substantial barriers to entry, but also the legacy of their consolidation during their former ownership by MEC-linked capital.

Post-1994 economic liberalisation saw significant long-term domestic outflows of capital described earlier, but short-term speculative capital inflows rose from 2.14 per cent in 1994 to 10.29 per cent by 1999 (Mohamed 2003). These were volatile portfolio inflows into domestic equities and bonds, rather than long-term foreign direct investment into the labour-absorbing productive economy. Relative to other (larger) emerging middle-income BRIC countries (Brazil, Russia, India and China), South Africa's is the only economy where the former exceeded the latter. Speculative inflows were catalysed by high mineral resource commodity prices, a soaring domestic stock market and comparatively high (hence attractive to foreign speculators) interest rates. They contributed to an outsized South African stock market, with the third highest stock market capitalisation to gross domestic product (GDP) ratios in the world (exceeded only by Hong Kong and Switzerland) (Masie 2015). These 'hot money' speculative inflows tempered South Africa's current account deficit,[2] but fuelled the growth of the financial services sector, with rapid asset (property, equity) price increases and a consumer spending boom. This boom was evident in the retail, services and property sectors from the late 1990s until the eve of the 2008 global recession.

Moreover, speculative global inflows and the growth of the domestic financial services sector intensified the local process of financialisation. Through the growing banking and financial services sector, this had a number of far-reaching consequences, including exacerbating economic volatility, crowding out domestic industrial and productive investment and whittling away at prospects for employment-intensive growth.

Global financial flows and the expansion of the financial services sector have amplified the racialised labour market differentials described above. The loss of low-skilled employment occurred in parallel with skilled workers benefiting from rapid employment growth in the consumer economy, along with the lucrative FIRE (finance, insurance, real estate) and telecommunications sectors (Teles 2012). The larger trajectory of growth, including the expansion of the financial services sector, has therefore functioned to deepen pre-existing allocations of economic opportunity. It has accentuated the gains of the winners, specifically the educated and skilled, in parallel with the creeping immiseration of the losers, namely the poor and low-skilled (Leibbrandt et al. 2010). Given the historical accretion of opportunity in South Africa, the former are disproportionately white and the latter overwhelmingly black.

The rise of financialisation has also seen non-finance firms increasingly engage directly with financial markets and by-pass banks. Banks have responded by deriving larger proportions of their profits from individual rather than corporate clients. These tendencies take on varied forms; in much of industrialised world, bank profits have become driven by housing mortgage growth. This phenomenon has some resonance with South Africa, where a surfeit of liquidity and historically low interest rates fuelled a housing price boom from the early 2000s. Much as it did elsewhere, equity from rising house prices bolstered consumer spending.

Capital inflows and rising domestic liquidity associated with the economic boom of the 2000s furthermore converged with banks (and other financial sector actors) reaching 'downmarket' to capture lower income customers. In the USA, this spawned the 'sub-prime' mortgage market, subsequent defaults in which infamously precipitated the 2008 Great Recession. In South Africa, this downward flexion into formerly disregarded low-income segments of the population entailed the growth of unsecured (that is, without asset-backed collateral) lending and consumer credit extension. The formal (regulated) unsecured lending market attracted new entrants (African Bank, Capitec and others), along with the established 'big four' banks. Expanding consumer credit extension has involved many other actors, including a wide range of 'non-finance sector' firms such as credit-based consumer goods retailers (clothes, furniture, appliances, jewellery). Freer access to credit has increased individual and household indebtedness, and provided a key arena in which processes of financialisation have intensified. These processes of debt-driven financialisation, and the inequality reinforcing distributional outcomes they generate, are the focus of the section that follows.

FINANCIALISATION IN SOUTH AFRICA: INDIVIDUALS AND HOUSEHOLDS

To this point, the dynamics of financialisation have been discussed in terms of their relationship to the larger macrostructural context. The argument is that the development and structure of the South African economy sees it marked by declining opportunities for the (disproportionately African) poor and unskilled. The labour market is therefore a key transmission mechanism between process of financialisation on one hand, and rising inequality on the other. Employment is a particularly important mediator of poverty and inequality in South Africa because of high levels of 'wage dependency' and scant opportunities for livelihoods or subsistence production outside the realm of markets and money (Bryceson 1996).

In this way, the appropriation of value associated with financialisation occurs within the realm of 'production', and inequalities flow from the highly differentiated positions individuals occupy in relation to it. This inequality-inducing dynamic remains prominent in South Africa, even if the gains derived from labour (and capital) markets are tempered by a wider 'distributional regime' (Seekings and Nattrass 2006) that includes some fiscal redistribution through the 'social wage' (subsidised utilities, basic public health, education and housing) and a widespread (by middle country standards) system of welfare grants. These ameliorative mechanisms hence serve to stabilise and perpetuate existing systems of production and distribution. However, the capture of value associated with financialisation plays itself out across a diverse range of other scales and sectors. It occurs at the microstructural level scale of persons and households: it inheres in the quality of their relationship to the larger economy, as manifest in household balance sheets (viz. household assets less liabilities). In the context of the post-apartheid growth of the financial system, credit extension and consumption boom of the 2000s, processes of financialisation drove an intensification of individual indebtedness.

Conceptually, financialisation through rising household indebtedness is different from the extraction of value in the sphere of production. Within production, finance typically (or at least hypothetically), entails investment, and commensurately receives a portion of the expanded value created. In contrast, financialisation through individual or household indebtedness takes the form of 'financial expropriation' (Lapavitsas 2009), the extraction of value from existing flows, within the sphere of circulation. Individuals are therefore not simply subject to financialisation as workers (or would-be workers) in the realm of production, but as consumers, borrowers, debtors and the holders of assorted financial liabilities and assets. Individuals increasingly serve as a nexus of profit for the financial system quite independently of their status as workers.

INDIVIDUAL AND HOUSEHOLD INDEBTEDNESS

South African household indebtedness rose during the economic boom of the early 2000s to 2008. The small net savings that historically characterised the average house-hold inverted by the mid-2000s, becoming indebtedness or 'dissaving' (reaching minus 3 per cent by 2006) (Teles 2012). Rising indebtedness, of course, represents the transfer of even larger shares of income to the financial sector.

In aggregate, the largest forms of debt on household balance sheets are mortgages. Mortgage debt grew in tandem with booming property prices, and significantly outpaced inflation (between 2000 and 2009 the mean national housing price increased by a nominal 348 per cent). South Africa's total household debt to disposable income ratio of 82.3 per cent on the eve of the 2008 Great Recession was significant in a small, open, vulnerable economy with high interest rates and a reliance on inflows of fickle foreign capital. Moreover, prior to the 2008 recession collateral from (and the psychological 'wealth effect' of) soaring property values bolstered consumer spending. Rocketing property prices were a significant manifestation of, and ultimately a contributor to, the asset bubbles associated with financialisation globally. Yet an important caveat is that these apply only to a minority of the South African population, the middle-class upwards owners of bank financed property (approximately 14 per cent of households lived in mortgaged residences in 2008 (Teles 2012)). In contrast, for the majority, ensnarement in the asymmetrical power relations associated with financialisation is essentially the tale of unsecured debt.

Before examining the rise of unsecured lending and consumer credit it is useful to briefly contextualise consumer consumption in South Africa. The post-apartheid explosion of individual debtness is partially explicable in terms of notions of consumption, identity and aspiration. The poor have long been incorporated into circuits of commodification, consumer markets and practices of 'emulative consumption' (Trigg 2001), and consumption is invariably bound up with social and cultural norms. In South Africa, the acquisition and display of the accoutrements of consumer modernity (clothes, cars, cellular phones and so on) has been 'boldly declared and invested with the iconography of a joyous emancipation' (Posel 2010: 159) as part of post-apartheid social citizenship. The relationship between race and the 'regulation of consumption' is therefore deeply inscribed. Historically, for instance, from the early colonial encounter 'Western' attire and patterns of domesticity were markers of an embrace of Christianity, Western education (Bank 2002) and 'respectability' (Ross 1999). Similarly, by mid-twentieth century the cosmopolitanism of North American influenced jazz culture was highly influential in the pockets of early, urban African modernity, such as in Sophiatown. Cultures of consumption and aspiration are particularly prominent in a highly unequal society such as South Africa, where prodigious wealth has long been displayed in close proximity to the poor, and conspicuous consumption is a valorised habit of its elites. The centrality of consumption is even affirmed in its negation, such as contemporary township youth street culture practices of *izikhothane*, the ritual destruction of luxury consumer goods (Italian shoes, cellular phones, fast food) as a performative act of conspicuous consumption (Jones 2013; Mnisi 2015).

Rising indebtedness in South Africa is moreover often variously attributed to consumer ignorance ('financial illiteracy') or simply feckless overindulgence. Yet this moral opprobrium serves to obscure the structural roots of indebtedness as a response to the growing squeeze on 'social reproduction' at household level. Globally, long stagnating working-class and middle-class wages, and rising income inequality, see financial intermediation play an increasingly important role in accessing healthcare, education and pensions. Rising household indebtedness thereby substitutes for the retreat of state provisioning – or, in a middle-income 'developing' country with high levels of poverty and inequality such as South Africa, the relative paucity of state provisioning. In this way, indebtedness is intertwined with the economic milieu of low levels of economic growth, high costs of living and, for the majority, chronic unemployment or underemployment.

INDEBTEDNESS AND UNSECURED LENDING

A major factor of impoverished South African household's indebtedness is unsecured lending (loans and consumer credit). The liberalisation of credit extension to low-income earners occurred in concert with the democratic transition. The 1990s lifting of the regulated interest rate caps on small loans, spawning the microloan industry, and drew the (overwhelmingly African) poor into formalised credit relations. This liberalisation was accompanied by reckless credit extension, legion abuses and rising personal indebtedness (James 2015), eventually leading to the 2005 promulgation of the National Credit Act (NCA). Applicable to all credit providers (banks, retailers, microlenders), the NCA sought to advance a 'market friendly' approach through the fostering of competition, clear disclosure of costs and capping of excessive interest rates. Yet its results have been, at best, rather uneven. Not only was continued, unchecked and reckless credit extension a driver of the 2010 implosion of African Bank, abuses remain widespread in what some characterise as South Africa's 'post-apartheid microcredit-driven calamity' (Bateman 2014). A full discussion of the array of post-NCA predatory practices and financial venality, is well beyond the ambit of this chapter but two specific examples are briefly discussed here: consumer credit insurance and 'garnishee' orders.

Although the NCA statutorily capped interest rates, they remained high and coexist with various permissible fees such as initiation and monthly fees. Moreover, loan costs (creditor's profits) readily metastasised into unregulated insurance, warrantees and other ancillary products, such as a miscellany of 'clubs', magazines and 'cash backs' that credit providers routinely conjure up. Take a single example of these, namely lightly regulated 'credit insurance' peddled with unsecured loan products: the premiums for this 'insurance' not only frequently exceed the principal interest (which it ostensibly 'insures') but these products have been systematically mis-sold – for instance, charging pensioners or the self-employed for retrenchment cover. Consumer ignorance assures credit providers of exceptionally low claim rates and high profits. So commonplace are exploitative practices in relation to credit insurance that even South Africa's largest furniture retailer, the Johannesburg Stock Exchange-listed Lewis group, was found guilty of illegal conduct by the National Consumer Tribunal. It refunded R64.1 million to customers, and attributed over R40 million of methodically mis-sold products to 'human error' (BD Live 2016)).

At the other end of South Africa's vast landscape of indebtedness is the collection of defaulters' debts. Notwithstanding the provisions of the NCA, credit extension in South Africa has long been predicated on the lenders' ability to collect, rather than a borrowers' ability to pay. It is manifest in mass indebtedness, where almost half of credit active consumers have 'impaired' records (eNCA 2015). In this context, the widespread use of emolument attachment orders and 'garnishee' orders on salaries to recover debt have long been characterised by egregious 'abuses' (Van Sittert 2013: 33) and systemic 'shortcomings and irregularities' (Van Sittert 2013: 41). These illegitimate salary deductions have been subject to successful public interest litigation against lenders (Maregele 2015). The abuses are remarkable not only for their extent, but also for how they systematically implicate a wide array of other actors such as debt collection agencies, legal firms and financial professionals. Quite apart from predatory marketers, retailers and lenders, the financialisation of the poor feeds an entire financial ecosystem, which includes credit bureaux, tracing agents and debt collectors, sheriffs, auctioneers, paralegals, lawyers and debt counsellors.

The ubiquity of financial expropriation through consumer indebtedness sees many of South Africa's largest consumer goods retailers derive substantial proportions of their profits from finance. Take the largest non-food retail group, Edcon: twice as large as its nearest competitor, with over 1 500 stores (including Edgars, Boardmans, Legit, Jet, Topshop and CNA) it makes approximately half its sales on credit, 47.3 per cent in 2014 (Edcon 2014), and a quarter of its profit from financial services. Similarly, market leading credit-based furniture and appliance retailer the JD Group (brands include Joshua Doore, Bradlows, Morkels, Russells) derived the majority of its profits (53 per cent) from financial services in 2014 (FinMark Trust 2014). Many of South Africa's leading retailers are essentially financial services companies that peddle clothes, furniture, appliances and jewellery as a necessary adjunct to their core business of credit extension. Geared towards credit extension, many retailers have ventured into touting other financial products such as funeral, life, asset, critical illness and credit life insurance.

So profitable is finance that even traditional non-credit extending retailers, such as supermarkets, have segued into financial services. South Africa's big four supermarket chains (Shoprite, Pick 'n Pay, Spar and Woolworths) offer an array of financial products including insurance, savings stamps, cash back facilities, third party bill payments and (some) even savings bonds, bank accounts and credit cards. They are not peripheral players either, with Shoprite holding an estimated 70 to 80 per cent of the money transfer market in South Africa (Finmark Trust 2014). These practices confound a neat distinction between finance and non-financial sector actors, and underscore the profitability and pervasiveness of finance.

INDEBTEDNESS AND INEQUALITY

Household debt can helpfully be thought of in terms of a three-part typology (Teles 2012). At the apex of a debt pyramid, is 'secured debt' with comparatively reasonable interest rates (typically a few per cent over the prime lending rates) underpinned by asset-backed finance (for example, property and vehicles) and typically accessed by the formally employed or middle classes upwards. The formal credit products held by this group of debtors are firmly within the purview of regulation, and therefore generally free of the worst excesses.

Below the upper tier of 'secured debt' is a middle tier of unsecured debt, without collateral, comprising expensive unsecured debt (store cards, furniture and personal loans) at commensurately higher interest rates. This makes up the bulk of the debt burden of the low-waged and working poor, accessible even to those with low incomes – even some beneficiaries of state welfare grants fall into this category of debtor.

The third and lowest tier of indebtedness includes forms of unregulated and informal borrowing, incurred by the unemployed and poor. South Africa's poor often hold a comparatively high number of financial 'instruments' (Collins 2008), ranging from various socially embedded arrangements such as informal savings groups (*umcalelo*), to extortionate informal (colloquially '*mashonisa*') loans at usurious interest rates.

The above typology is somewhat schematic. In reality, some porosity exists between categories, especially as higher-tier borrowers routinely access credit from the lower-tier sources. For instance, many middle-class South Africans hold unsecured debt. Moreover, informal borrowers and lenders routinely alternate roles, where borrowers become lenders and vice versa (James 2012). Notwithstanding this, the general tendency is for low-income borrowers to hold proportionally more unsecured, unregulated and higher-cost debt. They frequently pay higher interest rates than richer borrowers for similar types of debt such as consumer credit and unsecured loans (Teles 2012), a classic case of a 'poverty premium'. In these ways, indebtedness is characterised by highly 'regressive distributional outcomes' (Teles 2012: 213) and serves to perpetuate inequality. While inequality is obviously synonymous with the uneven distribution of assets and opportunity, the dynamics of financialisation mean it is also marked by higher costs and lower returns to the assets, including financial capital, that the poor possess.

To this point indebtedness in South Africa has been described in individual and household terms, but debt has powerful, aggregate socio-political consequences. Rising personal indebtedness, intertwined with the creeping crisis of impoverishment and household reproductive 'squeeze' alluded to earlier, generates pressures that are manifest in contested and fractious social, political and labour relations. Hence, several commentators suggest chronic indebtedness contributed to internecine conflict on South Africa's platinum belt in 2012 (Bond 2013) which culminated in the Marikana massacre.

FINANCIALISATION, DEVELOPMENT AND PUBLIC POLICY

To this point expanding processes of financialisation have been considered in terms of both their microstructural and household level impacts, and the resultant consequences for inequality has been reflected on. The concluding section briefly considers how these processes of financialisation articulate with larger public policy discourse and imperatives.

The notion of extending financial services to the formerly excluded (viz. 'financial inclusion') has intuitive appeal, and is a prominent theme in international development discourse (Sarma and Pais 2011). The archetypal example is microfinance, which ascended into the global poverty-reduction orthodoxy in the 1990s (Bayulgen 2008). It essentially consists of small developmental loans to groups of people (typically women), to enable them to overcome credit constraints and engage in productive activity. Historically, banks avoid low-income markets owing to proportionally high transaction costs and a paucity of collateral. But after two decades not only has multinational banking capital entered the microfinance sphere – even speculating in securitised microfinance debt (Soederberg 2013), many of the earlier developmental impacts attributed to microfinance have been subject to critical reappraisal (Bateman 2014). In South Africa, microfinance has had limited traction, partially because of the limited scope for leveraging microcredit into income-generating activity in the informal sector. Instead much debt in the South African context is used for consumption purposes, rather than directed to productive investment.

Where the discourse of financial inclusion does surface in South Africa is in attempts, exercised through moral suasion and regulatory fiat, to extend financial services to the historically excluded by low-cost bank accounts for the 'unbanked'. Although access to appropriate transactional, savings and credit instruments is a laudable developmental objective, 'financial inclusion' can often serve as a veil for the increased commodification of impoverished livelihoods and the rapacious expansion of financial markets. This is exemplified in the 2000s development mantra of 'making markets work for the poor' (Gibson et al. 2004), or the contemporary valorisation of 'social entrepreneurs'. In fact, it is often those with greatest of material interest in 'financial inclusion', namely corporate marketers, who most ardently invoke the discourse. Marketers have long sought to exploit (in the title of a seminal text) 'The fortune at the bottom of the pyramid' (Prahalad 2010) or, more recently, and with a local twist, service the township denizen practitioners of 'KasiNomics' (Alcock 2015).

Yet it is difficult to square the discourse of 'inclusion' with the fact that the poor have long populated the bottom tiers of South African marketers' canonical living standard measures typology. The African poor have long been cast as the 'emerging market', the 'informal market' or, in hair and personal care product markets, the 'ethnic market'. And no demographic is too impoverished or vulnerable to pursue. Consider a recent sordid Bloomberg headline: 'Welfare Kids' Funeral Cover Pits Insurers Against S. Africa' (Wild and Dzonzi 2016). It stemmed from two of the country's largest insurers (including Sanlam) attempting to litigate their right to directly deduct funeral policy premiums from the small welfare grants paid to impoverished children.[3]

Much of the shortcoming of financial inclusion talk is that it implicitly posits a problem in need of solving – 'exclusion' – but elides the reality that the impoverished and vulnerable are not excluded from the South African economy. They have long constituted entire market segments as consumers, customers, buyers, debtors, borrowers, clients, policyholders and subscribers. They are less excluded from markets, including financial markets, than they are incorporated into them, but often on highly disadvantageous and unfavourable terms (Du Toit and Neves 2007). It is the nature and quality of this inclusion that matters, and that determines the extent to which finance either ameliorates or exacerbates inequality.

CONCLUSION

This chapter has explicated the rise of financialisation and its manifestations in South Africa, and has described the country's racialised, inequality-inducing historical growth path and how it came to converge with global trends towards financialisation. These larger processes of financialisation have served to intensify inequality in South Africa through their constitutive effects on the labour market and the wider distribution of economic opportunity.

It followed on from this that financialisation of the poor is not limited to the realm of 'production' and employment, but increasingly includes the realm of circulation, including through the mechanism of individual and household indebtedness. In this way, systems and practices of 'financial expropriation' (Lapavitsas 2009) of the poor are no longer limited to workers, or at least workers in a formal 'productivist' (Ferguson 2015) sense. For the poor occupy diverse places within South Africa's larger distributional regime: they are remittance receivers and social grant beneficiaries, they are the precariously employed, informally employed, underemployed or altogether unemployed. Yet their estrangement from formal, remunerative work does not preclude them from being a source of value and profit to capital. Finance and financiers are increasingly able to sequester value from them.

South Africa, with its agglomerations of wealth, sophisticated financial infrastructure and long socio-political tolerance of extreme inequality, provides ample prospects for financialisation to extend its frontiers, to novel target groups or plumb greater depths in existing market segments. The extent to which this continues will ultimately determine the extent to which processes of financialisation persist in reinforcing inequality.

NOTES

1   Along with a multitude of other factors, such as skills deficits, biases towards capital-intensive production, and low productivity on the back of a volatile and overvalued currency.
2   A measure of the difference between a country's net income (including imports) and its exports.
3   At the time of writing similar evidence was emerging over the potential 'capture' of social grants, and grant recipients, by commercial interests contracted by the state to pay them.

REFERENCES

Aghion, P, Braun, M and Fedderke, J (2008) Competition and productivity growth in South Africa. *EcoNomics of Transition*, 16 (4), 741–768.

Alcock, GG (2015) *KasiNomics: African informal economies and the people who inhabit them*. Johannesburg: Tracey McDonald Publishers.

Ashman, S, Fine, B and Newman, S (2011) The crisis in South Africa: Neoliberalism, financialisation and uneven and combined development. *Socialist Register*, 47, 174–195.

Bank, L (2002) Beyond red and school: Gender, tradition and identity in the rural Eastern Cape. *Journal of Southern African Studies*, 28 (3), 631–649.

Bateman, M (2014) South Africa's post-apartheid microcredit-driven calamity. *Law, Democracy and Development*, 18, 92–135.

Bayulgen, O (2008) Muhammad Yunus, Grameen Bank and the Nobel Peace Prize: What political science can contribute to and learn from the study of microcredit. *International Studies Review*, 10 (3), 525–547.

BD Live (2016) Lewis to oppose new referral to consumer watchdog. *Business Day*, BD Live. http://www.bdlive.co.za/business/retail/2016/04/19/lewis-to-oppose-new-referral-to-consumer-watchdog.

Black, A and Gerwel, H (2014) Shifting the growth path to achieve employment intensive growth in South Africa. *Development Southern Africa*, 31 (2), 241–256.

Bond, P (2013) Debt, uneven development and capitalist crisis in South Africa: From Moody's macroeconomic monitoring to Marikana microfinance mashonisas. *Third World Quarterly*, 34 (4), 569–592.

Bracking, S (2015) *The financialization of power in Africa*. London: Routledge.

Bryceson, DF (1996) Deagrarianisation and rural unemployment in sub-Saharan Africa: A sectoral perspective. *World Development*, 24 (1), 97–111.

Collins, D (2008) Debt and household finance: Evidence from the financial diaries. *Development Southern Africa*, 25 (4), 469–479.

Devey, R, Skinner, C and Valodia, I (2005) The state of the informal economy. In S Buhlungu, J Daniel, J Latchman and R Southall (eds) *The state of the nation 2005–6*. Pretoria: HSRC Press.

Du Toit, A and Neves, D (2007) In search of South Africa's second economy: Chronic poverty, vulnerability and adverse incorporation in Mt Frere and Khayelitsha. *Africanus*, 36 (2), 145–174.

Edcon (2014) *Annual report Edcon Holdings Limited (for 52 weeks ended 29 March, 2014)*. Johannesburg: Edcon Holdings. http://www.edcon.co.za/pdf/annual_reports/annual_report_2014.pdf.

eNCA (2015) *SA impaired credit records at highest levels ever: Nzimande*. 4th October. https://www.enca .com/money/sa-impaired-credit-records-highest-levels-ever-nzimande.

Epstein, G (2005) *Financialisation and the world economy*. Aldershot: Elgar.

Ferguson, J (2015) *Give a man a fish: Reflections on the new politics of distribution*. Durham: Duke University Press.

Fine, B (2010) Locating financialisation. *Historical Materialism*, 18, 97–116.

Fine, B (2013) Financialization from a Marxist perspective. *International Journal of Political Economy*, 42 (4), 47–66.

Fine, B and Rustomjee, Z (1996) *The political economy of South Africa: From minerals-energy complex to industrialisation*. London: Hurst.

Finmark Trust (2009) *FinMark brief: The banking inquiry*. Johannesburg: Finmark Trust.

Finmark Trust (2014) *Retailers' motivation for offering financial services*. Johannesburg: Finmark Trust.

Gibson, A, Scott, H and Ferrand, D (2004) *Making markets work for the poor. An objective and an approach for governments and development agencies*. Johannesburg: ComMark.

Harvey, D (2005) *A brief history of neoliberalism*. Oxford: Oxford University Press.

James, D (2012) Money-go-round: Personal economies of wealth, aspiration and indebtedness. *Africa: The Journal of the International African Institute*, 82 (1), 20–40.

James, D (2015) *Money from nothing: Indebtedness and aspiration in South Africa*. Stanford, CA: Stanford University Press/Johannesburg: Wits University Press.

Jones, M (2013) Conspicuous destruction, aspiration and motion in the South African township. *Safundi*, 14 (2), 209–224.

Krippner, G (2005) The financialization of the American economy. *Socio-Economic Review*, 3, 173–208.

Lapavitsas, C (2009) Financialised capitalism: Crisis and financial expropriation. *Historical Materialism*, 17 (2), 114–148.

Lee, R, Clark, G, Pollard, J and Leyshon, A (2009) The remit of financial geography: Before and after the crisis. *Journal of Economic Geography*, 9, 723–747.

Leibbrandt, M, Woolard, I, Finn, A and Argent, J (2010) *Trends in South African income distribution and poverty since the fall of apartheid*. OECD Social, Employment and Migration Working Paper No. 101, Organisation for Economic Co-operation and Development.

Marais, H (2011) *South Africa pushed to the limit*. Cape Town: University of Cape Town Press.

Maregele, B (2015) Victory for consumers as court rules against salary deductions. 9 July 2015. *Mail & Guardian*. http://mg.co.za/article/2015–07–09-victory-for-consumers-as-court-rules-against-salary-deductions.

Masie, D (2015) How much is too much? Finance in South Africa. *New African*, 24 March.

Mnisi, J (2015) Burning to consume? Izikhothane in Daveyton as aspirational consumers. *Communicatio*, 41 (3), 340–353.

Mohamed, S (2003) *Capital inflows since the end of apartheid and the currency crisis of 2001*. Forum 2003 Papers. TIPS, Development Policy Research Unit, School of Economics, University of Cape Town.

Mohamed, S and Roberts, S (2006) *Questions of growth, questions of development*. Conference paper presented at TIPS/DPRU accelerated and shared growth in South Africa: Determinants, constraints and opportunities conference, 18–20 October, Johannesburg.

Philip, K (2010) Inequality and economic marginalisation: How the structure of the economy impacts on opportunities on the margins. *Law, Democracy & Development*, 14, 1–28.

Porteous, D (2003) The landscape of access to financial services in South Africa. *South African Reserve Bank Labour Markets and Social Frontiers*, 3, 1–6.

Posel, D (2010) Races to consumer: Revisiting South African's history of race, consumption and the struggle for freedom. *Ethnic and Racial Studies*, 33 (2), 157–175.

Prahalad, CK (2010) *The fortune at the bottom of the pyramid: Eradicating poverty through profits*. 5th edition. Upper Saddle River: Wharton School Publishing/Pearson Educational.

Roberts, S (2010) Competition policy, competitive rivalry and the developmental state in South Africa. In O Edigheji (ed.) *Constructing a democratic developmental state in South Africa*. Pretoria: HSRC Press. pp. 222–239.

Ross, R (1999) Missions, respectability and civil rights: The Cape Colony, 1828–1854. *Journal of Southern African Studies*, 25 (3), 333–345.

Sarma, M and Pais, J (2011) Financial inclusion and development. *Journal of International Development*, 23, 613–628.

Seekings, J and Nattrass, N (2006) *Race, class and inequality in South Africa*. Pietermaritzburg: UKZN Press.

Soederberg, S (2013) Universalising financial inclusion and the securitisation of development. *Third World Quarterly*, 34 (4), 593–612.

Teles, N (2012) *Financialisation in South Africa: Examining the financial conduct of non-financial enterprises, banks and households*. PhD thesis. London: SOAS, University of London.

Trigg, AB (2001) Veblen, Bourdieu, and conspicuous consumption. *Journal of Economic Issues*, 35 (1), 99–115.

Van Sittert, C (2013) *The incidence of and undesirable practices relating to 'garnishee orders'*. Report University of Pretoria Law Clinic, Faculty of Law. http://www.up.ac.za/media/shared/Legacy/sitefiles/file/47/327/2013 garnishee orders followup report.pdf.

Wild, F and Dzonzi, TA (2016) Welfare kids' funeral cover pits insurers against S. Africa. Bloomberg. 3 May. http://www.bloomberg.com/news/articles/2016–05–02/welfare-kids-funeral-cover-pits-insurers-against-south-africa.

THE POLITICS OF INEQUALITY

2

CHAPTER 5

Liberal democracy, inequality and the imperatives of alternative politics: Nigeria and South Africa

Samuel Ojo Oloruntoba

After many years of despotic and autocratic rule, African countries joined the third wave of democracy in the 1990s (Huntington 1991). The return to democracy on the continent was motivated by various factors, including revolutionary pressures from within in the form of protests, civil disobedience and violent struggles as well as external pressures from development agents which made democracy a primary condition of eligibility for development aid and assistance. Today, however, democratic governance in Africa is highly uneven, involving simultaneity in the pursuit of democratic consolidation, slight improvements over previous elections, cases of opposition political parties winning elections at different levels and development or strengthening critical institutions such as election management bodies and (to some extent) judiciaries. Bright prospects have been blighted by cases of leaders making attempts to change – or successfully changing – constitutions to stay longer in government, as well as intolerance of opposition parties, leading to what Diamond (2002) calls the retreat of democracy.

The variations in the practice of democracy and the forms of democratic governance have given rise to interpretations such as illiberal democracy, authoritarian democracy and hybrid democracy. There have also been serious concerns about the prospects of democracy fostering inclusive development in Africa, concerns borne out in the complexities in explaining the wide gap between the expectations of egalitarianism, inclusiveness and voice to the disadvantaged and the reality that liberal democracy has not been able to bridge such yawning gaps between rich and poor.

The two case studies in this chapter, South Africa and Nigeria, pose some similarities and contrasts in the structure of their economies; the composition of the elite base in society; the nature and character of the state's capacity to deliver on the promises of fostering inclusive development; institutionalisation of the political processes; and the relevance of political parties to policy making. The similarities can be seen in the size of their economies (two of the three biggest in Africa); the adoption of liberal democracy; patrimonialism (the client-patron relationship) in politics; and the nature of the economy. The differences can be seen in the form of colonialism they experienced (South Africa's settler colonialism and Nigeria's non-settler colonialism); the racial composition of South African society and the relatively developed auto-economy of South Africa as against the oil and resource-dependent economy of Nigeria.

Since South Africa's democratisation in 1994 and Nigeria's return to democratic governance in 1999, the basic tenets of liberal democracy (regular elections, universal adult suffrage, the supremacy of the rule of law, the protection of property and civil rights) have been observed in varying degrees. However, although there has been growth measured by gross domestic product (GDP) in both countries, the levels of inequality have correspondingly increased. Accordingly, the contradictions of growth without development, democracy without inclusion and participation without transformation call for a thorough analysis of those who are deriving benefits from electoral democracy and stress the urgency of developing alternative models to both liberal and electoral democracy.

The next section of this chapter examines democratic typologies, features and the debates around democracy's correlation with development. The third section situates the democratic experiences of Nigeria and South Africa in the context of their political economies and considers how these experiences affect the capacity for fostering inclusive development. I then make a case for alternative politics that is consistent with the socio-economic and political conditions of the two countries.

DEMOCRACY: FORMS, TYPOLOGIES AND THEORIES

The debate over the link between democracy and development has raged for years. Modernisation theory argues that, given the low level of political culture in newly independent countries, elected governments lack the required discipline and capacity to bring about development. It has therefore been assumed that undemocratic regimes lack the wherewithal to bring about development – which was considered a necessary condition for facilitating democracy (Lipset 1959). Huntington (1968) argued that the lack of political institutions and the legitimacy of the state created instability, thereby undermining development, noting that the most important political distinction among countries concerned not the form of government but the degree of governing. Consequently, political institutions and strong authority bases were needed to manage the various centrifugal and centripetal forces that tear a society apart or pull it together. Given the low level of political culture and the revolutionary pressures that attended the first decades of independence, modernisation theorists like Huntington considered the military as a social group capable of fostering order and bringing about development.

The failure of military regimes to realise the expected development and social change, the fall of the Soviet Union and the end of the Cold War led to what Ake (1994) called revolutionary pressures from below in the form of agitation for a return to democracy in African countries. The economic crisis of the 1980s and 1990s also created a unique opportunity for international financial institutions such as the World Bank and International Monetary Fund to intervene in restructuring the political economies of these countries. The high levels of debt which had been accumulated by African countries over many years necessitated the involvement of the external agencies in the reform of their economies, subject to meeting set conditions. One of the conditions was for countries to democratise through opening the political space, a demand imposed by the World Bank in the good governance agenda (Chan 2002).

It was in this context that South Africa's political system changed from a minority controlled apartheid government to a multiparty democracy in 1994 (Habib 2013). However, as I shall demonstrate later, the triumphalism of liberals such as Francis Fukuyama (who foresaw no form of political economic arrangements other than capitalism and liberal democracy), was too simplistic as it failed to grasp the complexities that have defined the art of governing over the past three decades. Rather than reaching its end as Fukuyama (1992) prematurely declared, history has continued to be made in various forms and patterns economically, socially and politically. Chan (2002: 8–9) puts the uncertainties around liberal democracy as a universal form of political arrangement this way:

> It is not at all a foregone conclusion that the collapse of authoritarian and communist regimes will lead to democracy. It is not only that in the process of democratisation, each step in one direction risks a reaction in the opposite direction. It is also that as democratisation proceeds, various intermediary forms are taking shape. Indeed, the celebration of 'liberal democracy' greatly exaggerates the coherence of the process of democratisation.

The lack of homogeneity in the forms and practices of democracy has given rise to different typologies such as liberal, electoral, electoral authoritarianism, competitive authoritarianism, uncompetitive or hegemonic democracies, illiberal democracies or ambitious democracies (Diamond 2002). In Diamond's earlier work, those regimes with multiparty electoral competition of some kind, with electoral authoritarianism and that are pseudo-democratic or hybrid and politically closed are classified as undemocratic (Diamond et al. 1995). Competitive authoritarianism may be either competitive or hegemonic depending on the degree to which civil liberties and the institutionalisation of the democratic process are allowed and the possibility that an opposition party will be allowed to compete on a level playing field in a free and fair election. Thus, contrary to the simplistic categorisation of democracies into liberal or illiberal as Huntington (1968) and Zakaria (1997) would have us believe, there have been several complexities in the form and practices of democracies, especially after the third wave. As Zakaria (1997) notes, constitutional liberalism, which embodies separation of powers, property rights, protection of liberties such as free speech, assembly and religion, is different from democracy.

Levitsky and Way's (2002) categorisation of new democracies that manifest dynamic features of authoritarianism and competitiveness has gained resonance among democracy scholars. They note that political systems descend into electoral authoritarianism when violations of the minimum criteria for democracy are so serious that they create an uneven playing field between government and opposition. While these regimes may permit elections, the governance processes remain authoritarian and centred around the personalities of the president or the prime minister, who use patronage systems to maintain loyalty among members of the ruling elites. Thomas Carothers (cited in Menocal et al. 2008) makes a distinction between hybrid regimes characterised by 'feckless pluralism' (regimes where there is considerable pluralism and competitive electoral processes, but where democracy remains shallow and troubled) and democracies characterised by 'dominant-power politics' where there is more space for political competition but one grouping dominates the system so that there is little prospect for a real alternation of power.

DEMOCRACY AND DEVELOPMENT: EXPLORING COMPATIBILITY

The complexities in grappling with the forms and typologies of democracy have not detracted from the popular expectation that it is the best form of government to bring about inclusive development. Although some liberal scholars argue that democracy is a consequence of economic development (see, for instance, Przeworski and Limongi 1997), there is no conclusive evidence that democracy leads to development. What is increasingly emerging is that authoritarian regimes are delivering more development outcomes for their citizens, with varying degrees of success. The cases of China and Singapore in Asia as well as Rwanda and Ethiopia in Africa are good examples (Joseph 2016).

The great expectation that democracy will bring about development was bolstered by the demise of communism. Scholars like Fukuyama thought we had reached an end of history, as it then appeared that with the triumph of the Anglo-American version of capitalism over Soviet-style communism modern society had reached the end of the evolutionary processes of political economy (Fukuyama 1992). However, barely two decades after such euphoric outbursts, Fukuyama and his co-travellers have become sober and realistic as they have had to come to terms with the failures of democracy to deliver public good for most of the citizens. For instance, Fukuyama (2013: 6) notes that:

> ... the inability to 'make democracy deliver' in terms of shared growth and broadly available public goods has in turn weakened the legitimacy of democratic governments. Conversely, the prestige of authoritarian countries like China and Singapore lies in their apparent ability to provide precisely these things, despite the absence of formal government accountability ... if we care about the health of democracies around the world, we must also care about the performance of their governments, that is, the quality of their state bureaucracies.

There is merit in this argument, but it appears too sweeping to assume that there is 'absence of formal government accountability in China and Singapore'. Although the governments of these countries did not display accountability to their electorates, they were nonetheless accountable to their populations through other mechanisms. In China, this was through the Communist Party. This remains the case today, with institutional mechanisms having been developed within the Communist Party to pursue and prosecute cases of corruption.

The gap between the expectations that democracy will bring about development and the reality of the failure to achieve this goal has increasingly led to distrust, suspicion and even frustrations with democratic governments in both developed and developing countries, with citizens' preference for democracy on the decline (Freedom House 2007).

> ... [the] ascendancy of liberal democracy is accompanied by a growing discontent in the established liberal democracies of the West with its practice operation, with demands for a more deliberative democracy, for ways to deepen democracy, to increase civic-ness, for teledemocracy, for keeping party politics in check, for overcoming public apathy and the recognition that democracy seems incapable of delivering on its promises, that there is a tension between democracy and the complexity of contemporary life (Chan 2002).

Liberal democracy and its variants have led to widened inequality and increased poverty among the citizens in both advanced and developing countries – but especially in the latter. As I explain in the subsequent section, this contradiction is encapsulated in the changes to the social structure of accumulation, the renewed imperial orientation of global capital and the deliberate establishment of transnational capitalist elites, whose main preoccupation is accumulation on a large scale (Robinson 2010, 2004).

In the case of Africa, Ake (1994, 1996) argues that despite all pretensions to the contrary, there was no development on the agenda of postcolonial elites as they did not know what development entails. He also argues that the history of state formation on the continent, the character of the state, the composition of the elites as well as the liberal form of democracy adopted was not conducive to development in its proper form. What Ake missed in the democracy-development debate are the international forces that have emerged to shape the global economy in the last three decades and how these forces shape global production, accumulation, consumption, interests and domestic politics in terms of their capacity for redistribution. His analysis also missed the influence of emergent transnational elites who successfully displaced, upturned or incorporated the national- ist elites that adopted the Fordist-Keynesian model of accumulation to bring about the 'golden age' of capitalism after the Second World War.

The crisis that ensued from the contradictions inherent in the Fordist and Keynesian regime of accumulation led to counter-hegemonic reactions from conservative elites in the developed countries who became engaged in a competition for state power – which they won and effectively used 'to push capitalist globalisation, to restructure national productive apparatuses and integrate them into the new global production and financial system' (Ake 1994: 2). The Thatcher-Reagan alliance of neoliberal orthodoxy produced a set of institutions and transnational elites that promoted the idea of TINA – 'There is no alternative to the market' (see Harvey 2007). The shift in orientation of the dominant elites led to 'a shift in discourse from national industrialisation and expanding internal markets to global market integration and macroeconomic, principally neoliberal policies that facilitated such integration' (Robinson 2010: 3). Robinson recognised four distinct but interrelated processes through which this new regime of capitalist expansion and surplus accumulation was institutionalised and internationalised:

> First was a new capital-labour relation based on the deregulation, informalisation, and
> 'flexibilisation' of labour. Second was a new round of extensive and intensive expan-
> sion. Extensively, the system expanded through the reincorporation of major areas
> of the former Third and Second worlds into the world capitalist economy, so that by
> the 1990s no region remained. Third, was the creation of a global legal and regulatory
> structure to facilitate what were emerging globalised circuits of accumulation, includ-
> ing the creation of the World Trade Organization. And fourth, was the imposition
> of the neo-liberal model on countries throughout the Third and the former Second
> worlds, involving structural adjustment programmes that created the conditions for
> the free operation of capital within and across borders and the harmonisation of accu-
> mulation conditions worldwide (Robinson 2010: 5).

It was essentially in the context of the above that liberal democracy became a necessity and a ready handmaiden for the expansion of global capital. To underscore this point, democracy became a conditionality for developing countries in their bids to access aid and development assistance from multilateral organisations. Regardless of irregularities in the conduct of elections, especially in developing countries, the international elec- tion observers almost always assert that such elections met local standards, leading to a phenomenon that has been termed the fallacy of electoralism which, according to Diamond (1996: 22)

> ... consists of privileging electoral contestation over other dimensions of democracy and ignoring the degree to which multiparty elections, even if genuinely competitive, may effectively deny significant sections of the population the opportunity to contest for power or advance and defend their interests or may leave significant arenas of decision-making power beyond the reach or control of elected officials.

To summarise, my core argument is that the formation of a transnational elite – whose overriding concern is the expansion of global capital and the integration of all parts of the world into its production circuit – has ensured that the state and the democracy that it adopts only serve the interests of capital and the members of the tiny elites. This explains why despite the expansion in the global economy over the past thirty years, inequality has continued to grow (Oxfam 2015; Piketty 2014).

This linearity provides some basis for comparison between Anglo-American based globalisation and the national social democratic projects that obtain in the Scandinavian countries. Whereas in the former there has risen a sharp rise in inequality and poverty, and reduction in provision of social services, the latter have done relatively better in lifting millions out of poverty (Ravallion 2009). In Asia, the cases of China and Singapore also show the necessity of ensuring a rethinking of the types of democracy that Africa needs in order to guarantee growth and development. The idea of a democratic developmental state has been mooted as a possible route to development, especially in South Africa (Edigheji 2010). However, this has not been possible owing to several factors, not least the differences in the domestic and international conditions that favoured the success of developmental states in South East Asia in the 1950s to 1990s (Evans 1998; Wade 1990). Lack of hegemony of the ruling elites in Africa and the nature of the political economy as well as the dependent nature of the state on global capital appear to have limited the prospects of building a democratic developmental state on the continent.

DEMOCRACY AND DEVELOPMENT: NIGERIA AND SOUTH AFRICA IN COMPARATIVE PERSPECTIVE

To explore how democracy has hindered or promoted development in Nigeria and South Africa, it is imperative to locate the two countries in their historical contexts as well as their placement in the hierarchy of power at the global level. This will help us to understand how the present realities are reflections of coloniality: a systematic reconstruction and continuity of colonial patterns of domination in knowledge, being and power (Ndlovu-Gatsheni 2013).

Although they historically experienced colonial domination in different ways, Nigeria and South Africa were both subjected to brutal forms of exploitation. Not only were their economies overtly integrated into empire in a dependent form, but the colonial state was not rooted in the society. It was authoritarian, violent and extractive in nature (Taylor 2014). The postcolonial state continues to manifest the characteristics of the colonial state. Lacking hegemony and base in the society, the post-independence elites continue to put on a Fanonian white mask over their black skins. As surrogates of the global imperial powers, they are joined with the members of the transnational capital class in an unholy unity of exploitation and expropriation of the resources of their people. As obedient servants of capital, many of them have uncritically accepted imposition of economic and political programmes which only benefit key actors in the game of global accumulation. In the two countries – as well as in many other African countries – the state and the elites have become kleptocratic and predatory (Joseph 2016).

Nigeria has had three experiences of democracy since gaining political independence from Britain on 1 October 1960. Barely six years into independence, the first military coup took place on 15 January 1966, followed by a counter-coup in July of the same year and a devastating civil war that lasted for three years. The second attempt at democracy was from 1979 to 1983, when another military coup took place. As Joseph (2016) argues, it was particularly instructive that Nigeria returned to democracy in 1979 when the third wave of democratisation had yet to take root in Africa.

Although the 1999 Constitution defines Nigeria as a welfarist state, successive governments since 1999 have followed the key prescriptions of neoliberal economic doctrine such as liberalisation, deregulation, privatisation of state-owned enterprises and the like. Successive governments have put in place various policies and development strategies which were geared towards fostering development. For instance, the Olusegun Obasanjo administration from 1999 to 2007 designed intervention and macroeconomic policies such as the National Poverty Eradication Programme, National Economic Empowerment Development Strategy, Consolidation of Banks and so on, as means of fostering development. The two administrations after this also embarked on what they called the seven-point agenda and the transformation agenda. While these interventions led to some growth measured by GDP, the trickledown effect was minimal. Figures from the National Bureau of Statistics show that the proportion of people in poverty in Nigeria reached 69 per cent in 2014. As I argue (Oloruntoba 2016), the National Poverty Eradication Programme of the Obasanjo administration was mired with undue corruption as it was hijacked by officials of the ruling Peoples' Democratic Party (PDP) to serve the interests of their cronies.

The class dimension of the political economy of Nigeria becomes conspicuous if it is considered that in the same country where the mass of people live in poverty, private jets owned by state governors (who could barely pay the salaries of civil servants) and politically connected businessmen (most of whom are not productive) dot the landscape (BBC 2014). What emerges is that the patronage network of corruption, fuelled with rents from the oil economy, has continued to foster inequality. The presidency itself has ten aircraft in its fleet. Despite the election promises by the present incumbent that some of the aircraft would be disposed of if he won the 2015 elections, the planes remain unsold.

DEMOCRACY AND DEVELOPMENT IN SOUTH AFRICA

The history of South Africa is one of institutionalised and racialised inequality culminating in apartheid, which entrenched white domination and differing standards of living, income, education, infrastructures and freedom of association and mobility along lines of race (Seekings and Nattrass 2006). Since 1994, the African National Congress (ANC)-led government has embarked on various measures to bridge the gap in inequality, especially along racial lines. However, due to historical and structural imbalances in the economy, education and other aspects of social services, both racial and class inequalities have continued unabated. Gumede (2015: 91–2) argues that 'even though inequality is a function of an under-transformed labour market and skewed structure of the economy in South Africa, the entrenched legacy of apartheid colonialism has ensured that it remains highly racialised'.

Democracy in South Africa has been dominated by the ANC. As Southall (2008: 281) has argued, the party was formed as a liberation movement which drew much of its strength from its moral underpinning in fighting for a just society. He stresses that the ANC 'opposed legalised racism, with a commitment to nonracialism and political equality for all … it could present itself as offering a home for all South Africans, of whatever race, colour or creed, so long as they were prepared to embrace democracy'. However, the noble goals espoused by the ANC in the struggle for democracy have long been abandoned under the party's post-1994 rule. From 1996, the ANC embraced an abrupt turn to neoliberalism, resulting in growing inequality – rendered worse by the spread of rampant corruption.

Unsurprisingly, given the gap in expectation and reality of the fruit of democracy, there is a growing discontent among supporters of the ANC. As Habib (2013) notes, the wind of discontent among ANC members is not limited to the top echelons of the party membership. The majority of black people, who voted the party into power and who see it as an agent for empowerment, remain poor and disillusioned. Young black South Africans have a distant emotional connection to the ANC as a liberation movement. Their major concerns are deliverables: transparent governance, improvement in the standard of living and services. It portends danger for the ANC in terms of mass support and the resultant electoral victory if it loses the emotional connection with the black South Africans born post-apartheid.

In both Nigeria and South Africa, the interest of the ruling class has trumped that of the majority of the citizens. The sheer size of the difference in the standard of living of the average citizen and the ruling elites – income, housing, health and so on – attests to the level of inequalities in the two countries.

IN SEARCH OF ALTERNATIVE POLITICS

Scholars of democracy as well as nongovernmental organisations (such as Afrobarometer and Freedom House) charged with monitoring the health of liberal democracy have expressed concern about the retreat of democracy, the failure of democracy to facilitate inclusive development, distrust of democracy and apathy to democracy (Diamond 2015; Fukuyama 2013; Freedom House 2007; Chan 2002). However, the retreat of democracy is not limited to the developing countries as the young population in advanced democracies are also losing interest in the rituals of four- or five-year election cycles with little or no improvement in their living conditions.

Various factors account for the contradictions inherent in liberal democracy with respect to its ability to bring about development. These factors include (1) the imposition of liberal democracy by the West as a conditionality for aid or even as part of the new form of civilising mission (see Ndlovu-Gatsheni and Dzinesa 2008); (2) the ineluctable connection between liberal democracy and the changing nature of the organisation of the global capitalist system, in which financialisation has replaced production, democratic politics has been subordinated to economics under a new utopia of market fundamentalism, and a new financial oligarchy has emerged which dictates policy preferences (Oloruntoba 2015; Stiglitz 2012); and (3) the disconnection between the practice of democracy and traditional institutions of governance as well as insensitivity to cultural specificities.

To tackle the gap between the expectations and the reality of democracy and development, it needs to be restated that democracy is not alien to Africa (Mamdani 1996). Thus, it is necessary to revisit the pre-colonial systems of governance (Nzongola-Ntalaja and Lee 1997), in which checks and balances constituted the core of kingship authorities, of the rotation of power among ruling houses and of the agency of the people in selecting the kings. Despite the limited space available for policy making in Africa, lessons from the East Asian and Scandinavian countries show that cautious engagement with the globalisation processes and subordination of economics to politics are two critical ways of escaping from the deleterious effects of market fundamentalism. Thus, reorganisation of the economy in a way that allows for job creation for both the high and the low-skilled are crucial for reducing inequality. Rather than the fixation with liberal democracy, the aim should be to foster developmental democracy in which the creation of social wealth (water; electricity, education and environment; agriculture; law and governance; transportation; and housing) become the core pursuit of the government (Joseph 2016).

CONCLUSION

This chapter has examined the disparity between expectations and reality in the deliverables of liberal democracy in Nigeria and South Africa. The high rate of inequality in the two countries has caused distrust in government and disillusionment about democracy.

My argument is that the nature of the political economies of the two countries, the organisation of politics and the international division of labour have created conditions for the reproduction of class disparity between the political elites and their cronies on the one hand and the masses of the people on the other, with class and race playing different roles in the two countries.

Given the contradictions within liberal democracy, especially in relation to its connection to the hegemony of neoliberal global capitalism in Africa, there is a need to think outside orthodoxy through the reorganisation of politics in such a way as to ensure redistribution, citizenship action, participation and inclusiveness. As Stiglitz (2012) reminds us, inequality has a price, which can manifest in the form of double movements (Polanyi 1947), violent protests (Bond 2015), possible revolution (Habib 2013), apathy to political process (Chan 2002) and a complete change in the existing order. In the case of South Africa, Terreblanche (2002) warns that if the privileged class among the racial groups in the 'rainbow nation' fails to accommodate the poor majority in the enjoyment of the dividends of democracy, it should prepare to experience what the two previous dispensations, the British and the Afrikaner colonialism went through: inevitable change, more far-reaching in scope and magnitude than anticipated. Although the Boko Haram and Niger Delta insurgencies in Nigeria may be attributed to religious and environmental issues, they cannot be divorced from the high rate of inequality in that country.

The future of liberal democracy lies in its ability to foster an inclusive society where access to socio-economic and political rights is guaranteed without regard to class, race or some initial conditions and privileges. While building a democratic development state appears limited in its practicality and usefulness, developmental governance (anchored in accountability, redistribution through progressive taxes, investment in education, health, water and infrastructure) and an interventionist state with the capacity for formulating appropriate trade and industrial policies are required to create access to economic opportunities. As Green (2008) has argued, in addressing the twin challenges of poverty and inequality two things are critical: effective states and active citizens. Although effective states can help in mediating the rampaging effects of neoliberal capitalism through a redistributive and empowering politics in which all members of the society have some form of identification and bearing, active citizens are necessary to perform their civic duties and put on the agenda the change from the politics of private accumulation to the politics of distribution or inclusion.

REFERENCES

Ake, C (1994) *Democratization of disempowerment in Africa. Issue 1 of CASS Occasional Monograph.* Lagos: Malthouse Press.
Ake, C (1996) *Democracy and development in Africa.* Maryland: Brookings Institution.
Bond, P (2015) Africans are rising against Africa 'rising'. Paper presented at the colloquium on global economic crisis and the social values organized by Mapungubwe Institute for Strategic Reflections, Pretoria, 30 September.

BBC (British Broadcasting Corporation) News (2014) Private jets in Nigeria, 5 May.

Chan, S (2002) *Liberalism, democracy and development*. Cambridge: Cambridge University Press.

Diamond, L (1996) Is the third wave over? *Journal of Democracy*, 7 (3), 20–37.

Diamond, L (2002) Thinking about hybrid regimes. *Journal of Democracy*, 13 (2), 21–35.

Diamond, L (2015) The democratic recession. *Journal of Democracy*, 26 (1), 141–155.

Diamond, L, Linz, J and Lipset, S (eds) (1995) *Politics in developing countries*. Boulder: Lynne Rienner.

Edigheji, O (2010) *Constructing a democratic developmental state in South Africa*. Pretoria: Human Science Research Council.

Evans, P (1998) 'Transferable lessons': Re-examining the institutional prerequisites of East Asian Economic Policies. *Journal of Development Studies*, 34 (6), 66–86.

Freedom House (2007) Map of freedom in the world. Available from www.freedomhouse.org/template.cfm?page363&year-2007 (accessed 14 April 2016).

Fukuyama, F (1992) *The end of history and the last man*. New York: The Free Press.

Fukuyama, F (2013) Democracy and the quality of the state. *Journal of Democracy*, 24 (4), 5–16.

Green, D (2008) *From poverty to power: How effective states and active citizens can change the world*. Great Britain: Oxfam.

Gumede, V (2015) Inequality in democratic South Africa. In X Mancu (ed.), *The color of our future: Does race matter in post-apartheid South Africa?* Johannesburg: Wits University Press.

Habib, A (2013) *South Africa's suspended revolution: Hopes and prospects*. Johannesburg: Wits University Press.

Harvey, D (2007) *A brief history of neoliberalism*. Oxford: Oxford University Press.

Huntington, S (1968) *Political order in changing societies*. London: Yale University Press.

Huntington, S (1991) *The third wave: Democratization in the late twentieth century*. Norman: University of Oklahoma Press.

Joseph, R (2016) *The Nigeria prospect: Democratic resilience and global turmoil*. Africaplus. Available from https://africaplus.wordpress.com/2016/03/31/the-nigerian-prospect-democratic-resilience-amid-global-turmoil.

Levitsky, S and Way, L (2002) The rise of competitive authoritarianism. *Journal of Democracy*. 13 (2), 51–65.

Lipset S (1959) Some social requisites of democracy: Economic development as political legitimacy. *American Political Science Review*, 53 (1), 69–105.

Mamdani M (1996) *Citizens and the subject: Contemporary Africa and the legacy of late colonialism*. Princeton: Princeton University Press.

Menocal, A, Fritz, V and Rakner, L (2008) Hybrid regimes and the challenges of deepening and sustaining democracy in developing countries. *South African Journal of International Affairs*, 15 (1), 29–40.

Ndlovu-Gatsheni, S (2013) Decolonial epistemic perspective and pan-African unity in the 21st century. In M Munchie, P Lukhele-Olorunju and O Akpor (eds) *The African Union ten years after*. Pretoria: African Institute of South Africa. pp. 385–409.

Ndlovu-Gatsheni, S and Dzinesa, G (2008) Liberal democracy and the African context: The experience of South Africa. In K Matlosa, K Prah, B Chiroro and L Toulou (eds) *The state, democracy and poverty eradication in Africa*. Johannesburg: EISA. pp. 91–110.

Nzongola-Ntalaja, and Lee, G (eds) (1997) *The state and democracy in Africa*. Addis Ababa: Africa World Press.

Oloruntoba, S (2015) Politics of financialisation and inequality: Transforming global relations for inclusive development. *Africa Development*, XL (3), 121–138.

Oloruntoba, S (2016) Democratization and poverty in Nigeria: Exploring the link between politics and poverty in middle income countries. In J May, G Wright and E Breathen (eds) *Poverty and inequality in middle income countries: Policy achievements, political obstacles*. London and New York: Zed Books/CROP, University of Bergen, Norway. pp. 123–142.

Oxfam (2015) *Wealth: Having it all and wanting more*. Great Britain: Oxfam. Available from https://www.oxfam.org/en/research/wealth-having-it-all-and-wanting-more (accessed 6 June 2016).

Piketty, T (2014) *Capital in the 21st century*. Boston: Harvard University Press.

Polanyi, K (1947) *The great transformation*. Boston: Beacon Press.

Przeworski, A and Limongi, F (1997) Modernization: Theories and facts. *World Politics*, 49 (2), 155–183.

Ravallion, M (2009) *A comparative perspective on poverty reduction in Brazil, China and India*. Policy Research Working Paper, 5080.

Robinson, W (2004) *A theory of globalisation capitalism: Production, class, and state in a transnational world*. Baltimore: Johns Hopkins University Press.

Robinson, W (2010) *Global capitalism theory and the emergence of transnational elites*. Working Paper No. 2010/02. Finland: World Institute for Development Economics and Research, United Nations University.

Seekings, J and Nattrass, N (2006) *Class, race and inequality in South Africa*. Pietermaritzburg: UKZN Press.

Southall, R (2008) The ANC for sale? Money, morality and business in South Africa. *Review of African Political Economy*, 35 (116), 281–299.

Stiglitz, J (2012) *The price of inequality. How today's divided societies endanger our future*. New York: W. W. Norton.

Taylor, I (2014) *Africa rising? BRICS-diversifying dependency*. New York: James Currey.

Terreblanche, S (2002) *History of inequality in South Africa: 1652–2002*. Pietermaritzburg: UKZN Press.

Wade, R (1990) *Governing the market: Economic theory and the role of government in East Asia industrialisation*. Princeton: Princeton University Press.

Zakaria, F (1997) The rise of illiberal democracy. *Foreign Affairs*, 76, 6.

CHAPTER 6

Liberalism and anti-liberalism in South Africa. Or, is an egalitarian liberalism possible?

Daryl Glaser

South Africa has a weak liberal tradition – but it has a strong anti-liberal one. Neither condition is especially difficult to explain in light of South African history. But the weakness of liberalism and strength of anti-liberalism both arguably carry costs. The weakness of liberalism has resulted in too shallow an embedding of liberalism's best insights within South African political culture; it has also forestalled the development of a radical, social or egalitarian liberal tradition which would counter inequality without sacrificing political and civil liberties. The absence of a radical liberalism has, in turn, deprived progressive politics of important intellectual and moral resources.

The weakness of South African liberalism should not be overstated. If liberal politics has remained marginal, liberal ideology scored significant victories in the 1990s. Actually, it scored two victories. One was the signing-up of South Africans to a Constitution that prescribes an essentially liberal-democratic polity; the other was the partial victory of classic free-market liberalism in economic policy making. These two victories need to be distinguished, at least from the vantage point of radical liberalism. The first victory marks the triumph of liberal-democratic precepts of political-system design, most of which have stood the test of the twentieth century and constitute the minimum requirements of any democratic system: direct, free, multiparty elections, universal adult franchise, constitutionally entrenched political freedoms, due process, separation of powers and political pluralism. The second is a victory of a classical liberal philosophy that regards private property and voluntary market exchange as fundamental anchors of individual liberty.[1] One problem for egalitarian liberals is that in South Africa the first liberal victory is conflated with the second (as, arguably, it is by Samuel Oloruntoba in Chapter 5 of this volume). The conflation is unsurprising, given the tendency of both Western free-market ideologues and orthodox Marxists to treat capitalism and liberal democracy as inseparable. But it is, many social liberals would argue, a dangerous conflation, placing democracy itself in the firing line of anti-'neoliberal' critique.

The weakness of South African liberalism rests in the fact that it has found its core constituency in a demographically marginal layer: Anglophone middle-class whites, and a small minority, even, of that group. Liberalism alienated, and alienated itself from, more radical forces (both leftist and nationalist) that commanded much larger popular followings. South African mainstream liberalism was characterised by several commitments that proved at odds with the radicalising mood of the mass-based anti-apartheid opposition from around 1940: scepticism about racial nationalism; hesitancy about majority rule; preference for reform over revolution; anti-Communism; and attachment to markets.

Anti-liberalism became a strong trend in opposition ranks partly in reaction against these conservative features of South African mainstream liberalism but it sprang from an additional source: rejection by certain black-led currents of white leadership in the anti-apartheid struggle. In these currents, liberalism became a name for all white opposition to apartheid, both liberal and Marxist. The elision enabled black critics to tar the white radical left with the brush of liberal paternalism. Ironically the ruling National Party also elided the two, viewing both liberalism and communism as harbingers of race mixing, secularism and black takeover. I myself argue for the possibility of a radical liberal position that straddles the liberal-socialist boundary. But black radical treatment of white communism and white liberalism as the same thing amounted to a deliberate effort to downplay stark ideological distinctions in the name of a larger project – affirming black leadership. Anti-liberalism as anti-whiteness should be distinguished from the anti-liberalism of the South African Communist Party (SACP). In the communist rendering, at least, there was a clear distinction between white liberals (problematic) and white communists (good).

In this chapter I will say something about the history of South African liberalism through to the present, evaluating its strengths and its weaknesses. Instead of offering a familiar leftist catalogue of liberal failings – or a conservative-liberal hagiography of a minority that was good but despised – I will argue for distinguishing the things that mainstream liberalism got right and wrong (and still does). I will also devote some effort to understanding (i) the tragic absence of a self-consciously egalitarian or social liberal tradition in South Africa, and (ii) the dangers of anti-liberalism.

LIBERALISM – DEFINITION AND GENEALOGY

That liberalism is internally diverse, containing both classical and more social variants, is standardly acknowledged in textbooks (though it may, tellingly, come as a surprise even to some reasonably well-informed South Africans).[2] It is important to identify, first of all, what binds liberalism's variants. Some liberal philosophers see its fundamental value as equality, others as individual liberty. It is, at a minimum, a belief in equal liberty, or an equal right to liberty. How ambitiously this liberty, or freedom, should be understood is a source of contention among liberals. All liberals, I suggest, acknowledge as a baseline some idea of equal formal negative liberty. Radical or social liberals generally seek to add something more 'substantive' to this liberty: for example, a commitment to creating real rather than merely formal equality of opportunity; or to creating the economic and social conditions that enable all citizens, including the least well off, to exercise their political and civil freedoms effectively. Radical or social liberals are also liable to accord substantive equality value in its own right, and not merely as a buttress to – or way of giving substance to – individual freedom. In light of these imperatives, liberal philosophers – especially those operating in the Anglospheric analytic tradition – have sought since the interventions of John Rawls in the early 1970s to elaborate egalitarian liberal theories. The status of property and the role of the state figure centrally in contention between classical and social liberals, with egalitarian liberals granting private property (at least beyond personal property) a lower level of protection than do classical liberals or, in American parlance, 'libertarians'. While libertarians treat the state as a necessary evil that should be restricted to maintaining order, protecting property and enforcing contracts, liberal egalitarians look to the state to redistribute wealth and income and regulate markets. Egalitarian liberalism merges with social democracy or democratic socialism, though I think that points of distinction remain between these traditions (Glaser 2014).

Although the term liberalism only came into use in the early nineteenth century, the tradition to which it refers emerged in Europe and North America in the later seventeenth and the eighteenth century as an opponent of royal absolutism, feudalism and mercantilism. It also attached itself to the Enlightenment, becoming associated with opposition to the established church and with currents of rationalism, empiricism and secularism. Against its various authoritarian opponents, liberalism upheld individual freedom and a sharpened distinction between public and private. It cherished the private as a sphere of voluntary exchange, personal autonomy and intimacy to be protected from interference by the state, organised religion and pressures of social conformity. Earlier liberals tended to justify these commitments by reference to natural right and social contract (an approach rejuvenated since the 1970s); in the nineteenth century, hard-nosed liberals emphasised the value of individual freedom in promoting utility or human welfare.

Liberalism has evolved – and fissured – in response to a range of historical developments, including the rise of democracy, the emergence of corporate capitalism, the challenge of socialism and demands for inclusion and liberation issuing from a range of subordinate groups. Liberalism's varied responses to these developments form the historical backdrop to the crystallisation over time of more or less conservative and socially radical liberalisms. A brief survey of these responses might be illuminating for an understanding of South Africa's conservative liberalism.

Many early liberals were suspicious of democracy, viewing it as a bearer of majority tyranny. Liberalism eventually reconciled with democracy under the sign of liberal democracy with its characteristic features of government by electoral consent, division of powers and impersonal rights-protective law. Some liberals continued to fear the masses, hewing to elitist forms of democracy; others embraced more participatory forms.

Corporate capitalism presented a problem for both free-market and socially minded liberals. The former were wary of corporate monopoly; the latter saw in corporations powerful and impersonal state-like organisations of the sort that individuals needed protection against. While the free marketeers called for more competition and less cronyism, they were largely reconciled to the capitalism of large corporate bureaucracies. So, arguably, were social liberals, who looked to the state primarily to redistribute the proceeds of corporate capitalism rather than to democratise production. This preference – for egalitarian redistribution over socialised property – shaped the 'new' liberal response to socialism. While all liberals opposed authoritarian collectivism – including its twentieth-century 'communist' manifestation – 'new' liberals came to share the Left's interest in social reform, laying the basis for an alliance, in countries like the UK and Canada, with social democracy. Free-market liberals rejected this socially meliorative trend in liberalism; indeed American free-market radicals came to call themselves libertarians precisely to distinguish themselves from a liberalism that they believed had (beginning with the New Deal) capitulated to statism and collectivism. While liberalism in the UK and North America took a more social form, it remained more classically liberal, and allied with conservatism rather than socialism, in Germany and in Australia.

Liberalism originated in Europe and North America as the project of free white men of the owning and upper middle classes. It was this tiny global minority that claimed for itself the benefits of equal liberty and government by consent. To some radical critics of liberalism, like Losurdo (2011), liberalism has remained forever marked by its elitist origin and its initial happy coexistence with, notably, slavery in the Americas and European colonialism, not to mention a franchise that excluded white women and working people even in its metropolitan heartlands. In contemporary critical theory liberalism has also figured as a champion of the Kantian rational subject, allegedly devised in the image of the Western male and exclusionary of putative bearers of irrationality and affect, such as women and 'savages'. It is certainly true that the liberal valorisation of the 'private' offered protection to unaccountable private power – notably of male household heads and capitalist owners. It is also true that the liberal fear of majority rule provided warrant for a narrowed bourgeois public sphere, one confined to the educated and 'enlightened'.

There was, however, nothing intrinsic to liberalism that required the restriction of its benefits to a tiny proportion of humanity. The liberal belief in equal rights offered itself as a banner for numerous groups, including the working class and women, claiming inclusion. If some liberals could assimilate captive black bodies in the category of private property, others were drawn to abolitionism by a liberal love of freedom and equality. Liberalism took hold in tandem with the modern nation state, and the proliferation of demands for national liberation, initially felt mainly in Europe and the Americas, were as much an accompaniment of the march of liberalism as was a European colonialism that sought to tutor the barbarians in civilised liberal ways. It was inevitable that colonial subjects would take up the liberal demand for national self-determination even if, by the later twentieth century, many preferred to do so under the banner of Marxism rather than liberalism. Nationalism, as we know, is available for quite diverse ideological appropriations. Liberalism refused its appropriation by the proponents of a 'collective' freedom that subordinated individuals to 'peoples' and 'nations', insisting that free peoples were necessarily also free as individuals. At the same time, some liberals, notably in South Africa, have seen minority group rights (and not merely individual rights) as a defence against collectivist or majoritarian domination.

To be sure, the concern to keep society out of the private was an impediment to the liberation of private subordinates that was inherent to liberalism itself. But, if so, it contended with liberal imperatives that pointed to different possibilities, including a rule of law that was understood, from the outset, as penalising certain horizontal infringements on the rights of others, including intimate others; the commitment to individualism, which resisted the reduction of human beings to private collectives like the family; the championing of equality and freedom; and voluntarism, which encouraged suspicion of coercive and irrevocable contracts, whether of employment or marriage. In any event, a liberal feminism developed that insisted on subjecting personalised power to scrutiny – if less sweepingly than its radical competitor. In a similar vein, Franklin Delano Roosevelt introduced measures requiring private corporations to recognise worker rights to unionise. Liberals may not have sought worker control, but the industrial relations model of the pluralistic firm seemed to fit liberal precepts comfortably enough. There is no evading the fact that liberalism is ultimately more cautious than radical liberation traditions about external protective intervention in the private realm, but that caution is not in every case unmerited. It is, after all, totalitarianism that erases the state-society distinction and, with it, the public-private one.

LIBERALISM IN SOUTH AFRICA

South African liberalism is stamped with its colonial origin. In this respect it is not fundamentally different from other imported European ideologies, including Marxism and Christianity. Like both of those ideologies, liberalism was transplanted initially via white settlers and (metaphorical or literal) missionaries, and then domesticated – even indigenised – in various ways. But liberalism's colonial imprint is deeper, its internalisation more superficial, than is the case with either Marxism or Christianity. Though all three served categories of white settlers and their descendants – sometimes in fighting battles with other whites, of different classes or ethnicities – liberalism alone among the three did not develop a significant black organised stream. There was no black liberal equivalent of the SACP (once it became more focused on mobilising blacks) or black independent churches. This is one reason why South African liberalism has been more conservative than some of its international counterparts. One possibility is that it was not amenable to the degree of radicalisation demanded by the temper of post-war anti-apartheid struggle, although the participation of armed liberal militants in the African Resistance Movement (ARM) might cause us to doubt this – as might the militancy of the 'slideaway liberals' of whose perfidiousness conservative liberals like Wentzel complained in the 1980s and 1990s (Wentzel 1995). In any event, liberalism was neither fully domesticated nor durably radicalised.

There were several ways that the colonial inscribed itself in liberalism. For one thing, early versions of it served white settlers in the Cape fighting for rights against autocratic Dutch and later British overlords. The late eighteenth-century struggle of the Cape patri-ots against the Dutch East India Company was fleeting (Giliomee 2003: 54–6); settler struggles with British colonial rulers in the early to middle nineteenth century scored significant victories, notably for freedom of the press and later for settler self-government (Keegan 1996: 96–9). It is notable, though, that these struggles never acquired a vigour comparable to that of American settlers against the British. In both North America and southern Africa, white settler self-government ultimately brought with it an intensified depredation against indigenous societies and entrenchment of coercive labour regimes.

Still, importantly, a strand of liberalism emerged in white society – initially in the Cape Colony – that sought greater protection for indigenous peoples. Christian missionaries in the 1820s and 1830s opposed the coercive indenture of Khoi labourers and sought to phase out slavery (Lewsen 1971; Keegan 1996: 75–128). After 1884, sections of the white political elite developed an interest in preserving the Cape nonracial qualified franchise and competed for African votes (Trapido 1968). Here were the origins of liberal racial paternalism. But the Cape's protective paternalism was 'shallow' (Keegan 1996: 127). It never challenged white political and economic supremacy and it gradually lost faith in the universalist ideal of full black assimilation into white society.

The early twentieth-century successor to white racial paternalism ended up impli-cating liberalism in the policy of segregation. Concerned that settler land expropriation might engender conflict and expose landless natives to white domination and a cultur-ally alien industrialism, prominent liberals argued in favour of setting aside reserves for 'separate' African development under overall white rule. Liberalism's flirtation with par-tition was abandoned only after the full iniquity of actual segregationist policy became clear (Dubow 1989: 7–8, 21–50). In the meantime it placed liberals in de facto alliance with mine owners and – once the latter had come to accept Natal-style indirect rule – Afrikaner nationalists.

Paternalistic protectionism continued to dominate South African liberalism until at least the 1950s and arguably beyond (Rich 1984; Dubow 2014). Between the two World Wars liberals busied themselves with research on race relations, with projects of black upliftment (here influenced by British Fabianism), with efforts to ameliorate govern-ment race policies and with serving as interlocutors between blacks and successive white governments. They never mounted an effective resistance to deepening institutionalised racism. After the exclusion of Africans from the common voters' roll in 1936 (a huge liberal defeat), some white liberals successfully stood for office as 'native representatives' in the white parliament. Their function was at best mildly ameliorative. Liberal optimism about market-driven integration jostled with fears of racial conflict. The colonial imprint remained deep.

Black liberalism also carried the imprint of colonialism. It was a form of politics that developed in an emerging black Christianised elite in a period overlapping the final defeat of independent black polities. Its exponents were engaged largely in defensive measures; they hoped, at least until after the protest against Union, to receive backing from the British imperial centre. Even after Union they struggled to defend the Cape franchise and to resist the deeper entrenchment of segregation. The African National Congress (ANC)'s pre-Second World War politics was primarily though not exclusively Christian, liberal and constitutionalist (Walshe 1970: 34, 187–92). Until the National Party took power in 1948, the black liberals could still hope to access the state through English speakers in the circle of power. Hertzog's segregationist measures, and then the rise of the Nats, were death blows to black liberal hopes. More radical alternatives increased their appeal to black oppositionists, including pan-Africanism and communism.

Liberalism might still have redeemed itself, implanting a major contending current in black African opposition politics. Post-War black radicalisation was, after all, influenced by the Atlantic Charter's emboldened liberalism. Internationally, liberalism had consummated its marriage with universal suffrage, and liberals were active in the US civil rights struggle. Some local liberals were radicalised by the advent of apartheid in 1948 and its subsequently tightening grip. Radical liberals appeared in the Torch Commando, Liberal Party and Black Sash, as well as within the Pan Africanist Congress (PAC). Some liberals were sympathetic to socialism or willing to engage in extra-parliamentary action (Van der Westhuizen 1994; Everatt 2009). Subsequently, liberals participated in the ARM (Du Toit 1994) and in the 1980s some worked with the United Democratic Front (UDF) (Wentzel 1995). While the ANC came to rely on Soviet bloc support, it also valued the solidarity of social democrats in Britain and Scandinavia. There were black liberals in the Liberal Party, some in the ANC itself.[3]

In the end, the possibility of a popular radical liberalism was confounded by several factors. The first was the sheer extent of disillusionment with liberal half measures in black society; these were bound to make it receptive to non-liberal currents such as nationalism and Marxism. Second (and black liberals notwithstanding), liberalism was associated predominantly with whites. Third, liberals were reluctant to associate with communist-linked organisations. In a common telling this marked its loss of radical courage; but in retrospect there were perfectly sound reasons to be wary of Marxist-Leninist regimes and movements. Liberal nervousness about violence was a fourth factor distancing liberals from a mass base (ARM notwithstanding). Indeed, a part of the tragedy of liberalism's conservatism and lack of mass base is that it could not influence black radical politics away from authoritarianism and the romance of violence. Conservative liberals must take some responsibility for this outcome. It was one thing to oppose Stalinism and armed struggle; another to back the apartheid regime as it destabilised southern Africa in putative anti-terrorist and anti-communist operations, as did the Progressive Party and certain liberal journalists. Finally, many liberals placed a faith in the capacity of capitalist growth to render apartheid and racial prejudice redundant. This encouraged liberal resistance to South Africa's international economic isolation, as indeed did the links between the Progressive Party and Anglophone capital.

In short, liberals were on the wrong side of too many strategic priorities in post-War radical black politics. Their voice was marginalised, for both good and ill.

LIBERALISM – INTO THE TRANSITION

Liberalism in South Africa was weak as a political movement, and remained so into the transition and beyond. Liberal businessmen and politicians began to flirt with the ANC amid the terminal crises of the later 1980s. But by the early 1990s there were only two major players in the field, the National Party (NP) and the ANC, with the spoiler camp dominated by the white Right and Inkatha. But despite the liberal movement's political weakness the constitutional settlement represented a triumph for liberal democracy. The political system enacted a liberal-democratic formula of universal franchise, free multiparty elections, constitutionalised political and civil freedoms and an independent judiciary. The ascendancy of liberal democracy had little to do with domestic liberalism. Not only was the latter politically weak, but it was a 'Johnny come lately' in the adoption of one person, one vote (1960 in the case of the Liberal Party, the late 1970s in the case of the Progressive Party). Even after embracing universal franchise, many liberals sought to hedge it with minority group protections. Mainstream South African liberalism was anchored in a privileged minority who, like nineteenth-century European liberals, viewed universal franchise with trepidation.

The ascendancy of liberal democracy was mainly a product of other developments. The end of the Cold War saw the collapse of Marxism-Leninism as an alternative governing formula. Samuel Huntington's 'third wave of democratisation' brought liberal democracy (at least in formal terms) to former communist states and sub-Saharan Africa. Rights-based liberal democracy looked better to white society than untrammelled majority rule. Certain organisations in the ANC camp, such as unions and civics, were reluctant to cede autonomy to the returning ANC and could find protection in liberal guarantees of free association. The ANC was itself internally influenced by lawyers and human rights advocates who supported a role for rights and courts. Finally, the ANC could look forward to winning elections under standard liberal-democratic rules; it thus had little reason to oppose these rules and it had a theory of revolution, the National Democratic Revolution, that could justify a tactical or strategic embrace of bourgeois democracy.

Obviously enough, the gross discredit into which 'real socialism' had fallen strengthened the hand of all of those inside and outside the ANC who favoured a liberal-democratic political system.

Not all liberals recognised their own ideological victory. The most conservative fretted about the choice in favour of constitutional as opposed to English-style common law; the recognition of horizontal rights; the weakness of federal provisions; the alleged retention of a Westminster-style 'winner takes all' system; and the entrenchment of socio-economic rights, which invited state economic intervention (Welsh 1998: 21; Jeffrey 1998). A few regretted the failure to gain recognition for group-based protections. A strand of South African liberalism had long looked to group rights and representation as alternatives to black majoritarianism.[4] Indeed when it came to group versus individual rights, the ANC was more classically liberal (in the sense of individualist) than some of the liberals. Conservative liberals had grounds for misgivings, judged purely in their own terms. The Constitution steered elected governments towards redistributive policy choices, and it talked of participatory democracy. To the extent that it was liberal, it represented a radical liberalism.

I have insisted on treating the ANC's adoption of 'neoliberal' economic policies as a separate matter. In important ways it was, of course, part of the same phenomenon. It too was influenced by the collapse of 'actual socialist' alternatives and by residual white bargaining power. Western governments and international lending bodies combined representative democracy with free markets in a 'good governance' formula that they expected emerging democracies to adopt. Like liberal democracy, the neoliberal turn was an ideological victory for liberalism that many conservative liberals failed to recognise – and, again, with some reason, because the ANC's embrace of neoliberalism was qualified and, especially after 2000, began to loosen.

There are good reasons, though, for keeping these liberal 'achievements' separate. There is no necessary relationship between liberal democracy as a political system and neoliberal economics. Historically, liberal-democratic states enacted many major gains for the working class and poor, not all of which have been reversed by neoliberalism and globalisation. Working and poor people themselves need the vote, and freedoms of expression and association, to organise independently and effectively in ways that they were not, incidentally, able to do in the so-called workers' states. To be sure, liberal democracies that push too far to the Left encounter capitalist resistance: capital flight and strike, middle-class agitation, Western pressure, *in extremis*, military coups. But capitalist power is a constraint on any kind of regime that chooses to live with capitalism: the profit imperative and hypermobility of capital will confine an authoritarian as surely as a liberal-democratic regime. There is nothing as such, in the idea of legislators freely elected by universal suffrage, that necessitates the election of pro-capitalist governments. And if there were, that would be a lethal problem for democratic socialism, because it is difficult to see how any democracy can operate without these 'bourgeois' provisions as a democratic baseline. There is, to be sure, no guarantee that socialists will win durable popular mandates in conditions of free choice; but that is just a way of saying that there are no guarantees of success for democratic socialism. Socialism can only ever be one project – one possible human future – competing with others in the democratic domain. This holds, even allowing that the domain itself, in its designs and biases, is never entirely neutral and always an object of contestation. In South Africa, the domain – the arena of contestation, as it were – carries a basically social-democratic bias, thanks to a progressive Constitution.

And so, yes, liberals won this double ideological victory: for liberal democracy and for neoliberalism. But these are achievements of different historical meaning and consequence, and all democrats should welcome the first even if they can reasonably disagree about the second.

Meanwhile, liberalism qua political movement soldiered on post-1994, donning and shedding garbs. The Democratic Alliance (DA) (nee Democratic Party, née Progressives), its principal bearer, is the product of a merger between the Progs' fairly conservative liberalism and the conservative reformism of the New National Party. Under Tony Leon, the DA tried on 'muscular liberalism', a model which insisted that liberalism should oppose the new dominant African nationalism as energetically as it did the old Afrikaner one. In the process, however, it projected itself, not always subtly, as the party of the racial minorities. Doing so proved strategically brilliant as an opening move; robust opposition to the ANC enabled the DA to scoop up white, coloured and Indian votes, consigning the Nats to irrelevance and propelling the DA from the electoral margins to official opposition status. But this achievement has also tainted the DA, associating it with anti-majoritarianism even as the party set out to expand support in the African population and, more recently, elected a black leader. Civil society liberalism has meanwhile retreated to redoubts like the SA Institute of Race Relations, the Helen Suzman Foundation and the Centre for Development and Enterprise. These organisations do useful research work, but they compose an essentially conservative liberalism – if not an actual current of Toryism in the case of personages like John Kane-Berman, RW Johnson and Franz Cronjé. Radical or egalitarian liberalism remains largely absent from the South African political scene.

To the extent that there is a notable current recognisable as radical liberal, it largely denies any liberal identity. I think here of, for example, the pro-human rights legal community which, both in academe and the courts, presents itself as a progressive critic of liberalism. In its framing, liberalism is unduly formalistic and prioritises freedom over equality; the radical 'legalitarians', by contrast, build on the insights of critical legal studies to insist on a jurisprudence that is transformative and 'substantive' or, put another way, that works actively to create a socially just order.[5] Viewed in these terms, we might suspect the radical lawyers of by-passing free ideological choice and seeking to entrench socialism through the back door, but this does not strike me as an accurate account of what the radical lawyers and rights activists say and do in practice. Whatever their framing, they are doughty defenders of the Constitution's commitments to freedoms of expression, association and assembly – that is, of a range of classical liberal political and civil rights (whose belonging to liberalism they nevertheless challenge). The liberal freedoms they most energetically reject (see, for example, Pieterse 2005) are those that radical liberals themselves, if they do not actively contest, confer the weakest protections upon: namely rights in property and private contract.

There is also a radical liberalism, if by other names, in the area of civil society activism. The very idea of an autonomous civil society is identifiably liberal in its genealogy (Keane 1988). Some voluntary organisations are specifically radical-liberal in the things they care about. The Institute for Democratic Alternatives in South Africa (Idasa), now disbanded, fitted this bill nicely; so do the Right2Know Campaign and the Freedom of Expression Institute. So too, in a different register, do organisations such as the Institute for Justice and Reconciliation (IJR) and the Ahmed Kathrada Foundation (AKF). These organisations are radical in their emphasis on social justice and equality; Right2Know, for example, couples its critique of state censorship and secrecy with a demand for a more pluralistic, community-oriented media. At the same time their spokespersons defend vigorously a range of liberal freedoms, and the IJR and AKF are recognisably liberal in their insistence on dialogue and nonracialism, even as they rightly hold that these must be rooted in advances towards social justice.

Anything approximating *self-consciously* radical liberalism remains in the margins. In 2013, David Bilchitz and I hosted a conference at the Constitutional Court on 'egalitarian liberalism', which we intended would stimulate a discussion on the contribution that liberal theory could make to creating a more equal society while preserving political and civil liberties. The conference was fascinating, but quite a number of the presenters and attendees seemed unconvinced that liberalism, even in its radical egalitarian permutation, had much to offer South Africa. In 2014, the American-based (originally Caribbean) black thinker Charles Mills presented a paper at Wits University entitled 'Liberalising illiberal liberalism'. He took Rawlsian liberalism to task for neglecting race in its rather abstract pontifications, and in particular Mills thought liberals should concern themselves more with restorative justice (including racial restorative justice) than with perfecting ideal norms of distributive equality. This line might have been expected to appeal to students and academics grappling with decoloniality, yet Mills's concern to rescue liberalism from itself generated bemusement in the audience. More recently, Chantal Mouffe has visited South Africa and, in her Wits presentation, affirmed that her famous conception of 'agonistic democracy' is not intended as a refutation of liberalism but as a way of radicalising it, specifically by placing more emphasis on contestation than on the rational agreement she understands writers like John Rawls and Jürgen Habermas to hanker after. Once again, these pro-liberal affirmations encountered puzzlement in the radical audience present, notwithstanding that Mouffe has long been, as the event chairperson put it, at the forefront of international Left thought. These episodes confirm that liberalism remains a tainted brand in South Africa. The progressive liberalism that is almost a commonplace in British and North American political theory, at least among analytic philosophers, finds little resonance here. (Indeed, analytic philosophy has itself come under attack for its association with Kantian liberal universalism.)

That there are radical liberals who eschew the l-word raises questions about how much turns on a label. If the radical liberal substance is there, does nomenclature matter? I return to this question later.

ANTI-LIBERALISM IN SOUTH AFRICA

In leftist and black-nationalist circles in South Africa, liberalism is a dirty word. Its badness has acquired a taken for granted character in swathes of activism, academia and the political elite.[6] The global advent of 'neoliberalism' has a lot to do with the contemporary sway of anti-liberalism, as has dissatisfaction with the nonracial cum multicultural discourse of the 'rainbow nation' that cast a misleadingly reassuring glow over post-1994 nation building. Many radicals blame neoliberalism and nonracialism for the persistence of sharp racial and class inequalities post-apartheid. They consider liberalism's political expression, in the DA and assorted think tanks, wholly incapable of offering a progressive alternative to the ANC government. The freighted history of South African liberalism gravely handicaps any effort to popularise progressive forms of liberalism.

Still, there is no one anti-liberalism. Several component strands of leftist and 'black' anti-liberalism can be distinguished. First, there is anti-liberalism as anti-capitalism. Here anti-liberalism draws on an assumption shared by many of liberalism's friends and enemies, that liberalism is inseparable from capitalism. In this telling, liberalism forms a part of the ideological superstructure of capitalism, fostering an illusion of individual freedom, equality and democracy in societies characterised by inequality, exploitation and the alienation of political power from civil life. During the apartheid period liberalism came under Marxist scholarly criticism for its faith that capitalism and white racist domination were inimical, and that the evolution of the former would erode the latter, obviating any need for revolutionary overthrow of apartheid or for radical social change. For anti-capitalist anti-liberals, post-apartheid 'neoliberalism' is liberalism redux, a hyper-capitalism overlaid with thin democracy.

Second, there is anti-liberalism as anti-reformism. Here liberalism is cast as a particular temper: timid, afraid of violence, fearful of the masses. Liberal reformism is also understood as a commitment (naive, devious or both) to peaceful and gradualist methods of addressing social problems. Because deep-seated problems require radical solutions, liberalism is viewed as incapable of winning needed transformations. Construed as devious, liberals set about deliberately pacifying the masses in order to protect interests hiding behind a liberal ideological facade; construed as naive, they espouse a shallow sentimentality, refusing the realities of power and the need to dirty one's hands.

Third, there is anti-liberalism as anti-individualism. Here, in fashionable cultural criticism, is liberalism as bearer of the universal autonomous rational subject, a projection onto the world of what is in fact a particular Western white male subject – a subject alien to many non-Western cultures dominating supposedly less rational non-European or lower-class beings. For exponents of 'African socialism', liberal individualism was foreign to African communalism and bound up with coldly instrumental reason, in contradistinction to African warmth and expressiveness. Anti-liberalism as anti-individualism has thus overlapped anti-liberalism as anti-rationalism, a fourth anti–liberal type.

Finally, there is anti-liberalism as anti-whiteness. Here liberalism figures as an instrument of white domination over blacks. If 'liberals' challenge white domination – as they challenged segregation in the US or apartheid in South Africa – this was in order to gain admission for blacks into the illusory equalities of a white-privileging world. Moreover, liberalism legitimated white influence in struggles that should properly be black-led. Downplaying the benefits they derive from systemic racism, white liberals seek undeserved credit for being the defenders, even 'saviours', of black underdogs. Though complicit in racial domination, they seek to dictate how blacks should respond to their own oppression, typically with militancy-dampening results. White Marxists are not spared this line of attack. For black consciousness advocates, whites who adopt class analysis are liberals in denial about the primacy of racial oppression, using Marxism to claim a place in the revolutionary sun.

South African anti-liberalisms have their specific habitats. Anti-capitalist anti-liberalism is prominent in all leftist currents, from the SACP to black consciousness. So is anti-reformist anti-liberalism. Both Marxists and Africanists criticise liberal individualism, although orthodox Marxists are suspicious of traditional communalism as an alternative. Orthodox Marxists certainly don't go along with the critique of Western rationalism and empiricism, since they think of themselves as pro-scientific modernisers; the critique however appeals to supporters of Negritude and African socialism and to critical theorists within the academy. Finally, the conflation of whites and liberals is made by black consciousness and Western Cape Trotskyists, but rejected by nonracialists in the SACP. Africanists of the 1950s opposed white involvement in black struggles, but generally identified their white radical adversaries as communists rather than liberals, and the PAC was indeed keener to work with the Liberal Party than the ANC or white leftist SA Congress of Democrats (Van der Westhuizen 1994: 90).

Anti-liberals certainly had telling points to make about the limits of liberalism in South Africa. Radical or egalitarian liberals will, however, grant greater weight to some anti-liberal complaints than others. They share with anti-liberals a critique of market fundamentalism and property fetishism, even if they are not, usually, in favour of overthrowing capitalism. They would surely dismiss, as I do, the equation of liberalism with whiteness, even while conceding that South African liberalism has been too white. They will defend reformism against revolution, but insist that a radical reformism is possible. They will defend individuality though not atomistic individualism.

Anti-liberalism is vulnerable to criticism itself, including from a progressive standpoint. Its central failing is that it renders progressive politics more amenable to illiberalism and authoritarianism – or at least it does so on certain plausible readings. A part of the problem here is that the anti-liberals do not always clarify exactly what they are against.

THE PRICE OF ANTI-LIBERALISM – OR, WHAT *EXACTLY* ARE THE ANTI-LIBERALS ANTI?

As noted earlier, some ostensible anti-liberals champion values and institutions (including a number of constitutionally entrenched individual political and civil freedoms) that liberal democrats endorse. When they criticise liberalism, these 'anti-liberal liberals' tend to target features that many social liberals themselves consider worthy of criticism. The liberalism they reject largely equates to free-market libertarianism rather than egalitarian liberalism. Some of their supposedly anti-liberal commitments (including their commitment to the regulation of markets, provision of social insurance and a social minimum, and the attainment of distributive fairness) are shared by egalitarian liberals. The anti-liberal liberals referenced here are particularly those located in the legal and human rights communities.

If anti-liberal liberalism is a thing, this raises questions. How much of the disagreement is about naming rather than substance? Why go to the barricades in defence of a 'name'? Saddled with the fact of liberalism's local reputational damage, why not choose another label? There are, after all, labels (social democracy and democratic socialism) with which liberal egalitarianism enjoys a close affinity and which are easier to sell in progressive circles.

If one is to be fastidious, one might object that the anti-liberal Left's claim to equal ownership of political and civil liberties – their claim that these values are intrinsic to their own non-liberal alternatives – is somewhat tendentious as a matter of historical accounting. It is clear that counter-majoritarian rights protections developed in the milieux of seventeenth and eighteenth century Euro-American liberalism, and a matter of record that these rights were dismissed by many Marxists as bourgeois (or, where not dismissed, treated as mere instruments of revolutionary struggle). Nor can anyone doubt that the rights-respecting grade of the 'actual socialist' regimes of the previous century was poorer than that of the Western liberal democracies – certainly when it comes to political and civil rights, arguably also with respect to social rights, especially if we compare 'actual socialist' regimes to European social democracies.

But the historical record matters less than what is at stake now. Let us assume that what is at stake is the following: social or egalitarian liberals seek a social order that preserves the so-called 'bourgeois' civil and political liberties, while also seeking greater distributive equality and social protection than is currently available under Western welfare capitalism (especially in its present retreat). They may take a Rawlsian view that a certain list of essential basic liberties should enjoy 'priority', or they may take the view that liberty and social rights are indivisible. In either case, they oppose trading liberal-democratic political freedoms for putative social welfare advances, believing such trade-offs to be unacceptable but also, for the most part, unnecessary. Their basic conviction is that a strong defence of liberal political and civil freedoms can be joined to the pursuit of radical social goals. The question, then, is whether South Africa's leftist anti-liberals share the liberal-egalitarians' rejection of authoritarian means of pursuing the radical social objectives that both traditions share.

Certainly, some do not. The SACP is heir to a long tradition of supporting Marxist-Leninist one-party states. Its general secretary, Blade Nzimande, continues to deploy a Leninist vocabulary against supposedly individual and formal liberties, insisting on the priority of social rights.[7] The same holds for many in the ANC and, even more so, to the Left of the ANC, in organisations like the Economic Freedom Fighters. Many on the Left continue to think of constitutional democracy as a sell-out, an unavoidable tactical-strategic compromise or as (at best) the superstructural form appropriate to the national-democratic revolutionary phase. On the far Left there are those, still, who hold out for the chimera of replacing parliaments with a supposedly higher form of democracy, such as a proletarian democracy of workers' councils. Those who argue along these lines are straightforwardly in opposition to liberals. More seriously, they are potentially architects of a totalitarian future redesign of South Africa's polity.

The far-Left Utopians deny that political freedoms will be absent from their communist future. But it is usually easy to expose the hollowness of this denial. When pressed, how many will agree that in their communist society citizens will be entitled to organise pro-capitalist parties and win popular mandates to implement pro-capitalist policies? How many accept the direct election of leaders and legislators in conditions of genuine political choice? Most have in mind a democracy confined to pro-socialist elements, or one in which participatory democracy is employed to harness popular energy for socialist tasks. Most lack a theory for how to extend their deeper democracy to higher tiers of government in large territories, falling back on opaque and unworkable schemes of pyramidal upward delegation.

There is undoubtedly a role for liberals, egalitarian or otherwise, in warding off *this* kind of future. It is the anti-liberal liberals – the de facto radical liberals who disown the liberal label – who present the more interesting case. It ought not to matter to the egalitarian liberal whether *these* anti-liberals reject (what they call) liberalism, because they defend the institutions and values that matter to liberal egalitarians. I nevertheless offer two reasons why their facial rejection of liberalism *might* matter. First, at least some of the anti-liberals, some of the time, do downplay the political and civil liberties in ways that leave them potentially exposed. At least some of them would grant non-elective institutions such as courts a level of authority in deciding aspects of an economic and social policy that goes beyond what democratic politics can comfortably accommodate.[8] Second, rhetorical attacks on liberalism potentially place liberal political and civil liberties in danger, precisely because left-authoritarians (such as those in the SACP) *do* consider these liberties to be liberal, and moreover because they, like the anti-liberal liberals, conflate liberalism with their shared enemy, namely neoliberalism. In attacking or even just disowning liberalism, liberal anti-liberals link hands with those who (unlike themselves) actually do think that South Africa needs to give less attention to formal, procedural freedoms and more attention to substantive, outcome-related freedoms – in other words, with precisely those who make the sorts of arguments that were used, during the Cold War, to justify Marxist-Leninist totalitarianism.

Two further points in favour of keeping the liberal name: if South African progressives do not want to be thought of as liberal, most will also not want to be judged *illiberal*. Illiberalism is a disposition and temperament marked by intolerance and narrow mindedness. In a violent and polarised country like South Africa there may be mileage still in the promotion of a liberal temperament, or at least the condemnation of an illiberal one.

There is also an association in many minds between liberalism and personal freedoms admired by progressives, one that posits liberalism as the opposite of social conservatism. Most contemporary leftists celebrate, for example, the freedom to give expression to non-normative sexualities among consenting adults. Cultural radicals might question whether sexual freedoms are necessarily liberal (or whether liberals think about them sufficiently radically), but they bear liberal hallmarks, including an implicit valorisation of the autonomous subject. Located in these two juxtapositions –to illiberalism or conservatism – liberalism might still find political traction.

Finally, a point can be made about what anti-liberalism cuts itself off from. There is a large political theory literature, primarily in the analytic tradition, devoted to thinking about the requirements of social justice. A good many of its participants think of themselves as egalitarian liberals. The literature is partly about abstract principles, but also inserts itself into concrete policy debates about basic income grants, the detailed entailments of rights to housing or healthcare, the design of social insurance schemes, and so on. The debate about the purposes of equality (whether it is fairness, dignity, utility, democracy), the goods needing to be equalised (welfare, resources, capabilities, power, the social bases of self-esteem) and about the extent of equality that is desirable (sufficiency, priority, brute luck neutralisation, fair equality of opportunity, absolute equality) is impressively sophisticated. It is also rich in policy implication.[9]

The literature enjoys advantages over the rival, ostensibly egalitarian creed of Marxism (or at least over orthodox Marxism; 'analytic Marxism' participates in the literature). One is that it attends to 'circumstances of justice', that is, conditions in which goods are scarce and need to be assigned according to some distributive principle, contrary to the Marxist prediction of a communist abundance that supersedes distributive questions. It is thus relevant to the real world. Second, it engages moral and ethical questions for which Marxism is poorly equipped. Orthodox Marxism is sceptical about moral talk, and thus avoids discussion of the necessary moral limits to what can be done to individuals in the name of revolutionary goals. Third, the literature tends to focus on the sphere of distribution rather than on production. While this invites the charge that it ignores structural power, it frees philosophers to think about what distributions are just, rather than fetishising particular economic and productive structures. It also frees philosophers to worry less about the technical meaning of exploitation, so that they do not have to worry about whether non-productive welfare recipients are exploiting the working class. And it frees them to imagine distributive norms that are potentially more radically egalitarian than those that might result from working class control of the means of production per se, as Kymlicka notes (2002: 166–201).

The analytic political philosophy field is broad enough to attract Marxist and other (non-liberal) radicals. Its terms and preoccupations might, however, seem irrelevant to radicals who focus on struggle and power, prefer critique to reconstruction or stick closely to orthodox Marxism. Some anti-liberals dismiss this whole field for its association with formal logic and normative justification. At the same time, if egalitarian analytic philosophy *does* offer valuable insights to those engaged in designing a just society (as I hold it does), then outright rejection of this literature is denying progressives something of value.

LIBERALISM AND RACE

An assessment of liberalism in South Africa must include a consideration of its relationship to race. Liberalism has two points of weakness here. One is historical: liberalism set out as the ideology of free white European and American men of the middle and upper classes. It coexisted with, scandalously sometimes legitimated, slavery, colonialism and segregation. The second is conceptual: in valorising the individual, it ignores the communally and culturally embedded character of human beings, including their racial identities, experiences and claims. It posits abstract persons guided by impersonal justice rather than real people with particularised relations, commitments and strategies of conflict resolution. This is a criticism made of it by feminists, who add that it insulates private power from critical interrogation. The point already made in response is that liberalism denotes a set of equal freedoms that all can benefit from, and that a fair amount of progressive struggle has been about bringing excluded and subordinate subjects under liberalism's beneficial cover. Liberalism, moreover, has intellectual resources for interrogating unaccountable private power, whether of employers or patriarchs. To this one can add that liberal multiculturalists, spearheaded by writers like Kymlicka (1995), have attempted to re-theorise liberalism to enable it to accommodate group associations, and to accommodate, subject to certain provisos, the claims – to group representation, rights and self-government – that flow from it.

South African liberalism carries a special burden in respect of race. This is partly because its champions have been disproportionately white, and partly because many defended policies and plans fell short of granting full equality to blacks. As earlier noted, some South African liberal thinkers embraced group pluralism rather than abstract liberal individualism, but primarily in order to protect racial minorities from the black majority. Today, liberals are charged with propagating a colour blindness that is either naive or cynical, and incapable of recognising deep and ongoing racial inequality. Previously, white liberal ethno-pluralists sought protection in minority group protections; now, they seek protection in the pretence that race does not exist, and that formal equality or nonracial redistributive measures can adequately meet black demands for affirmation and redress.

Liberalism has work to do on this front; while an ideal of nonracialism can be defended (construed in a certain way), colour blindness cannot be. Liberalism must grant a role to racial restitution and race-based affirmative action. Absent such accommodation, it will fail to win the backing of the black middle class, parts of which look to policies based on racial recognition to facilitate their upward mobility. It will also fall short in egalitarian terms, because simple colour blindness will likely perpetuate remediable racial injustices and inequalities.

Still, the learning need not all be unidirectional. Liberals voice legitimate concerns about the subsuming of individuals under group identities and the subjection of individuals to the arbitrary powers of group and cultural leaders. Along with Marxists, liberal egalitarians also raise necessary questions about the limits of inter-group redistributions as a way of addressing inequality in the round. Reification of inter-group equalisation might result in neglect of intra-group inequalities. Moreover, liberals express reasonable worries about the divisiveness of race politics. The aspiration to nonracialism – to inter-racial friendship and solidarity, civic nationhood and the comprehension of persons as individuals in their own right rather than as group ciphers – remains legitimate.

CONCLUSION

Liberalism is a diverse tradition, a familiar fact often not given its due in simplistic dismissals of liberalism by South African progressives. Some liberal currents correspond exactly to the neoliberal stereotype, but other currents are radical and egalitarian, and potentially allied to social democracy and democratic socialism. South African liberalism, however, bears the imprint of its colonial origin, reflected into the present in a conservatism and disproportionate whiteness. There has never developed a large, durable and adequately self-theorised South African current of egalitarian liberalism. Instead, and not entirely mysteriously, South African history has yielded assorted anti-liberalisms. While liberalism is open to legitimate criticism, and South African liberalism perhaps more than most, anti-liberalism is, it has been argued here, a problematic response whose prevalence leaves South African left-wing politics cut off from important international debates about justice and open to authoritarian and ethno-nationalist appropriations.

NOTES

1   Both victory claims require qualification. The liberal-democratic political system prescribed by the Constitution is not purely procedural or electoral. Entrenched socio-economic rights tether liberal-democratic processes to social-liberal or social-democratic outcomes, while the constitutional requirement of participatory democracy inflects the process in a radical-democratic direction. The victory of liberal economic ideology is also qualified. Neoliberalism's ascendancy grated against constitutional commitments to redress and social protection. Neoliberal policies have been partly offset by strong labour protections, mass provision of housing, electricity, water and other public goods, and by social grants.

2   See for example Heywood (2007: 43–62). The more redistributive and welfarist liberal strands are characterised variously as 'modern', 'new', 'twentieth-century', 'social', 'socialist' and 'egalitarian' liberalism, in contrast to 'classic', 'nineteenth-century' and 'libertarian' liberalism. 'Neoliberalism' represents a revival of the latter.

3   Prominent black liberals included Selby Msimang, Jordan Ngubane and Archie Gumede.

4   Prominent liberal exponents of group-based solutions in South Africa have included RFA Hoernlé, ID MacCrone, Hermann Giliomee and Lawrence Schlemmer. Liberals adopting this view have viewed South Africa and other ex-colonies as 'multiracial' or 'plural' societies not amenable to the

sorts of individualist solutions applied to homogenous Western societies. They have sought solutions instead in various kinds of partnership, power-sharing or consociation among race groups (Giliomee 1989; Dubow 2014; Soske 2015).

5   For a good representative examples of this literature see Haysom (1992), Mureinik (1992) and Liebenberg (2010).

6   For academic critiques of liberalism in South Africa, see for example Legassick (1972), Rich (1984), Mngxitama et al. (2008).

7   Thus Nzimande (2007) has called for a debate on the balance between 'freedom of expression and human rights'. On another occasion (using terminology somewhat inconsistent with the previous quote) he attacked liberal 'human rights fundamentalism' (News24.com 2009). Nzimande (2009) has also attacked those who champion media and academic freedom but downplay the need to 'transform' the media and academia into institutions that better serve the masses. He lambasts the media for playing an 'oppositional' rather than 'informational' role, the universities for perpetuating 'racialised, patriarchal and elite forms of knowledge production'.

8   For a discussion of the extent and limits of the socio-economic powers of courts, see Pieterse 2004.

9   For examples see Anderson (1999), Arneson (1999, 2000), Dworkin (2011), Cohen (1989), Crisp (2003), Daniels (1990), Parfit (1997), Rawls (2001), Sen (2009).

REFERENCES

Anderson, ES (1999) What is the point of equality? *Ethics*, 109, 287–337.

Arneson, RJ (1999) Equality of opportunity for welfare defended and recanted. *The Journal of Political Philosophy*, 7 (4), 488–497.

Arneson, RJ (2000) Luck egalitarianism and prioritarianism. *Ethics*, 110, 339–349.

Cohen, GA (1989) On the currency of egalitarian justice. *Ethics*, 99 (4), 906–944.

Crisp, R (2003) Equality, priority, and compassion. *Ethics*, 113, 745–763.

Daniels, N (1990) Equality of what? Resources, welfare, or capabilities? *Philosophy & Phenomenological Research*, 50, 273–296.

Du Toit, A (1994) Fragile defiance: The African resistance movement. In I Liebenberg, B Nel, F Lordan and G van der Westhuizen (eds) *The long march: The story of the struggle for liberation in South Africa*. Pretoria: Haum.

Dubow, S (1989) *Racial segregation and the origins of apartheid in South Africa, 1919–36*. Basingstoke: Macmillan.

Dubow, S (2014) Uncovering the historic strands of egalitarian liberalism in South Africa. *Theoria*, 140, 7–24.

Dworkin, R (2011) *Justice for hedgehogs*. Cambridge: Cambridge University Press.

Everatt, D (2009) *The origins of non-racialism: White opposition to apartheid in the 1950s*. Johannesburg: Wits University Press.

Giliomee, H (1989) The communal nature of the South African conflict. In H Giliomee and L Schlemmer (eds) *Negotiating South Africa's future*. Basingstoke: Macmillan.

Giliomee, H (2003) *The Afrikaners: Biography of a people*. Cape Town: Tafelberg.

Glaser, D (2014) Liberal egalitarianism. *Theoria*, 140, 25–26.

Haysom, N (1992) Constitutionalism, majoritarian democracy and soco-economic rights. *South African Journal on Human Rights*, 8, 451–463.

Heywood, A (2007) *Political ideologies: An introduction*, 4th ed. Basingstoke: Palgrave Macmillan.

Jeffrey, A (1998) The new constitution: A triumph for liberalism? Some doubts. In RW Johnson and D Welsh (eds) *Ironic victory: Liberalism in post-liberation South Africa*. Cape Town: Oxford University Press.

Keane, J (1988) *Democracy and civil society*. London: Verso.

Keegan, T (1996) *Colonial South Africa and the origins of the racial order*. London: Leicester University Press.

Kymlicka, W (1995) *Multicultural citizenship*. Oxford: Clarendon Press.

Kymlicka, W (2002) *Contemporary political philosophy: An introduction*, 2nd ed. Oxford: Oxford University Press.

Legassick, M (1972) The rise of modern South African liberalism: Its assumptions and social base. In *Institute of Commonwealth Studies collected seminar papers on the societies of Southern Africa in the 19th and 20th centuries*. London: ICS.

Lewsen, P (1971) The Cape liberal tradition – myth or reality? *Race*, 13 (1), 65–80.

Liebenberg, S (2010) *Socio-economic rights: Adjudication under a transformative constitution*. Durban: Juta.

Losurdo, D (2011) *Liberalism: A counter-history*. London: Verso.

Mngxitama, A, Alexander, A and Gibson, NG (eds) (2008) *Biko lives! Contesting the legacies of Steve Biko*. Basingstoke: Palgrave Macmillan.

Mureinik, E (1992) Beyond a charter of luxuries: Economic rights in the constitution. *South African Journal on Human Rights*, 8, 464–474.

News24.com (2009) Nzimande on a tightrope. News24.com, 13 May. Available from http://www.news24.com/SouthAfrica/Politics/Nzimande-on-a-tightrope-2009 05 13 (accessed 20 April 2010).

Nzimande, B (2007) Decisive working class intervention is of absolute necessity. Address to the COSATU Central Committee, Esselen Park, 18 September. *COSATU Daily News*. Available from http://groups.google.com/group/cosatu-daily-news/web/necessity-of-decisive-working-class-intervention-b-nzimande-18-september-2007 (accessed 20 April 2010).

Nzimande, B (2009) Defend and deepen the April 22 electoral victory: The tasks of the SACP and the working class after the elections. *History Matters*, 10 May. Available from http://historymatters.co.za/2009/05/10/blade-nzimande-and-the-way-forward/ (accessed 20 April 2010).

Parfit, D (1997) Equality and priority. *Ratio*, 10 (3), 202–221.

Pieterse, M (2004) Coming to terms with judicial enforcement of socio-economic rights. *South African Journal on Human Rights*, 20 (3), 383–417.

Pieterse, M (2005) Towards a reconciliation of contract law and constitutional values: *Brisley versus Afrox revisited*. *South African Law Journal*, 122, 865–895.

Rawls, J (2001) *Justice as fairness: A restatement*. Cambridge, MA: The Belknap Press.

Rich, PB (1984) *White power and the liberal conscience: Racial segregation and South African liberalism*. Johannesburg: Ravan Press.

Sen, A (2009) *The idea of justice*. Cambridge, MA: The Belknap Press.

Soske, J (2015) The impossible concept: Settler liberalism, pan-Africanism, and the language of non-racialism. *African Historical Review*, 47 (2), 1–36.

Trapido, S (1968) African divisional politics in the Cape Colony, 1884 to 1910. *Journal of African History*, 9 (1), 79–98.

Van der Westhuizen, G (1994) The liberal party of South Africa, 1953–1968. In I Liebenberg, B Nel, F Lordan and G van der Westhuizen (eds) *The long march: The story of the struggle for liberation in South Africa*. Pretoria: Haum.

Walshe, P (1970) *The rise of African nationalism in South Africa*. Craighall: AD Donker.

Welsh, D (1998) Introduction: The liberal inheritance. In RW Johnson and D Welsh (eds) *Ironic victory: Liberalism in post-liberation South Africa*. Cape Town: Oxford University Press.

Wentzel, J (1995) *The liberal slideaway*. Johannesburg: South African Institute of Race Relations.

CHAPTER 7

Equality and inequality in South Africa: What do we actually want? And how do we get it?

Roger Southall

South Africa is heralded for its achievement of formal political equality for all its citizens. Today, however, there seems to be growing discontent with the democratic settlement arrived at in 1994. Two overlapping charges predominate. One is simply that the settlement's noble sentiments are being undermined, intentionally or otherwise, by either or both the political and economic elites. The other suggests that the settlement was drastically incomplete in that, despite the transfer of political power to a majority government, it failed to address the domination of the economy by a white elite.

What is really at stake here is the response to inequality or, more precisely, the extreme level of inequality which continues to characterise South Africa. A host of reports indicate that South Africa has failed to dislodge itself from the unenviable position of being one of the most unequal countries (perhaps *the* most unequal country) in the world, its Gini coefficient having increased from 0.61 in 1994 to 0.64 in 2014 (IRR 2016: 313). Indeed, the extremes of inequality have increased rather than decreased under democracy. According to Oxfam (2014), whereas in 1993, the richest 10 per cent of the population had a combined annual income of US$36 billion, by 2011 this had grown to US$69 billion. In comparison, the poorest 10 per cent had a combined income of US$1 billion, this remaining constant over the seventeen years. Meanwhile, this gross inequality is heavily racialised, with the rich being overwhelmingly white and the poor almost exclusively black.

The dimensions of this gross inequality are shaped by space, class and gender as well as race. Statistics abound, but in general blacks are far more likely to be unemployed, to live in poverty, to be poorly housed and educated, to have lower life expectancy and, overall, to suffer far more constrained life chances than whites; women, especially black women, suffer more limited life chances than men; and unemployment, poverty and their associated disadvantages are more extreme in rural rather than urban areas, especially in the former bantustans.

Although views vary regarding whether the generous remuneration packages earned by some among the corporate elite are a just reward for globally scarce skills, there is general denunciation of the extremes of inequality. Few politicians, whatever their affiliations, avoid any chance to pledge their commitment to addressing inequality alongside poverty and unemployment. However, when it comes to why and how inequality should be tackled, there is considerable disagreement. Unsurprisingly, that disagreement also tends to be heavily racialised. Despite indications that inequality is becoming increasingly class-based rather than race-based (Nattrass and Seekings 2016; Southall 2016), blacks tend to be more radical and impatient in their proposed solutions, whites more conservative and cautious.

The purpose of this chapter is to reflect upon what South Africans actually mean when they urge the necessity of greater equality, and the ways which are often put forward to achieve it.

THE DEBATE ABOUT INEQUALITY

What precisely is it that different protagonists in the debate about inequality actually want? Should inequality in South Africa be tackled because it is unjust, or is it rather that the extremity and racialised nature of inequality is socially dangerous and constitutes a major threat to democracy and political stability? Do protagonists in the debate simply want to narrow or abolish racial inequalities, or do they want to abolish inequality entirely? If it is just a reduction of inequalities that is wanted, what extent of inequality should be regarded as acceptable? Furthermore, if some degree of inequality is acceptable, is this implying, first, that it is inevitable, and/or second, that it is actually desirable for societal benefit as a whole?

Even by a simple posing of such questions it becomes obvious that South Africans are likely to disagree about the reasons and remedies for inequality. Nonetheless, it is important that such questions be asked.

Frankfurt (2015) points to how many Americans across the political spectrum are increasingly worried about growing inequality in their country. However, he goes on to argue that this is not because they wish to achieve economic equality but rather because they have some inherent sense of what is *fair*. In other words, it is not economic inequality in itself that is worrying them. They are unlikely to be bothered about *degrees* of inequality among the rich, nor are they likely to be enthusiastic about *absolute* equality if this were to be an equality of poverty. However, what does concern them is the perception that growing inequality is *unjustly caused* by some imbalance within the political economy or by the actions of elites – and they are troubled by what they perceive to be the *consequences* of inequality, whether these be that it leads to higher rates of crime, that it corrodes democracy or that it detracts from the general happiness of society.

South Africans are likely to concur with this line of argumentation, while placing particular emphasis upon the injustice and dangers of the continuing depth of racial inequality. Black South Africans in particular are likely to argue that black poverty is a product of a bitter history – of white conquest, white appropriation of black land, white exploitation of black labour, and wholesale imposition of discriminatory laws upon blacks that deprived them of opportunities while opening them up for whites. Even if whites disagree (perhaps suggesting that, for all its sins, past white domination facilitated South Africa's industrialisation), many will be concerned (perhaps with Julius Malema's Economic Freedom Fighters (EFF) in mind) that black resentment of racial inequality is leading to political instability, undermining democracy, and threatening a racial conflagration. So, if black South Africans are likely to be disposed towards economic redistribution because it would correct past wrongs, white South Africans may be more disposed to accept its wisdom on pragmatic grounds, in terms of their own interest and that of their children. Whatever their differences, therefore, South Africans would appear to have much in common regarding the desirability of addressing the yawning inequalities which characterise their society.

For a start, there is probably near universal agreement among South Africans about the good sense of combating poverty, most of which is black. However, beyond individual actions (whether inspired by guilt, moral, religious or pragmatic motivations) which may alleviate the lot of the poor, there are more systemic reasons for addressing inequality. Scanlon (1996, 2014) offers four such reasons which should resonate with South Africans.

The first is that 'economic inequality can give wealthier people an unacceptable degree of control over the lives of others'.[1] This goes to the heart of much of the present popular dissatisfaction with the huge differentials in wealth. First, there is mounting criticism that, notwithstanding strategies such as black economic empowerment (BEE), the political settlement has left economic power in the hands of white-owned companies, and that this is used to subvert the will of a majority government. The strongest critique is that whereas the African National Congress (ANC)'s liberationist history imbued it with socialist aims, these were sacrificed on the altar of capitalism after 1994 as a result of intense pressures placed upon the new government by 'white monopoly capital' – in other words, the economically powerful continue to dictate what strategies may and may not be followed, and impose their version of 'common sense' upon those within government who are responsible for steering the economy. As a result of this perspective, there remains huge distrust of 'white capital' among the ranks of the ruling party and its allies. Even though the response of business is that the ANC has in fact acquired significant economic power via its control of the country's parastatals, there is a widespread sense that a white oligarchy continues to dictate the country's history behind the scenes.

This leads on to a second risk attached to inequality, namely that 'economic inequality undermines the fairness of political institutions'. The supposition that overweening economic power enables the rich to unduly influence (if not actually to buy) politicians is a commonplace. In South Africa today, there is much concern about 'state capture'. This has become current in political debate because of the activities of the Gupta family. Arriving in South Africa from India in 1993, the Guptas appear to have ensnared Jacob Zuma in a web of obligation which they have manipulated to establish a formidable economic empire which, in essence, feeds off the state via acquisition of contracts. Furthermore, it would seem that they have used their influence to ensure appointment of particular individuals to senior positions within the state and the parastatals, thereby establishing a patronage network which functions to further their interests (Public Protector 2016). In response, the Zuma faction within the ANC tends to argue that hostility to the Guptas is driven by 'white monopoly capital', which had previously 'captured' the state under apartheid. Whatever the position taken, the debate about state capture indicates wide concern about the illegitimate use of economic power.

Beyond state capture, there is a further danger, especially where inequality is so visibly racialised. Politicians may seek to avoid accountability by blaming inequality for policy failures. For instance, the government is prone at times to blame the massive failures of the public school system upon the legacies of apartheid, without reference to its own culpability for the continuation of poor quality schooling for the majority of black children. Similarly, politicians may seize upon inequality to propose simple solutions to complex problems to drum up political support. In this regard, for instance, Julius Malema's EFF proposes appropriation of white land without compensation, without reference to the generally disastrous impact upon food security of the land seizures in Zimbabwe,[2] and nationalisation of the banks, without reference to the ANC's extremely chequered record of control over parastatals. This is not to say that radical structural reforms are not required; but it is to say that politicians may misuse the facts of inequality to justify the pursuit of irresponsible policies.

The third cost of inequality which Scanlon identifies is that it undermines the fairness of the economic system itself. There are two types of argument involved here. The first is that inequality dictates different life chances for the rich and the poor. This is particularly evident in South Africa. To state the obvious, black children born in impoverished areas are likely to be condemned to inadequate nourishment in their formative years, to attend poorly functioning schools, and hence end up either unemployed or in low-paid, unskilled jobs. In contrast, middle-class children, of whatever background, enjoy adequate nutrition and are funnelled through the upper tiers of the educational system to emerge with qualifications that favour advantaged entry into the labour market.

The second type of argument is that contemporary capitalist systems are systematically geared to reproduce inequality. Oxfam (2016) has identified free market fundamentalism at the core of global economic policy making as having driven an agenda of 'deregulation, privatisation, financial secrecy and globalisation'. This has enabled an increasing return to capital rather than labour; the blossoming of a 'spider's web' of tax havens and 'an industry of tax avoidance'; and a 'race to the bottom' (Oxfam 2016: 4) as governments lower taxes on the rich and large corporations in order to attract capital investment. As a result, while the overall share of income going to wages is shrinking, the incomes for the top 1 per cent have risen consistently, as has the remuneration of executives below them. CEOs of top companies regularly earn anything between 300 and 500 times more than the average workers in their employ.

Oxfam's report chimes with the argument of Piketty (2014) that the world is returning to the stark levels of inequality that existed before the First World War. In the early 1900s, inequalities in the advanced capitalist countries were extreme, with the richest decile owning something like 90 per cent of societal wealth. In the wake of the two world wars, the richest decile lost out to an emergent middle group, representing nearly half the population, who collectively came to own a quarter to a third of nations' wealth. Today, however, inequality has begun to reassert itself, so that in the USA, the richest decile owns over 70 per cent of national wealth, while the poorest 50 per cent owns just 4 per cent. Less extreme but not dissimilar distributions of income and wealth are to be found in Europe.

Piketty contests the analysis of Marx that levels of inequality and exploitation by the rich of the poor would lead to the collapse of capitalism under the weight of its internal contradictions. Capitalism has survived its crises because of the rise of modern economic theory and the diffusion of scientific knowledge. Even so, these advances 'have not modified the deeper structures of capital and inequality' (Piketty 2014: 1). Indeed, inequality is inherent in the laws of motion of capitalism:

> When the rate of return on capital exceeds the rate of growth of output and income, as it did in the nineteenth century and seems quite likely to do again in the twenty-first, capitalism automatically generates arbitrary and unsustainable inequalities that radically undermine the meritocratic values on which democratic societies are based (Piketty 2014: 1).

Indeed:

> The resurgence of inequality after 1980 is due largely to the political shifts of the past several decades, especially in regard to taxation and finance. The history of inequality is shaped by the way economic, social and political actors view what is just and what is not, as well as by the relative power of those actors and the collective choices that result (Piketty 2014: 20).

Yet having sounded the alarm, Piketty goes on to say that:

> There are nevertheless ways democracy can regain control over capitalism and ensure that the general interest takes precedence over private interests, while preserving economic openness and avoiding protectionist and nationalist reactions (Piketty 2014: 1).

In other words, inequality can be reversed through policy. Against that, however, there is no natural, spontaneous process to prevent destabilising, inegalitarian forces from prevailing. While trends towards greater equality (such as the diffusion of technical knowledge and skills between 'advanced' and less developed countries) may exist, they tend to be countered by powerful forces pushing in the opposite direction.

This leads to Scanlon's (2014) final argument about inequality which is that 'workers, as participants in a scheme of cooperation that produces national income, have a claim to a fair share of what they have helped to produce'. While Marx would argue that capitalists' drive to maximise surplus value will lead them into inevitable class conflict with the workers they exploit, the rejoining argument is that the distribution of surplus-value is amenable to trade union action and bargaining between capital and labour. It might be argued that any outcome of wage negotiations is more often than not a product of power differentials between employers and employees, yet it is also likely to be strongly influenced by what either party regards as 'fair'. Are wages keeping up with inflation? Are wage increases allowing for an incrementally improving standard of living? Or is worker 'greed' threatening the profitability of business and ultimately threatening their own long-term interests?

While noting that there are likely to be competing ideas of what is 'fair', Scanlon cites the difference principle of John Rawls, according to which inequalities in wealth and income are justifiable if and only if these inequalities cannot be reduced without worsening the position of those who are worse off. While this implies that all those involved in the production process should share in improved profitability and productivity, on the other hand it also suggests that some degree of inequality may be necessary and inevitable.

It is this latter suggestion which lies at the heart of free market arguments that while the remuneration of the executives who run large companies looks extravagant to ordinary workers, it can be justified because of the rare talents and skill that they possess. It is also argued that the possibility of huge financial returns encourages the innovation and change which is at the heart of economic progress (so in other words, without inequality, economies would go backwards) (Tovey 2014).

These arguments should not be dismissed, if only because it would be absurd to dismiss material reward as an incentive to work. Yet here the Rawls argument would seem to kick in as a standing rebuke to the widening gulf between those at the top of the corporate world and the workers they employ. As has been pointed out with regard to corporate salaries in South Africa (Massie et al. 2014), the remuneration of top executives seems to reflect power differentials within corporations rather than economic rationality, as company remuneration committees are often staffed by individuals whose self-interest dictates that they leverage senior managerial salaries upwards. The result is that in recent years executive pay levels in South Africa have been in excess of such rates internationally. Even if the need for pay differentials is accepted, there is clearly need for debate about how wide gaps should be and how a narrowing of differences might lead to a greater sense of societal fairness and hence political stability.

This leads on to considerations about how inequality in South Africa has been and should be addressed.

TACKLING INEQUALITY – REMEDIES AND LIMITATIONS

Two broad approaches predominate in debates about how to tackle inequality in South Africa: reparations and redistribution. Although they overlap, they are conceptually quite distinct, and each presents its own dilemmas.

Reparations – compensations for history

Many black South Africans feel that they, their families and their ancestors are owed recognition and compensation for present and past suffering by the present beneficiaries of South Africa's history of racial oppression. Black poverty is ascribed to white wealth, and the argument made that the social chasm which divides blacks from whites can never be breached without proper acknowledgement and, as far as possible, the overturning, of the sins of the past.

The conviction that black South Africans had been subject to huge injustice and human rights abuses was central to the activities of Truth and Reconciliation Commission (TRC). However, the TRC referred only to offences committed during the period of apartheid, and did not attempt to reach back deeper into South African history. Nonetheless, it established the principle that there could be no healing or reconciliation of victims and abusers without reparations, even though it acknowledged that reparations could never fully compensate for suffering. It proceeded to recommend five forms of reparations: urgent interim reparations for victims in need of emergency assistance; individual reparation grants; symbolic measures to acknowledge victims; community rehabilitation programmes; and institutional reforms to ensure that perpetration of human rights violations would not be repeated (Sooka 2004; Fernandez 1999).

Subsequently, although the government was to be strongly criticised for its limited implementation of such measures, the principle of reparations – of the need to compensate those (individuals or communities) who had suffered under apartheid – was to be enshrined in law and practice. Financial payments were to be made to those who had suffered gross human rights abuse at the hands of the state and there was to be considerable symbolic acknowledgement of victims in the form of commemorative monuments. In addition, the government's land reform policy, as well as introducing strategies for land redistribution, provided for restitution of land to those dispossessed of it after 1913 as a result of racially discriminatory laws or practices (or payment of financial compensation in lieu). The pursuit by the government of such policies as equity employment and BEE, which seek redress, are also guided at least in part by the logic of reparations. Generally, however, widespread criticism has been made that the government's actions in response to the TRC's recommendations have fallen far short of what has been needed. Indeed, many complain that reparations have taken second place to reconciliation (allowing whites off the hook) and the government's fear of offending 'white capital', with particular bitterness aroused by the government's opposing attempts by activists to demand reparations from foreign companies (on the ground that their past investments in South Africa had made them complicit with apartheid) in US courts (Daly 2003; Howard-Hassman 2008).

It is difficult to distinguish popular dissatisfaction with the government's reparations policies from unhappiness with its performance more generally. Nonetheless, given that the majority of blacks remain poor and racial inequality remains so visible two decades into democracy, it is not surprising that the demands for economic reparations appear to be getting louder. In 2011, for instance, Archbishop Desmond Tutu picked up on a proposal for whites to pay a wealth tax, telling a white audience that they had all benefited from apartheid: 'your children went to fancy schools, you lived in posh suburbs' (Williams 2011). More forcefully, the demand for restorative justice lies at the heart of the EFF's demands for the seizure of white land and the nationalisation of the white-owned command posts of the economy.

Qunta (2016a), a black consciousness-influenced lawyer, has recently published a manifesto for reparations which is illustrative of wider demands for racial redress. She argues that South Africa's historically 'engineered inequality', alongside the economic dominance of the white minority, presents a looming danger of self-destructive political instability: 'the notion that a racial conflagration in South Africa was avoided in 1994 is a fallacy; it was merely postponed' – unless 'urgent material steps are taken to deal with these risks'. Accordingly, it follows that it is in the self-interest of whites to make reparations. She goes on to suggest three particular ways in which such reparation might be made.

First, restitution should be to made for the past appropriation of black land. Calculations should be made (by 'skilled professionals') of the current value of land taken from Africans since 1652. However, because it is unfair that black taxpayers should bear the cost of such restitution, it should not be the state but a specially established 'reparations fund' which pays. Second, white-owned companies and individual whites should pay over a proportion of their profits and incomes for a specific period to this reparation fund. Third, the reparation fund would be controlled by an independent board comprising private and public stakeholders, and run by professional individuals. Beyond restitution for land, it should target key interventions that would rescue present and future generations of blacks from poverty.

Qunta, with good reason, complains about the complacency of a large body, if not the majority, of whites (2016b). Her approach feeds into widespread perceptions of growing racial polarisation, which have been fuelled by extensive media coverage of racist insults to blacks by white individuals. Whether or not these perceptions are genuinely reflective of an underlying reality does not detract from an appreciation of the widespread sense of alienation experienced among many who feel excluded from the benefits of the democratic settlement. In short, if the demand for economic reparations is growing, it is only as part of a much wider pattern of protest, notably by young black South Africans, against felt injustice. However, while it is obviously important that calls for reparation should be heeded, rendering them practicable remains complicated.

The motivation for reparations is that those who have benefited from past racial exploitation should make recompense, symbolic and material, to the victims of this history. Inherent in such a demand is the quest for recognition of the justice of the claim by the perpetrators of such oppression, if they are still alive, and also by the present beneficiaries of this past – this linked to an apology. To some (limited) extent, this has already been realised, with, for instance, the Dutch Reformed Churches having confessed that their support for apartheid was a sin. Yet while institutions such as churches are in a position to make an apology, and while particular individuals may seek absolution from those to whom they may have done direct harm, the idea of a collectivity of individuals (and in this case, what is usually meant is 'whites') making an apology is much more complicated.

Who is to represent 'whites' to make such an apology when whites are, in practice, a highly diverse group – divided along lines of class, ethnicity and religion – and who are highly unlikely to agree, in any case, whether an apology is needed? Would it be expected that some whites, perhaps Afrikaners, should be expected to apologise more than others? Who would decide upon the actual distribution of guilt and the degree of apology that might be due? While black South Africans would doubtless welcome any such apologies if they were to perceive them as honestly made, they are unlikely to accept that symbolic apologies are sufficient.

The issue of material reparations is no less difficult to address. For a start, who exactly should pay reparations? Should all whites pay, or only some, regardless of different degrees of involvement in past oppressions by their ancestors? Should younger generations of whites be required to make material recompense because of the sins of their parents and grandparents? Would whites who have immigrated since 1994 be equally required to make material reparations? Would any attempt to secure reparations from whites extend to chasing those who have fled democracy to live in Vancouver, Perth or Wimbledon? In any case, as Qunta acknowledges, it is highly unlikely that singling out whites as a racial group to pay reparations would be allowable under the Constitution – which is why she concedes that reparations should be made by whites on a voluntary basis. However, while this might well have symbolic value, it is highly unlikely that what would be, in effect, the imposition of a voluntary tax would do much to resolve the issue of inequality.

Even beyond the issue of 'who' should pay, there is the problem of 'how much' should be paid – and for what and in what form. Is it really possible to calculate, with any exactness, the amount of recompense that should be paid? While historians would likely concur that today's racialised inequality is a product of history, how should this be balanced out against the 'development' of South Africa in terms of the country's industrialisation and the construction of common goods such as roads, railways and schools (even if the latter are enjoyed differentially by different racial groups)? Again, how much present racialised inequality should be ascribed to past racial exploitation as opposed to policy errors by the democratic government? And how would the costs of corruption, generally perceived to have ballooned in recent years, be factored in to any such calculations?

It is true that provision has been made for the restitution of land to those unfairly dispossessed of it since the introduction of the National Land Act of 1913. This relates specifically to those who were dispossessed under homeland consolidations, forced removals from 'black spots', the Group Areas and related laws. As such, because its policy is relatively focused, the government has enjoyed some success, having restored 3.079 thousand hectares of land to over 371 000 households, alongside having made financial compensation payments of over R80 million to other claimants, between 1995 and 2014 (IRR 2016: 283). Even so, the land restitution process has not been unproblematic. The authorities have needed to ascertain the historical validity, not only of any claims, but also (not infrequently) of rival claims. Further, if the objective of restoring land to its prior owners (whether individuals or communities) is to enable them to escape poverty, then restitution needs to be accompanied by other strategies, and often extra capital, to ensure that it becomes sustainable. Meanwhile, of course, owners of land subject to restitution have had to be financially compensated (albeit not necessarily at market prices), as guaranteed under the Constitution.[3] This involves the considerable irony that black taxpayers are themselves paying indirectly to finance reparations. There is also the other factor, whether morally just or not, that the very threat that agricultural land may be subject to compulsory purchase for restitution purposes constitutes a disincentive to investment in the further productivity of the land by the existing owners.

Consider the even greater difficulties which would attend Qunta's proposal of calculating the value of land taken from Africans since 1652. Even if the objective were not to return land to the descendants of previous African owners (a highly contested issue), the 'skilled professionals' responsible for calculating land values would be unlikely to come to any agreement, especially as they would, almost undoubtedly, be hired by contesting parties. Meanwhile, if it would be difficult to calculate land values, imagine how even more complicated it would be to calculate the value accruing to past employers, firms or individuals as a result of the discriminatory 'cheap black labour' policies pursued by one white government after another.

This does not mean that the pursuit of reparations should be abandoned, but for reparations to be viable those seeking them need to be able to identify specific perpetrators of past abuses (rather than generic groupings such as 'whites'); to identify specific individuals or communities (rather than blacks at large) who have suffered from abuses; and to be able to specify what the particular damages are that have been done to them. It will also be necessary to find some credible way of quantifying the financial compensation that should be due, this in turn, requiring that specific periods be identified during which injuries or hurts were inflicted (rather than reaching back endlessly into history). Such, indeed, has been the strategy pursued by human rights lawyers Richard Spoor and his associates to gain compensation for mineworkers who contracted occupational lung diseases as a result of their working on gold mines. Ultimately, after defeats in lower courts, Spoor achieved a resounding recent victory when the Constitutional Court found in favour of the claim of an individual mineworker, Thembekile Mankayi, for compensation against a particular firm, Anglo-Gold Ashanti. This in turn led the Court to grant permission for the lawyers to pursue class actions on behalf of other mineworkers who had contracted silicosis or tuberculosis against gold producers in general. Potentially, such class actions could act on behalf of as many as 100 000 mineworkers against thirty-two firms (Nicholson 2016).[4]

Other such specific claims could be lodged against companies in other sectors of industry. Even so, the scope for such actions is limited – especially where the cost of reparations payments might end up bankrupting existing companies, thereby compelling them to close down and contributing to further unemployment. Spoor has pointed out that if compensation – 'conservatively priced' at R1 million a head – were to be paid out to each of 100 000 mineworkers, it might bankrupt the gold mining industry. Accordingly, a financial settlement is the likely result if class action suits are successfully pursued. In other words, reparations are likely to require trade-offs – between the wrongs of the past and the needs of the present.

It is such reasons that Howard-Hassman (2008), although strongly sympathetic to the claims of Africans for the harm caused by the slave trade, colonialism, and neocolonialism, believes that for legal, political and practical reasons, pursuit of financial reparations for Africa is not good strategy. As in South Africa today, it makes better sense to struggle for social justice.

Redistribution and the pursuit of social justice

If Scanlon's arguments are accepted as valid, then the need for redistributive justice follows. The primary motivation is simply that the extreme levels of inequality which obtain in South Africa are socially unjust. Yet the principle has sound pragmatic backing. Extreme inequality erodes social cohesion. The quest for happiness in South Africa is increasingly pursued behind high walls and electric fences, as those with resources seek to protect themselves against those without. Such inequality is strongly associated with high levels of stress, anxiety and aggression. Unsurprisingly, South Africa performs poorly in increasingly sophisticated happiness studies (ranking a miserable 142nd out of 151 countries in the Happy Planet Index conducted by the New Economics Foundation in 2012), providing backing to generic studies (for example, Wilkinson and Pickett 2009) which demonstrate the deleterious effects of inequality upon human well-being. The thrust of such analysis is that it is not just the poor who suffer in unequal societies, but the rich and better-off as well.

It would be wrong to disavow the considerable achievements of ANC governments in the provision of housing and services (such as water and electricity) to disadvantaged communities, alongside the remarkable expansion of social grants. Such provision has been accompanied by increased spending on healthcare and education, with considerable emphasis upon expanding access for the black poor. However, what matters in terms of the present argument is not whether such policies have been effectively pursued (clearly, their impact has been highly uneven) but whether they have gone beyond the alleviation of the worst aspects of poverty as their developmental objective.

The ANC has placed much emphasis upon the need for 'transformation'. This supposedly suggests the revolutionary change of the existing socio-economic system. However,
in practice transformation has focused upon the deracialisation of capitalism. This has
centred around policies such as equity employment and BEE, thereby increasingly opening up the apex of society to black people and challenging white privilege. This is versed
in terms of the pursuit of employment profiles in institutions in both the public and private sectors which reflect the racial profiles of the population at large. Today, therefore,
the ANC celebrates the 'transformation' of the public sector, which is now approaching
'demographic representivity', while lamenting the considerably slower pace to transformation to be found in the private sector. Nonetheless, despite these differentials the ANC
claims the considerable expansion of the black middle class and the increased representation of blacks in the top ranks of the corporate sector as one of its greatest achievements.
What this implies is that while the ANC has remained concerned to satisfy the basic
needs of its popular constituency, the thrust of its emphasis upon 'transformation' has
been on expanding black access to the present class system, rather than fundamentally
altering its shape and structure. To put it another way, the ANC has sought to produce a
more racially heterogeneous, middle-class society (Southall 2016).

If this seeks to even out unfairness, it does not necessarily tackle the problem of unfairness at its roots. It is the widespread sense of this unfairness which is driving the current
crescendo of social discontents which range from the EFF's populist demands, the lodg-
ing of wage demands by unions that business declares are wildly excessive, and students'
demands for free education and 'decolonisation' of the universities. These provide a backdrop to the sheer anger of those who feel so thoroughly marginalised by the current
system that they embark upon the destruction of community property, such as university
and school buildings. It is no wonder that Qunta fears a looming social conflagration.

All this indicates the urgency of the pursuit of greater equality. There are three major
issues to be taken into particular account. The first is that, contrary to arguments that the
democratic settlement was simply a fraudulent attempt to maintain elite power, the genuinely transformative potential of the Constitution needs to be reasserted. This was spelled
out by the former chief justice Pius Langa in 2006 when he argued that the Constitution
provided a platform for achieving 'substantive equality', by which he meant:

> a complete reconstruction of the state and society, including a redistribution of power
> and resources along egalitarian lines. The challenge of achieving equality within this
> transformation project involves the eradication of systemic forms of domination and
> material advantage based on race, gender, class and other grounds of inequality. It also
> entails the development of opportunities which allow people to realise their full human
> potential within positive social partnerships (Langa 2006 cited in De Vos 2013).

There are constraining factors on how this potential of the Constitution may be realised, from the articulation of transformative jurisprudence by the judiciary through to

institutional factors such as the capacity and willingness of the state to carry through substantively equalising policies (Albertyn 2007). In other words, while there are manifestly multiple grounds for social discontent, the target should not be the Constitution (the legal expression of the democratic settlement) but the parties, people and policies which have failed to maximise its potential for radical social change. In other words, central to present popular struggles should be the demand for accountability – and, again, the Constitution provides all the necessary tools. Some, such as the right to media freedom, are freely exercised, yet there are many others (such as the obligation of Parliament to keep the executive in check) which have been deliberately blunted. After all, while notionally in favour of accountability, elites seek to deflect it when it threatens their interests (Hoffman 2011).

If substantive equality (which encompasses equalities of both opportunity and outcome) is the goal, then the second issue is how to realise it. It is here that the present ideological impasse, embodied in crude oppositions of socialism and capitalism which pervade the policy discourse in South Africa, proves particularly unhelpful. Instead, adoption of a social justice paradigm should be accompanied by thinking that is simultaneously radical (far-reaching in its scope) and pragmatic (does it work?). This implies abandonment of existing shibboleths by both Left and Right. In a country where state-owned industry is earning a reputation for inefficiency and financial failure, traditional notions of nationalisation, involving highly centralised controls over production, will need to be re-thought. Alongside appreciation of the virtues (but not the excesses) of private enterprise, new options – such as decentralised production, perhaps even involving public private partnerships, as well as worker cooperatives – should be explored. Meanwhile, the virtues of the recently approved national minimum wage will need to be carefully assessed against any negative effects on employment. Consequently, greater urgency should attend the necessity of land reform, inclusive of adoption of innovative models such as shared (established/emergent farmer) ownership, profit-sharing and cooperative enterprise.

On the Right, insistence on the rights of ownership and exclusive managerial control of companies should make way for official insistence upon options like employee share-ownership and worker representatives on boards (and particularly on corporate remuneration committees to rein in the remuneration earned by high-flying executives). While any strategy which encourages enterprise among the poor should be given strong support (and this might involve extensive abandonment of restrictive rules which numerous economists claim are hampering small business), any pretence that high growth rates will solve the problem of unemployment should be abandoned for, quite simply, they can't and they won't. Yes, South Africa desperately needs more jobs, but it even more urgently needs multidimensional opportunities for the poor to earn decent and dignified 'livelihoods', cobbled together from a mix of opportunities. In the communal areas, this must surely require the reversal of present ANC policies involving the strengthening of traditional leaders which strangle local citizenship and democracy and replacing them with strategies that genuinely empower the rural poor.

Finally, serious consideration needs to be given to taxing wealth. This will inevitably be countered by those who argue the wrongheadedness of socially engineered attempts to tackle inequality. The arguments will vary. Most commonly, while it may be conceded that economic growth particularly favours those at the top, it will be asserted that nonetheless it benefits everybody. Or it will be argued that any form of redistribution will lead to capital and skills leaving the country, leading to the greater impoverishment of all. This argument is usually linked to citations that South Africa has a very small tax base, and hence that there is limited scope for raising higher levels of revenue. According to one economist, there was only a small pool of income taxpayers who earned more than R750 000 in 2010–2011, so an increase in the rate of tax for such people from 35.2 per cent to 40 per cent would have raised only an additional R8.1 billion (Keeton 2014). However, such calculations may seriously underestimate the scope for increasing taxation upon the rich.

Forslund (2012) argues that tax rates for the better-off have actually declined since 1994, and that they could easily afford higher rates of taxation. Had tax levels been maintained at higher, earlier levels, the state would have raked in a further R125 billion in 2010–2011 alone. Second, Forslund cites a huge level of noncompliance among 'high net worth individuals' (HNWIs). Although only 2 000 individuals declared a taxable income above R5 million during the period from 2008 to 2011, the revenue authorities suspected that about 9 300 such South Africans were evading tax. Meanwhile, institutions such as Credit Suisse regularly report that there are anything between 70 000 and 200 000 South African US$ millionaires, and that in 2012, there were as many as 116 000 South Africans within the global top 1 per cent of wealth holders. Whether or not such individuals are actually resident and liable to tax in South Africa is a moot point but, even if Forslund over-estimates the potential for drawing more HWNIs into the tax net, there is clearly considerable scope for doing so and for simultaneously raising the rates of tax at the highest levels. Further, even if increased high-end income taxes were to be deemed as likely to prompt high-earners to flee to less onerous tax regimes, existing taxes on unearned incomes, such as capital gains tax, could be increased, while serious consideration could also be given to the imposition of taxes on the transfer of shares (the Tobin tax), a form of levy which is increasingly practicable given that such transactions are now almost all done electronically.

Finally, even if it is true – as many economists convincingly argue – that serious inroads into poverty and inequality can only be made through such long-term strategies as improving human capital, the imposition of higher taxes on the wealthy would have major symbolic value in a country of such extreme inequality. It would also serve as a necessary counter to what Piketty insists is the *inevitable* tendency of free market capitalism to widen rather than diminish inequality.

FINAL CONSIDERATIONS

Alarm bells are sounding about the injustice and dangerous consequences of the extent of inequality, especially insofar as it takes a racialised form. How long can South Africa continue to tolerate the persistently high levels of revolt which exist among the poor? How long can the political settlement of 1994 continue to hold and not be overturned by some popular revolution? True, such a revolution might be genuinely transforming – yet it might as easily degenerate into tyranny. Accordingly, even if it proves impossible to convince elites of the justice of some sort of radical change, it should not be so difficult to convince them on grounds of self-interest, dictated by fear of political upheavals and the potential destruction of their wealth.

Beyond such considerations, the tackling of inequality suggests the need for a paradigm shift – towards the prioritisation of social justice. This should not be to favour 'equality' *rather than* growth, but rather a more equalitarian quality of such growth. This is not as utopian as it sounds at first. When even the International Monetary Fund and World Bank start worrying about the extremes of global inequality we may assume that some major re-thinking about the trajectory of capitalism is afoot, and that the economic orthodoxy which has gripped the world in thrall for the last forty years cannot continue to hold. In South Africa, meanwhile, the increasing fluidity of popular opinion, signalled by the steady erosion of enthusiasm for the ANC, suggests the arrival of a new political moment – opening the way for the consideration of new possibilities.

South Africa needs to move beyond the blandness of calls for a less unequal society and ask hard questions about the nature of the society that is desired. How fast and how far should the drive for equality go? Should racial equality be prized above the pursuit of a more equal society more generally? To what extent may a degree of inequality be necessary for collective well-being? There will be no easy answers, yet the debate should be guided by the conviction that a more equal sharing of wealth will lead not only to a more just, but a happier and more stable society.

NOTES

1 Citations from Scanlon (2014) which is essentially a condensation of Scanlon (1996).
2 Although the complexity of the land reforms in Zimbabwe must be acknowledged, and the trope that it has been a total failure has been challenged (Scoones et al. 2010), the fact remains that many Zimbabweans have been rendered heavily dependent for their survival on humanitarian aid.
3 Under clause 25, Ch. 2 of the Constitution (the Bill of Rights), compensation for property expropriated in the public interest is required to be 'just and equitable', having regard to the current use of the property, the history of its acquisition, the extent of state subsidy and capital improvement represented in the property, and the purpose of the expropriation, as well as its market value.
4 The gold mining companies have given notice of their intention to appeal the judgement.

REFERENCES

Albertyn, C (2007) Substantive equality and transformation in South Africa. *South African Journal of Human Rights*, 23 (2), 253–276.
Daly, E (2003) Reparations in South Africa: A cautionary tale. *University of Memphis Law Review*, 33, 367.

De Vos, P (2013) Pius Langa: A man who knew the meaning of change. *Daily Maverick*, 25 July.

Fernandez, L (1999) Reparations policy in South Africa for the victims of apartheid. *Law, Development and Policy*, 3 (2), 209–222.

Forslund, D (2012) *Personal income taxation and the struggle against inequality and poverty*. Cape Town: Alternative Information and Development Centre.

Frankfurt, H (2015) *On inequality*. Princeton: Princeton University Press.

Hoffman, P (2011) Democracy and accountability: Quo Vadis South Africa? In Daniel, J, Naidoo, P, Pillay, D and Southall, R, *New South Africa Review 2: New paths, old compromises?* Johannesburg: Wits University Press, 83–99.

Howard-Hassman, R (2008) *Reparations to Africa*. Philadelphia: University of Pennsylvania Press.

IRR (Institute of Race Relations) (2016) *South Africa survey 2014/15*. Johannesburg: IRR.

Keeton, G (2014) Inequality in South Africa. *The Journal of the Helen Suzman Foundation*, 74, 26–31.

Massie, K, Collier, D and Crotty, A (2014) *Executive salaries in South Africa: Who should have the say on pay?* Johannesburg: Jacana.

Nattrass, N and Seekings, J (2016) *Poverty, politics and policy in South Africa: Why has poverty persisted after apartheid?* Johannesburg: Jacana.

Nicholson, G (2016) Silicosis: Court backs class action. *Daily Maverick*, 13 May.

Oxfam (2014) *Even it up: Time to end extreme inequality*. www.oxfam.org? ... ?cr-even-it-ip-extreme-inequality-291014-en.pdf.

Oxfam (2016) *An economy for the top 1%: How privilege and power in the economy drive extreme inequality and how this can be stopped*. www.oxfam.org.

Piketty, T (2014) *Capital in the twenty-first century*. Cambridge, MA: The Belknap Press.

Public Protector (2016) *State of capture*. Report 6 of 2016. Mg.co.za/article/2016–11–02-breaking-read-the-full-state-capture-report.

Qunta, C (2016a) How to avoid conflagration. *Sunday Independent*, 8 May.

Qunta, C (2016b). *Why we are not a nation*. Johannesburg: Serita sa Sechaba.

Scanlon, T (1996) *The diversity of objections to inequality*. The Lindley Lecture, University of Kansas. https://kuscholarworks.ku.edu/ … /The%Diversity%20of/20%Objections%20to%In.

Scanlon, T (2014) *The 4 biggest reasons why inequality is bad for society*. http://ideas.ted.com/the-4-biggest-reasons-why-inequality-is-bad-for-society/.

Scoones, I, Marongwe, N, Mavedzenge, B, Mahenehene, J, Murimbarimba, F and Sukume, C (2010) *Zimbabwe's land reforms: Myths and realities*. Johannesburg: Jacana/Woodbridge, Suffolk: James Currey.

Sooka, Y (2004) South Africa, its past, human rights and reparations. In *Keynote at the public seminar on reparations*. Wits Institute for Social and Economic Research. 6 July.

Southall, R (2016) *The new black middle class in South Africa*. Johannesburg: Jacana/Woodbridge, Suffolk: James Currey.

Tovey, M (2014) *The social function of inequality*. Mises Institute: Austrian Economics, Freedom and Peace. http://mises.org/library/social-function-economic-inequality.

Wilkinson, W and Pickett, K (2009) *The spirit level: Why equality is better for everyone*. London. Allen Lane.

Williams, M (2011) *Tutu calls for wealth tax on whites*. http://www.iol.co.za/news/politics/tutu-calls-for-wealth-tax-on-whites-1116744.

SOCIAL DIMENSIONS
OF INEQUALITY

CHAPTER 8

Analysis must rise: A political economy of falling fees

Stephanie Allais

This chapter explores some of the complexity of the debates around the funding of higher education in South Africa, and how it intersects with inequality – both counteracting and complicit in increasing inequalities in society. The specific context is student protests, under the banner of #FeesMustFall, which rocked universities in South Africa in 2015 and 2016, and seem likely to continue in 2017. The chapter argues that while there are convincing principled arguments for fee-free higher education as a mechanism to create equality in the student body, as well as to decommodify higher education, doing away with a component of fee payments for university education in contemporary South Africa could leave most if not all stakeholders in South African universities today with worse outcomes, and may aggravate inequality. This is based on two analyses that have been inadequately dealt with in the current debates. The first is that while elite higher education systems are politically untenable in democratic societies, mass higher education systems play into labour market inequalities in complex ways, and massification has negative as well as positive effects on society. The second is that the unintended consequence of doing away with fees is likely to be a substantial weakening of our top institutions, with – if the arguments for the public good role of higher education hold – negative consequences for society overall.

OVERVIEW OF THE PROTESTS AND RESPONSES TO THEM

South Africa's university system is located in a context of extreme and widespread poverty; extreme inequality; a racialised labour market with a historic and current built-in dependence on cheap labour; extremely high unemployment; high levels of insecure work; and widespread dissatisfaction with the government. Admission to university education has expanded dramatically over the past twenty years. Funding from the fiscus has risen in real terms, but higher education inflation has risen faster than inflation in general, in part due to a weak exchange rate, and expansion has seen large numbers of poor and poorly prepared students enter the system (DHET 2016). In short, a crisis has long been brewing in the university system.

Despite some aspects peculiar to South Africa, many of the trends in South African higher education are typical of an international picture. Participation in higher education has dramatically expanded around the world in the last two decades (Schofer and Meyer 2005). The crises facing South Africa – increased student numbers, poorly prepared students, demoralised staff, declining state expenditure per student – are very much international trends (Trow 2000). All over the world a range of different funding models which have worked until recently are collapsing or facing strain as participation is greatly increasing (Barr 2004; Oketch 2016). More costs are being pushed to families whose incomes are declining and who, in many instances, are not reaping substantial labour market rewards for their degrees and certificates (Collins 2013).

South African universities responded by raising fees and class sizes over time. The former meant that the proportion of fees to government subsidy has grown considerably. On average, state funding now amounts to about 40 per cent of university budgets, down from 70 per cent fifteen years ago (DHET 2014). The lowest university fees (average tuition only) for degree study are around R20 000 at universities such as Walter Sisulu and Cape Peninsula University of Technology, while average fees at the top universities range from around R45 000 at the University of the Witwatersrand (Wits) to R50 000 at the University of Cape Town (UCT) (DHET 2016). This is increasingly unaffordable to lower middle-class families, many of whom are highly indebted, although still relatively cheap for the wealthy middle-class families who spend what is easily double – and in many cases far more – on high school fees.[1]

Wits announced an 11 per cent fee increase in September 2015. This triggered an explosion of student protest on campuses around the country, culminating in a march of an estimated 10 000 university students and staff to the Union Buildings in Pretoria, the seat of the presidency, on 23 October 2015. By the end of the day President Jacob Zuma had announced that there would be no fee increase for the 2016 academic year. In real terms, this was a fee reduction, with inflation running at around 4.5 per cent and a weak exchange rate raising many university costs beyond inflation.

No announcements about fees were made by any university before the local government elections in August 2016. The ruling African National Congress (ANC), after a poor showing at the polls, quickly released a statement supporting a freeze on fee adjustments as part of a broader statement from its national executive committee meeting.[2] About a month later the minister of higher education announced that it would provide additional financial support to enable universities to raise fees up to 8 per cent: government would pay the difference between the 2015 fees and increased 2017 fees for all students from households earning below R600 000 a year. This was rejected by many students as inadequate – it did not do away with fees altogether. Major protests erupted again on most campuses, many of which were closed for several weeks, and some of which only partially completed the academic year.

In 2015 the student's victory was widely seen as a significant gain by a powerful student movement, with wide support from the public and a significant number of academic staff. The mobilisation of so many students, unified across traditional party-political and student organisation lines, the achievement of their short-term goal (no fee increase for 2016), and the obtaining of an additional R6.9 billion from the fiscus for university education in the context of a fiscal squeeze, were remarkable achievements. Others were that the president appointed a judicial commission of inquiry to explore the feasibility of fee-free higher education, and that serious pressure was put on government to deal with corruption and inefficiencies in the National Student Financial Aid Scheme (NSFAS). In 2016 the situation was less clear, with a heated national debate about both the aims and the methods of the student protests, as well as the responses from institutions and government (see Booysen 2016 for an overview of some of the debates).

INDIVIDUAL GOODS, PUBLIC GOODS, AND FISCAL PRIORITIES

One compelling argument for doing away with fees is that having a sale price, even if it is for only part of the cost, distorts the nature of education, as students believe they are purchasing a product, and start to view themselves as consumers as opposed to scholars acquiring and developing knowledge. Commodification makes services more easily accessed by those who have money, and potentially reinforces inequalities throughout society. However, public funding can come with many strings attached, and formal autonomy may not be sufficient to protect universities from state interference.

The argument in favour of fees that has dominated public policy, particularly in the developing world, is that in poor countries rates of return are relatively much higher for graduates, which makes fiscus-based funding regressive (Cloete 2015a; Pillay 2010; Psacharopoulos 1994). Cloete (2015b) similarly argues that there is a relationship between inequality and returns to higher education – the higher the inequality, the higher the returns to individuals. In South Africa currently, for every one hundred individuals in a particular age cohort, roughly ten graduate with a degree. Relative expenditure from the fiscus on these individuals is substantial already, even when they are expected to top up part of their study costs, and they go on to enjoy substantially better labour market outcomes than the other 90 per cent of the age cohort into which they were born. A key factor is the kind of jobs available to non-higher education graduates.

A difficulty here is that it is not clear how to distinguish between the public good role of university education, and the individual good role, in terms of what they cost, and what proportion should be funded by whom. And while the rates of return argument can be seen to hold for moments in time (and arguably does hold in South Africa today), it is a highly contingent relationship in an economic and labour market context which is changing fast.

A similar problem applies to one of the key arguments against fees: that universities are a public good. Universities develop knowledge for everyone – from cures for diseases to beautiful pieces of music – and educate people, such as teachers and nurses, who benefit society as a whole. Such a view can be seen as corroborated by research which finds higher education beneficial for economic growth (see, for example, Valero and Van Reenen 2016) and for social development including improved levels of health (see, for example, Furnée et al. 2008).

But '… the discourse on higher education finance has often ignored to discuss a threshold on the context-specific dimensions of cost-sharing' (Oketch 2016: 530). How would an appropriate threshold be determined? In other words, how big a higher education system should taxpayers, who only benefit indirectly and who have pressing immediate survival needs, be prepared to pay for? One obvious solution is to use academic achievement criteria to set a threshold, but this in fact plays into inequalities as school achievement is substantially predicted by socio-economic status. In South Africa only a tiny minority of students from income deciles one to seven qualify for higher education; the data is imperfect but the trends are very clear (Van den Berg 2015): in the main, the 20 per cent of an average age cohort who are at university are the richest 20 per cent of the cohort. Further, for poor countries in general, poverty interacts with gender inequality, to make poor women the least likely to access higher education (Ilie and Rose 2016). Academic merit also does not assist when larger and larger numbers of students qualify for higher education: on what grounds should fiscal allocations go to this and not to other social spending?

Neither the private nor the public good arguments provide a clear principled way of determining how many members of any given society should be funded by society as a whole to participate in university education.

The case for universal welfare is compelling. Means testing can be both humiliating for individuals and costly to administer. One particular problem with them is that student protestors have argued that the poor have a significantly different campus experience to the rich because of the number of administrative hurdles that they have to clear, and that such divisions between groups of students is contrary to the spirit of creating a student body unified around a common project of knowledge acquisition and development. But again, this does not assist us in thinking through why it is higher education and not, say, food or housing that should be supplied to everyone for free.

There are many competing demands on the fiscus, such as a national health service and a basic income grant, both of which would immediately benefit poor people who will never benefit directly from university education. As stated above, well over 80 per cent of students who qualify to apply for degree study come from the top two income deciles; there is minimal educational provision post-school for the remaining 80 per cent of the age cohort.

Even if we consider only the competing educational claims on the fiscus, the case for increasing higher education funding is contestable. Approximately 600 000 children finish school in South Africa each year, about 50 per cent of those who enrol in primary school; their options for continuing education lie in universities or technical and vocational colleges (TVET). There are limited educational opportunities available for those who don't complete or who fail school, mainly through what have recently been named 'community education colleges'. Currently there are about 1 112 000 enrolments in higher education (970 000 in public universities and 142 000 in private); 789 500 in TVET (710 500 in public and an estimated 79 000 in private); and about 275 300 in community colleges (DHET 2016). Government estimates that nearly 19 million South Africans of twenty years of age and older could benefit from the expansion and quality provision of community education and training programmes (DHET 2013; National Planning Commission 2011; Stats SA 2016).

Technical and vocational colleges are currently underfunded by 40 per cent in terms of the reported enrolment based on existing funding models. The community college sector, which remains little more than a vision, incorporates a chronically underfunded adult basic education sector barely able to function. The estimate of required funds to even set up a viable community education system for people unable to attend universities and TVET colleges is about R40 billion (DHET 2016).

The #FeesMustFall movement has not won any breakthrough to increase the size of the fiscus – only to redeploy funds. In practice, this has meant taking money away from social services for much poorer sections of the population. Activists inevitably distance themselves from this, and state that the fiscus can and should be increased. But the focus of the protests and demands has not been increasing the size of the fiscus ('We won't go back to class until the nuclear deal is cancelled') but increasing the size of the slice given to higher education.

South Africa could increase taxation progressively – since 2000 tax bracket adjustments have greatly exceeded inflation (Forslund 2012). And a huge amount is lost to corruption and vanity projects. Dealing with corruption is indisputably a pressing national priority, and Forslund's (2012) argument that much corruption could be prevented by building a stronger state and eliminating a tender-based system is compelling. But until this has been achieved money which has been stolen by corrupt officials is not available to be part of budget allocations or planning.

Regardless of whether the fiscus is increased, we need both principled (in terms of fairness) and practical (in terms of how it will actually work and the likely outcomes on the system) grounds for increasing the allocation given to higher education. One consideration mentioned above which invites further exploration is the interaction of higher education with changing labour markets.

GOOD AND BAD

Internationally, the last five decades – the same decades that have seen the international massification of higher education – have seen dramatically rising inequality. Data from many countries suggests that graduates have in the main benefited. Does this imply that increasing the number of university-educated people will lead to more people benefiting from higher wages? If this were the case, it would follow that massive expansion – requiring massive funding in a population of mainly poor people – would be a policy priority, but we may be confusing symptoms with causes if we reach this conclusion.

Education levels have risen faster than knowledge requirements in most jobs (Livingstone 2012) and technological change has not been the driving force in rising credential requirements (Collins 1979, 2013). Schofer and Meyer (2005: 900) point out that 'the rapid expansion of higher education in the 1960s does not coincide with especially large historical changes in occupational structures, job skill requirements, or labour market demands that would create a need for massive expansion of higher education'. The developed world has seen an increasing trend for graduates to take jobs previously seen as non-graduate – what Teichler (2009) calls 'almost' graduate jobs.

Is South Africa different? Bhorat et al. (2016) argue that the South African labour market is oversupplied with individuals with low levels of education, while there is, they suggest, a growing need for skilled individuals. They attribute this to erosion of the primary sector and growth in capital-intensive industries. Similarly, Makgetla (2016) argues that South Africa has a shortage of graduates relative to other middle-income countries.

'As enrolment at tertiary institutions has increased during the last decade, especially among black students, more young graduates have become unemployed' (Pauw et al. 2006: 22). But the conclusion reached by these and other South African economists is that the suggestion that content of the education system is inadequate for the needs of the labour market, and not that the labour market actually cannot absorb more labour.

Bhorat et al. (2016) based their argument for skill-biased growth partly on the sectors which are growing in the economy and partly on showing that labour market outcomes for graduates are better than for non-graduates. They also contend that in areas that do not require education workers with no education are being replaced by those with education. But this does not prove their argument; it merely shows that employers use education as a screening device. They also point out that there is growth in the 'technical' category, but that it has mainly been absorbing people with degrees. Their explanation for this is that there is inadequate preparation at vocational college level. But technicians are unlikely to be trained by universities. It seems more likely that what they are observing is a simple matter of qualification inflation in the context of a large reserve army of the unemployed.

Qualifications are not used only as an indicator of potential productivity, but also as a general screening device by employers. This leads to qualification inflation whereby potential workers are obliged to strive for higher and higher levels of qualifications to improve their place in the job queue. Moore (2004) demonstrates, for example, that in the UK over the course of the twentieth century absolute levels of education rose for all population groups – meaning that more working-class people acquired higher levels of education than ever before. But relative differences in educational attainment did not change at all over this period; middle-class people simply acquired higher levels of education. Similarly, in the US, one of the frontlines of higher education massification, degree-completion is heavily dominated by middle- and high-income families, and much enrolment at the relatively lower end of the socio-economic spectrum is in two-year community college programmes (Marginson 2016). Goldin and Katz (2007) classically showed in the USA the importance of the *relative* supply of skills over the course of the twentieth century as a major factor in shaping income inequality across more and less educated groups. In some periods, factors such as the unionisation of less-skilled groups also played a role.

Massification means many people are getting more higher education, but what they are getting is of varying quality, with contingent relationships with the labour market (Wheelahan 2016). In South Africa, one example of this is that students from wealthy backgrounds tend to enrol in the natural, mathematical, engineering and health sciences, and have considerably higher throughput rates, while their poorer counterparts are more likely to be enrolled for diploma programmes in business, commerce and the human or social sciences (Cosser 2015).

Labour market outcomes are shaped by socially determined rules which don't ignore but are not primarily about the qualities of individuals, including those qualities obtained through education. One clear sign that this is changing is higher education in the USA, where holding a PhD, the pinnacle of academic achievement, is no longer a guarantee of a permanent job or even a reasonably paying job (Newfield 2010). This should question any faith that increased levels of education improve salaries and working conditions because education in itself enhances productivity. Being very well qualified has not prevented the academic workforce in the USA from being casualised, because wages and job security are not only related to productivity – they are profoundly related to power. Creating a surplus of available workers is a well-established strategy of reducing the relative power of employees, and indeed Makgetla (2016) explicitly states that we should expand higher education in order to reduce the salaries of graduates.

Even if this were desirable, it is not clear that it will happen. As Keep and Mayhew (2014) argue in relation to the UK labour market, where there is a huge gap between the top-end and bottom-end occupations, there is an intense struggle for the good jobs. All education does in such a context is 'alter the number of competitors in the race' (Keep and Mayhew 2014: 772) without changing the rules of the game.

Sociological and economic analyses show that higher education can both reinforce stratification and counteract it, but it is more likely to play the former role. Riviera (2015: 3) argues: 'Higher education has become one of the most important vehicles of social stratification and economic inequality in the United States.' This is in line with the historical role of universities. Castells (2009) points out that universities have historically played three major roles in society: that of the production of social values and legitimation; the selection of elites; and the training of the labour force. As a societal function, selection of elites has been, Castells argues, more important than the other functions, despite the official goals being labour force training and research and innovation. Marginson argues while this creates a false impression of a meritocracy, it is a public good of sorts because it 'avoids an open violent struggle for social position in the manner of, say, the late Roman Republic' (Marginson 2011: 424). Similarly, Collins (1979, 2013) maintains that the main role education in general plays in liberal capitalist economies is absorbing surplus labour by entrenching the narrative that higher education is a necessity.

The ways in which higher education interacts with the reproduction of elites has changed with massification, and in some instances is calling into question the legitimacy of higher education as primary determinant of good labour market rewards. Some of these changes can be seen in the increased stratification within higher education – a symptom of which is the recent rise of international systems which attempt to rank universities according to certain criteria (Allais 2017). And we see a response in elite labour markets: of drawing ever-finer distinctions between institutions and programmes, and the introduction of mechanisms such as unpaid internships, study abroad programmes, and so on. As Castells (2009) points out, while the Ivy League institutions in the US, the *grandes écoles* in France, and Oxbridge in the UK may be of slightly higher quality than many other universities, and of dramatically higher quality than many more, it is implausible that these difference in quality can account for the fact that 90 per cent of the business and polity elites in these countries come from these universities. This has been described as a 'beauty competition' in which elite workplaces and top universities create a mutually reinforcing elite selection device which has the outward appearance of a meritocracy (Brown et al. 2011).

In some regards, the ways in which education interacts with labour markets has negative effects on individuals (and education systems, as it leads to constant pressure for curriculum reform). This does not mean that education is not also both a public and private good, but we need to be cautious about thinking that massive educational expansion and funding should be the primary focus of public policy.

On what grounds can decisions be made, then? One factor which has received insufficient attention in the various proposals for doing away with fees is the effects on the system of the models proposed. As two vice-chancellors contended in a national newspaper recently, not getting fee payments from the rich runs a 'risk of creating improved access to poor quality higher education' (Mabizela and Ballim 2016). Is this plausible?

EFFECTS ON THE SYSTEM

The South African higher education system is fragile, with the better institutions clinging marginally to international standards for education and research by placing enormous pressure on academic staff, and the other institutions clinging marginally to producing education and research of an almost adequate standard, with some of them in constant crisis, many highly unstable, with falling enrolments, high failure rates and management crises (DHET 2014).

Funding systems almost always have unintended consequences. One simple example is that when student enrolments form the main source of subsidy, institutions are incentivised to increase enrolments beyond capacity – and when subsidies are based on completion the incentive shifts to passing as many students as possible.

South African universities are public but fee-based, with a three-way funding model. The first component is the direct state subsidy, given on the basis of student enrolment, student graduation, research which is published in recognised outlets, and for specifically designated programmes and projects. The second component is student fees, which vary from institution to institution as public universities are autonomous. NSFAS provides financial assistance to very poor undergraduate students. Through this scheme, students' upfront fees are paid through a loan which is interest free while they are studying. Interest (below commercial lending rates) kicks in a year after successful completion. Students who complete in the minimum time have 60 per cent of their loan converted into a bursary. Students who do not complete, or who do not earn above the prescribed threshold, do not have to pay back their loan. By 2015, 16 per cent of undergraduate students were supported through NSFAS, and another 7 per cent of students obtained other types of financial support such as bursaries for trainee teachers (DHET 2016). There have been many practical problems with this scheme (some of which have improved in recent years) including weak management and corruption at university and national level; a low qualifying threshold which excludes students from lower middle-class families; and university practices of spreading the funding more thinly than the government allocation per student to accommodate more students, thereby leading to accumulating student debt. Further, NSFAS has covered only fees, not the full cost of study, leaving a large number of additional costs for very poor students, and leading to student hunger and homelessness (Ministerial Working Group 2013). A so-called third stream of income is obtained from donors, research grants, the beneficiation of intellectual property, university-owned enterprises, and others. This is not large in most universities.

The higher education system is relatively expensive compared to that of other countries, because of a low throughput rate: about 50 per cent of students who enrol in our universities drop out before graduation (DHET 2014). Compounding this is a weak schooling system (which make higher education and TVET even more expensive as they have to factor in remedial education) and the weakness of the TVET system which makes it an undesirable alternative to university education. It suggests that effective use of taxpayers' money would be better achieved by a substantial reduction of enrolments, thereby preventing large numbers of underprepared graduates and improving the quality of education (because of lower student to lecturer numbers). This, of course, could be argued to be unfair because of the relationship between socio-economic status and achievement at school.

It is widely maintained that South Africa underfunds its universities as a percentage of gross domestic product (GDP) (DHET 2014, 2016) although as Pillay (2016) points out these comparisons are complex and can be misleading depending on what kinds of education are included in the calculations, with which types of countries comparison is made, and whether comparisons of other types of spending are also included.

Although the percentage of spending on higher education has now (at the time of writing) increased, all universities are worse off than they were before the protests. The shortfall created by the 0 per cent increase of 2015 was funded in the richer universities partly from their own funds, leading to cuts in research budgets, post-doctoral positions, and so on. In poorer universities the DHET used an allocation intended for infrastructure at these same institutions, as well as an allocation of R800 000 000 which had been budgeted for support of the development of new black and female academics. Other government departments were top-sliced for the balance, in a fiscally constrained environment with an economy teetering on the brink of recession (DHET 2016). There have been many losses to the system caused by the protests, with damage to property estimated by the DHET at nearly a billion rands,[3] as well as an unquantifiable loss of teaching and learning time.

The numbers bandied about in popular debates about abolishing fees have centred around the DHET's estimate that, with current student numbers, removing fees for all undergraduate students would require about R70 billion a year, about R42 billion more than the current budget, with year-on-year increases for inflation and growth in the system (envisaged as approximately 10 per cent a year). But this is *only* the amount needed to cover what is currently paid for by fees. It also does not factor the cost of supporting poor students for the full cost of study (Ministerial Working Group 2013) – arguably a more important priority if equity is a key concern. It would not compensate for the historical erosion of systemic funding (DHET 2016). More crucially, it does not include the additional funding required by the system: for example, the funding required for student accommodation, estimated at about 300 000 new beds, or funds required to provide better student support, better care for rape victims (as well as systems for preventing rape), better and more accessible healthcare facilities, and so on.

Another practical difficulty with straight fiscus-based funding is wound up in the unpleasant reality of South Africa's past and present. Like higher education systems internationally, South Africa's higher education system is stratified. And while, as in all such hierarchies, there may be some aspects of prejudice and false perceptions at play, and some degree of self-fulfilling prophecies in which the best students and best staff seek out the institutions with the best reputations, what is not disputable is that there is dramatically varied quality across the institutions. A taxation-based system is easier to administer than a sliding arrangement of fees and financial aid, and avoids the stigmatisation of means-testing. But fee-based systems protect higher education from fiscal erosion, and enable the extraction of additional payments from the rich directly at the point of interface with the system, where they more likely to be willing to pay. The threat of fiscal erosion is not remote, as Cloete (2015a) demonstrates in research on African countries which provided free higher education with additional funds given to students for living expenses. This is one of the reasons that experts have suggested that taxation-based systems have proved very difficult to maintain (Barr 2004; Pillay 2016).

What complicates the debate in South Africa about how much money different institutions do get and how much they should get is that the hierarchy of institutions in South Africa is tied up with apartheid, so that the top universities were historically white and many of them still, today, have substantially larger proportions of white students than the proportions of white people in the population at large – and one of them, Stellenbosch, is still predominantly white with very low numbers of black African students. The bottom universities were historically black, set up as second-rate ethnically based colleges as part of the Bantu Education system. They still have almost entirely black student bodies, and enrol the poorest students. They need substantial additional funding to bring them up to standard, and some of them have been plagued by mismanagement and crisis.

The difference in fees across institutions maps to a considerable extent this hierarchy of perceived and actual quality: the most prestigious institution, UCT, has the highest fees. It is by no means to say that all courses at UCT are equally excellent, or that there are no excellent programmes at institutions with lower fees but on the whole the institutions providing better quality education charge more (however, the subsidy paid by the state per institution per student per field of study is the same).

A system which is purely fiscus-based, and in which there is no exchange of money at the point of registration to study, would give all institutions the same income. Institutions which cannot manage the funds they currently receive would get increased income; institutions which can manage the funds and are struggling to provide a reasonable standard of education would get increased income and potentially improve in quality; the institutions producing the most research and the best graduates would get substantially less income than they are able to in a fee-based system.

All of the above means at least three likely negative outcomes from a shift to a purely fiscus-based system:

- First, a reduction in the funds available to give more financial support to the poor, in terms of full cost of study, as well as funds available to provide better academic and social support to inadequately prepared students.
- Second, fiscal erosion is likely over time, and an underfunded system is likely to be the result, with worse conditions for students and staff overall. This would lead to staff leaving, and the most academically capable and the wealthiest students starting a flight towards private or overseas universities, which will in the long term greatly weaken public higher education in South Africa.
- Third, a fiscus-based system will provide all institutions with the same funding per student – but institutions are not the same. Activists will argue that the highest funding should be given to all, instead of the lowest, but it seems hard to make a case that the high fees levied by, say, UCT, could be paid for by the state for students to study at some of the more dysfunctional institutions. It would also be an unfair request to taxpayers – particularly in light of other fiscal priorities.

One possible alternative which deals with the first problem but not the second is a model similar to that in the UK, where fees are levied – thereby allowing different institutions to have different costs – but are not paid directly by students until they are working. This, however, is premised on funds being available upfront from the government. It is also likely to be rejected by student protestors as creating a burden of debt.

CONCLUSION

In the main, the principled arguments for fee-free university education take inadequate account of context, and the ways in which higher education interacts with labour markets in a context of extreme inequality, as well as not dealing adequately with other social priorities which affect more poor people more directly, and the likely effects on our universities. Policy solutions aimed at educational institutions and systems which do not address the root causes of inequality and poverty, and which assume that changing access to education (as well as the nature of education) is key to addressing inequality and poverty are likely to have negative consequences for education systems without disrupting, and potentially in some ways deepening, inequality. If the #FeesMustFall activists are unable to locate their struggles within a broader struggle which directly addresses inequality and poverty, they are simply engaged in an attempt to alter the relative power of different groups within an existing game, not changing the rules of the game. They could thus contribute both in the medium and long term to an overall worsening of South African universities as well as to inequalities in South African society, with a slight improvement in material conditions for one group of students in terms of basic survival, but deteriorating provision of education for this group and others.

While in principle the right thing to support is the goal of decommodification as well as for the need for universal services without means-testing, Oketch's (2016: 535) argument for flexible tuition fees supported by income-contingent loans in African countries – which could incorporate schemes based on graduates working in return for financial support while studying – seems the best medium-term solution in the absence of substantial change to the structure of the economy. There are very few signs that the South African state is capable of or interested in such change. The major opposition is a centre-right party focused above all on clean governance, with no clear vision for social and economic development outside of a neoliberal trajectory. Unfortunately, the absence of such policy change is likely to aggravate the feeling of generational betrayal experienced by the youth, leading to increasing focus on universities as the problem and potential solution. As Cloete (2015b) argues, the lower middle-class and poor students 'know that the development project has failed them. They also know they are not part of the "rainbow" group and, above all else, that the university, not the state, is their last chance of finding their way into the middle class.' In other words, pressure on the university system is going to increase, and a weak government inclined to short-term populist solutions may respond without regard for medium-term or long-term consequences. While skills shortages in key areas will remain, in general, labour markets are requiring more and more preparation for a lower and lower starting wage and for fewer and fewer available jobs. We could be headed for more government funding for small groups to produce no better labour market outcomes.

NOTES

1   By way of comparison, many fee charging public schools charge similar fees to those of the bottom end of the higher education system, while private school fees go up to R200 000 a year.
2   www.anc.org.za, accessed 31 January 2017.
3   https://www.dailymaverick.co.za/article/2017-01-26-blade-nzimande-hopes-2017-can-stabilise-higher-education, accessed 31 January 2017.

REFERENCES

Allais, S (2017) Towards measuring the economic value of higher education: Lessons from South Africa. *Comparative Education*, 53 (1), 147–163.
Barr, N (2004) Higher education funding. *Oxford Review of Economic Policy*, 20 (2), 264–283.
Bhorat, H, Cassim, A and Tseng, D (2016) Higher education, employment and economic growth: Exploring the interactions. *Development Southern Africa*, 33 (3), 312–327.
Booysen, S (ed.) (2016) *Fees must fall: Student revolt, decolonization, and governance in South Africa*. Johannesburg: Wits University Press.
Brown, P, Lauder, H and Ashton D (2011) *The global auction: The broken promises of education, jobs, and incomes*. Oxford: Oxford University Press.
Castells, M (2009) *The role of universities in development, the economy and society*. Lecture, University of the Western Cape.
Cloete, N (2015a) *The ideology of free higher education in South Africa: The poor and middle class subsidising the rich* (Kagisano No. 10. Student Funding). Pretoria: Council on Higher Education.
Cloete, N (2015b) *The third force in South African higher education activism*. Cape Town: CHET.
Collins, R (1979) *The credential society*. New York: Academic Press.
Collins, R (2013) The end of middle-class work: No more escapes. In I Wallerstein, R Collins, M Mann, G Derluguian and C Calhoun (eds) *Does capitalism have a future?* Oxford and New York: Oxford University Press. pp. 37–70.
Cosser, M (2015) *Differential pathways of South African students through higher education: Settling for less, but learning to like it*. Unpublished PhD thesis, University of the Witwatersrand, Johannesburg.
DHET (Department of Higher Education and Training) (2013) *White paper for post-school education and training: Building an expanded, effective and integrated post-school system*. Pretoria: DHET.
DHET (Department of Higher Education and Training) (2014) *Report of the ministerial committee for the review of the funding of universities*. Pretoria: DHET.
DHET (Department of Higher Education and Training) (2016) *Submission to the presidential commission on the feasibility of fee-free higher education and training*. Pretoria: DHET.
Forslund, D (2012) *Personal income taxation and the struggle against inequality and poverty: Tax policy and personal income taxation in South Africa since 1994*. Cape Town: Alternative Information and Development Centre.

Furnée, CA, Groot, W and van den Brink, HM (2008) The health effects of education: A meta-analysis. *The European Journal of Public Health*, 18 (4), 417–421.

Goldin, C and Katz, LF (2007) *The race between education and technology: The evolution of US educational wage differentials, 1890 to 2005*. Working Paper 12984. Cambridge, MA: National Bureau of Economic Research.

Ilie, S and Rose, P (2016) Is equal access to higher education in South Asia and sub-Saharan Africa achievable by 2030? *Higher Education*, 72 (4), 435–455.

Keep, E and Mayhew, K (2014) Inequality – 'wicked problems', labour market outcomes and the search for silver bullets. *Oxford Review of Education*, 40 (6), 764–781.

Livingstone, DW (2012) Debunking the "knowledge economy". The limits of human capital theory. In DW Livingstone and D Guile (eds) *The knowledge economy and lifelong learning. A critical reader*. Rotterdam: Sense. pp. 85–116.

Mabizela, S and Ballim, Y (2016) Populism will be the death of decent higher education for the poor. *Business Day Live*. 15 August. Retrieved from http://www.bdlive.co.za/opinion/2016/08/15/populism-will-be-the-death-of-decent-higher-education-for-the-poor.

Makgetla, NS (2016) Four workable fees options to open university access. *Rand Daily Mail*. 16 August. Retrieved from http://www.rdm.co.za/business/2016/08/16/four-workable-fees-options-to-open-university-access.

Marginson, S (2011) Higher education and public good. *Higher Education Quarterly*, 65 (4), 411–433.

Marginson, S (2016) The worldwide trend to high participation higher education: dynamics of social stratification in inclusive systems. *Higher Education*, 72 (4), 413–434.

Ministerial Working Group (2013) *Report of the working group on free university education for the poor in South Africa*. Pretoria: Department of Higher Education and Training.

Moore, R (2004) *Education and society: Issues and explorations in the sociology of education*. Cambridge: Polity.

National Planning Commission (2011) *National development plan. Vision for 2030*. Pretoria: Republic of South Africa, Presidency.

Newfield, C (2010) The structure and silence of the cognitariat. *Edu-Factory Web Journal*, 2010 (January), 10–26.

Oketch, M (2016) Financing higher education in sub-Saharan Africa: Some reflections and implications for sustainable development. *Higher Education*, 72 (4), 525–539.

Pauw, K, Oosthuizen, M and van der Westhuizen, C (2006) Graduate unemployment in the face of skill shortages: A labour market paradox. Conference paper presented at *Accelerated and shared growth in South Africa: Determinants, constraints and opportunities*, 18–20 October 2006, Birchwood Hotel and Conference Centre Johannesburg, South Africa.

Pillay, P (2010) *Higher education and economic development*. Cape Town: Centre for Higher Education Transformation.

Pillay, P (2016) Financing of universities: Promoting equity or reinforcing inequality. In S Booysen (ed.), *Fees must fall: Student revolt, decolonization, and governance in South Africa*. Johannesburg: Wits University Press. pp. 256–268.

Psacharopoulos, G (1994) Returns to investment in education – a global update'. *World Development Update*, 22 (9), 1325–1343.

Riviera, LA (2015) *Pedigree: How elite students get elite jobs*. Princeton, NJ: Princeton University Press.

Schofer, E and Meyer, JW (2005) The worldwide expansion of higher education in the twentieth century. *American Sociological Review*, 70, 898–920.

Stats SA (Statistics South Africa) (2016) *2015 general household survey*. Pretoria: Stats SA.

Teichler, U (2009) *Higher education and the world of work: Conceptual frameworks, comparative perspectives, empirical findings*. Rotterdam: Sense.

Trow, M (2000) *From mass higher education to universal access: The American advantage*. Research and Occasional Paper Series: CSHE.1.00. San Francisco: Berkeley.

Valero, A and Van Reenen, J (2016) *The economic impact of universities: Evidence from across the globe*. Working Paper 22501. Cambridge, MA: National Bureau of Economic Research.

Van den Berg, S (2015) *Funding university studies: Who benefits?* Kagisano No. 10. Student Funding. Pretoria: CHE.

Wheelahan, L (2016) "College for all" in Anglophone countries – meritocracy or social inequality? An Australian example. *Research in Post-Compulsory Education*, 21 (1–2), 33–48.

CHAPTER 9

Education, the state and class inequality: The case for free higher education in South Africa

Enver Motala, Salim Vally and Rasigan Maharajh

The state of tumult in our universities continued at the end of 2016, despite the announcement by the minister of higher education that the 8 per cent increase in fees demanded by universities would be subsidised by the state. The amendments to the national budget at the end of October did not deal with the fundamental challenges, but referred only to the implications for funding of the no-fee increase and the additional funding allocated to augment the National Student Financial Aid Scheme (NSFAS) to provide for the 'missing middle' (RSA 2016). The national budget did not address the key demand for publicly funded education for all – not even fee-free education for the poor. A significant amount of the increase will be provided to the NSFAS. Hart (2016: 1) – distinguished professor at Wits University – reminds us that:

> The failure of state funding to keep pace with growing student numbers has generated the cruel arithmetic of steadily increasing fees. Far from providing a solution, NSFAS is a part of a vicious circle through which inadequate government funding drives up fees, necessitating more support for low-income students. Furthermore, this support is by definition inadequate to the extent that increasing the NSFAS comes at the expense of direct funding to universities, and thus pushes up fees even further. It is little wonder, then, that many black university students feel as though they have been handed a poisoned chalice.

For the year 2015–2016, South Africa's state budget for universities, including funding for NSFAS, continued its decline to 0.72 per cent of gross domestic product (GDP) (RSA 2016: 7), considerably below the international average and even less than the continental average despite the growth of student numbers.[1] This chronic underfunding of tertiary education and the ongoing protests and police/private security reaction raised the ire of hundreds of academics who staged a national day of action on 7 October 2016. They demanded an increase of at least 1.5 per cent of the GDP towards directly funding tertiary education, pointing out that the government has created a funding crisis at universities. Underfunding, they argued, has also led to a reduction in student and academic support programmes, high lecturer-student ratios and large class sizes – and has negatively affected the quality of education.

Higher education in South Africa is chronically underfunded and has been the subject of much criticism (DHET 2014). The minister of higher education has accepted the need to access additional resources for higher education. Indeed, the commission of inquiry into higher education and training (henceforth 'the Fees Commission') appointed by the president will inevitably be required to examine this issue carefully. Similarly, the existence of egregious levels of social inequality in South Africa requires little further elaboration as South Africa consistently ranks among the most unequal societies on earth (Southall 2016).

Yet, there are, as we shall argue, important misconceptions in some of the arguments about the chronic underfunding of education and the phenomenon of social inequality as it affects 'poor' and 'middle' class access to higher education. These misconceptions can lead to narrow conceptualisations of the role of higher education and its relationship to social systems. The questions raised by students and other participants in the struggles around education are not simply about education alone, nor can they be resolved solely by better education policies, plans and strategies, or by merely increasing state budgets for the higher education system.[2] There are more fundamental considerations because in reality the student struggles raise questions about the very nature of the 'decolonisation' and 'transformation' of post-apartheid society and how 'national development' and its political, socio-economic and cultural goals are to be realised.

In this chapter we concentrate on one issue alone – the debate around the question of free higher education and whether it should be provided for the 'poor' or more universally 'for all'. We know that there is a raft of other issues that have been raised in the recent events around the role and purposes of universities, bringing into focus conceptions of the decolonising of the university and simultaneously of its curriculum, forms of leadership and management, the racism and gender violence which has characterised university life at many campuses, outsourcing of work, the commodification of knowledge and the limited nature of its conceptions of scholarship and pedagogy, together with issues about intra-institutional inequality, matters concerning the governance of institutions, the 'culture' of universities, language and other pertinent issues.[3]

Ours is a more focused examination relating to the interpretations of what might be included in any remit about the costs of education.[4] The focus on this issue is central to the debates, not only about the transformation of universities but also about its relationship to social change, inequality and society more generally. As we will show, the underlying rationale for opposing free higher education for all is misconstrued. These misdirected approaches are reliant on an assessment of the quantum of available government finances for higher education in South Africa, and reflect a particular orientation to the role of education in society. In our view, this opposition to a more universal approach to free education reflects a particular perspective about the form of social reorganisation that is prefigured through it.[5]

Although we draw on the South African experience in particular to illustrate our arguments we have no doubt that in the context of the debates about higher education globally our approach to these issues has much wider application and meaning. Contestation around higher education and its social role is not unique to South Africa, either historically or at this time. Over the last few years there have been similar stirrings and public protest in many countries. These struggles are not only about the rising costs of higher education but also raise questions that go to the core of the socio-cultural and intellectual project that is represented by the process of knowledge production and its dissemination in society – and in particular about the role of the institutions of higher education in that regard.

We approach this issue from the perspective of alternative social choices, values and purposes – not only for education but as a precondition for the realisation of the broader purposes of a democratic society. Discussions about education are inseparable from an examination of the dominance of those approaches that have disengaged education from its broader social remit, either deliberately or by omission. We are critical of the reduction of educational issues to the remit of economic ends alone. Such instrumental approaches arise from the paralysing discourses about education as a 'human resource', avoiding any focus on the relationship between education and social relations.

We begin with an examination of the arguments of the proponents of the view that free higher education is not achievable for all. Two fundamental arguments support this view. They refer firstly to the quantum of financial resources available to the higher education ministry and secondly to the argument about privileging an entrenched minority of 'rich' students.

THE ARGUMENTS AGAINST FEE FREE 'FOR ALL'

In an article entitled 'The flawed ideology of "free higher education"', Cloete (2015a) argues that despite its 'revolutionary appeal' the idea of free education is both 'financially impossible and morally wrong, as free higher education privileges the rich'[6] in the context of a developing country. He argues in favour of 'affordable' higher education for all, making a case for differential costs for separate groups of students, supposedly addressing inequality through such an approach. He points to the distinction between the idea of 'free higher education for the poor' and 'for all' and asks whether the latter is achievable, answering as follows:

> The short answer is: *'No, and there is not enough money in any developing country for free higher education.'* … The examples they usually cite are Norway, Finland and Germany – the richest and most developed countries in Europe – but never Africa or Latin America.[7]

Cloete examines government's contribution to the costs of education relative to students' contribution, and provides data about the comparative expenditures for higher education in various countries. He points to the reality that the proportion of the GDP spend on higher education in South Africa is markedly below that of many other developing economies, let alone developed ones.

Cloete proposes the establishment of what he calls a 'war room',[8] inter alia, to deal with systemic inefficiencies and the prescribing of higher fees for the 'rich' since 'for the rich, higher education in South Africa is a bargain' (Cloete 2015b: 9).' He strongly prescribes support for the 'missing middle' to avoid 'Arab Spring type uprisings' and because '[T]he "missing middle" is not only the backbone of higher education worldwide, but a productive and well-educated middle class is also the glue that holds society together' (Cloete 2015b: 10).

Elsewhere, drawing on neoclassical economics and human capital theory, he asserts that the undergraduate education system is 'too expensive', unable to produce 'highly skilled graduates (to drive down the exorbitant rates of return); neither can it absorb large numbers of successful (academically and materially) poor students'. For Cloete (2016a: 4), the present mode of funding of higher education 'is not only morally questionable, but also a lose-lose situation for the poor students and the economy'.

Vice-chancellors, too, have aligned themselves with the pro-free education 'for the poor' approach while rejecting the wider approach of free education for all instead of making common cause with the latter's advocates or even remaining open to these views. Habib and Mabizela's (2016) orientation is to call on the private sector to 'better fund our students, to partner with government and universities so that we can collectively generate the high-level skills and knowledge we need to move our economy forward'. They berate those who ignore the 'many concessions' made by government and the universities concerning funding (Habib and Mabizela 2016: 3).

Minister Nzimande has supported the idea of free education for poor students unequivocally and has made public pronouncements about this issue on several occasions. For Nzimande too, the idea of free higher education for all is simply 'impossible' (Shange 2016) and, moreover, 'populist'.

> You can't have free higher education for everyone in a capitalist society … That would be saying that as I, as a minister, government must pay for my child … I must pay for it myself because I can afford it … You would be taking money from the poor to subsidise the rich. That is my view.

A CRITIQUE OF ARGUMENTS AGAINST FREE EDUCATION 'FOR ALL'

The argument about fiscal limits

The first of these arguments is based on assertions about the limits of the quantum of money required to support those who had previously been excluded from higher education by apartheid. It rests on the assumption that there simply is not enough money to do anything other than what is envisaged by NFSAS expanded to cover the 'missing middle' and other contingent costs. It is against free higher education for all but not supported (to the best of our knowledge) by any empirical evidence about affordability. In effect, we are simply asked to accept the unqualified assertion that it is unaffordable on the grounds, inter alia, that it would be fiscally reckless since there is no likelihood of expanded fiscal provision through the prevailing tax base; poor economic growth; and the competing demands on the state's resources. Even in the most advanced capitalist economies, it is argued, not everyone is enabled to achieve higher education and there are other institutional issues pointing to the alleged failure of universities to manage resources effectively. In other words, unaffordability is arrived at without any examination of the state's resource capabilities except in relation to the present allocation for higher education in particular and without reference to how and what choices are made by institutions in the distribution of state and other resources. It is simply an assertion based on what could be presently allocated by the fiscus. There is no rigorous scrutiny of the underlying premises of the fiscal strategy. In effect, we are left with no more than a pragmatic response and the judgement that the call for free education is not possible. And yet there are always resources for other choices made by government. These include the purchase of weapons, vanity projects such as World Cup soccer stadiums and costly investments in non-renewable energy generation.

We believe that the issue of student fees is much less about such pragmatic approaches, and uncritically restricts higher education's role to what might be achieved on the basis of the quantum of resources available in an untransformed pattern of state expenditure. We think that a perspective less submissive to fiscal realism (and pointing to the reformulation of social goals especially, as these concern the 'case for higher education') is necessary – whatever its complexities. This would require an interrogation of the state's fiscal capacity more broadly; a critical examination of its political and social choices and processes and an examination of what interests are dominant in present policy and practice. The fallibility of the claims about unaffordability lies in their inability to ask the question about what goals need to be achieved – that is, about the nature of the society envisaged in the prescriptions about fiscal rectitude. Whether free education is unaffordable is hardly a neutral or technical determination. Arguments by Cloete (2016a; 2016b) and others about the chronic underfunding of higher education do not seek to fundamentally examine the responsibility of democratic states regarding the provision of education. They accept the theoretical and policy imperatives of the ideas of fiscal discipline untrammelled by a critical examination of its underlying ideological, political and social premises, negating the possibilities for any meaningful social change.

The comparisons to postcolonial states are devoid of any contextual or historical analysis because they ignore the body of contemporary and historical writings which examines the impact of colonisation and post-colonial economic, financial, trade and other regimes on post-colonial governments in Africa and elsewhere. Even a perfunctory reading of these texts about 'how the west destroyed the global South's best shot at development' (Hickel 2016) will show how the objectives of postcolonial nationalist and other governments were ruined by a host of structural adjustment and other policies led by global lending agencies supported by the power and military capabilities of predatory Northern states. Hickel reminds us:

> After the end of European colonialism in Africa and Asia, and with the brief cessation of US intervention in Latin America, developing countries were growing incomes and reducing poverty at a rapid pace. Beginning in the 1950s, countries like Guatemala, Indonesia, and Iran drew on the Keynesian model of mixed economy that had been working so well in the west. They made strategic use of land reforms to help peasant farmers, labour laws to boost workers' wages, tariffs to protect local businesses, and resource nationalisation to help fund public housing, healthcare, and education. This approach – known as 'developmentalism' – was built on the twin values of economic independence and social justice. It wasn't perfect, but it worked quite well.

Hickel refers to Robert Pollin's research showing that these 'developmentalist' policies gave rise to sustained growth rates of 3.2 per cent for at least two decades. They provided a check on the appetite of multinational corporations for cheap labour, raw materials and an easy access to the type of consumer markets that characterised colonial rule.

Cloete and others pay little attention to the considerable arguments about the larger developmental role of education in democratic states, arguments once made by some of the purveyors of the views now referring to fiscal considerations a priori. The arguments made in the 'case for higher education' often pointed to the complicity of weak clientilist postcolonial states trapped in the ideological presuppositions of global policy advisory and financing institutions. These included the commodification of education and user-pays ideas, subverting the public good and using global corporate capital power over nation states, trade regimes and financial systems (Mamdani 1993).

Long before Piketty (2015) provided the evidentiary material for the rise of global inequality there was already a great deal of consternation about the impact of the World Bank and International Monetary Fund policies on education. The underlying ideology of the approach adopted by the opponents of fee-free education for all (whether they realise it or not) is echoed by the policy pronouncements of governments whose choices are dictated by a particular orientation to macroeconomic policies. These policies prioritise cost containment regardless of its consequences for the delivery of public goods, and generally favour the role of private capital against the interests of the poor and marginalised communities. Certain types of mega-capital projects funded by the state are not struck by the considerations of limited resources, while others are. The logical consequences of austerity approaches applied to public services are their privatisation and an erosion of their capacity to fulfil their public mandate. It is appropriate therefore to ask the following questions: Is the global corporate world less powerful now? Are the prescriptions of the neoliberal regimes less prevalent? Is state capture by market fundamentalism less pronounced and is inequality less egregious? What exactly is the conceptual basis for the *volte face* in the perspective of those erstwhile exponents of the ideas of 'public good' who now proclaim the cause of fiscal rectitude and rebuke those who are 'irresponsible' for seeking free public education for all?

The idea of limited resources is itself based on a particular history of economic orthodoxy in support of corporate capital. These neoliberal policies are never open to proper interrogation and public and democratic scrutiny as they are mostly driven and planned by a coterie of officials, bureaucrats and consultants who have little knowledge of and interest in citizenship and democratic rights or about the role of a democratic state in its delivery of public goods and services, including education. The justification for these macroeconomic policy approaches lies in the ideological flagship of neoliberal dogma derived largely from a particular interpretation of neoclassical economic theory (Harvey 2010; Ha-Joon 2014).

The critical issue for us is not simply about the funding of education as an end in itself but as essential to the achievement of the socio-political, cultural and transformative goals of a society. Interventions by the state towards the full cost of education must be seen as a lever for wider social ends, as even the fullest funding of education will not by itself resolve the contradictions of post-apartheid/racial capitalism in South Africa. Policies that are designed to provide for the full cost of study are essential to the goals of a democratic and socially just society. Educationists and other critical thinkers can show the way towards such a society by pointing to the relationship between the wider view of education and training and the necessary goals of democratic social transformation – an issue we return to later.

Against selective affirmation

The second and related argument is about free higher education for the poor rather than for all (which would ostensibly disadvantage the poor and privilege the rich). This argument is ultimately based on an interpretation of the state's role in engendering the affirmation of historically disadvantaged individuals so that more such individuals are provided access to an expanded middle class – an approach, as we will show, that is ultimately selective and misconstrues the wider role of education in society. It argues that class mobility is necessary for poor students and not for rich ones who are already mobile by virtue of their class status. Ancillary to the above argument is that as it stands higher education is for privileged members of society and free education for all will further privilege them.

Somewhat ironically, this reasoning is consciously about the need to augment the middle class by supporting entry into it by those who have in the past been excluded from it. The concern about widening the relative advantage of the middle classes is in effect ostensibly resolved by providing greater access to that very class by increasing the numerical proportion of black middle classes relative to that which exists historically. This process of 'affirming' those who will now enter this social class, we have to assume, is acceptable – indeed desirable – for those who were forcibly excluded by history. In that sense it is avowedly about the creation of a middle class and not about how unequal social relations are reproduced; not about whether social class differentiation is itself desirable in the first instance or whether these relations need to be reconsidered more fundamentally. In effect it is about the continued application of the present approaches to affirmative action without reference to its contradictions (Alexander 2013).

The present approaches to affirmation are simply inadequate in their conceptualisation and in practice. Few students who don't come from private or well-resourced urban schools make the grade for admission into university courses, and even fewer for some highly prized courses. It is ultimately a proportionately small percentage of poor students who gain entry to the first year of study at universities.

Besides the historical and context-related issues there is a host of costs and other difficult hurdles for working-class urban and rural families – predominantly black students. These not only bar access to higher education but also – as the throughput figures show – result in high rates of exclusions *after admission*, based on 'push-out' for debt, unpaid fees, social, psychological and other conditions that affect even those who have managed to secure admission into the first year of study.[9] In effect, those who do make it are a relatively small minority of the poor since, as is generally agreed, the financial resources needed for higher levels of admission are simply not available beyond a certain defined limit.

Consequently, fiscal latitude alone will have a limited effect on the question of access for the poor in the absence of a more thoroughgoing approach to restructured social relations. The support for a limited reorganisation of social relations (largely based on colour criteria and even more limited in relation to gender and geographic location), is an argument essentially about widening access to (nonracial) middle-class status. This approach, as one can see, is about upward social mobility for a select number based on affordability and interprets social affirmation without reference to the wider considerations of historical justice or the reconceptualisation of social relations more fundamentally. It is not dissimilar to that in social systems where meritocratic social policies prevail – in which merit (attained and recognised by dint of higher education, tenacity, business sense, hard work and other such attributes) allegedly provides the opening to limitless opportunities. Such an approach moreover is based on the idea that 'people's success in life depends primarily on their individual talents, abilities, and effort' and that those who don't make it fail because of the 'bad choices' they make. In reality though, even this selective affirmative and funding approach is hardly generous as the record of the NSFAS and its limitations has shown. The policies and process of affirming those students who are poor (and the criteria for this have been the subject of criticism), continues to limit access even to the very students for whom it is intended, since fees alone are only a part of the costs associated with the opportunity for higher education.

These distracting approaches therefore constitute a barrier to the fundamental question about what role education might have in a social system that must be radically transformed. In our view, even if a small minority of parents has the resources, that can hardly be a major criterion for national planning, or obviate the necessity for free public education.[10] These policies are largely for a small and selected minority of the population – in this case an admittedly wider but nevertheless socially defined aspirant middle class. We leave aside for the moment the complaint that in fact the present reality in respect of affirmative action is even more limited and that – since it is dispensed largely on the basis of patronage – it is often the preserve of those called 'tenderpreneurs' and in effect to a select few individuals and families.

Whatever the philanthropic or ethically penitent imperatives of the prescriptions about supporting the poor (as envisaged in the arguments of those opposed to fee-free for all), they are no less a seductive trap since they avoid the more fundamental issue of social redistribution and equality. The real problem with the selective affirmation approach is its failure to reckon with a framework of values that is inherent in all class, gender, racist and geographic conceptions of access to public good – such as in the case of privatised education – even with the most liberal curriculum. The problem, therefore, with the fee-free for the poor approach is that its effect would be to entrench class and social division more firmly and permanently in society.

Upward social mobility may or may not itself be a problem. Without the necessary social agency of students, academics, community activists and all those socially conscious and committed to an alternative society (and a clearer conceptualisation of the role of education in that), instability in the public education system; the conflict between institutional managers, students and parents; the closure of institutions; the sacrifice of learning time; and a whole host of other negative effects are assured.

THE ALTERNATIVE – DEMOCRATIC SOCIAL AND POLITICAL CHOICE

Education has the pre-eminent role in the development of public consciousness and value systems and is the process of generating new knowledge useful for engagement about social, scientific and environmental issues together with the competencies necessary for participation in complex modern societies and the skills required for socially useful livelihoods and work. Ideas about efficiency and effectiveness are much too often predicated on a particular reading of the value and purposes of education and a set of assumptions intent on ascribing the principal (sometimes exclusive) defining role to considerations of economic and fiscal efficiency. Ironically, these accounts of the role and purposes of education sometimes refer to a framework of rights – even constitutional rights – even while they interpret these in ways that are limited to a juridical discourse, mystifying its real purposes in a welter of rhetorical declamations.

Our approach is based on a different conceptualisation of why free higher education is necessary. Its starting point is neither selective affirmation nor fiscal stringency. Fiscal considerations are not determined a priori to trump democratic social choice, and social policy is not dependent solely on an examination of fiscal responsibility abstracted from any discussion about social and political choice. Fiscal questions are not ignored but placed in their proper place following determinations arising from questions about the nature of society envisioned and what role education and other social rights would play in arriving at such a society. Most importantly, we defer to a set of democratic, political and social choices which arise from an ecological, humanistic and solidaristic philosophy based on some fundamental considerations.

The public good represented by public education is not simply about a pro-poor approach or limited by the tenets of constitutionalism, since we problematise the very issues which are largely avoided by pro-poor approaches – issues about social class, racism, gender discrimination and oppressive social relations and power. We seek to further democratise decisions concerning the overall issues of planning and the use of resources. We favour a concept of citizenship which engenders ideas about cooperation, collegiality, social sharing, social responsibility and caring – and not the conceptions of citizenship that reduces them to 'subjects' or 'clients'. Our view is predicated on the idea of social equalisation and not on selective affirmation. We regard education from its earliest stages as necessary to a range of intellectual and social attributes to enable citizens to develop meaningful, productive and socially useful relationships, knowledges and lives for themselves, their communities and the nation. Most importantly this approach seeks to bring all of society – not only the historically disadvantaged – into the process of social reorganisation. It implicates those who are presently endowed with wealth in the process of social reorganisation, and those who are not. Such reorganisation depends on wealth redistribution through a systemic focus on the nature, causes and effects of inequality in society. It regards universities and other educational institutions, the agency of students, academics and all those seeking alternatives to the present, as critical to this process. It does not regard class, racialised and gendered relations as a given, but places these very relations under scrutiny. It is therefore not based on the continuities of class relations by virtue of the affirmation of some, and not the majority, in society.

This approach also seeks to problematise the relationship between the state and global corporate capitalism, while advancing ideas about inclusive social relations not based on privilege and the effects of racism, class, gendered oppression and exploitation. We are critical of the narrower commodification and managerialist ideologies relating to the availability of public goods and the processes of privatisation accompanying them. These ideologies trump and reshape the capacity of the state to favour the hand of market mechanisms (or so-called 'public-private partnerships') in ways that insert the agendas of private gain into the domain of public good and open the door to 'user-pays' approaches to the provision of services to a democratic citizenry.

Our orientation is likely to attract the charge of naivety, a charge sometimes laced with false pragmatic solutions and derisive criticisms about left-wing ideas, which are impossible to achieve in practice, referring to the ideological position of those who are charged with such naivety, while simultaneously proclaiming their own innocence in this regard. In some ways we regard the stance taken by such realists as much more damaging to the possibilities for transformation than of the adherents of right-wing ideologies. The criticisms against fee-free higher education for all represent not only a failure of the political and social imagination but also an abandonment of the critical intellect. It is unremittingly subservient to the given framework of social relations which it regards as unassailable. Supposedly pragmatic approaches serve only the predilections of conservative approaches, deepening existing relations of power and inequality. The alternatives we propose are about setting a conceptual framework around which practical possibilities can be built. They are not about the seizure of power but about the mobilisation of public will and democratic accountability as a minimum condition for possibilities toward transformation. They provide a framework for thinking more rigorously, philosophically and politically about universal free education and the provision of the full costs of study as a constitutive condition for democracy and the public good.

WHAT CAN BE DONE?

We set out several proposals that could be considered, based on our submission to the Fees Commission. Subsequent to our submission, several significant and considered submissions aligned to the 'free education for all' approach were assembled, including proposals by #WitsFeesMustFall and Equal Education.[11]

We are fully cognisant that fee-free higher education *by itself* cannot resolve the contradictions wrought on society by corporate global capitalism and its social consequences, but we regard these proposals as important both symbolically and in practice because they provide an alternative framework for thinking about the role of education in society, and they give content to a set of transitional demands which can widen access to higher education especially for working-class and rural communities. To that extent, they could be useful to prise open the possibilities for achieving the broader social goals envisaged here and push back the dominant neoliberal approaches to policy and practice.

1. One approach to public funding of university education could be based on a set of fairly simple principles, and we draw on various writers on this subject (Moss 2015). For instance, it could be agreed that no student who meets the requirements for admission to a university course should be excluded for financial reasons. Students should be funded for the costs of study which should cover registration and other fees, costs of meals and accommodation, travel and books. In addition, universities should receive a subsidy per student from public funds which is sufficient for its recurrent operations – to ensure what has been called both financial and epistemic access to university education.

2. A determined state could reasonably rethink (for instance) the structure of personal taxation which could be levied for the very top income earners in the country. This income bracket could generate a substantial increase in available public

revenue.[12] An approach which concentrates on the structural aspects of inequality and uses tax revenues for the purpose is preferable to the idea of a differentiated approach to the rich and poor. It supports the idea that those identified with the top 'net-worth' pay for their children's education through taxation, and the distribution of public funds, rather than through an individually based 'wealthy-user-pays' model. Contrary to the dominant view, user-pays mechanisms are consistent with market-led approaches to the commodification of education. They do not equalise the costs of education between rich and poor, and are in fact punitive for the poor. The view that the rich can afford to pay fees obfuscates the larger issue of transforming social relations. The approach we suggest is also a more democratic model of public interest and public funding than individual philanthropy or subsidy. We do not here set out the more detailed arguments around approaches to taxation but would refer in this regard to the ideas set out by Forslund (2015) and Rudin (2015).[13] The further implication of this approach is that all students are regarded as beneficiaries of public funding and participants in a system prioritising the public good. As such, students should be expected to contribute to society when leaving university – possibly through community service and by working in public institutions after graduation. In effect, equal participation in the benefits of public funding by virtue of citizenship would support the creation of socially cohesive attitudes among students. Such an alternative approach to that seeking to differentiate between rich and poor students would have consequences for far-reaching structural and systemic change.

3. The government needs to increase the funding by at least an aggregate amount equal to the ratio achieved in the Organisation for Economic Cooperation and Development (OECD) countries to address the chronic underfunding of the higher education system.

4. Consideration must be given to the difference between a progressive realisation of the goal of free higher education for all, relative to a deliberate or gradualist approach. A determination should be made about the exact time frame for the achievement of fee-free education for all, together with the relevant milestones to be achieved for that purpose. In other words, such an approach will ensure a set of binding covenants about the achievement of free education for all, the effective mechanisms by which this would be achieved and the process for its monitoring. Here the approach adopted in Article 13 of the United Nations International Covenant on Economic, Social and Cultural Rights is instructive. Article 13.2 recognises not only the availability of free education in the primary education but also:

> Secondary education in its different forms, including technical and vocational secondary education, shall be made generally available and accessible to all by every appropriate means, and in particular by the progressive introduction of free education; (c) Higher education shall be made equally accessible *to all, on the basis of capacity, by every appropriate means, and in particular by the progressive introduction of free education.*[14]

5. The idea of 'progressive' should be interpreted more meaningfully as we have suggested – and not left to the caprice of individual policy decision makers without reference to a deliberate approach.

6. Dedicated research must be undertaken about costs of quality public education – from early childhood to higher education – and especially to facilitate and open debate to show what democratic choices could be made informing fiscal and other policy decisions about the provision of education and other public goods and the potential sources of such funding – including through, but not limited to, a system of wealth taxes. Such research could examine these issues comparatively.

7. Similarly, and in order to place the right to free education for all in its proper social context, serious consideration might be given to the idea of responsible public service and citizen work by the recipients of its benefits. This could, if applied consistently, engender greater social consciousness about the important relationship between knowledge and society and especially its role in resolving some of the intractable social and environmental issues facing all societies. Such a 'fellowship' would not only develop forms of social solidarity but develop a new consciousness beyond the narrow and largely self-interested limits imposed by the requirements of the formal job market.

We do not pretend that these goals are achievable immediately. The approach adopted towards the stated goals – democratically and socially driven – would be based on a process to get there and be dependent on both the social and political agency required. Especially important would be the avoidance of choices left to 'experts,' 'advisers' 'consultants' and the agents of global institutions. Indeed, the failure to reckon openly with the extraordinary power and dominance of global corporate interests in shaping both the agenda for public education and the values which these foster and reproduce would result inevitably in a continuation of social inequality, oppressive relations and catastrophic environmental effects. The perspectives of those most affected by the policy choices related to higher education as a public good must be properly engaged. This would call for colloquiums, dialogues, workshops and debates at every university with communities that are outside the university to broaden the impact of democratic dialogue and alternative visions and practices. In such discussions, questions about the wider role of higher education in relation to a more rigorous conception of social transformation (or 'decolonisation') would be central.

The protests on campuses during 2016, even if sometimes inchoate, are no less than a demand for a different society – one based on a fundamentally different set of values from the values that are pervasive and dominant in social systems driven by globalised corporate capitalism – greed, the commodification of all social goods, the destruction of public assets, and the generation of rampant social-economic inequality and dystopia. We reiterate the importance of the public good attributes of higher education, and reject the neoliberal assumptions and attempts to commodify education.

Flooding campuses with security force personnel is not a sustainable solution and strengthens the hand of those who are frustrated and desperate. We unequivocally condemn arson, including the torching of buildings and libraries, but reject equating legitimate protests with arson. Demonising those who support free education does not bring us closer to a sustainable solution. Hundreds of students have been imprisoned and many suspended without due process simply on suspicion of involvement in these acts. This merely aggravates frustration and contributes to a vicious cycle of violence. Elsewhere we wrote that:

> Neither smoke from police stun grenades, burning buildings nor officialdom's smoke and mirrors will solve the problem … It is clear to us that very little will be resolved without reference to this critical demand [of free education]. All the minister has done is to kick the can further down the road, deepening students' disquiet and provoking conflict on campuses.[15]

Times of social upheaval and change call for creative and imaginative leadership. Thus far we have seen a spectacular failure of imagination and a forlorn and unfortunate resort to the apartheid-era practice of *kragdadigheid*. It failed then and it will fail now. We need to be deeply concerned with the complex questions of *how* and *when* universal free and quality public education from early childhood education to higher education can be achieved, not *if* or *whether* it can be achieved.

NOTES

1   From 2012 data, the proportion of GDP for Brazil is 0.95 per cent, Senegal and Ghana 1.4 per cent, Norway and Finland over 2 per cent and Cuba 4.5 per cent. In South Africa, the 2015–2016 budget for higher education is R30 billion. If the government were to spend 1 per cent of GDP on higher education, this would amount to R41 billion – an additional R11 billion and almost *four times the reported shortfall* due to the 0 per cent increase.

2   In the book *Education, Economy and Society* (Vally and Motala 2014) the authors challenge the resurgent neoclassical and human capital theory assumptions related to the link between education and economic growth and that more and better education and training will automatically lead to employment.

3   There is a new consciousness encouraging solidarity among significant numbers of youth that speaks more and more to the intersectionality of class exploitation, racism, different forms of oppression and patriarchy in concrete ways. This has over time expanded to include issues about privatisation, the perverse pursuit of rankings and competitiveness, inequalities between universities and the 'decolonising' of the curriculum.

4   Our approach would favour the more encompassing approach though here, as will become plain, that is not the burden of the argument we make, as we argue that much more fundamental issues need to be resolved before meaningful judgements about the quantum of costs can be resolved.

5   Use of these categories of analysis by the proponents of 'fee-free for the poor' compounds the problem since no definitional boundaries are set in the use of who is poor and what is not beyond the quantitative definitions set out in the NSFAS framework for the purpose of supporting students

who fall within its categories of funding support. The working group on fee-free university education (DHET 2013) for the poor had a similar problem defining the poor as those households earning less than the lowest SARS tax bracket.

6   Page 1 – later re-asserting on page 10 that it is 'financially, empirically and morally wrong'.

7   The italics are our own.

8   The 'war room' as suggested by Cloete is to be composed of 'representatives from a number of other ministries, experienced business leaders and a few academics.' David Cooper responds (personal correspondence 8 November 2015): 'In my view this is exactly the global solution-type of government/business/academic elites who have since the 1980s given us the new form of global capitalism across a range of policies including in higher education. This framework underlies (i) the thinking of our 1996 National Commission of Higher Education (in which Cloete played a leading part) which so under-stressed the issues of equality in our university system that we have now the serious and almost irreparable divisions between our new system of 26+ university institutions; (ii) the new system of outsourcing at our universities … and (iii) a serious lack of transformation of our university curricula (especially in the social sciences) which are still deeply rooted in our colonial past.'

9   Dickinson (2015) makes the following apposite points: 'Many of the students entering South African universities are bright but underprepared by schools in townships and rural areas. This compounds the problem of inadequate funding by imposing a burden on already stretched academic resources. It also limits students' abilities to raise funds by working part time … Students from the new black middle class may be better prepared, having come out of private or well-resourced public schools. But their families are juggling competing demands on their resources with limited intergenerational transfer of resources that established middle classes can utilise.'

10   This apart from the inevitable problems of definitional questions about who is rich and the administrative requirements of complicated criteria, and the inevitably unintended and perverse effects of any bureaucratic system in this regard.

11   All these alternatives can be accessed here: http://www.educationpolicyconsortium.org.za/content/portfolio/review-6-funding-free-education.

12   For instance, in supporting this sort of extension to progressive taxation, Stiglitz (2015) has suggested that a 5 per cent increase to the tax rate of the top 1 per cent of earners in the USA would raise as much as US$1.5 trillion over ten years.

13   For Forslund (2015), 'To further increase revenue the Treasury could reintroduce the 45 per cent tax bracket for incomes above R1 million. It would yield R5–6 billion (based on the 2014 tax statistics). An important point must however be made about our millionaires. In 2013, there were about 4 200 individuals registered for an income of R5 million or more. Their average income (3 337 tax forms assessed) was R9.5 million, and the tax they paid was R3.7 million per person. Capgemini's World Wealth Report (2014) estimates that 'there are about 48 800 high net worth individuals (HNWI) in South Africa. An HNWI has an income of more than R7 million, or R70 million in accumulated wealth. If only 10 000 of these HNWIs paid income tax like the 3 337 income millionaires did in 2013, instead of hiding outside the tax system, this would yield an additional R37 billion in tax revenue.'

14   Section 13.2.5, our italics.

15   https://theconversation.com/free-education-is-possible-if-south-africa-moves-beyond-smoke-and-mirrors-65805.

REFERENCES

Alexander, N (2013) Affirmative action and black economic empowerment in post-apartheid South Africa. In *Thoughts on the new South Africa*. Johannesburg: Jacana Media.

Capgemini (2014) World Wealth Report. https://www.worldwealthreport.com/.

Cloete, N (2015a) The flawed ideology of 'free higher education'. *University World News*, Global Edition Issue 389.

Cloete, N (2015b) Fees should not fall for all. *Ground Up*. 8 November. http://www.groundup.org .za/article/fees-should-not-fall-all_3475/ (accessed 1 May 2016).

Cloete, N (2016a) For sustainable funding and fees, the undergraduate system in South Africa must be restructured. *South African Journal of Science*, 112 (3/4), 1–5.

Cloete, N (2016b) *Free higher education: Another self-destructive South African policy*. Cape Town: Centre for Higher Education Trust.

DHET (Department of Higher Education and Training) (2013) *Report of the working group on free fee university education for the poor in South Africa*. Pretoria: Department of Higher Education and Training.

DHET (Department of Higher Education and Training) (2014) *Report of the ministerial committee for the review of the funding of universities*. Pretoria: Department of Higher Education and Training.

Dickinson, D (2015) Fee protests point to a much deeper problem at South African universities. *Daily Vox*, 20 October.

Forslund, D (2015) The political budget crisis and alternatives to austerity, Part Two, 5 November. http:// www.dailymaverick.co.za/opinionista/2015-11-05-the-political-budget-crisis-and-alternatives-to-austerity-part-two/#.V0LkWzV96M (accessed 5 January 2016).

Ha-Joon, C (2014) *Economics: The user's guide*. London: Bloomsbury Press.

Habib, A and Mabizela, S (2016) *Societal response required to address challenges facing the higher education sector*, 21 February. https://www.wits.ac.za/news/latest-news/general-news/2016/2016-02/ societal-response-required-to-address-challenges-facing-the-higher-education-sector.html.

Hart, G (2016) Inequalities increase as fees rise. *Mail & Guardian*, 21 October. http://mg.co.za/article/ 2016-10-21-00-inequalities-increase-as-fees-rise (accessed 25 November 2016).

Harvey, D (2010) *The enigma of capital and the crises of capitalism*. New York: Oxford University Press.

Hickel, J (2016) *How the west destroyed the global South's best shot at development*. http://thought-leader.co.za/jasonhickel/2016/03/09/how-the-west-destroyed-the-global-souths-best-shot-at-development/ (accessed 5 May 2016).

Mamdani, M (1993) University crisis and reform: A reflection of the African experience. *Review of African Political Economy*, 58, 7–19.

Moss, G (2015) Free education, public funding and democratic accountability. *Politicsweb*, 12 November. http://www.politicsweb.co.za/news-and-analysis/free-education-public-funding-and-democrat-ic-accou (accessed 10 December 2015).

Piketty, T (2015) *Nelson Mandela annual lecture 2015*. Johannesburg: Nelson Mandela Foundation. https:// www.nelsonmandela.org/news/entry/transcript-of-nelson-mandela-annual-lecture-2015 (accessed 30 April 2016).

RSA (Republic of South Africa) (2016) *Medium term budget policy statement*. Tshwane: National Treasury.

Rudin, J (2015) No fees: Breathe fire into Ubuntu. *Mail & Guardian*, 27 November.

Shange, N (2016) Free higher education for all impossible – Nzimande, 3 December. http://www .news24.com/SouthAfrica/News/free-higher-education-for-all-impossible-nzimande-20151203 (accessed 1 May 2016).

Southall, R (2016) Inequality in South Africa: The immediate enemy. Unpublished.

Stiglitz, JE (2015) *The great divide: Unequal societies and what we can do about them*. New York: W. W. Norton & Company.

United Nations General Assembly (1976) *International covenant on economic, social and cultural rights, adopted by General Assembly resolution 2200A (XXI) of 16 December 1966 entry into force 3 January 1976, in accordance with article 27*. http://www.ohchr.org/EN/ProfessionalInterest/ Pages/CESCR.aspx (accessed 13 May 2016).

Vally, S and Motala, E (2014) *Education, economy and society*. Pretoria: Unisa Press.

CHAPTER 10

Still waiting: The South African government's pending promise of equality for people with disabilities

Jacqui Ala and David Black

From a constructivist perspective the causes and manifestations of inequality are multidimensional. Different populations affected by systemic inequality are disadvantaged through a convergence of socio-economic, cultural and political factors that are also historically and contextually bound. Moreover, inequality is not experienced the same way either horizontally between different groups or vertically among people within the same group. Constructivism allows for a more nuanced understanding of the causes and consequences of inequality for particular groups within society.

Relatively little attention has been paid by development studies to issues concerning people with disabilities, in South Africa and elsewhere. In the transitional and immediately post-apartheid years of the 1990s, some progress was made by government in addressing the development needs of people with disabilities – indeed, South Africa was regarded internationally as a leader in addressing the rights of the disabled. However, this focus has waned. We will argue in this chapter that the accommodation of people with disabilities in the South African political economy was critically compromised by the country's post-apartheid embrace of several key policy choices. Most fundamentally, South Africa's initial vision of a society built on social democratic principles has been eroded by the awkward marriage of neoliberal economics to these ideals – a step initially marked by the abrupt abandonment of the Reconstruction and Development Programme (RDP) for the Growth, Employment and Redistribution (Gear) strategy in

1996 (see Naidoo 2010; Marais 2011). In this context, the adoption of a development framework based on human rights and social justice was unable to be effectively implemented, and the government's commitments to people with disabilities concomitantly waned. The steady spread of corruption and maladministration has only served to make the situation worse.

DISABILITY AND INEQUALITY IN SOUTH AFRICA

Despite variations and nuances in the manifestations of inequality, it can be firmly observed in South Africa – as elsewhere – that disabled people are typically the *most* disadvantaged within the various social categories of difference and inequity (Yeo and Moore 2003; Graham et al. 2013; Loeb et al. 2008; Leibbrandt et al. 2010). Despite wide-ranging constitutional and legislative provisions aiming to guarantee the rights of people with disabilities in South Africa, the disabled remain marginalised socially and economically.

Seekings and Nattrass (2015) argue that post-apartheid South Africa instituted various policies and initiatives aimed at redressing social and economic inequalities as well as decreasing poverty. The expansion of social grants to vulnerable groups such as pensioners, the disabled and children has come to serve as the foundation of government's efforts to decrease poverty. The social grants paid to people with disabilities are high, relative to the child care grant. Government has made considerable progress in expanding the number of disability grant recipients since 1994. The number of disability grants grew from less than 600 000 towards the end of the 1990s to 1.4 million in 2007 (Seekings and Nattrass 2015: 139) This dropped to 1.1 million by 2014 owing to more stringent governmental vetting of recipients to curb fraud (also see Ferreira 2015). Thus, relative to other poor households those receiving grants may appear to be economically better off (Seekings and Nattrass 2015: 147–50) but in practice these grants do not translate into any substantial advantage, as this income will typically be spent on caring for the disabled family member (MacGregor 2006). People with disabilities officially constitute approximately 7.5 per cent of the South African population (Census 2011) – a percentage which disability rights advocates view as a significant underestimate (see also World Bank 2017). The majority of the disabled struggle to access healthcare and schooling, are unemployed and live in poverty. Due to the lack of adequate state services for people with disabilities, households with a disabled member spend much of their disposable income on caring for them, compounding household economic vulnerability, whereas households in higher income brackets are better able to absorb such expenditure and are able to provide more resources and care to their disabled members through their access to typically superior private services. Thus, class further exacerbates inequality among people with disabilities, as do race and gender. In addition, without adequate education and transportation it is difficult for most disabled people in South Africa to find and maintain employment. The mechanisation of many industries and the decrease in semi-skilled employment opportunities also contribute to relatively higher unemployment rates among this demographic.

CONCEPTUAL MODELS OF DISABILITY AS A SOURCE OF INCLUSION OR EXCLUSION

There are three distinct paradigms into which the response of society towards people with disabilities can be categorised: the welfare/charity, medical and social models. The first two models share a view of disabled people as passive or vulnerable recipients of rehabilitation and charity initiatives provided for them by others. In the medical model, disability is equated with illness, disease and imperfection and the focus is on preventing, treating, curing or ameliorating disability (Yeo and Moore 2003). Although these objectives are not in themselves unnecessary or undesirable, the way they are implemented is often disempowering. The opinions and decisions of medical professionals are privileged over the right of disabled people to autonomy over the management of their condition. In other words, medical professionals have the discretion to determine what is good for a disabled person. Taken to its logical conclusion, the association of disability with disease has distinct eugenic overtones in that the ultimate objective is to eradicate or occlude imperfection. Creating links between disability, disease and imperfection results in disability being stigmatised as 'unacceptable'.

The welfare/charity approach also deprives disabled people of agency. Disability is perceived as rendering a person incapable of functioning autonomously within society – it is society's duty to provide care and shelter. Once again, disabled people are effectively denied involvement in decisions as to what shape or form assistance should take, further entrenching their subaltern status and stereotyping them as incapable of meaningfully participating in social, economic or political life. It is now widely accepted that both the medical and the welfare approach effectively establish and/or reinforce inequality between disabled people and the rest of society.

In contrast, the social model prioritises equal rights for people with disabilities and is strongly grounded in the principle of inclusivity, on the premise that they should be active members of the polity with the right and the expectation of self-representation. Disability should not curtail political, social or economic access. The social model relocates disability in an active space, and in a way which differs fundamentally from the previously dominant medical and welfare models. The corollary to the social model in terms of state policy and expenditure is that it requires active state intervention, after consultation with disabled people's organisations (DPOs) in civil society, to formulate legislation, policy and programmes to ensure equal access to resources and infrastructure. However, to provide disabled people with equitable socio-economic and political access has significant cost and capacity implications. Moreover, if seen in terms of the neoliberal cost-benefit equation where the input cost for providing this access must be commensurate with benefits received (often narrowed to purely financial returns) then these costs could be deemed unaffordable by both public and private spheres. Although both the medical and welfare models require public expenditure, their exclusive focus on individualised outcomes may mean that they are perceived as more cost-effective, whereas in reality these individualised programmes are often more expensive to administer than policies guided by a social understanding of disability, and usually only reach a minority of the disabled community, typically located in urban settings (Yeo and Moore 2003).

How disability is defined is influenced by which of the three models is subscribed to. In this chapter we subscribe to the more inclusive bio-psycho-social definition used by the World Bank's 2011 World Report on Disability that draws on the medical and social models:

> Disability is the umbrella term for impairments, activity limitations and participation restrictions, referring to the negative aspects of the interaction between an individual (with a health condition) and that individual's contextual factors (environmental and personal factors) (World Bank 2011: 3).

DISABILITY IN THE POST-1994 CONTEXT

After 1994, the social model that was implemented was that advocated by the South African disability rights movement, mobilised through Disabled People South Africa (DPSA), who played an active role in the struggle against apartheid and thereby positioned themselves to advance the rights of disabled people in the new South Africa. Through a combination of effective lobbying and a deep-seated commitment on the part of the African National Congress (ANC) to establishing an equitable, non-discriminatory post-apartheid state, this model was embraced by the leadership of the new democracy. As early as 1992 a collaboration between disability rights activists and Lawyers for Human Rights produced the Disability Rights Charter of South Africa which would become the basis for the 1997 Integrated National Disability Strategy (INDS) White Paper. Both documents seemed to put South Africa firmly on a trajectory to operationalising a social model of disability (Dube 2005), in line with the equality rights embedded in the 1996 Constitution. The INDS set out a framework to enable government and society to think and act inclusively in terms of development planning, programme implementation and service delivery (Dube 2005). To reinforce the priority which the ANC government placed on the rights of the disability community, the Office on the Status of People with Disabilities (OSPD) was established in 1997, located initially within the office of the vice-president and later moved, under Thabo Mbeki, to the presidency. This gave it access to all government departments and was supposed to enable it to guide government with respect to the inclusion of disability in all legislation, policies and programmes (Yeo and Moore 2003).

Not only were disabled people's rights guaranteed within the 1996 Constitution, and elaborated in the INDS, but this emphasis on the inclusion of disabled people as active participants in all spheres of life was also embedded within a host of other statutes. The mechanism of mainstreaming as a way of comprehensively ensuring equality and, where necessary, redress for disabled people is evident in the fact that there is hardly any legislation that *exclusively* focuses on disability; instead the actions to achieve disability rights have been incorporated in all legislation deemed necessary for this purpose. This again testifies to the synergistic relationship between government and activists during the first ten years of democracy. Indeed, a number of key leaders of the disability rights movement were co-opted into government service – a development which seemed at the time to portend a decisive step forward for disabled South Africans but which ultimately seriously weakened the capacity of the movement to mobilise pressure and hold state agencies to account. Key legislative landmarks pertaining to the discussion and analysis in this chapter include:

1. The *Broad-Based Black Economic Empowerment Act of 2003* which addresses the economic empowerment of black people as well as disabled people.
2. The *Children's Act of 2003*, with specific clauses prohibiting discrimination on grounds of a child's or its caregiver's disability. It also calls for the creation of enabling environments within which to respond to children's special needs.
3. The *Cooperatives Act of 2005*, designed to facilitate the provision of support for emerging cooperatives and specifying disabled persons as one of the categories requiring attention to promote greater equity and participation in these ventures.
4. The *Employment Equity Act of 1998*, which prohibits discrimination in the workplace on the basis of disability, and designates disabled people as one of the groups who require affirmative action to ensure equitable employment opportunities. Quotas and reporting criteria to ensure the implementation of these provisions were also established, with a target of 2 per cent of staff employed being persons with a disability.
5. The *Labour Relations Act of 1995*, establishing fair labour practice and expressly forbidding discrimination based on arbitrary grounds such as disability.
6. The *National Building Regulations and Building Standards Act of 1997*, requiring that any built environment insofar as possible be fully accessible to and safe for disabled people.
7. The *National Education Policy Act of 1996*, which states that no person should be denied the opportunity to receive an education, notably due to disability. The South African School Act of 1996 goes further, requiring that as far as reasonably possible education should provide for students with special needs and endeavour to provide facilities that are accessible to physically disabled students (Ngwena et al. 2013). In the Education White Paper 6 released in 2001, government mapped out a twenty-year plan to make the schooling system inclusive for all learners. In response to its own audit which concluded that 280 000 children and youth with disabilities were not going to school, the government undertook to systematically ensure that all disabled learners would be accommodated at a school. It envisaged enrolling most disabled students in

'mainstream schools'. However, government also undertook to enhance those special needs schools that already existed as well as to build more of these types of schools (Human Rights Watch 2015). A cap on class sizes was also recommended, commensurate with the types of special needs learners being taught.

8. The *Skills Development Act of 1998*, together with the Skills Development Levies Act of 1999, which creates a framework for national skills development. Working in tandem with the Employment Equity Act it identifies disabled people as a group requiring specific intervention and monitoring and thus sets skills development targets with the aim of securing their inclusion (Ngwena et al. 2013).

9. The *National Land and Transport Act of 2009*, containing regulations, requirements and time frames for the purposes of ensuring that disabled people have access to vehicles and facilities, particularly with regard to public transportation.

10. The *Promotion of Equality and Prevention of Unfair Discrimination Act,* designed to enforce the non-discrimination and protection of human dignity provisions set out in sections 9 and 10 of the 1996 Constitution and specifically outlawing discrimination against disabled people. The Act also made provision for the establishment of Equality Courts which have been extremely helpful in providing redress for people with disability who have experienced discrimination in areas under legislative purview (Ngwena et al. 2013).

11. The *Social Assistance Act of 2004,* outlining criteria that allow people (specifically including the disabled) to claim social assistance from the state.

These and other legislative advances were reinforced at the international level by South Africa's early ratification of both the United Nations Convention on the Rights of Persons with Disabilities (UNCRPD) and the Optional Protocol to the Convention in 2008, only a year after they had been opened for signature (White Paper 2015). These important steps forward for the rights of the disabled globally were underpinned conceptually by the social model of disability, providing international validation and reinforcement for the legislative and institutional steps taken domestically.

On paper, then, South Africa has created a progressive dispensation for its disabled citizens, firmly aligned with the social model that should by this stage (twenty years after the adoption of the INDS) have substantially improved the socio-economic status of people with disabilities. In practice, however, these expectations have been largely unfulfilled. The lives of the vast majority of people with disabilities, especially those located in rural and peri-urban areas, are defined by poverty, unemployment, continued social discrimination, severe education and skills deficits, and serious limitations in the range of state medical and social services available to them (these stark ongoing inequities are elaborated on later in this chapter). Moreover, the high-level political commitment that had seemed so hopeful in the first decade of democracy has proved to be far less robust than anticipated. At the end of the Mbeki presidency, the OSPD was integrated with programming concerning women and children into the Department of Women, Children and People with Disabilities, diminishing its standing as a high-level priority of the presidency within a relatively marginal department. At the beginning of President Zuma's second term of office, disability was effectively relegated to the Department of Social Development, to the surprise and distress of leading DPOs, expressed during interviews undertaken by the authors in August 2015. In spite of espousing a social model of disability therefore, South Africa seemed to be reverting to a welfare-medical model (Loeb et al. 2008). Meanwhile, the once unified and influential disabled people's movement was increasingly splintered into multiple disability-specific service providers struggling to sustain their activities and initiatives in an increasingly competitive funding environment.

POLICY CHOICES AND CONSEQUENCES FOR PEOPLE WITH DISABILITIES IN SOUTH AFRICA

In South Africa, in an often told story, the onset of the new, rights-centred democratic era in 1994 coincided with the apex of neoliberal globalisation. Seekings and Nattrass (2015) argue that the model embraced by the ANC government in post-apartheid South Africa was social democratic, in light of its strong socio-economic equality and redress agenda. However, in 1996 this model was fused with the Gear policy framework with its decidedly neoliberal orientation, which was in turn carried through subsequent national development policies (Marais 2011). This created a hybrid model in which social democracy and neoliberalism coexisted. While the two are not necessarily incompatible in the goals they seek to achieve, the means by which they pursue these and the socio-economic implications thereof are frequently in opposition to each other. This policy evolution has led to the re-channelling of aspirations toward reconciliation and restitution through neoliberal policy modalities. The growing entrenchment of patronage in the form of crony capitalism has further eroded government's ability to deliver on the scope of social development initially promised (Andreasson 2006; Beresford 2015).

Ironically, despite proclaiming to value individual rights and freedoms, neoliberalism has served to limit or even to erode the socio-economic status of people with disabilities (Yeo and Moore 2003; Russell and Malhotra 2009). Cuts in state spending on welfare, medical and education services have resulted in people with disabilities either having to pay private institutions to acquire services that were once provided free or at a subsidised cost or, in the case of those who cannot shoulder these costs, effectively losing access to these benefits. Russell and Malhotra (2009) refer to this as the commodification of disability in which people with disabilities are perceived, like the elderly, as exploitable markets where profits can now be made by providing goods and services no longer available in the public sector. In this way, neoliberalism is tacitly supportive of the medical model of disability as it touts medical treatment as a way to manage disability while simultaneously profiting from this process. Similarly, it is implicitly supportive of the charity model by celebrating and indeed relying on the role of corporate philanthropy to underwrite opportunities for people with disabilities. The irony of these trends is that at precisely the moment when the rights of South Africans with disabilities were entrenched constitutionally and institutionally in accordance with the precepts of the social model of disability, the capacity of the state to give effect to these provisions was fundamentally compromised. This exacerbated the challenges facing a state apparatus that would have been hard-pressed, under the best of circumstances, to meet the needs and expectations of the many black South Africans whose rights and opportunities had long been systematically suppressed. As a result, the demographic effects of South Africa's new era of opportunity for people with disabilities have been strikingly limited. By way of illustration, the following section outlines the persistent gap between legislative aspiration and policy impact in two crucial issue areas: education, and employment and income.

DEMOGRAPHIC OVERVIEW OF THE DISABLED POPULATION IN SOUTH AFRICA

The 2011 Census estimate of people with disabilities constituting 7.5 percent of the South Africa population excludes people with psychosocial disorders, certain neurological conditions, intellectual disabilities and children under the age of five. Moreover, the high degree of stigmatisation associated with having a disabled household member may also have resulted in non-reporting. In light of these factors the 2011 Census concedes that it may have undercounted the number of disabled people. The DPSA (ENCA 2014) and Human Rights Watch maintain that the figures that they have collected are higher than that of the Census (Human Rights Watch 2015).

The 2011 Census data indicates that the Free State and the Northern Cape have the highest populations of people with disabilities (11 per cent), followed by North West (10 per cent), the Eastern Cape (9.6 per cent), Limpopo (9 per cent), KwaZulu-Natal (8.5 per cent) and Mpumalanga (7.0 per cent). The Western Cape (5 per cent) and Gauteng (5 per cent) have the lowest rates. More females (8.5 per cent) than males (6.5 per cent) have disabilities. When disaggregated by race, the incidence of disability is highest among black Africans (7.8 per cent), followed by whites (6.5 per cent), coloureds (6.2 per cent), Indians (6.2 per cent) and 'others' (5.6 per cent). Except for the age group five to nine years, which had a 10.8 per cent prevalence rate, disability is positively correlated with age. The age group ten to fourteen years has a 4.1 per cent prevalence rate, with rates declining slightly or remaining constant until fifty to fifty-four when it rises to 12.2 per cent and steadily increases to a peak of 53.2 per cent in the eighty-five and over age group range (Census 2011).

The 2011 Census revealed that out of the six functioning domains through which disability is measured, disability relating to sight was the most prevalent (11 per cent), followed by cognitive disabilities (4.2 per cent), hearing difficulties (3.6 per cent) and finally communication (2 per cent), self-care (2 per cent) and walking difficulties (2 per cent).

EDUCATION

The provision of early childhood development programmes, together with primary education to all children, is one of the fundamental objectives of the Department of Basic Education – an objective which, as noted above, is embedded in various pieces of legislation. It is also an important component of government's socio-economic development strategies. Government claims that it has attained a 100 per cent enrolment rate at primary school level as mandated by the Millennium Development Goals (schooling is compulsory from seven to sixteen years). As noted above, South Africa subscribes to the principle of inclusion; thus most children with disabilities should be allowed, and enabled, to attend mainstream schools. Government is also committed to accommodating students at specialised schools if the severity of their disability renders mainstream schooling unsuitable. Inclusive education allows a disabled learner to go to a school within their neighbourhood or community. It should also make it more affordable for these learners' parents, as 80 per cent of schools are 'no fee' owing to the low economic status of the community in which they are located.

In spite of the government's claim to have achieved 100 per cent primary school enrolment, the table below drawn from the 2011 Census data reveals that a significant number of disabled students do not attend school. The under-representation of disabled learners is prevalent across the education spectrum from early childhood development to tertiary education, where it is most acute.

Moreover, in line with the assumptions of intersectionality, highlighting the layering of marginalisation and discrimination on the basis of categories of social identity, the data indicates that this exclusion is also gendered, with fewer female disabled learners participating at all levels of education. There is also an urban-rural divide, with fewer

Table 10.1: Percentage of disabled learners not attending education facilities, disaggregated by type and extent of disability as well as age group

	5–6 years		7–13 years		14–19 years		20–24 years	
	Moderate	Severe	Moderate	Severe	Moderate	Severe	Moderate	Severe
Seeing	12.5	18.7	3.9	7.2	15.3	18.1	66.4	69.3
Hearing	15.3	22.6	5.2	22.6	18.8	23.2	73.5	73.4
Communication	16.9	25	8.1	23.5	25.1	42.7	73.8	80.5
Walking	18.7	35.5	9.5	30.9	23.4	40.1	73.4	78.5
Remembering	14.4	18.7	5.3	14.5	21.6	36.9	72.6	79.3
Self-care	6.6	14.4	3.7	7.2	19	34.6	70.7	78.6

Source: Census 2011.

learners in rural and farming areas able to access education across the board. In terms of race, coloured and then black African learners are most under-represented, indicating a lack of progress towards racial equality for disabled people.

The government's numerous legal and policy instruments for disabled learners have not been effective in achieving their stated objectives. In 2015, Human Rights Watch (HRW) produced a report entitled 'Complicit in exclusion: South Africa's failure to guarantee inclusive education for children with disabilities,' which analyses the reasons for the absence of disabled learners. The report reveals the large and persistent disconnect between policy and practice.

Despite signing onto the United Nations Convention on the Rights of the Child, which calls for the provision of free basic education for all children, South Africa has adopted a more neoliberal stance towards fee payment. Education is not free. The amount payable depends on the socio-economic status of the family of each learner. In practice, this leads to schools in poor areas being designated 'no fee' schools while learners in areas deemed middle and upper class are expected to pay fees. However, no designated government special needs school is categorised as a 'no fee' school because they are located in more affluent areas. The HRW report also found that very few schools, especially in rural areas, were willing and/or able to accept disabled students. Most of the moderately and severely disabled learners the HRW interviewed were turned away from mainstream schools. Learners who were allowed into mainstream schooling had to pay for special assistants to help them with their learning as well as with physical access to their surroundings. Not being able to go to mainstream schools within their community means that disabled learners from poor communities are unable to benefit from fee waivers. Furthermore, attending school in suburban areas means having to find and pay for suitable transportation. South Africa lacks an integrated public transport system; consequently the majority of the school-going population relies on taxis – and taxis charge double to transport a wheelchair and are unreliable in dropping off and picking up disabled students. The additional transportation costs are frequently unaffordable for caregivers, and the risks associated with taxi transport are also a deterrent. Thus, the caregiver grants provided are usually insufficient to cover all schooling-related costs.

There is a misalignment between government's repeated commitment to mainstreaming and support for disabled learners on the one hand, and its practices on the other. In the 2014–2015 budget more money was allocated to the building and equipping of special needs schools than was allocated for inclusive education. The amounts budgeted for disabled students by province are quite small, usually no more than 3 per cent of the total provincial spending on education, with the majority allocated to special schools (Human Rights Watch 2015). Despite increased funding to build and equip special schools, the number of places required by disabled learners cannot be accommodated in these institutions alone. With inadequate funding for transforming existing schools' infrastructure and providing educational resources for disabled learners, inclusive public learning environments have extremely limited capacity, and large numbers of disabled students are turned away or placed on waiting lists.

The small budgets allocated to the needs of disabled learners means there is a short-age of the equipment and personnel required to assist with learning and navigating the learning environment. In the authors' interviews with representatives of the South Africa Guide Dog Association and BlindSA (August 2015), both noted that government is no longer employing orientation and mobility practitioners who assist the visually impaired to navigate new environments. According to BlindSA, despite White Paper 6 committing government to providing each visually impaired learner with their own Braille textbook per subject, this has not occurred, resulting in the pursuit of a court order to force com-pliance. In spite of government's declaring SA Sign Language an official language, there are too few interpreters to meet the needs of deaf students. The HRW report also found that where disabled students attended mainstream schools these schools often failed to provide individualised learning plans, in contravention of UNCRPD and government policy. Few teachers in mainstream schools are equipped to teach in an inclusive envi-ronment, and very little support was available to learners. Without support, children are often victims of bullying. Universal design for learning is not incorporated into teaching to the degree necessary to make inclusive education a reality. Ultimately, the convergence of these deficits in schooling results in many students dropping out.

The 2015 White Paper on Disability emphasises the tax deductions available to caregiv-ers of disabled children who themselves cover the costs of school fees, medical expenses, related therapies and assistive devices. However, what is not mentioned is that only part of the amounts paid will be reimbursed, and in addition, as Bruno Druchen from the South Africa Disability Alliance pointed out (authors' interview), these benefits are only meaningful to families who have employment and who pay tax (with only 4 788 334 South Africans taxpayers in 2015–2016 (SARS 2016)). It is the employed who can secure better care and support for disabled children, further exacerbating pre-existing class and racial inequalities.

According to the DPOs interviewed for this chapter, the services available to learn-ers in the university sector are usually relatively comprehensive and of good quality, but because of the attrition rates at lower education levels few disabled students reach tertiary education. Moreover, post-school learnerships and skills development for the disabled are very limited.

Currently, then, there is a persistently high level of inequity between the quality and affordability of education available to able and disabled learners. Disabled learners who have access to both monetary and social capital are able to secure world-class education privately; but the consequence of not being able to secure adequate education sets the majority of disabled people at a further disadvantage when seeking employment.

EMPLOYMENT AND INCOME

The 2011 Census data indicates that the likelihood of a disabled person finding employ-ment depended on type of disability, severity of disability, gender, race and location.

Table 10.2: Disabled people employed as percentage of the South African labour force disaggregated by level of representation and gender

	2010		2012		2014	
Level of representation	Male	Female	Male	Female	Male	Female
Top management	1.2	0.3	1.4	0.4	1.5	0.5
Senior management	0.7	0.1	1.2	0.5	1.2	0.5
Professional	0.6	0.4	0.8	0.5	0.9	0.5
Technical	0.5	0.3	0.8	0.5	0.7	0.5

Source of data: *Commission for employment equity annual report* 2014–15, South African Department of Labour.

Employment was highest among people with disabilities related to sight whereas people with severe disabilities found it hard, in general, to find work. More disabled men than women were employed. Fewer black disabled people were able to find jobs than white disabled people, who had the highest employment rates relatively. Employment rates for urban disabled people were higher than those in rural areas – except for those in farming regions, who actually had relatively high employment rates. These same factors also account for income variability among disabled people who are employed.

The 2014–2015 Employment Equity Report indicates that the current total percentage of disabled persons employed is 1.2 per cent (see Table 10.2), which is still below the 2 per cent minimum target set by the Employment Equity Act. When disaggregated by level of representation within the labour force it is only at top management that the 2 per cent quota is being approached. This is also the only level in the above table that has seen consistent, though marginal, increases across the 2010–2014 period. As one moves up the spectrum of levels of representation the presence of disabled people employed increases. Between 2012 and 2014 the technical level saw a slight decline for men. Overall, women are less represented at all levels, with hardly any increase between reporting periods.

Figure 10.1 indicates that most sectors, aside from state-owned enterprises and agriculture, have not met the 2 per cent target set by the Act. Among state-owned enterprises are some that cater specifically for the employment of disabled people. However, they usually make minimal or no profit and in terms of the neoliberal agenda this represents inefficient government expenditure. Thus, there is an increasing push for these initiatives to either become cost-effective and increase income generation or be shut down (Brown 2016; Peyper 2016). As the agricultural sector requires a large amount of semi-skilled and unskilled labour, it offers greater opportunities to disabled people, most of whom fall within this skills range because they have been unable to access higher levels of education.

All the DPOs interviewed raised employment as one of the greatest challenges facing people with disabilities. Cathy Donaldson of BlindSA attributed the problem partly to the shrinkage of jobs available to the blind because technological advances (for example,

Figure 10.1: Disabled people employed by job sector as a percentage of the entire labour force

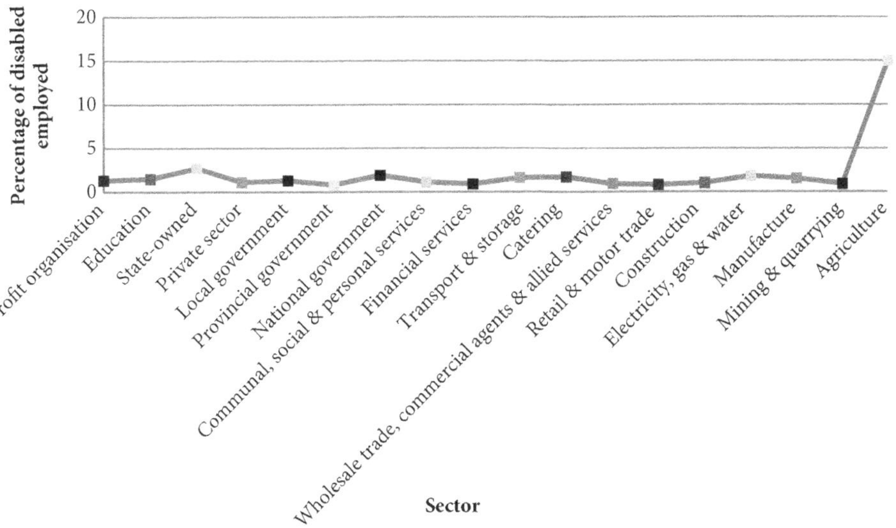

Source: *Commission for employment equity annual report* 2014–15, South African Department of Labour

in switchboard operation) have replaced the need for human labour. Many of the workshops for the blind were closed through lack of demand for the goods they manufactured (woven goods, for example). We surmise that much of this economic activity was unable to compete with cheaper and more plentiful foreign imports. Ari Seirlis of the Quad-Para Association of South Africa stated that the majority of their members were unemployed. One of the biggest hindrances faced by physically disabled people when seeking employment was reliable and affordable transportation that could accommodate their disabilities. A service that collected and dropped off the disabled was only available in Cape Town and Durban, and was insufficient to meet demand. Very few suitable transportation services were available in the rural areas. The bus rapid transport system was seen as a step forward but was only available in a few cities and was still not sufficiently extensive in coverage. Both BlindSA and the South African Guide Dog Association noted that much of South Africa's physical infrastructure (notably, street crossings and pavements) was difficult for disabled people to navigate. Using public transport in high crime areas was a risk for visually impaired people who are easy targets for criminals. To create employment, DeafSA has entered a joint venture for a hotel in Newlands, Cape Town, staffed by roughly 30 per cent deaf employees, in every department (Willis 2015). Bruno Druchen, national director of DeafSA, believes that the hotel helps to eradicate the commonly held view that disabled people are incapable of more than menial employment. This finding correlates with the literature on how disabled bodies are seen as mis-fitting in a neoliberal system in terms of ability to work (Kumar et al. 2012; Mladenov 2015; Garland-Thomson 2005). Eradicating these misperceptions would enable people with disabilities to secure the loans and investment required to be entrepreneurs.

As government is doing very little to create and/or support employment opportunities for disabled people, it now portrays its major contribution to their economic well-being as the social grants system. This – together with the movement of the government lead on disability from the Office of the President, to the Ministry of Women, Children and People with Disabilities to, most recently, the Ministry of Social Development – conveys that despite its policy rhetoric espousing the social model of disability, the placement of state resources suggest that the de facto model embraced is a welfare one. All DPOs interviewed stated that government gave no reason for the relocation of disability to the Department of Social Development and had undertaken no consultations with DPOs prior to the move. This contradicts the emphasis on self-representation that is central to the social model.

Indicative of South Africa's high levels of inequality and low levels of employment, coupled with its poor record on economic development, the 2015 South African budget allocated R11.5 billion to social grants over the next three years. The 1 058 328 beneficiaries of disability grants receive R1 510 per month; 145 030 people get care dependency grants of R1 510 to enable them to support dependent children with severe disabilities. A grant-in-aid of R320 per month is available to pay for any assistance needed by a disabled or elderly person. Currently, 165 692 people are eligible for this grant (SASSA 2017). The cost of caring for a disabled household member absorbs much of the disabled income available to those with middle and low incomes (Graham et al. 2013; Loeb et al. 2008; News24 2015). The 2011 Census revealed that those in the lower income range in particular had low consumption habits. The expense associated with disability makes these households economically vulnerable. The quality and range of accessible services in the government sector is extremely variable and generally inadequate. QuadPara SA noted, for example, that government healthcare services were particularly under-equipped to treat and rehabilitate spinal cord injuries. HRW noted that it was especially difficult for children in rural areas to obtain wheelchairs and a variety of auxiliary services to help accommodate their disability. However, as South Africa has private medical care available to those who can afford it, disabled people in this tier can access a wider range of treatments and assistive devices than those reliant on the state.

A specific example is the Gauteng Health Department's austerity-driven December 2015 decision to close down the Life Esidimeni Care Centre, which provided full-time care facilities for people with severe psychiatric disorders as well as cognitive disabilities. The Gauteng Health MEC stated in October 2015 that the Department wished to reduce the number of psychiatric patients resident in full-time care facilities by discharging those it felt could be cared for by their families. The remainder who could not be discharged would be redistributed to other facilities, one of which is a facility whose primary purpose is to care for disabled children. The group consists of more than 2 000 patients with ages ranging from twenty-four to a hundred-and-one. The South African Depression and Anxiety Group representing the families of the patients tried to obtain a court interdict to stop the relocation of patients to facilities unequipped to deal with many of the disabilities prevalent in the group, and family members also stated that they were not equipped to provide full-time home-based care to those patients released. The court denied the application and the release or relocation of patients is proceeding (Raborife 2015). It has turned out to be disastrous. In little over a year ninety-four patients had died from various forms of neglect in sixteen out of the twenty-seven nongovernmental organisations (NGOs) patients had been placed in (Makgoba 2017). A government commission of inquiry found that none of the twenty-seven NGOs selected by provincial government to received patients had licences to provide healthcare services for mental health patients. Officials sold the initiative to nongovernmental organisations (NGOs) primarily as a business venture with government, underplaying the importance of facilities being able to provide professional psychiatric healthcare services (Makgoba 2017). Thus, at most facilities staff lacked training to care for patients. Many were overcrowded. Most failed to provide patients with adequate food, shelter and medical care. Head of the commission of inquiry, Malegapuru Makgoba, found that the decision to transfer patients was inadequately planned, resulting in rushed and chaotic implementation. Provincial funding for the initiative was woefully insufficient. He stated that the cost rationale, a major factor that drove the decision to de-institutionalise, should not have been placed above patients' rights to dignity and access to healthcare (Makgoba 2017). This example is indicative of the shift of burden from the state to the community that so often takes place as part of the neoliberal project to cut state expenditure, at the expense of the disabled persons and the community which now has to care for them.

CONCLUSION

As is reflected in these examples, the rights-based and legislated commitments to equalising opportunities for the disabled have been largely unfulfilled, reflecting the limitations of public sector capacity and political will as well as the related repercussion of the neoliberal policy orientation that has predominated in the post-apartheid era.

The emphasis on democratic South Africa's failure significantly to alter the deep inequities faced by its disabled citizens should not be taken as dismissing the importance of the constitutional, legislative and institutional gains made since the end of apartheid. Reinforced by South Africa's eager acceptance of the UNCRPD, they mean that government has signed on to clear standards of behaviour and can be held to account when it fails to live up to these standards. In certain sectors, such as higher education, relatively significant (though uneven) advances in awareness, advocacy and service provision have been made. Institutional structures such as the South African Human Rights Commission, though under-resourced and relatively weak politically, have nevertheless attempted to raise awareness among employers and others concerning their obligations and to act on individual complaints regarding the denial of the rights of people with disabilities. These rights provisions and legislative requirements create the basis on which the gap between aspiration and implementation can be exposed, and government agencies (among others) held to account. Yet in practice, as we have seen, these same agencies and actors have, in the era of neoliberalism, lacked the capacity, resources and resolve to significantly narrow this gap.

In late 2015 and early 2016, after nearly a decade of apparent drift, several steps were taken that seemed to signal high-level interest in reinvigorating efforts towards equality for disabled South Africans. The White Paper on the Rights of Persons with Disabilities adopted by Cabinet in late 2015 seemed firmly to renew the government's commitment to an encompassing, holistic effort to promote equality for disabled citizens, explicitly premised on the social model (see especially pp. 48–123). Although the ability of government to operationalise this ambitious vision is doubtful, there is no doubting the progressiveness of its stated aspirations. In March 2016, this was followed by a Disability Rights Summit and the launch of a Presidential Working Group on Disability (Presidency 2016). While these developments were accompanied by revealing divisions between the South African Disability Alliance, composed of most of the country's leading national disability associations, and the long-standing but significantly diminished DPSA (see My Newsroom 2016), they seem on the face of it to portend the renewal of the early promise and commitment on the part of the government to full inclusion for the disabled.

At the time of writing it is too soon to tell what will come of these initiatives. Based on the foregoing analysis, however, compounded by the country's increasing political, economic and social strains, it is improbable that their expansive vision can be substantially fulfilled so long as the country remains locked into a predominantly neoliberal policy logic and the governance structures that flow from it. Only a more unapologetically interventionist and equality-promoting state can be expected to operationalise, support and sustain the necessary efforts toward greater equality and inclusion.

REFERENCES

Andreasson, S (2006) The African National Congress and its critics: 'Predatory liberalism', black empowerment and intra-alliance tensions in post-apartheid South Africa. *Democratization*, 13 (2), 303–322.

Beresford, A (2015) Power, patronage, and gatekeeper politics in South Africa. *African Affairs*, 114 (455), 226–248.

Brown, J (2016) *Economy and treasury sounds SOE alarm*. http://www.fin24.com/Economy/treasury-sounds-soe-alarm-20160930 (accessed on 3 April 2016).

Census 2011 (2014) *Profile of persons with disabilities in South Africa*. Report No. 03-01-59. Pretoria: Statistics South Africa. Available from http://www.statssa.gov.za/publications/Report-03-01-59/Report-03-01-592011.pdf.

Dube, A (2005) The role and effectiveness of disability legislation in South Africa. *Disability Knowledge and Research*, 1–89.

ENCA (2014) *Over 2.8m people in SA live with disability*. 9 September. https://www.enca.com/self-declaration-key-accurate-disability-figures (accessed 3 June 2015).

Ferreira, L (2015) *Separating myth from reality: A guide to social grants in South Africa*. Available from https://africacheck.org/factsheets/separating-myth-from-reality-a-guide-to-social-grants-in-south-africa/ (accessed 28 November 2016).

Garland-Thomson, R (2005) Disability and representation. *PMLA*, 120 (2), 522–527.

Graham, L, Moodley, J and Selipsky, L (2013) The disability–poverty nexus and the case for a capabilities approach: Evidence from Johannesburg, South Africa. *Disability & Society*, 28 (3), 324–337.

Human Rights Watch (2015) *Complicit in exclusion: South Africa's failure to guarantee an inclusive education for children with disabilities*. USA: Human Rights Watch.

Kumar, A, Sonpal, D and Hiranandani, V (2012) Trapped between ableism and neoliberalism: Critical reflections on disability and employment in India. *Disability Studies Quarterly*, 32 (3), 1–18.

Leibbrandt, M et al. (2010) *Trends in South African income distribution and poverty since the fall of apartheid*. OECD Social, Employment and Migration Working Papers, No. 101.

Loeb, M, Eide, AH, Jelsma, J, Toni, M and Maart, S (2008) Poverty and disability in Eastern and Western Cape Provinces, South Africa. *Disability & Society*, 23 (4), 311–321.

MacGregor, H (2006) 'The grant is what I eat': The politics of social security and disability in the post-apartheid South African state. *Journal of Biosocial Science*, 38 (1), 43–55.

Makgoba, M (2017) *The life Esidimeni disaster: The Makgoba report*. http://www.politicsweb.co.za/documents/the-life-esidimeni-disaster-the-makgoba-report (accessed 26 May 2017).

Marais, H (2011) *South Africa pushed to the limit: The political economy of change*. London: Zed Books.

Mladenov, T (2015) Neoliberalism, postsocialism, disability. *Disability & Society*, 30 (3), 445–459.

My Newsroom (2016) *SADA walks out of disability caucus on the eve of President Zuma addressing the disability summit*. 10 March. http://www.mynewsroom.co.za/sada-walks-out-of-disability-caucus-on-the-eve-of-president-zuma-addressing-the-disability-summit/ (accessed 17 March 2016).

Naidoo, J (2010) *Fighting for justice: A lifetime of political and social activism*. Johannesburg: Picador Africa.

News24 (2015) *SA disabled trapped in cycles of poverty*. Available from http://www.health24.com/News/Public-Health/sas-disabled-trapped-in-cycles-of-poverty-20151125 (accessed on 6 April 2016).

Ngwena, C, Grobbelaar-du Plessis, I, Combrinck, H and Kamga, SD (2013) *African disability rights*. Yearbook Vol. 1. Pretoria: PULP, 307–340.

Peyper, L (2016) *SOEs no longer relevant will be phased out, says Zuma*. http://www.fin24.com/Economy/soes-no-longer-relevant-will-be-phased-out-says-zuma-20160211 (accessed 28 April 2016).

Presidency, Republic of South Africa (2016) *Opening address by President Zuma to the disability rights summit and launch of presidential working group on disability, Irene, Pretoria*. 10 March. http://www.thepresidency.gov.za/pebble.asp?relid=21733 (accessed 17 March 2016).

Raborife, M (2015) *Families of mentally ill relatives saddened by dept's move*. News24 http://www.news24.com/SouthAfrica/News/families-of-the-mentally-ill on 2016–03–08 (accessed 10 April 2016).

Russell, M and Malhotra, R (2009) Capitalism and disability. *Socialist Register*, 38 (38), 1–18.

Seekings, J and Nattrass, N (2015) *Policy, politics and poverty in South Africa*. Basingstoke: Palgrave Macmillan.

South Africa Department of Labour (2014–2015) *Commission for employment equity annual report*, Pretoria: South Africa Government Printers.

SARS (South African Revenue Services) (2016) Tax statistics. http://www.sars.gov.za/About/SATaxSystem/Pages/Tax-Statistics.aspx.

SASSA (South African Social Development Agency) (2017) *Statistical report 4 of 2017*. Available from http://www.sassa.gov.za/index.php/statistical-reports (accessed 26 May 2017).

Willis, J (2015) Deaf hotel staff deliver a world first in Cape Town. *The Guardian*, 30 April. https://www.theguardian.com/sustainable-business/2015/apr/30/deaf-hotel-staff-deliver-a-world-first-in-cape-town (accessed 14 August 2017).

World Bank (2011) *World report on disability*. Malta: World Bank.

World Bank (2017) *Disability*. http://www.worldbank.org/en/topic/disability (accessed 5 June 2017).

Yeo, R and Moore, K (2003) Including disabled people in poverty reduction work: 'Nothing about us, without us'. *World Development*, 31 (3), 571–590.

CHAPTER 11

Big fish in small ponds: Changing stratification and inequalities in small towns in the Karoo region, South Africa

Doreen Atkinson

Small towns are anything but simple, despite the general media image of bucolic villages inhabited by gentle rustic folk living a slow and relaxed life. A small town may include as many social classes, categories, schisms and tensions as in any typical metropolis, but these fractious fragments are coalesced into a small population inhabiting a small area. People rub shoulders with people they like, or people they loathe, on a daily basis. Within these narrow spatial parameters, social classes develop even more subtle and powerful ways of keeping their distance from one another, or interacting on terms which both sides find congenial or tolerable. Small towns are polities in their own right; there are systems of decision making and resource allocation, and there are overt or latent tensions about the ways in which these functions are implemented. Complex ladders of social status serve to distinguish and separate different groups.

Small towns are also affected constantly and profoundly by their regional, national and international contexts. Some local people migrate to the cities to advance their education, and return with more skills and influence; other locals straddle town life and city life, juggling professions and livelihoods in several different localities. Many local townspeople use regional or city networks to advance their livelihoods and local influence. Some local people are adept at riding new international economic waves, adjusting to new opportunities such as game farming, tourism, retail or credit provision; other small-town people are hopelessly trapped within the narrow confines of the village.

This chapter explores the dynamics and prospects of different groups in the arid Karoo region of South Africa – a vast area of about eighty towns that makes up almost 45 per cent of South Africa's land surface. Based largely on my two decades of work and interaction in Karoo towns, the chapter suggests numerous social dynamics, simultaneously increasing and reducing inequality, and creating new forms of social cohesion and competition. These towns offer many opportunities for future social research.

DEFINING STRATIFICATION IN SMALL TOWNS

Small towns in South Africa differ greatly in their racial, ethnic and class profile. These towns were often shaped by their colonial origin, their role in apartheid planning, their economic function and their location near cities or in remote areas. Different typologies of small towns have been developed; for example, one can distinguish between towns with a strong agricultural profile and those which focus more strongly on agro-processing, mining and tourism (Toerien and Marais 2012). For almost every town, my conclusions may require further reflection, and for almost every argument there may be exceptions. Yet there appear to be some defining features of Karoo towns, which are explored below.

A 'small town' can be defined as a stand-alone town surrounded by farmland or environmental reserve land. There is no definite upper limit to the population of a 'small town' other than intuitive sense. In the Karoo, the upper limit is probably about 50 000 (Beaufort West). However, there are some lower limits, in that a small town must at least have *some* inhabitants who are not involved directly in agriculture; there must be some 'urban' activity such as retail, commercial services or personal services. Any settlement without such basic features would be considered a rural hamlet or farm settlement.

Small towns, as a spatial geo-type, have at least three main characteristics: (a) substantial agricultural land in the vicinity and therefore some nature-based economic activities; (b) some government services; and (c) some urban-based private sector activity creating opportunities for jobs and incomes. How these three factors play out – changes which strengthen or undermine them, or ways in which they provide mutual support – determines the economic trajectories of different towns. This, in turn, affects the nature and degree of social inequality, and people's ability to advance their prospects and to escape poverty traps.

In South Africa, a broad comparison with the economic profiles of metropoles and deep rural areas (the erstwhile communal 'homelands') highlights the distinctive economic patterns of small towns. Metropoles have relatively higher levels of manufacturing (typically based on private investments), whereas deep rural areas have relatively higher levels of traditional land ownership (based on communal property systems). In contrast, small towns – such as in the Karoo region – tend to be surrounded by commercial farms, and they contain a significant number of privately owned urban businesses (such as shops and guesthouses). Small towns do not have much manufacturing (with a few rare exceptions), but there are usually other fairly significant sectors such as retail, financial services and tourism.

Another contrast between these three spatial types – metropoles, deep rural areas and small towns – is the proportion of government expenditure (either on government officialdom or on social grants) within the local economic mix. Generally, the metros have large government expenditures which are fairly small in comparison with a robust private sector; and the deep rural areas have small government expenditures which are large in the context of depressed rural economies in traditional areas. The small towns are situated roughly midway on this continuum, with some government expenditure (municipal offices, schools, police stations, clinics, magistrates' courts), alongside fairly vigorous privately owned businesses. In the Karoo, the ratio of private sector investment to government expenditure differentiates robust towns from weak towns. In economically depressed towns (such as Pearston and Loxton), the private sector is relatively small, and equalled or even overshadowed by government expenditure (particularly via social grants), while in stronger towns (such as Cradock or Graaff-Reinet) the private sector is healthier.

In Karoo towns, the public and private sectors are very interdependent, at least partially because they are in close physical proximity (in contrast to dispersed rural settlements). Government officials spend their salaries at local shops, and the private sector offers alternative employment, particularly to spouses and offspring of government officials.

During the last twenty years Karoo towns retained much of their inherited racial, linguistic and status identities, and these are proving surprisingly resilient in the face of significant economic changes. However, there have been two major systemic shifts. Firstly, there has been a major change in the racial profile of the middle class, as public sector opportunities have been closed off to whites and opened up for Africans and coloureds. This, in turn, has required local white people to strengthen their private sector resources, for the sake of their economic survival. Secondly, small towns are not nearly as isolated as they were in 1994. Many innovative local people have plugged into regional or national economic systems, through migration, commuting, tourism and political influence (De Jong and Verkoren 2012). Karoo towns are no longer isolated economic islands but key nodes within broader networks of economic and political exchange. Cities such as Bloemfontein, Kimberley and Port Elizabeth loom large in the life of many Karoo residents.

Are the new social dynamics leading to an increase or decrease in social and economic inequality in small towns and their hinterlands? This chapter reflects on two broad trends in Karoo small towns. Firstly, it uses National Income Dynamic Study (NIDS) data to show that inequality has largely declined in rural areas, owing to the constant out-migration of poor people to the cities as well as steady or growing levels of government expenditure which support local incomes (notably social grants). This nationwide *quantitative* profile is then complemented with *qualitative* observations from Karoo towns, to show that social and economic stratification remains significant, although subject to rapid social changes.

STUDYING SMALL TOWNS IN SOUTH AFRICA

Small towns are poorly placed in general data analysis because they are sometimes, in the public mind, regarded as 'rural' and sometimes as 'urban'. The definition of 'urban' is a complex one. To add to the complexity, the South African census definition changed significantly between 1996 and 2001 (Stats SA 2001); this has made longitudinal analysis very difficult and often misleading. The 2011 Census usefully distinguishes between towns and farmland, but the 2001 Census did not.

The NIDS surveys, hosted at the University of Cape Town, have brought some rural-urban spatial distinctions back into their analysis. In these surveys, these terms are still used rather vaguely. The surveys sometimes distinguish between 'rural informal' (referring to traditional 'homeland' areas) and 'rural formal' (including commercial farmland and, presumably, small towns, although this is not made entirely clear (Daniels et al. 2013: 6)).

The NIDS data shows that rural-urban migration is a constant theme in post-1994 South Africa (Leibbrandt et al. 2010: 15). The rural population has shrunk as a proportion of national population (from about 51 per cent in 1993 to 40 per cent in 2008). The levels of poverty in rural areas have remained largely static (at around 77 per cent of the rural population). But the percentage of poor people living in rural areas has declined (from around 70 per cent in 1993 to around 57 per cent in 2008), and this group has increased significantly in urban areas (from about 30 per cent of poor people to about 43 per cent). This shows clearly that many poor rural people have migrated to the cities.

But not all poor people migrate to large cities, where jobs need to be found and where many goods and services have to be paid for. In rural areas and small towns, many services do not require money. People travel by foot instead of taxis or buses, and extended families look after children on a no-fee basis. Even though the average household income from the labour market for households living in rural areas is lower than that of urban households, rural households were often better off than the households in urban informal areas between 2008 and 2012 (Daniels et al. 2013: 6). This suggests that some poor people in small towns and rural areas prefer to stay where they are rather than migrate to urban areas – and particularly if they have access to social grants. The temptation to move to the cities is typically one felt by ambitious working-age job seekers, leaving their elderly and young family members in the small towns as part of a safety net. The remittances further help to reduce economic inequalities in small towns and to explain why the rural Gini coefficient (measuring the extent of inequality) is lower than in urban areas, and in fact has shown a decreasing trend between 1993 and 2008, while the urban Gini has increased (Leibbrandt et al. 2010: 32).

In South Africa generally, 'between race' inequalities remain stubbornly high (Leibbrandt et al. 2010: 21), with Africans having a much greater share of poor people, but the interracial gap is narrowing because of the increase in African, coloured and Indian incomes over the past three decades (Leibbrandt et al. 2010: 16; Seekings and Nattrass 2006: 307). At the same time, inequality *within* the black group is increasing significantly (the black middle class is forging ahead, while other black people are falling into poverty traps). These dynamics can be clearly seen in Karoo towns, where social stratification no longer follows clear racial lines.

CHANGING SOCIAL STRATIFICATION IN KAROO TOWNS

The end of apartheid has brought a major growth in individual freedom to vast swathes of society (the previously disenfranchised). This is part of an international trend which can be termed 'individualisation': 'Freed of traditional constraints of faith, tradition and class, the modern individual ... is expected to engage actively on their own life project, setting personal goals and monitoring their performance' (Walker 2006: 70). For many African and coloured people, this growth in choice has offered welcome new options for education, jobs and investment; however, for many others it has led to poor choices (often based on inexperience), and has resulted in indebtedness, unemployment, inadequate education, substance addiction and worsened poverty (Seekings and Nattrass 2006). As elsewhere, these same trends are playing out in Karoo towns, but some of the local dynamics are somewhat different from those of large cities.

In Karoo towns, four important new social categories stand out. First, there are local African and coloured political elites who have settled into municipalities and owe their success to their political-party affiliations. Second, there are young adult professionals (typically African and coloured) who accept government jobs in small towns, sometimes with the intention of moving to the cities later; they have income streams but few assets. Thirdly, there are elderly investors (typically white people) who spend their lifetime earnings (often earned in larger cities) by starting a rural niche industry – for example, in tourism, art or crafts; they have assets which deliver a steady income stream. Finally, there are very vulnerable people (of all race groups) who are falling into poverty traps, without assets or income, and relying on a very fragile social support system to keep afloat.

We therefore have to understand a complex interplay of income streams, asset accumulation, government support and social networks. These are the drivers of changing patterns of social stratification in the Karoo, and they have resulted in six key trends. Often, the evidence is still impressionistic, and requires more systematic analysis in future.

TREND 1: VULNERABLE AND CONTESTED INCOME STREAMS

Levels of income and wealth in Karoo towns are more constrained than in urban areas; local product markets are thin and job opportunities highly contested. Some Karoo towns are clustered around a single substantial enterprise (such as the hotel in Britstown); other towns, such as Cradock, have a fairly diverse array of enterprises; and some towns (such as Nelspoort near Beaufort West) have hardly any enterprises at all. Many Karoo towns are in economic decline for numerous reasons, including the demise of rail transport

(Noupoort), and the change in retail patterns which have caused financial leakages to larger towns and cities (Aberdeen, see Atkinson 2009).

Securing a reliable and ample income is, not surprisingly, a major aspiration for many local residents. The labour market (skills, jobs and wages) is always a crucial determinant of income (Deaton 2013: 190). Income earned through work remains a critical determinant of inequality in South Africa (Leibbrandt et al. 2010: 34). People without a good education through lack of ability or social background are likely to fall behind or resort to other means, such as politics, to secure an income. As few Karoo towns offer post-school training (Graaff-Reinet is an exception), this is a real constraint on people's earning capacity.

Internationally, there has been a trend towards declining real wages – particularly for manual work, for work not protected by trade unions, or for work exposed to competition from immigrants (Deaton 2013: 195). Karoo towns are weak on all these scores. Manual workers such as farm workers earn low wages (although sometimes supplemented by goods in kind), and they are vulnerable to unemployment through climatic, seasonal or economic fluctuations (Aliber et al. 2007). Declining employment in agriculture further undermines local incomes and multipliers in Karoo towns. Where farm workers, hampered by low skills, lose their farm-based jobs, they have little option but to eke out a living in shack settlements on the peripheries of towns. Such farm-to-town migration is partly based on 'push' factors (farm workers losing their jobs), and partly on 'pull' factors (farm workers or their families attracted by social services and Reconstruction and Development (RDP) houses in towns). In the process, Karoo towns have ballooned, placing increasing pressure on housing and infrastructural services (Nel et al. 2011).

There are hardly any trade unions in small towns (except in municipalities and schools, and such staff are already middle class); and many towns host immigrants from elsewhere in South Africa and the rest of Africa, which drives down wages. In Karoo towns, some families have a low and vulnerable wage income, exacerbated by lifestyle-based diseases (such as hypertension) and poverty-related illnesses such as TB and HIV (Walsh and Van Rooyen 2015). In these contexts, the importance of effective social services (mainly social grants and well-functioning clinics and schools) as corrective measures against poverty can hardly be overstated.

TREND 2: DIVERSIFICATION OF ECONOMIC ASSETS IN SMALL TOWNS

The fragile income streams in Karoo towns are also being altered by new investment patterns. New economic opportunities create fresh pathways of upward social mobility, particularly in retail, tourism, transport and nature conservation. Many small towns have seen a significant growth in tourism, mainly in hospitality services, but increasingly in attractions worth visiting (Atkinson 2016). New jobs have opened up in enterprises which require human contact – shop assistants, tourism, restaurants or healthcare (Atkinson and Ingle 2010). These jobs are often held by women, reinforcing local family incomes.

In those small towns where tourism has developed significantly it has been a boon to poor families – jobs in tourism enterprises are often better-paid than farming or retail jobs, and they involve some training and skills acquisition, creating future options for workers, who can move to another job or even to another town or the city.

In addition to local jobs and new investments, government services – municipalities, police stations, schools, clinics, social work and post offices – also provide a steady flow of revenue into Karoo towns, supporting local businesses which, in turn, offer local conveniences: a virtuous cycle. However, size matters. In very small towns, government services are limited, and provide only a few white-collar jobs. In large municipal jurisdictions, small outlying towns have a significant disadvantage, as municipalities have their head offices in larger towns.

The private sector, including privately owned farms and urban enterprises, is critical to Karoo towns. However, business owners can experience shocks too, as fluctuating rates of return and economic cycles can severely challenge business profitability. Some agricultural families have many children and have to split inheritances, and some entrepreneurial investments are inherently risky. Nevertheless, fixed assets such as farms and urban properties provide a use-value and are a buffer against risk because they can be tailored to new economic activities. Where property-owners invest in the local small-town economy jobs are created and local livelihoods and economic multipliers are stimulated.

In Karoo towns, the (more affluent) white commercial farmers still function as the rural aristocracy, with large farms that provide fairly reliable income despite droughts and economic fluctuations. They also have opportunities to diversify. However, there is a significant and growing difference between 'cash farmers' and those mired in chronic debt (Ortmann and Machethe 2003). Successive agricultural risks (drought, declines in the price of primary products, increases in the price of inputs, poor agricultural training systems) have hammered many dedicated producers. The number of farms in South Africa has halved in thirty years (Aliber et al. 2007). An ongoing difficulty in the commercial agricultural sector after 1994 has been the lack of government support in terms of science, technology, disaster management, rural infrastructure and tariff protection, and this has greatly increased the risks of farming (Vink and Kirsten 2003: 17). Since 2000, farmers have faced steep electricity price increases and input price hikes owing to a weakened currency. The Karoo agricultural economy is dominated by sheep production, and once the post-war wool boom waned the region suffered a long, slow decline (Conradie et al. 2009). Farmers have survived only by bolstering their position through highly effective producer companies and by local innovation such as alternative energy systems. Farmers who cannot manage these risks may sell up and leave the farming sector – following an international trend, as many farmers face ever increasing input prices and low product prices (Buckland 2004: 65).

Many Karoo farmers have diversified their economic activities in order to stay afloat. Some run their farms as a part-time activity while conducting a profession in the local town or in larger cities. Several have completed degrees in agriculture – a valuable skills base and a social network within which they can seek employment in enterprises such as agricultural retail or engineering. A university degree also provides opportunities to find spouses with a tertiary education and qualifications in teaching, nursing, tourism and architecture who can supplement farming incomes by establishing an enterprise or profession in a nearby town or city. This helps to smooth income streams and reduce risk. On-farm diversified activities include boutique agricultural products, tourist accommodation, recreational facilities and restaurants. These can enable families to hang on to their farms in volatile agricultural conditions.

In this context, the black beneficiaries of land redistribution grants do not fare so well. Many have experience as farm workers or taxi drivers, and they launch into agriculture with a measure of government financial support but they often do not have the benefit of agricultural studies at university. These new farmers face an ongoing battle for survival, without the complementary skills and networks of their white peers. Their new wealth base – the farm – may become an albatross rather than an eagle, dragging them into new cycles of debt and vulnerability. In the South African rural landscape, the significance of 'owning a farm' depends substantially on how it was obtained (inherited, purchased or received by government grant); what commercial and technical skills are available to work the land; what operating capital is available; what resources the spouse can muster; and what social networks help to support the farming enterprise.

Economic capital is always supported by social capital. It is at this point that a key residue of the apartheid system intrudes: white Karoo farmers create ongoing social capital through their farmers' unions and their churches, as well as their children's school affiliations. These networks are grounded on middle-class values and lifestyles. On occasion, white commercial farmers may reach out to their new black neighbours to provide advice and support, but this would not be a meeting of social equals – it would be a gesture of goodwill to a struggling person who does not really belong to the same social circle. A key question is whether farmers' unions, intended to be a meeting-ground of agriculturalists, can (or want to) overcome these racial and class divides. This typically varies from place to place, depending on the local interracial atmosphere as well as the dedication of social champions (black as well as white) who deliberately reach out to one another and help to break down social barriers. In this way, inherited social institutions such as agricultural associations can reproduce old social structures, but they may also create the opportunities for human agency and new social systems.

TREND 3: GOVERNMENT RESOURCES OFFER NEW OPPORTUNITIES – FOR SOME PEOPLE

The new professional class of Karoo towns are typically black people, working for provincial governments and municipalities. Ageing white officials have been largely replaced by younger black African and coloured officials, who bring new ways of doing things and new social networks. This has opened opportunities for black people in the public and private sectors because the new officials are more amenable to affirmative action tendering practices. The new government-business nexus has been a force for reducing inequality – at least between black and white people. Where officials see their long-term future in a small town they may purchase properties – although many officials prefer to rent homes as they are aiming at future careers in the bigger cities. Government offices bring important revenue streams (salaries and capital expenditure) to the towns, as well as new social dynamics – which remain poorly researched.

There are at least three discernible dynamics in the changing status of black African and coloured people in municipalities. The first, and most clearly evident, is the politics of patronage and job access that results from 'political deployment'. In many Karoo towns, political power has been captured by party-based elites. (The African National Congress (ANC) and the Democratic Alliance (DA) are the two most prominent parties in the Karoo, and a much deeper analysis is required of the style of governance in ANC-controlled and DA-controlled municipalities.) The practice of 'deployment' in ANC branches has contributed to politicising municipalities, not only at the level of councillors but also in officialdom, as senior officials become accountable to the political structure rather than to the local residents. Key municipal tasks, such as local economic development, tourism, gender relations and community development have become useful sinecures for local elites, sometimes with little regard to skills, aptitude or experience. Officials have often been guilty of poor decisions, inappropriate allocation of government resources or even an unwillingness to take decisions at all. The benefits to these modest-means recruits have significantly outweighed the benefits to the population at large.

A second group consists of local black middle-class families who have, through generations, survived segregationist restrictions and have diversified into sectors such as education, transport and construction. Where these family members have joined political organisations they are particularly well-placed to find jobs in desegregated and restructured public-sector institutions (Mabandla 2015). They also tend to invest in their children's education (often post-school), which makes them suitable candidates for local public sector jobs.

Finally, there is a new class of committed and professional black officials, who may have benefited from affirmative action principles (favouring black appointments), but who also secure their official jobs largely on the basis of merit and technical skills rather than (primarily) 'political deployment'. As middle-level jobs open up in municipalities and front-end offices of provincial departments, a new cohort of younger, professional and progressive officials are entering public service. In practice, they are often frustrated by the increasingly entrenched political patronage systems established by older 'deployed' officials and councillors.

The favouring of certain groups in distributing municipal largesse is certainly not new in South African history. Before 1994, only white people could own businesses in 'white' areas (outside the 'homelands'), and therefore any contracting of government businesses was allocated by law to white people. Within this racial category, small towns were likely to favour certain social 'inner circles' (such as local Broederbond chapters).

After 1994, the 'changing of the guard' in the government services has had important social consequences in Karoo towns. Many municipal officials are linked informally with new black entrepreneurs, by family networks, government contracts, political support and sometimes patronage and corruption. Professional standards in small towns are often lower than in the cities, simply because of a smaller pool of experts or qualified staff to compete for jobs. The opportunities for undue social or political influence in appointing staff or issuing contracts are widespread. Such cosy relations between government agencies and certain social groups very often subvert well-meant public policies. Broad-based economic growth may be undermined by rent-seeking, inter-factional conflict and ever more vicious competition for shares of a limited pie.

The rapid rise of this new government-linked middle class has created an ever-larger gap between salaried officials and the poorer black people who have not managed to secure a foothold in local employment or patronage systems. This also creates widespread social anxiety. In many cases, local politicians are drawn from the ranks of the working class or the unemployed, and have little experience of organisational management or business development. Becoming a municipal councillor has become an important political reward for loyal party members, regardless of their leadership abilities or developmental experience. Local officials and councillors feel threatened and embattled by potential competitors, and cling to their posts with inordinate desperation. Some mayors use municipal largesse to create a flotilla of jobs (personal assistants, community liaison officers) to employ their loyal political supporters. Any shift in local political power may open the floodgates to new challengers for municipal jobs, and hence many municipal officials resort to political stasis at any price.

Some of the advantages enjoyed by the new 'bureaucratic bourgeoisie' are cumulative, as political influence and government jobs promote social networks linked by ties of community, language and family. This creates opportunities for upward social mobility, strengthened by 'marital homogamy', the selection of partners with similar levels of education (Esping-Andersen 2006: 16). These families can afford much better education for their children, who are often sent away to schools in larger towns; their children, in turn, start moving in more affluent middle-class circles or migrate permanently to larger cities. In some cases, the speed of social advancement has been remarkably fast, with ambitious black people in Karoo towns stretching their new middle-class social and political networks into the cities where they gain access to even more opportunities, although links with their home towns remain important for family and symbolic reasons.

Some young people – of all race groups – remain in the Karoo towns, often because they lack the resources to escape, or are socially vulnerable, or are very emotionally attached to their families. These young people have to rely on their local social networks to access jobs in shops, government offices or tourism enterprises. In many cases, such social networks are still racially defined: young white people are employed in white-owned business, and young black people help out their family members in black-owned local enterprises or secure a position in the public sector. Church networks are important mechanisms for finding jobs. The only real racial integration takes place in larger enterprises, usually in larger Karoo towns, where white-owned private sector companies such as hotels, supermarkets or spas recruit black staff at various levels. From the perspective of racial contact and integration, new investments in new sectors make an important contribution to breaking down social barriers in small towns.

TREND 4: 'POST-PRODUCTIVIST SMALL TOWNS'

A new generation of energetic entrepreneurs has moved into Karoo towns from the cities, attracted by intangibles such as a rustic atmosphere, the neatness or architectural heritage of a town, the social solidarity provided by a church or cultural group and the reliability of water, electricity or broadband.

Some of these investors are fairly young (in their thirties or forties), and have already accumulated capital, business networks and experience in the cities. Many are in their fifties, or are retirees, investing their life savings in a rural enterprise such as tourism or crafts. Some of these people grew up in small towns, and have always wanted to return to their roots, or they have cultivated a fantasy (sometimes inspired by *Country Life* magazine) about returning to attractive small towns to pursue creative careers. Internationally, they form part of a 'creative class', inventing livelihoods out of innovation and artistic flair. Some Karoo towns have seen many of these well-heeled and stylishly countrified investors (Ingle 2010; Hoogendoorn and Nel 2012). They flow against the predominant rural-to-urban migration stream, and are therefore sometimes referred to as 'reverse migrants' or 'counter-urbanisers'. Their clienteles are typically urbanites or even foreigners, often spurring new ripples of in-migration.

This counter-intuitive type of migration is part of an even more far-reaching national trend, called 'rural post-productivism'. Rural areas and small towns diversify from primary agricultural production into lifestyle, tourism, ecological conservation, arts and crafts, thereby stimulating new economic sectors. In Karoo towns, these investors are typically white, middle class and visible. They make their presence known through upgrading local properties (particularly heritage buildings), advertising their enterprises and raising real estate prices. This, in turn, stimulates local activities such as construction, retail and business services. The investors bring new financial capital and a range of new ideas and social influences. New liberal values enter these towns; for example, gay people are often quite at home in Karoo towns and have made significant investments (Steytlerville's Karoo Theatrical Hotel, hosting cabaret performances, is a memorable example). New jobs and opportunities are created for (some of) the poor, although the number of employed people is small in relation to the large cohort of the unemployed.

The social consequences have varied widely in Karoo towns. Some of these new tourism and post-productivist initiatives tend to take place in isolation from the local black communities, who often still lack of the right kind of information, awareness, knowhow, networks and finance to benefit. A new kind of social schism characterises successful small towns, separating the new investors from the white old-timers as well as the local black communities. In other towns, the new arrivals have launched philanthropic projects, often linked to arts-and-crafts themes, and are having a notable impact on local black communities (Smithfield and De Aar being notable cases).

At the same time, there is a lingering racial schism in small towns. In the cities, white and black middle-class people have created shared spaces in the corporate sector but this is lacking in small towns, and hence the interface between the white and black middle classes still often needs to be encouraged and managed. Local black families, of middle-class means, tend to invest in sectors such as transport (taxis or vehicle maintenance), catering and personal services (such as hair-dressing). These are typically very small micro-enterprises, growing in experience and confidence but poorly linked to the post-productivist tourism sector. The relationship between the new white post-productivist class and the local black business class deserves much fuller investigation. Some small towns, such as Somerset East, have managed to build interracial linkages by means of dynamic chambers of commerce and local economic development associations, but this is still the exception to the rule.

TREND 5: SOCIAL PATTERNS REINFORCE POVERTY TRAPS

Karoo towns have a category of ultra-poor, often in dysfunctional households, in a classical 'poverty trap', defined as persistent poverty enduring over a period of time (Von Fintel 2015: 5).

Not all black people have access to government jobs or political influence, and they cannot capitalise on the lucrative commercial opportunities opening up. For farm workers and domestic servants without scarce skills or useful family networks employment is little more than intermittent and short-term. In Karoo towns, some people face multiple disadvantages: living or growing up in dysfunctional households or broken homes, enrolling in poorly functioning schools, dropping out of school, without inspiring role models or marketable skills, and without social networks to open up opportunities.

Poverty is increasingly becoming deracialised. Karoo towns also have elderly white people with limited incomes and meagre pensions, and they are slowly sliding into poverty traps. Some younger white people without effective networks are following them down the social ladder. High rates of teenage pregnancy are typical of 'formal rural' areas and small towns (Kara and Maharaj 2015: 73). Teenage pregnancy is compounded by absent fathers, or fathers unwilling to share financial responsibility for raising their children. Some towns are experiencing 'boomtown' conditions, owing to the rapid roll-out of renewable energy projects; in some towns, the phenomenon of 'sun babies' (illegitimate offspring of short-term contractors) has become prevalent. Many Karoo towns also have high levels of foetal alcohol syndrome (Urban et al. 2008), which virtually closes off any opportunity for social advancement for afflicted young people.

Social exclusion may result from multiple deprivation, particularly where social safety nets no longer function adequately. Poverty leads people to engage in illegal means of raising income: housebreaking, stealing livestock, peddling drugs and prostitution.

A criminal record almost invariably results in unemployment. Compared to the cities, small towns are typically very disadvantaged in terms of social support services, such as nongovernmental organisations (NGOs), alcohol and drug treatment centres or criminal rehabilitation. It is difficult for people on the margins of society to work their way back to social normality, because of the lack of expert support systems.

A real challenge, for Karoo towns, is the quality of schooling. Schools not only build technical and cognitive skills, but also create social skills and networks (Esping-Andersen 2006: 31). Many competent and ambitious teachers are tempted to seek careers in the cities, often leaving local schools staffed by teachers with limited skills or dedication. This contributes directly to long-term poverty and inequality in small towns. Early childhood education services, in particular, are critically important to break the cycle of poverty. Significantly, a growing number of Karoo towns have vibrant educational NGOs established by philanthropists – either long-time Karoo residents (Hantam School near Colesberg) or people who moved from the cities.

Social grants offer another important avenue out of severe poverty and social exclusion. They help to keep a large cohort of poor, vulnerable people in the small towns (thereby discouraging migration to the peri-urban squatter camps of the cities). The effectiveness of social grants should be measured along two entirely different scales. The first is the impact on poor households, particularly for children receiving child support grants, and the foster grants. Several analyses have pointed to the beneficial effects of grants in assisting children (Coetzee 2014; Leibbrandt et al. 2010: 63). This has particular significance for small towns: it enables working-age people to migrate to the cities in search of work, leaving children behind in the care of the grandparents, in a relatively safe environment. This, in turn, enables remittances to local families.

The second key impact of social grants works through local economic multipliers. Typically, grants and pensions are used for food and for school-related necessities such as uniforms (Leibbrandt et al. 2010: 64) which support small-town retail stores and indirectly sustain local jobs. Without social grants, businesses in many small towns would simply become unviable. Social grants help to sustain Karoo towns.

TREND 6: RACE, ETHNICITY AND LANGUAGE

Local small-town people function in dense social networks, and these networks are deeply influenced by linguistic identities. Karoo towns typically have several ethnic groups. Because of the 'cheek-by-jowl' nature of small towns, people from different language groups can hardly avoid each other in public places. Language can therefore play an important role in linking people (through multilingualism), as well as separating people, where people either cannot speak another language or do not want to learn or speak it, or they speak in ways which reinforce status barriers (see Laponce 1987: 26).

Under apartheid, Afrikaans was dominant in Karoo towns. Since 1994, indigenous languages have increasingly 'come into their own' and are a convenient communication tool in certain settings. Afrikaans has been virtually worked out of government institutions, and English has been strengthened in the tourism sector. Having some mastery of English often helps in securing a job. This further shapes new patterns of inclusion, exclusion and dominance in institutional settings. In some Karoo towns, such as Calvinia, local people feel that community relations are generally good (Rule and Fryer 2012). A great deal depends on the quality of local leadership (Toerien and Marais 2012: 5). Unlike large cities, Karoo towns still operate on a 'human scale', where a few inspired leaders can greatly improve race relations and social cohesion. Prince Albert is a notable example.

CONCLUSION

Karoo towns present a very complex and fluid picture of historical cultural patterns still remaining in force, with new class dynamics taking hold. White middle-class farmers and entrepreneurs are expanding their economic activities, creating more diverse economic regions. New well-heeled white investors interact with very poor rural people in close geographic proximity; 'old-timer' farmers rub shoulders with urban tourists; new and ambitious black officials have to stamp their authority on conservative and suspicious local white populations; and 'cadre-deployed' political veterans need to manage and watch out for a new class of young professional black officials. There are lucrative new opportunities. For black and white people, becoming big fish in such small ponds requires flexibility, innovation, risk-taking, diversification and effective networking abilities.

At the same time, some African, coloured and white people have fallen into poverty traps, often reinforced by a constrained labour market and poor-quality public services, notably education. It is not clear yet whether this ultra-poor class is growing. Most likely, some of this class are indeed working their way out of their dire straits, particularly where they encounter a conscientious teacher or social worker nearby. Many others are sinking deeply into social isolation, exclusion and criminality.

Each Karoo town is a microcosm – a social petri dish of postcolonial class patterns, ambitious new elites, new entrepreneurs and a new officialdom dispensing new systems of patronage and defending their privileges, all overlaid uncomfortably by parallel systems of racial networks and linguistic identities. Occasionally, local development champions reach out to potential collaborators in other racial groups, but it is still a challenge to create synergies and networks between white and black middle-class sectors. Karoo towns offer a cornucopia of future research opportunities.

REFERENCES

Aliber, M, Baipheti, M and Jacobs, P (2007) Agricultural employment scenarios. In R Hall (ed.)*Another countryside? Policy options for land and agrarian reform in South Africa*. Programme for Land and Agrarian Studies, University of the Western Cape, Bellville.

Atkinson, D (2009) Economic decline and gentrification in a small town: The case of Aberdeen, Eastern Cape. *Development Southern Africa*, 26 (2), 271–288.

Atkinson, D (2016) Is South Africa's Karoo Region becoming a tourism destination? *Journal of Arid Environments*, 127, 199–210.

Atkinson, D and Ingle, M (2010) A multi-dimensional analysis of local economic development in Graaff-Reinet, Eastern Cape. *Journal for New Generation Sciences*, 8 (1), 11–28.

Buckland, J (2004) *Ploughing up the farm: Neoliberalism, modern technology and the state of the world's farmers*. London: Zed Books.

Coetzee, M (2014) *Do poor children really benefit from the Child Support Grant?* www.econ3x3.org.

Conradie, B, Piesse, J and Thirtle, C (2009) What is the appropriate level of aggregation for productivity indices? Comparing district, regional and national measures. *Agrekon*, 48 (1), 9–20.

Daniels, RC, Partridge, A, Kekana, D and Musundwa, S (2013) *Rural livelihoods in South Africa*. Cape Town: SALDRU, University of Cape Town. SALDRU Working Paper Number 122/NIDS Discussion Paper 2013/4.

Deaton, A (2013) *The great escape: Health, wealth and the origins of inequality*. Princeton: Princeton University Press.

De Jong, T and Verkoren, O (2012) Commuting to and from small towns in the hinterland of Cape Town metropolitan area, Western Cape Province. In R Donaldson and L Marais (eds) *Small town geographies in Africa*. New York: Nova Press.

Esping-Andersen, G (2006) Inequality of incomes and opportunities. In A Giddens and P Diamond (eds) *The new egalitarianism*. Cambridge: Polity Press.

Hoogendoorn, G and Nel, E (2012) Exploring small town development dynamics in rural South Africa's post-productivist landscapes. In R Donaldson and L Marais (eds) *Small town geographies in Africa*. New York: Nova Press.

Ingle, M (2010) A 'creative class' in South Africa's arid Karoo region. *Urban Forum* 21 (4), 405–423.

Kara, R and Maharaj, P (2015) Childbearing among young people in South Africa: Findings from the National Income Dynamics Study. *Southern African Journal of Demography*, 16 (1).

Laponce, JA (1987) *Languages and their territories*. Toronto: University of Toronto Press.

Leibbrandt, M, Woolard, I, Finn, A and Argent, J (2010) *Trends in South African income distribution and poverty since the fall of apartheid*. Paris: Organisation for Economic Co-operation and Development (OECD), www.oecd.org/els/workingpapers.

Mabandla, N (2015) Rethinking bundy: Land and the black middle class – accumulation beyond the peasantry. *Development Southern Africa*, 32 (1), 76–89.

Nel, E, Hill, T, Taylor, B and Atkinson, D (2011) Demographic and economic changes in small towns in South Africa's Karoo: Looking from the inside out. *Urban Forum*, 22, 395–410.

Ortmann, G and Machethe, C (2003) Problems and opportunities in South African agriculture. In L Nieuwoudt and J Groenewald (eds) *The challenge of change: Agriculture, land and the South African economy*. Pietermaritzburg: University of Natal Press.

Rule, S and Fryer, S (2012) Calvinia: Exploratory study of the workings of a Karoo town. In R Donaldson and L Marais (eds) *Small town geographies in Africa*. New York: Nova Press.

Seekings, J and Nattrass, N (2006) *Class, race and inequality in South Africa*. Durban: University of KwaZulu-Natal Press.

Stats SA (Statistics South Africa) (2001) *Investigation into appropriate definitions of urban and rural areas for South Africa: Discussion document*. Report no. 03–02–20, Pretoria.

Toerien, D and Marais, L (2012) Classification of South African towns revisited. In R Donaldson and L Marais (eds) *Small town geographies in Africa*. New York: Nova Press.

Urban, M, Chersich, MF, Fourie, L, Chetty, C, Olivier, L and Viljoen, D (2008) Fetal alcohol syndrome among Grade 1 schoolchildren in Northern Cape Province: Prevalence and risk factors. *The South African Medical Journal*, 98 (11).

Vink, N and Kirsten, J (2003) Agriculture in the national economy. In L Nieuwoudt and J Groenewald (eds) *The challenge of change: Agriculture, land and the South African economy*. Pietermaritzburg: University of Natal Press.

Von Fintel, M (2015) *Social cohesion and mobility in post-apartheid South Africa*. PhD thesis, University of Stellenbosch.

Walker, R (2006) Opportunity and life chances: The dynamics of poverty, inequality and exclusion. In A Giddens and P Diamond (eds) *The new egalitarianism*. Cambridge: Polity Press.

Walsh, C and van Rooyen, F (2015) Household food security and hunger in rural and urban communities in the free state province, South Africa. *Ecology of Food and Nutrition*, 54 (2).

LAND AND ENVIRONMENT

4

CHAPTER 12

Spatial defragmentation in rural South Africa: A prognosis of agrarian reforms

Samuel Kariuki

South Africa is the most unequal country in the world, and the gap between rich and poor is growing. In 2013, the richest 4 per cent of South African households earned 32 per cent of the country's total income, next to 66 per cent of households receiving less than a quarter (21 per cent) of all income (Visagie 2013). One of the core indicators of South African inequality and poverty is unequal land ownership, spatial fragmentation, tenure insecurity, a dualistic agriculture sector tilted in favour of large-scale farmers and agribusinesses to the neglect of smallholder producers, and economic exclusion based on race, place and class, all of which form part of apartheid's historical legacy.

This chapter seeks to analyse some of the broad contours of South Africa's rural economic transformation in a context where structural changes in the agricultural sector that are characteristic of the industrial agricultural model (land consolidation, corporate concentration, financialisation, capitalisation, intensifying duality in agricultural value chains, informalisation of the labour force and increasing uptake of foreign juristic persons in land acquisition and agro-corporations) could potentially undermine the very constitutional promise of redress to be achieved through a progressive land policy regime in favour of an inclusive and 'deracialised' rural economy. This constitutional promise is set out in the Bill of Rights (Chapter 2 of the Constitution), particularly section 25 and section 27.

In examining increasing inequality and persistent poverty in rural South Africa, particularly in land ownership and in the context of the industrialisation of the farming sector, this chapter aims to demonstrate the urgent need for bold and decisive reforms promoting rural structural transformation. These reforms must change the current trajectory of the agricultural sector if the state is to fulfil its constitutional obligations and achieve the National Development Plan's (NDP's) objectives of inclusive and sustained economic growth and development, food security, poverty eradication and a significant reduction in inequality (NPC 2012).

With dangerous levels of unemployment, poverty and inequality continuing to rise as major sectors such as mining and manufacturing stagnate, the role of agriculture in boosting the overall economy and uplifting living standards for the poor is increasingly important. A shift away from the prevailing agricultural industrial model and its associated structural changes (as discussed below) is particularly salient in light of the mounting evidence that sustained economic growth is not possible in the context of extreme inequality (Dabla-Norris et al. 2015).

DEFINING THE CONCEPT OF SPATIAL DEFRAGMENTATION

Although it is commonly used in discussing structural reform in South Africa, it is difficult to find a clear definition for the concept of spatial defragmentation. As articulated by Kuethe (2012: 16), fragmentation 'relates to the discontinuities between subgroups within some larger population'. The same author differentiates between different kinds of fragmentation, including ecological, political, social and spatial fragmentation:

> Ecological fragmentation addresses such topics as maintaining biodiversity and preserving natural landscapes … High degrees of political fragmentation are associated with the division of an area into numerous administrative units with little collaboration among them … A population with a high degree of social fragmentation is characterised by limited connections between subgroups, such as groups formed by common culture, language, race, or income level … which lead to increased levels of economic disparity and social inequality. Spatial fragmentation … addresses the discordance of land use activities and the physical properties of space (Kuethe 2012: 16–17).

Spatial defragmentation as used in this chapter incorporates all the above elements, as apartheid divided the country not only along ecological, political, racial, economic and geographic lines, but has also shaped how land is held and used throughout the country. Apartheid created different kinds of spaces, characterised by starkly different forms of spatial inequality stubbornly enduring to the present day. Therefore, spatial defragmentation here refers to the dismantling of apartheid geography, and the reintegration of rural and urban economies.

THE SPATIAL IMPRINT OF COLONIALISM AND APARTHEID

South Africa's spiralling levels of inequality are rooted in its protracted history of race-based land dispossession, economic exclusion and exploitation. This history resulted in severe spatial and economic segregation, in which the core, consisting of approximately 87 per cent of the land, was designated for white and state ownership, while the remaining periphery was designated for black occupation in so-called 'native reserves'. Blacks residing in the core were forcibly removed from their homes into peripheral areas (today consisting mostly of what is referred to as the communal areas), and permitted to enter 'white South Africa' only for employment purposes.

The vast majority of white South Africans reside in cities and towns, and on privately owned commercial farmland with secure tenure rights and well-established infrastructure. Also found within the white commercial farming areas are large numbers of black South Africans (approximately 2.7 million people as of 2011), most of whom lack secure land rights and provide their labour to farm owners for low wages and under poor working conditions (Visser and Ferrer 2015). The former reserve areas are home to another estimated 16.5 million mostly tenure-insecure black South Africans, of which 59 per cent are women (Weinberg 2013). Millions more black South Africans are found in informal rural and peri-urban settlements that have rapidly developed outside the towns and cities owing to continued evictions of farm dwellers, as well as other forms of land alienation and a dearth of opportunities in the communal areas. A substantial number (32.4 per cent) of food-insecure South Africans live in these informal areas (Oxfam 2014).

Correspondingly, the former reserve areas score the lowest on all dimensions of the multiple deprivation index, including access to public services, education, clean water and sanitation, adequate housing, food security and health (Stats SA 2014). Unsurprisingly, South Africa's highest rates of unemployment, infant mortality and illiteracy, as well as lowest levels of asset ownership and income, are also concentrated in the ex-bantustans and former reserve areas (UNDP 2014). Stalled agricultural and industrial development, low levels of productivity, and increasing pressure on already scarce land and resources form poverty traps in which the absence of upward mobility opportunities means that social and economic marginalisation is transferred from one generation to the next.

More generally, the great divide between rural and urban areas is evident in the fact that more than two-thirds of rural residents lived below the poverty line in 2011, compared to fewer than a third of urban residents, with poverty levels in rural areas (at 68.8 per cent) more than double those in urban areas (at 30.9 per cent) and of a far more severe kind (Stats SA 2011, 2014). These statistics are especially informative to the analysis of trends in urbanisation. Despite the substantial out-migration from rural areas, South Africa still has a large rural population, with over 182 local municipalities classified as rural and only 52 municipalities as urban, out of which 8 are the metros. In 2011, the predominantly rural provinces of KwaZulu-Natal, the Eastern Cape and Limpopo comprised nearly 43 per cent of the population, even though together they cover less than 32 per cent of the country's surface area (Stats SA 2011).

Intrinsically intertwined with the stark urban/rural divide is the increasing inequality seen in South Africa, with the nation's Gini coefficient rising from 0.64 in 1995 to a high of 0.7 in 2012 (Sharma 2012). The 2011 Census estimated that more than nine out of ten poor people in the country were black South Africans (Stats SA 2011). In 2012, the average income of white-headed households was over 5.5 times that of African-headed households: R387 011 and R69 632 respectively (Stats SA 2012). It is now widely agreed that the main drivers of income inequality are labour market outcomes (UNDP 2014). This is largely because wages of the lowest income workers have not increased in real terms since before independence, whereas earnings of the country's highest paid workers have increased substantially (Cole 2015).

Empirical evidence indicates that economic inequality hinders economic growth and poverty alleviation, exacerbates other forms of existing inequalities (such as those between women and men), and is unsustainable in the long run (Murray-Prior and Ncukana 2000; Dabla-Norris et al. 2015). On the other hand, low levels of income inequality have been correlated with inclusive economic growth, in which every per cent of growth is accompanied by a significant level of poverty reduction (Ferreira and Ravallion 2008). These findings highlight the urgency of reforms that effectively tackle the structural basis of inequality and poverty in South Africa – namely the continuation of spatial fragmentation and exclusion of rural residents from the benefits of economic growth.

The need for structural change was most recently articulated by Minister Rob Davies in May 2016 during the Department of Trade and Industry's launch of the eighth iteration of the Industrial Policy Action Plan 2016/2017–2017/2018 (government's rolling action plan for reindustrialisation of the South African economy). One of the overarching messages of Davies's speech was that overcoming the 'deep-seated structural problems that characterise our economy' requires interventions that engender 'sustainable localisation'. This entails growing the labour-absorbing sectors of society (including agriculture) and developing the capacity of local manufacturers (including agro-processing) which, in turn, will create jobs, increase incomes and boost demand for locally produced products, thus translating into a 'virtuous cycle of growth' (DTI 2016). From a land reform perspective, redistribution of land must be carried out within a broader approach to structural reform and sustainable development that changes the current inequitable and exclusive patterns of accumulation in order to result in broad-based meaningful employment and wealth creation.

SKEWED LAND DISTRIBUTION

Population and land distribution statistics are telling of the extremity of the spatial fragmentation and inequality that stand in the way of inclusive growth and development. In 1911, approximately 6 million people lived in South Africa, including just under 4.7 million black Africans, coloureds and Indians next to approximately 1.27 million whites. The apartheid blueprint created by the 1913 and 1936 Land Acts translated into over 70 per cent of South Africa's land (87 million hectares) being controlled by less than 1 per cent of the population in 1994, while approximately 2 million black households farmed on a small scale in the former reserve areas, which consisted of less than 15 per cent of the country's land (13 million hectares) (PLAAS 2012; Cochet et al. 2015).

By mid-2015, South Africa's total population had risen to just under 55 million people, with more than 90 per cent classified as black Africans, coloureds and Indian/Asians and only 9 per cent of the population classified as white (Stats SA 2015a). Despite significant population growth and the introduction of land reforms in the post-1994 era, the great extent of South Africa's agricultural land is now owned by even fewer (mostly) white and internationally owned corporates. This means that the majority of South Africans who need rural or urban lands for agricultural, residential and other social and productive purposes are unable to gain access to land. Extreme poverty is exacerbated by the limited availability of suitable land for farming and grazing purposes.

While around 82 million of the country's 122 million hectares of land is considered potential commercial agricultural land, only 12 per cent is classified as arable and only 3 per cent regarded as high potential agricultural land. South Africa has experienced a significant decline of arable land available to produce food (as much as 30 per cent between 1994 and 2009). The Department of Agriculture, Forestry and Fisheries (DAFF 2015b) estimated that as much as 3.38 million hectares of arable land has been converted to non-agricultural uses (mining, game farms and urban expansion) by 2011.

A BI-MODAL AGRICULTURAL SECTOR

Closely interlinked with apartheid's legacy of skewed land distribution and consequent poverty and inequality is the bi-modal nature of South Africa's agricultural sector. On one hand, a well-established flourishing commercial sector consists of a relatively small number of commercial farmers and agribusinesses that own the greater part of agricultural land under freehold title. Benefiting from extensive state support throughout most of the twentieth century, this large-scale commercial sector uses advanced technology to cultivate and process a wide range of commodities, has a well-developed input, processing and wholesale sector, competes successfully in local and international markets, and generates significant employment and export earnings (Sandrey and Vink 2008).

On the other hand, an underdeveloped, historically disadvantaged small-scale sector consisting of more than 2 million households engages mainly in subsistence production on environmentally degraded land (most of which is located long distances from markets in the former reserve areas) held under insecure tenure (Cochet et al. 2015). Constrained by limited access to quality arable land, services, irrigation systems and other technology, smallholder communal farmers are confined to cultivating basic crops and raising livestock mostly for household consumption, with little opportunity to develop viable farming enterprises capable of withstanding the increasing economic pressures affecting the agricultural sector in the post-1994 era. The consolidation of agricultural land and concentration of capital has further intensified the already highly dualistic nature of the agricultural sector (RSA 2014).

STRUCTURAL CHANGES AND EMERGING TRENDS IN THE AGRICULTURAL SECTOR

Liberalisation and deregulation reforms in the agricultural sector began in the final decades of apartheid and rapidly accelerated throughout the 1990s. The reforms took different forms including significant reductions or complete cancellation of direct state subsidisation of farmers and the abolition of systems concerned with agricultural marketing and price regulation – and altering the status of state cooperatives, financial institutions and other structures concerned with agricultural development.

Closely linked with the factors discussed above, new trends have emerged in the commercial agriculture sector: corporatisation, consolidation and concentration of agricultural land and capital; increasing conversion of farmland into non-agricultural uses; mounting foreign ownership of land; northward expansion of South African agrarian capital; and financialisation of the sector. These trends have undermined rural transformation and deepened the dualistic nature of South African agriculture.

Although liberalisation reforms were justified on the basis of ending state transfers to the already highly privileged white commercial sector, and the need to break down monopoly on agricultural markets, they had the opposite effect. Market deregulation resulted in further corporate concentration of agricultural capital (Visser and Ferrer 2015). Reforms enabled numerous cooperatives to privatise, consolidate and reinvent themselves as Johannesburg Stock Exchange-listed agribusinesses. Together with other domestic agribusiness giants that came out of apartheid and multinationals, formerly state-run and now privatised cooperatives have come to dominate the entire agriculture value chain not only in South Africa, but throughout the rest of the continent (Cochet et al. 2016). This is due to the vertical and horizontal integration of agricultural firms within the agro-food system through major acquisitions and mergers that have been made during the privatisation process. It has resulted in the inability of smaller enterprises along the value chain to compete, especially entry-level black entrepreneurs historically disadvantaged in terms of experience, skills and networking opportunities.

Agricultural deregulation and liberalisation have also translated into further consolidation of the country's farmland. Next to well-established large-scale commercial farmers who accumulated enough capital during apartheid to withstand the withdrawal of state support and the opening of markets to global competition, most small-scale farmers (white and black alike) have struggled to compete successfully with their better-off domestic counterparts and international firms absent of state support. With the phasing out of agricultural marketing boards in 1996, commercial farmers faced greater market risks next to dramatically reduced support and increasing legislative requirements. Insolvent white farmers could no longer fall back on the state to bail them out, and had to either adapt or go under. Many have consequently been bought out by larger agricultural firms, with a major decline in the number of these farmers since 1996.

This decline is evident in the statistics. In 1971, there were 90 422 commercial farming units in South Africa (Aliber et al. 2007). By 1996, this number had declined to an estimated 60 000 units, which continued to decrease to 45 818 in 2002 and 39 966 by 2007 (Visser and Ferrer 2015). Today the number of commercial farming units is estimated at between 29 000 and 40 000, depending on the source (DAFF 2015a; Cochet et al. 2015). Land concentration in certain subsectors has been especially drastic following deregulation. For instance, the dairy industry experienced a 41 per cent reduction in the number of dairy farms between 1997 and 2006 (Visser and Ferrer 2015).

Coupled with this decline is the corresponding trend of growth in the average farm size. The average size of South African farms exceeding a turnover of R300 000 grew from 1 450 hectares in 1997 to just below 2 500 hectares in 2015 (Cochet et al. 2015). This rise of so-called 'mega-farms' – witnessed around the world in developing countries as part of the trend of increasing foreign investment in farmland – is yet another element of the agricultural industrialisation model. As in many other developing countries, the increase of mega-farms in South Africa is resulting in increasing reliance on capital assets such as mechanisation and subsequent substantial labour shedding within the sector, as well as major land-use changes, further dispossession of rural inhabitants and an increasingly monopolised sector (Saravia-Matus et al. 2013).

Even those who make the case for large-scale commercial agriculture problematise the concentration of farmland into massive industrial agricultural units. For instance, in asking whether mega-farms are a sensible approach for African governments to engender sustainable development, Collier and Dercon (2013: 3) conclude: 'While commercialisation of African agriculture is desirable, the mega-farms are fundamentally geopolitical rather than commercial, and are therefore not an appropriate vehicle for African societies.' Mega-farms are viewed by these authors as inefficient, inequitable and disadvantageous for society.

Occurring alongside the phenomenon of mega-farms is the emergence of significant monopolies over agricultural inputs (particularly seeds, pesticides and fertilisers) by large transnational corporations which are buying out or into South African companies and dominating input supply chains. Take seeds for instance: only ten of the largest seed companies hold rights to nearly two-thirds of the country's registered seed varieties. At the top of this list is Pannar, a South African-owned company that in 2012 merged with Pioneer Hi-Bred, a subsidiary of the US-based company Du Pont, and Monsanto, also a US-based company (African Centre for Biosafety 2014).

Such monopolisation diminishes options for both smaller producers and consumers, as monopolistic corporations have the power to engage in price setting and influence agricultural policies favouring the agricultural industrial model. As such, the contribution of multinationals to an increasingly monopolised, inequitable and exclusive commercial agricultural sector, with all of its structural changes as discussed herein, has been extremely destructive for local small producers.

Again, the case of seeds is telling. While genetically modified seeds are promoted on the basis of improved production yields and thus higher profits for farmers, such outcomes are highly dependent on fertiliser, pesticide and irrigation use. Frequent use of these inputs are unaffordable and out of the reach of most small-scale farmers in South Africa, as is yearly purchase of hybrid seed varieties (which are designed for one-time use). Smallholders are thus unable to compete with 'mega farmers', who use hybrid seed varieties together with the other required inputs to boost yields (African Centre for Biosafety 2014).

The sharp reduction in number of farming units can be attributed to other factors, including the choice of large-scale producers to exit farming and enter into other sectors of the economy because of increased pressures in the agricultural sector since 1994; the trend of converting farmland (in both the freehold and communal areas) to non-agricultural uses such as mining, game farms, golf courses, housing developments and holiday estates; and increasing foreign ownership of land (Hall 2009, 2011; DAFF 2015b). The exact amount of land held by foreign individuals and corporate entities remains unknown, although the Department of Rural Development and Land Reform (DRDLR) is currently developing legislation to both determine the extent of and regulate foreign acquisition of agricultural land. In 2007, a panel of experts appointed by the former Department of Land Affairs (DLA) to investigate this issue reported that around 3 per cent of land (or just under 300 000 hectares) was owned by foreign persons. This figure, however, excludes land owned by foreign legal entities, and the reality is expected to be much higher (DLA 2007). 'Foreignisation' of South African agriculture is not limited to land. There are agribusinesses along the entire value chain (see the example of Pannar above). South Africa is now being seen as the 'gateway into Africa' by a wide range of foreign investors.

The aforementioned trends have also led to land speculation and higher property values in rural areas (DLA 2007). Inflated land prices and speculation translate into a seller's market, posing even more obstacles for land redistribution. This is closely related to yet another way in which the agricultural sector has been restructured – the financialisation of the South African and wider global economy. Financialisation of the South African agricultural sector has seen capital directed into finance and consumption as opposed to the productive investments necessary to create jobs, develop rural industry and overcome inequality (UNDP 2014). The country's farmland is being purchased and held for speculative and other non-productive purposes by both domestic and transnational private capital (such as various forms of institutional funds, financial institutions and agribusinesses) (Hall and Cousins 2015). This trend has been accentuated post-2007 – agricultural land has been promoted as a new and lucrative asset class in response to the major hikes in prices of food and non-food commodities (Ducastel and Anseeuw 2013). Another key trend closely related to the corporatisation and financialisation process is the recently intensified trend of northward economic expansion of agrarian capital into the rest of Africa. South African farmers and other enterprises along the agricultural value chain have sought new opportunities for capital accumulation across the border since 1994 (Miller et al. 2008).

IMPLICATION OF THE STRUCTURAL CHANGES AND CHANGING TRENDS IN AGRICULTURE TO RURAL REFORM

As noted above, smaller commercial farmers have suffered considerably under the dereg-ulated and liberalised sector, with many forced out of production. This is not only evident in the drastic decline in commercial farming units, but also in the sharp rises in levels of indebtedness of smaller white farmers. Left without state financing mechanisms to help capitalise operations, these producers have had to borrow from commercial banks at much higher interest rates than provided by the Land Bank under apartheid. Farmers paid almost R3 billion in interest charged on nearly R30 billion-worth of loans in 2002, with total farming debt growing to R36.7 billion by 2006 (up from about R18.18 billion in 1994) (Hall 2009; Chisasa and Makina 2012). By 2010 it reached nearly 57.1 billion, with most of this debt owed to commercial banks in 2011 (DAFF 2012). The highest share of this debt is owed by farming enterprises generating less than R300 000 in gross annual income. These smaller commercial farms have provided the bulk of agricultural employ-ment in South Africa, yet many have either collapsed or been sold owing to insolvency (Hall 2009). '[The] solvency position of the farm sector is currently at its worst position for over three decades' (Visser and Ferrer 2015: 73).

In sum, the impacts of deregulation and liberalisation on farmers in the former reserve areas and other target land reform beneficiaries has been far worse than those felt by smaller white commercial farmers. The combination of historical disadvantage and neo-liberal restructuring of the agricultural sector has meant that the estimated millions of smallholder producers in communal areas face massive barriers to establishing competi-tive primary and secondary agricultural enterprises.

The most affected by these structural trends are probably farm workers and their families. The agricultural workforce has been restructured in two main ways since 1994: substantial reduction in labour and the casualisation and externalisation of the labour force. The sector is estimated to have lost 1.1 million jobs between 1994 and 2012 (IDC 2013). However, the total gross value of agricultural production and net incomes of farm-ers have increased in recent years (June 2011 to June 2015), particularly for large-scale commercial producers, many of whom are found in provinces experiencing the sharpest decline in agricultural employment (DAFF 2012, 2013a, 2013b, 2014, 2015c, 2016).

As increasing numbers of smaller commercial farmers go under, choose to exit farming or convert farms to non-agricultural land uses, farm workers lose their jobs. Additionally, heightened land consolidation and market monopolisation have translated into a dimin-ished reliance on labourers as mechanised methods of production are increasingly employed. Even in certain subsectors that are unable to mechanise – such as fruit farms – the agricultural workforce has been downsized (Visser and Ferrer 2015). The consoli-dation trend has significantly accelerated since the early 1990s. Between 1993 and 2002, approximately 150 000 agricultural jobs were lost, with agricultural employment total-ling 627 000 in 2002 (Hall 2009). Between 2002 and 2012 another 858 975 workers in the agricultural, forestry and fishing sector were retrenched, the sector's total employment decreasing from 1.52 million to 661 025 in this decade (Visser and Ferrer 2015).

Although by the end of 2015 total agricultural employment was back up to 860 000, it still amounts to only about 2.53 per cent of South Africa's working age population in mid-2015 (Stats SA 2015b, 2015a). It also masks the trend towards increasing casualisation and externalisation of farm labour that has followed democratisation in 1994. Next to the massive expulsion of workers – which for many has meant not only the loss of income but also loss of homes, land and social networks, often with no alternative employment to be found – farm owners have replaced permanent employees with short-term contracted (often seasonal) workers. Casualisation of agricultural labour has also been accompanied by externalisation of workers, who are employed via brokers or other intermediaries instead of directly by farm owners. Hall and Cousins (2015: 3) write that these trends have 'meant the creation of an increasingly off-farm, casual labour force, especially in the core sector of horticulture – a footloose workforce of people in informal settlements dotted around farming districts.

Beyond the socio-economic implications of continuing land consolidation, increasing farm sizes and mechanised production, there are significantly negative environmental implications of the agricultural industrial model. Large-scale industrial farming is water intensive and contributes to a higher carbon footprint for South Africa owing to greater use of fossil fuels and electricity for powering machinery and petroleum-based fertilisers and pesticides. Corporate farming in South Africa also often involves practices such as massive land and forest clearing, intensive monoculture production, factory livestock production and conversion of farmland into non-agricultural land uses, all of which significantly increase global greenhouse gas emissions. Largely because of these practices, agriculture contributes 5 per cent to the country's total net greenhouse gas emissions (Blignaut et al. 2014).

As highlighted by key global institutions, industrial agricultural production methods drastically accelerate global warming (even more so than the global transportation sector) and are therefore unsustainable. There is a crucial need for application of more agro-ecological methods as commonly practised on small-scale farms (IAASTD 2008). Labour-intensive small-scale farms are now widely viewed as more climate friendly and sustainable as they rely on people power as opposed to heavy machinery, use less chemical inputs, and most often produce for local markets and direct consumption. Carbon emissions from sustainably run small-scale farms are as much as one-half to two-thirds per acre of production less than large-scale industrial agriculture (IPCC 2007). The small-scale agro-ecological methods of production carry significant potential for sequestering carbon dioxide already present in the soil and atmosphere (Vandermeer et al. 2009). For these reasons, consensus is emerging that shifting from reliance on industrial farming to small-scale production will minimise agriculture's contribution to global warming. However, rather than structural transformation of the economy through land and agrarian reform, the past twenty-two years of democracy have witnessed increased dominance of large-scale corporate farming in the country, further exacerbating inequality, poverty and unemployment.

Notable gains have been made in poverty alleviation and improvement of households' welfare, with the most progress made since democratisation in the provision of electricity, water access, sanitation and housing (Cole 2015); and there are significant decreases in people living below the food poverty line. Nonetheless, as observed by the NDP of 2012, reductions in rural poverty can mainly be attributed to substantial expansion of the state's social grants system, with recipients increasing from 3 million in 2000 to 15 million by 2011 (Stats SA 2014). It is estimated that half of rural households depend on social grants and/or remittances to sustain livelihoods, compared to one in six households in urban centres (NPC 2012). These grants play a pivotal role in helping the most vulnerable members of society to meet their basic needs. However, there are questions about the affordability and sustainability of the social welfare system.

LARGE-SCALE FARMING NEXT TO SMALLHOLDERS

The view that larger sized farms are better able to realise economies of scale, and are thus more efficient and viable than smaller sized farms, is a principle philosophy underlying the agricultural industrial complex. The dominant view that large farm size synchronises with greater efficiency underpins the agricultural industrial model, and has significantly thwarted rural economic transformation and further entrenched rural poverty and inequality. The consolidation of farmland into fewer hands and larger farms has intensified dualism in the agricultural sector, as well as exacerbated rural unemployment (RSA 2014). Noting that as much as 75 per cent of poor people in developing countries live in rural areas, the World Bank's 2008 World Development Report, entitled 'Agriculture for Development', highlights that the vast majority of the world's rural residents (86 per cent in 2008) depend on agriculture as an important livelihood resource (World Bank 2008).

The 2008 report places much emphasis on the need to support small-scale farmers in sub-Saharan Africa and beyond. The experiences of certain Asian and Latin American countries provide ample evidence of the poverty-reducing and transformative potential of agriculture if policies are tilted towards the needs of small-scale producers and other rural residents. Take China for example. In the second half of the twentieth century, China implemented various land and other reforms aimed at securing tenure, stimulating the production of smallholder farmers, promoting rural industry and diversifying rural incomes. The country also invested heavily in educating and developing skills in the rural population, and provided extensive subsidisation and protection to its small-scale farmers (including by establishing state credit facilities for these producers). As a result, the country experienced impressive economic growth and drastically reduced its number of poor citizens, while also creating a more equitable country (Fan and Chan-Kang 2005).

Harnessing agriculture's employment-creation potential is especially urgent in light of what the NDP refers to as the 'youth bulge', where there exists a high proportion of working-age people next to a high dependency ratio due to the majority of the working-age population not having employment (NPC 2012). In the next two decades, South Africa will see its youth population (between fifteen and twenty-nine years) grow to over 14 million. As the NDP avers, the country has reached a 'sweet spot' of demographic transition with a relatively large number of working-age residents together with low numbers of young and old. Some economists refer to this as a 'demographic dividend' in which a large economically active population can 'increase economic output and invest in technology, education and skills to create the wealth needed to cope with the future aging of the population', in turn contributing to overall poverty and inequality reduction (NPC 2012: 98).

However, if not effectively taken advantage of by 2030, the nation's 'demographic dividend' poses one of the greatest threats to social stability as this large working-age population turns into elderly pensioners dependent on social assistance to meet their basic needs. In the agricultural sector, this window is closing – evident in the ageing cohort of farmers, whose average age in 2012 was estimated to be sixty-two (Hancock 2015). While there are ample numbers of youth to fill the places of retiring farmers, studies have indicated low participation rates and interest levels of the young in agriculture despite the high levels of youth unemployment (SACAU 2013). This is partially a result of pervasive landlessness, land-shortage and tenure insecurity among rural black South Africans, who also lack the necessary resources and skills to make a successful entry into the sector. It is also due to negative attitudes of youth towards farming (FAO 2013).

Research has indicated that many young people see agriculture as a last resort and perceive farm work to be characterised by drudgery, riskiness, limited financial return and work for the elderly, uneducated and poor (SACAU 2013). Despite this perception, studies have shown that the demand for land among rural South African youth is high, with most wanting land to grow food, bolster incomes and have a secure place in which to live (HSRC 2005). The generational crisis of the South African agricultural sector could be addressed through policies that not only support labour-absorbing small-scale agriculture but also provide rural black youth with the skills, education and other necessary capabilities to find, secure and maintain quality employment and become successful agro-entrepreneurs.

The urgent need to alter South Africa's current structure of commercial agriculture in favour of small-scale farmers, and thus counteract destructive trends of land consolidation and mega-farms, monopolisation of the agricultural value chain by multinationals and conversion of farmland to non-agricultural uses is supported by major multilateral organisations such as the United Nations, who declared 2014 the International Year of Family Farming. In complementing this, the Food and Agriculture Organisation's (FAO) (2014) report showed that family farming is the principal method of agricultural production around the globe (with more than 500 million of the 570 million farms in existence worldwide classified as family farms); is responsible for producing 80 per cent of the world's food in value terms; and, together, the largest employer in the world (Lowder et al. 2014: 2).

CONCLUSION

Apparent in the great spatial disparities, unequal land ownership patterns and dualistic agricultural regime characterising South Africa, rural transformation and historical redress has not taken significant effect in fully meeting the constitutional imperative on land dispossession. The substantial labour shedding seen in the agricultural sector has also been accompanied by a decline in unskilled employment in the mining sector, which employed an estimated 500 000 people in 2013, down from approximately 830 000 in 1997 (Gwatidzo and Benhura 2013; NPC 2011). Paired with the decline in farm employment, the retrenchment of mineworkers has hit rural African residents of traditional labour-sending areas (the peripheral communal areas) particularly hard, further deepening poverty and inequality. Increasing evidence affirms that ending structural inequality and rural poverty through bold agrarian reforms is an essential step in realising sustained and inclusive economic growth, given the current reality of South Africa's contracting economy.

Following global trends, there has been a renewed focus in South Africa on the potential for the agricultural sector to serve as the engine for rural development. The refocus by government to promote an integrated and inclusive rural economy gives emphasis to land and agrarian reform, and in particular the contribution of small-scale agriculture to the rural economy. In order to effectively reverse the apartheid spatial geography of segregated development and alienation of land, rural development, land redistribution and tenure reform initiatives must be targeted towards capturing the immense amount of human and resource capital potential available in the periphery. At the core of rural development and tenure reform should be a concerted attempt to restructure the national economic and spatial framework through a combination of policies focused on development of rural areas and strategic land acquisition.

This requires a shift away from the agricultural industrial model and the attendant trends that have resulted in significant transformations of the agricultural sector, albeit not in the direction intended within the framework of land and agrarian reform. While the extent of these trends is not yet fully known, they hold significantly negative implications for poor rural black South Africans. As has been demonstrated through this paper, the large-scale corporate farming model is not sustainable and is completely unsuited for the South African context, where land and agrarian reforms are urgently needed to address the spatial fragmentation, inequity, food insecurity, poverty and unemployment still all too apparent in society.

In order to effectively pursue radical changes in property relations, we must continue critically to examine the viability of the large-scale corporate farming model. The main argument advanced by proponents of this model, namely that large-scale commercial farms contribute to national food security, is unconvincing, particularly in light of the fact that 14 million South Africans go to bed hungry on a regular basis (Oxfam 2014). While it is true that only the top 20 per cent of commercial farms produce as much as 80 per cent of the value of agricultural production (Kirsten 2011), this is not an indication of the contribution of large-scale farms to national food security but, rather, evidence of the sector's increasingly monopolised and inequitable nature.

Widely acknowledged by a diverse range of stakeholders, including government, community based organisations (CBOs) and nongovernmental organisations (NGOs), certain farmers' organisations and academics, a new model of agricultural development is urgently needed in South Africa. Such a model must engender broad inclusive agrarian transformation, in which millions of African households living in communal areas and on commercial farms are enabled to expand their own production activities and incrementally build agricultural skills and resources. This cannot be achieved without drastic restructuring of the highly concentrated food system, and agricultural landholdings (in which mega-farms are divided into smaller family-sized farms) are rapidly transferred to the rural poor and other land reform beneficiaries, comprehensive support is provided to producers and a more equitable pattern of land and wealth distribution is created.

Momentum has advanced towards such a shift under the auspices of the 2011 Green Paper on Land Reform, which proposes a paradigm shift in dealing with the question of land and agrarian transformation by overhauling the entire policy, institutional and legal infrastructure that has underpinned land and agrarian reform in the past twenty-two years (DRDLR 2011). The overhaul of land and agrarian reform proposed by the 2011 Green Paper exemplifies government's recognition that major structural reforms are required to effectively tackle the triple challenges of poverty, unemployment and inequality.

Thus far, change is tangible, as seen through passage of recent legislation emanating from the Green Paper such as the Spatial Planning and Land Use Management Act (SPLUMA) (Act 16 of 2013), Property Valuations Act (Act 17 of 2014) and the Restitution of Land Rights Amendment Act (RLRA) (Act 15 of 2014). While SPLUMA offers mechanisms for improving coordination and consistency in state spatial planning and more sustainable land use, the Property Valuations Act signifies a dramatic shift away from the willing buyer/willing seller model of land acquisition as it enables the state to acquire land at below-market prices – as opposed to the commonly inflated prices paid for land in the past. This is especially important in light of the need to accelerate land redistribution.

If carried through and implemented properly, these new laws and other proposed reforms offer much potential for the revitalisation of broad-based agricultural reforms as a vital means for addressing inequality in South Africa, and could engender substantial rural employment and livelihood creation – but this requires equitable land distribution and a new model of agricultural development focused on labour-absorbing methods of production and attaining food security and sovereignty to bring about inclusive growth in rural areas. Policies promoting large-scale intensive corporate agriculture as the only option for developing a solid agro-industrial base will have to give way to those that enable the successful development, participation and competition of smallholder producers and smaller agri-businesses – mixed farming and production regimes. A diversified multisectoral approach, based on integration of the different forms of tenure and different farm sizes, must be developed to create scope for integrating household smallholder schemes into the land reform and rural development programmes.

REFERENCES

African Centre for Biosafety (2014) *Africa: An El Dorado for South Africa's business giants*. www.acbio
    .org.za (accessed 5 February 2016).
Aliber, M, Baipheti, M and Jacobs, P (2007) Agricultural employment scenarios. Unpublished draft
    report. Pretoria: Human Sciences Research Council.
Blignaut, JN, De Wit, MP, Knot, J, Midgley, S, Crookes, DJ, Drimie, S and Nkambule, NP (2014)
    *Sustainable agriculture: A viable option for enhanced food and nutritional security and a sustain-
    able productive resource base in South Africa*. http://www.sagreenfund.org.za/wordpress/wp-
    content/uploads/2015/09/Sustainable-Farming-in-SA-Lit-Review-Asset-Research.compressed.
    pdf (accessed 9 January 2017).
Chisasa, J and Makina, D (2012) Trends in credit to smallholder farmers in South Africa. *International
    Business and Economics Research Journal*, 11 (7), 771–784.
Cochet, H, Anseeuw, W and Freguin-Gresh, S (2015) *South Africa's agrarian question*. Johannesburg:
    HSRC Press.
Cole, M (2015) *Is South Africa operating in a safe and just space?* Oxfam Research Report.http://
    policy-practice.oxfam.org.uk/publications/is-south-africa-operating-in-a-safe-and-just-
    space-using-the-doughnut-model-to-555842?http://policy-practice.oxfam.org.uk/publications/is-south-
    africa-operating-in-a-safe-and-just-space-using-the-doughnut-model-to-555842?intcmp=RM_
    SADoughnut (accessed 15 March 2016).
Collier, P and Dercon, S (2013) *African agriculture in 50 years: Smallholders in a rapidly changing world*.
    http://www.fao.org/3/a-ak983e. http://www.fao.org/3/a-ak983e.pdf (accessed 5 June 2016).
Dabla-Norris, E, Kochhar, K, Ricka, F, Suphaphiphat and, N and Tsounta, E (2015) *Causes and conse-
    quences of income inequality: A global perspective*. International Monetary Fund. http://www.imf.
    org/external/pubs/ft/sdn/2015/sdn1513.pdf (accessed 22 March 2016).
DAFF (Department of Agriculture, Forestry and Fisheries) (2012) *Abstract of agricultural statistics*.
    Pretoria: DAFF.
DAFF (Department of Agriculture, Forestry and Fisheries) (2013a) *Trends in the agricultural sector
    2012*. http://www.nda.agric.za/docs/statsinfo/Trends2012.pdf (accessed 9 January 2017).
DAFF (Department of Agriculture, Forestry and Fisheries) (2013b) *Economic review of South
    African agriculture 2012/13*. http://www.nda.agric.za/docs/statsinfo/EcoReview1213.pdf (accessed
    9 January 2017).
DAFF (Department of Agriculture, Forestry and Fisheries) (2014) *Economic review of South African agri-
    culture 2014*. http://www.senwes.co.za/Files/main_productsservices/agriservices/2015/Economic
    Review2014.pdf (accessed 9 January 2017).
DAFF (Department of Agriculture, Forestry and Fisheries) (2015a) *2015/16 to 2019/20 strategic plan*.
    http://www.daff.gov.za/doaDev/topMenu/DAFF_SP_per cent20complete.pdf (accessed 22 March
    2016).
DAFF (Department of Agriculture, Forestry and Fisheries) (2015b) *Draft policy document on the preser-
    vation and development of agricultural land*. Pretoria: DAFF.
DAFF (Department of Agriculture, Forestry and Fisheries) (2015c) *Economic review of the South
    African agriculture 2014/2015*. http://www.daff.gov.za/Daffweb3/Portals/0/Statistics per cent20
    and per cent20Economic per cent20Analysis/Economic per cent20Analysis/Economic per cent20
    Review_2014_15.pdf (accessed 9 January 2017).
DAFF (Department of Agriculture, Forestry and Fisheries) (2016) *Economic review of the South African
    agriculture 2015/2016*. http://www.daff.gov.za/Daffweb3/Portals/0/Statistics per cent20and per
    cent20Economic per cent20Analysis/Statistical per cent20Information/Economic per cent20
    Review per cent202015_2016.pdf (accessed 9 January 2017).

DLA (Department of Land Affairs) (2007) *Report and recommendations by the panel of experts on the development of policy regarding land ownership by foreigners in South Africa*. http://lamosa.org.za/resources/FOREIGN per cent20LAND per cent20REGULATION per cent20REPORT.pdf (accessed 9 January 2017).

DRDLR (Department of Rural Development and Land Reform) (2011) *Green paper on land reform*. Pretoria: Government Printer.

DTI (Department of Trade and Industry) (2016) *Minister Davies' speaking notes at the launch of the Industrial Policy Action Plan 2016/17–2018;/19*. http://www.dti.gov.za/editspeeches.jsp?id=3728 (accessed 9 January 2017).

Ducastel, A and Anseeuw, W (2013) *Agriculture as an asset class: financialisation of the (South) African farming sector*. http://iippe.org/wp/wp-content/uploads/2013/06/Antoine-Ducastel-Agriculture-as-an-asset-class.-Financialisation-of-the-South-African-farming-sector.pdf (accessed 18 December 2015).

Fan, S and Chan-Kang, C (2005) Is small beautiful? Farm size, productivity, and poverty in Asian agriculture. *Agricultural Economics*, 32 (1), 135–146.

FAO (Food and Agriculture Organisation) (2013) African youth in agriculture, natural resources and rural development. *Nature & Faune*, [online] 28 (1). http://www.fao.org/docrep/019/as290e/as290e.pdf (accessed 9 January 2017).

FAO (Food and Agriculture Organisation) (2014) *What do we really know about the number and distribution of farms and family farms worldwide?* http://www.fao.org/docrep/019/i3729e/i3729e.pdf (accessed 9 January 2017).

Ferreira, F and Ravallion, M (2008) *Global poverty and inequality: A review of the evidence*. http://elibrary.worldbank.org/doi/pdf/10.1596/1813-9450-4623 (accessed 18 March 2016).

Gwatidzo, T and Benhura, M (2013) *Mining sector wages in South Africa*.http://www.lmip.org.za/newsletter/item/mining-sector-wages-south-africa (accessed 18 December 2016).

Hall, R (2009) Dynamics in the commercial farming sector. In R Hall (ed.) *Another countryside*. Cape Town: Institute for Poverty, Land and Agrarian Studies.

Hall, R (2011) The next Great Trek? South African commercial farmers move north. In *International conference on global land grabbing* [online]. Brighton, UK: Land Deals Policy Initiative. https://www.iss.nl/fileadmin/ASSETS/iss/Documents/Conference_papers/LDPI/4_Ruth_Hall_Final.pdf (accessed 18 March 2016).

Hall, R and Cousins, B (2015) Commercial farming and agribusiness in South Africa and their changing roles in Africa's agro-food system. In *Land grabbing, conflict and agrarian-environmental transformations: Perspectives from East and Southeast Asia: An International Academic Conference* [online]. Chiang Mai: Chiang Mai University and others. https://www.iss.nl/fileadmin/ASSETS/iss/Research_and_projects/Research_networks/LDPI/CMCP_D7_Hall_and_Cousins.pdf (accessed 9 January 2017).

Hancock, T (2015) Ageing SA farmer cohort could prompt food shortages, consolidation – Deloitte. *Engineering News* [online]. http://www.engineeringnews.co.za/print-version/aging-sa-farmers-could-lead-to-food-shortages-consolidation-deloitte-2015-03-02 (accessed 9 January 2017).

Human Sciences Research Council (HSRC) (2005) *Who wants land reform? Preliminary results of a survey study*. Pretoria: HSRC.

IAASTD (International Assessment of Agricultural Knowledge, Science and Technology for Development) (2008) *Agriculture at a crossroads: Synthesis report*. http://www.unep.org/dewa/agassessment/reports/IAASTD/EN/Agriculture per cent20at per cent20a per cent20Crossroads_Synthesis per cent20 Report per cent20(English).pdf http://www.unep.org/dewa/agassessment/reports/IAASTD/EN/Agriculture per cent20at per cent20a per cent20Crossroads_Synthesis per cent20Report per cent20(English).pdf (accessed 9 January 2017).

Industrial Development Corporation (IDC) (2013) *South African economy: An overview of key trends since 1994.* https://www.idc.co.za/reports/IDC per cent20R&I per cent20publication per cent20-per cent20Overview per cent20of per cent20key per cent20trends per cent20in per cent20SA per cent20economy per cent20since per cent201994.pdf https://www.idc.co.za/reports/IDC per cent 20R&I per cent20publicationper cent20-per cent20Overview per cent20of per cent20key per cent20trends per cent20in per cent20SA per cent20economy per cent20since per cent201994.pdf (accessed 9 January 2017).

IPCC (Intergovernmental Panel on Climate Change) (2007) *Climate change 2007: Fourth assessment report of the intergovernmental panel on climate change.* https://www.ipcc.ch/publications_and_data/publications_ipcc_fourth_assessment_report_wg2_report_impacts_adaptation_and_vulnerability.htm (accessed 9 January 2017).

Kirsten, J (2011) *Agri-food chains in South Africa: Global challenges and structural changes.* http://www.nbi.org.za/Lists/Events/Attachments/48/Kirsten_Agri-food_Chains_In_South_Africa.pdf (accessed 4 June 2016).

Kuethe, TH (2012) *Spatial fragmentation and the value of residential housing.* http://pubag.nal.usda.gov/pubag/downloadPDF.xhtml?id=54240&content=PDF http://pubag.nal.usda.gov/pubag/download PDF.xhtml?id=54240&content=PDF (accessed 5 June 2016).

Lowder, SK, Skoet, J and Singh, S (2014) *What do we really know about the number and distribution of farms and family farms worldwide?* http://www.fao.org/docrep/019/i3729e/i3729e.pdf http://www.fao.org/docrep/019/i3729e/i3729e.pdf (accessed 9 January 2017).

Miller, D, Saunders, R and Oloyede, O (2008) South African corporations and post-apartheid expansion in Africa – Creating a new regional space. *African Sociological Review,* 12(1), 1–19.

Murray-Prior, R and Ncukana, L (2000) Agricultural development in South Africa: Some preliminary thoughts. In *Links, land and identities conference.* Perth: Curtin University of Technology.

NPC (National Planning Commission) (2011) *Diagnostic report.* Pretoria: Government Printer.

NPC (National Planning Commission) (2012) *National development plan 2030 – our future, make it work.* Pretoria: Government Printer.

Oxfam (2014) *Hidden hunger in South Africa: The faces of hunger and malnutrition in a food-secure nation.* https://www.oxfam.org/sites/www.oxfam.org/files/file_attachments/hidden_hunger_in_south_africa_0.pdf (accessed 16 March 2016).

PLAAS (Programme for Land and Agrarian Studies) (2012) *The distribution of land in South Africa.* http://www.plaas.org.za/sites/default/files/publications-pdf/No1 per cent20Fact per cent20check-per cent20web.pdf   http://www.plaas.org.za/sites/default/files/publications-pdf/No1 per cent-20Fact per cent20check per cent20web.pdf (accessed 27 February 2016).

RSA (Republic of South Africa) (2014) *Twenty year review – South Africa 1994–2014: Background paper – Rural transformation.* Pretoria: Government Printer. http://www.dpme.gov.za/publications/20 per cent20Years per cent20Review/20 per cent20Year per cent20Review per cent20Documents/20YR per cent20Rural per cent20Transformation.pdf http://www.dpme.gov.za/publications/20 per cent20Years per cent20Review/20 per cent20Year per cent20Review per cent20Documents/20YR per cent20Rural per cent20Transformation.pdf (accessed 17 March 2016).

SACAU (Southern Africa Confederation of Agricultural Unions) (2013) *Youth in agriculture - Synthesis report for Madagascar, Malawi, South Africa, Zambia and Zimbabwe.* http://www.sfoap.net/fileadmin/user_upload/sfoap/KB/docs/SACAU-YOUTH per cent20SYNTHESIS.pdf (accessed 9 January 2017).

Sandrey, R and Vink, N (2008) *Case study 4: Deregulation, trade reform and innovation in the South African agriculture sector.* OECD Trade Policy Working Paper No. 76. http://www.oecd.org/southafrica/41091441.pdf (accessed 9 January 2017).

Saravia-Matus, S, Delince, J, Gomez, S and Paloma, Y (2013) *An overview of (international) large-scale land transactions (LSLT) in the context of food security.* http://publications.jrc.ec.europa.eu/repository/handle/JRC81127 (accessed 18 February 2016).

Sharma, S (2012) *Rising inequality in South Africa: Drivers, trends and policy responses.* http://www.consultancyafrica.com/index.php?option=com_content&view=article&id=1142:rising-inequality-in-south-africa-drivers-trends-and-policy-responses-&catid=87:african-finance-a-economy&Itemid=294 (accessed 4 June 2016).

Stats SA (Statistics South Africa) (2011) *Census 2011 statistical release.* Pretoria: Stats SA.

Stats SA (Statistics South Africa) (2012) *Income and expenditure survey 2010/2011.* Pretoria: Stats SA.

Stats SA (Statistics South Africa) (2014) *Poverty trends in South Africa: An examination of absolute poverty between 2006 and 2011.* Pretoria: Stats SA.

Stats SA (Statistics South Africa) (2015a) *Mid-year population estimates, 2015.* Pretoria: Stats SA.

Stats SA (Statistics South Africa) (2015b) *Quarterly labour force survey: Quarter 4, 2015.* Pretoria: Stats SA.

UNDP (United Nations Development Programme) (2014) *The impacts of social and economic inequality on economic development in South Africa.* New York: UNDP.

Vandermeer, J, Smith, G, Perfect, I and Quintero, E (2009) *Effects of industrial agriculture on global warming and the potential of small-scale agroecological techniques to reverse those effects.* Ann Arbor, MI: The New World Agriculture and Ecology Group. https://viacampesina.org/en/index.php/publications-mainmenu-30/797-effects-of-industrial-agriculture-on-global-warming-and-the-potential-of-small-scale-agroecological (accessed 9 January 2017).

Visagie, J (2013) *Who are the middle class in South Africa? Does it matter for policy?* http://www.econ3x3.org/article/who-are-middle-class-south-africa-does-it-matter-policy (accessed 16 March 2016).

Visser, M and Ferrer, S (2015) *Farm workers' living and working conditions in South Africa: Key trends, emergent issues, and underlying and structural problems.* http://www.bittergrapes.net/wp-content/uploads/2016/10/ILO-rapport.pdf (accessed 9 January 2017).

Weinberg, T (2013) Overcoming the legacy of the Land Act requires a government that is less paternalistic, more accountable to rural people. *Focus on Land,* 70, 28–36.

World Bank (2008) *Agriculture for development.* Washington, DC: International Bank for Reconstruction and Development. https://siteresources.worldbank.org/INTWDRS/Resources/477365-1327599046334/8394679-1327614067045/WDROver2008-ENG.pdf (accessed 9 January 2017).

CHAPTER 13

Mining, rural struggles and inequality on the platinum belt

Sonwabile Mnwana

In South Africa, the Gini coefficient per capita (including salaries, wages and social grants) stands at a staggering 0.7. The richest 20 per cent of the population accounts for over 60 per cent of the national consumption while the poorest 20 per cent accounts for just 4.3 per cent of consumption (Stats SA 2014). The gross domestic product (GDP) per capita stands below R50 000 (NDP 2012). The national income distribution is also vastly skewed. The richest 20 per cent of the population earns about 70 per cent of the income, while the poorest 20 per cent take home a miserly 2.3 per cent of national income (NDP 2012).

The picture is even drearier in the former 'homeland' areas,[1] where more than 16 million Africans live on communal land, under tribal ('traditional') authorities with weak tenure rights to land and its natural resources, high poverty levels, poor public services and limited infrastructural development. Women continue to be the most affected social category (NDP 2012). In 2011, 68.8 per cent of people living in rural areas were poor, while the figure for urban dwellers living in poverty was 39.9 per cent (Stats SA 2014: 33). With the highest levels of poverty reported in largely rural provinces – Limpopo (63.8 per cent), Eastern Cape (60.8 per cent) and KwaZulu-Natal (56.6 per cent) (Stats SA 2014: 36) – the legacy of the social, economic and political exclusion of Africans during apartheid still holds a firm grip over Africans in the former 'homelands'. But intra-rural inequality remains less examined, particularly in how it connects the emerging modalities of resistance to mining expansion in communal areas. This chapter attempts to narrow the gap.

The chapter examines the emerging forms of rural struggles that continue to unfold in South Africa's former 'homeland' areas where platinum mining takes place. It provides an empirical account of how social relations over landed property have significantly shifted as a result of platinum mining expansion on rural land. Drawing on detailed ethnographic research conducted in two rural communities in North West and Limpopo provinces, the chapter demonstrates how the mining expansion has produced new forms of dispossession, differentiation and struggles over mining revenues. The findings also reveal resistance to mining expansion. I argue that mining-led dispossession, struggles over land and mining revenues, inequality and intensified local tensions render the rurally based platinum industry less fulfilling when held against its policy requirement of improving the lives of the rural poor.

This work is part of a detailed ethnographic study conducted between 2013 and 2015 in the villages under the Bakgatla-ba-Kgafela (henceforth Bakgatla area) and Langa Mapela (Mapela area), traditional authority areas in the North West and Limpopo provinces respectively.[2] Methods included in-depth interviews, observations, analysis of documents and several visits to the South African National Archives in Pretoria. During the different stages of data collection, the research team participated in a range of activities including *makgotla* (village meetings), youth gatherings and court cases that dealt with land and chieftaincy disputes.

RURAL STRUGGLES AND SOCIAL DIFFERENTIATION

Land is not only the material means of survival for millions of Africans; it has also become the subject of intense contestation in many postcolonial states in Africa where the nature and legal status of land tenure rights of families occupying rural land remains quite weak. Most rural land is defined as 'communal' and is held under customary tenure systems.

In South Africa, the land tenure rights of indigenous communities in the former homelands,[3] as elsewhere in most postcolonial sub-Saharan African countries, are extremely precarious, capricious and ambiguous. This situation is rooted in the history of massive land dispossession of all indigenous communities during colonial and apartheid periods and the imposition of significantly distorted meanings of customary property rights (Claassens 2008a, 2008b, 2011; Mnwana 2014). The post-apartheid state and other powerful actors further complicate the issue by generally defining African rural property rights and control over resources as 'communal' (Cousins 2008), shared by groups who are defined as political units – 'tribes' under the control of chiefs.

This system of denial of private property rights and enforcement of chiefly authority over African property rights was endemic in the colonial state's system of indirect rule (Mamdani 1996: 109). Such a system was significantly influenced by the social Darwinist theoretical framework which greatly shaped administrative and policy thinking during twentieth-century British colonial rule (Delius 2008: 213). Since (according to colonial officials influenced by this strand of thinking) Africans were 'at a lower level of social evolution', the property rights of Africans were deemed 'communal', not private or individual (Delius 2008). Social Darwinism greatly influenced the colonial ideological position and policy practice on African land tenure, and also promoted a generally problematic idea that all Africans were chiefly subjects and thus members of tribes. Colonial laws in South Africa rendered it impossible for the rural poor in the former homelands to have communal tenure without the control of tribal authorities – but such a belief is not only ahistorical but also groundless. The colonially derived versions of customary rights and governance mechanisms, albeit legally ambivalent and administratively laborious, were to be kept intact and sustained through colonial declarations and the two major 'Native' Land Acts of 1913 and 1936.[4]

It was these historical processes that led to intense struggles over land. Such struggles have intersected with processes of differentiation, exclusion and inequality at different historical moments. Therefore it is crucial at this juncture to outline some of the key debates on African struggles over land and natural resources, particularly how inequality at a local level influenced these struggles. Scholars provide detailed accounts of how rural land in Africa has increasingly become the focus of contestation.

The first set of arguments revolves around the question of negotiability of customary land rights. In the 1960s and 1970s, the dominant approach of the state was administratively oriented and largely influenced by the modernist school of thought which sought to do away with customary tenure and advocated private (mostly individual) titling of rural land. Customary landholding was deemed to be counter-developmental as it was seen as a hindrance to private investment and rural development. But customary tenure proved quite resilient as individual titling proved too expensive, and many landholders opted for customary and other informal land tenure systems (Chanock 1989; Amanor and Ubink 2008: 9). The drive towards titling and registration of rural land became even more contentious and unpopular when the private sector and foreign investor-driven neoliberal policies of the 1980s (which promoted individual titling) were found to be poorly grounded empirically. Studies funded by the World Bank in various countries established that there was no clear empirical connection between 'titles to land and long-term investment to land', and they recommended that customary land be administered at a local ('community') level (Amanor and Ubink 2008: 10). Such a shift has been largely bolstered by the view that customary property systems at a communal level are consensus-driven, dynamic, adaptable and negotiable and tend to evolve over time (Chanock 1989; Berry 1993; Deininger 2003).

But it is within this very negotiability and adaptability of customary landholding systems that the roots of rural inequality, social differentiation and conflict tend to be found. This marks the second set of arguments. Scholars have increasingly mapped out contours of differentiation within the customary tenure systems in different parts of Africa. Peters (2004), for instance, argues that land relations in parts of Africa are rooted in highly unequal social relationships. For Peters, the escalating reports on competition and conflict over land point to a need to reorientate our analysis towards understanding that there are winners and losers in the processes of negotiating land transactions that are governed through customary systems (2004: 304). As such, continues Peters, the lauded flexibility and negotiability of African customary landholding systems tend to be limited to certain social categories (the ruling elite, powerful groups) and exclude others (women, youth 'outsiders', 'foreigners', 'non-citizens', ethnic 'strangers', the poor). For Peters, a move towards a concerted empirical effort should be made to identify classes of the landed and the landless, particularly where values for landed resources and resulting social competition rise dramatically as a result of commodification of such resources (Peters 2004: 269–70, 293; Woodhouse 2003). Such a phenomenon is, in essence, a form of dispossession of the marginalised social groups.

Other studies conceptualise rural land and natural resource struggles as contestation over meaning to demonstrate how the elite and other powerful actors utilise ideology, historical memory, culture, ethnicity and other tools at their disposal to extend and legitimise their political and private control over communal land and natural resources and to exclude other social actors (Berry 1989; Shipton and Goheen 1992; Peters 1984). Therefore, conflict over rural land becomes a 'struggle over resources, over wealth and power is … engaged via a struggle over meaning' as evidenced in the 'legal and legislative contexts: that a category of person or act becomes defined in one way rather than in another is clearly a victory of one meaning over another' (Peters, 1984: 35).

The challenge of addressing the insecurity of tenure rights in the former homeland areas is not only one of the significant failures in South Africa's land reform programme, but a fundamental aspect of the proliferating rural land struggles. Central to this paradox is the inability of the state and other powerful actors to recognise the diversity of land tenure situations in rural South Africa (Cousins 2007). Cousins (2007: 282) raises the seminal question of 'how to recognise and secure land rights that are clearly distinct from "Western-legal" forms of private property but cannot be characterised as "traditional" or "pre-colonial", given the impacts of both colonial policies and of past and current processes of rapid social change'. Such a question is central to the main challenges that underpin the ongoing conflicts and inequalities rooted in claims over communal land rights in South Africa, particularly in situations where rural land is the focus of mining expansion.

MINING EXPANSION AND RURAL RESISTANCE

The platinum industry in South Africa, which has become prominent since the decline of gold mining, has shifted the geography of post-apartheid mining expansion. Unlike gold mining, which largely operated in urban areas and was responsible for the establishment of major cities, platinum mining largely occurs on rural land occupied by impoverished black communities in the North West and Limpopo provinces. Communal land in South Africa's densely populated former homeland areas has increasingly become the focus of platinum mining expansion. South Africa accounts for over 80 per cent of the world's known platinum group metals reserves. The massive, platinum-rich rock formation, the Bushveld Igneous Complex (often referred to as 'the platinum belt') spreads beneath a vast swathe of rural land which falls under the political jurisdiction of several traditional – 'tribal' – authorities. Extreme poverty, high unemployment, poor education standards, and a lack of basic services are among the miserable legacies ravaging these tribal authority areas which fell under the Bophuthatswana and Lebowa bantustans during apartheid (Mnwana and Capps 2015).

In an attempt to redress past injustices, the post-apartheid government has introduced some radical legislation and measures in the mining sector, particularly dealing with the historical racial exclusion of Africans from mine-ownership structures, and the relationships between the mining companies and local communities (Mnwana and Capps 2015). The Minerals and Petroleum Resources Development Act of 2002 (MPRDA) is the key piece of legislation in this regard. Through it, the state has promoted a range of measures, including black economic empowerment (BEE), mine-community partnerships, continued royalty payments, and social labour plans as requirements for mining companies (Mnwana 2015). Communities that previously received royalty payments for mineral rights on their land have been encouraged by the state to convert their royalties into equity shares (Mnwana 2014). Several communities have also entered into other complex deals with mining companies which operate on their land. Local chiefs, as assumed custodians of communal resources, have become mediators of mineral-led development and mining deals.

The rural focus of the mining industry in post-apartheid South Africa has been characterised by significant resistance. Ordinary community members who feel marginalised and excluded continue to resist mining expansion into their ploughing and grazing land. Mining capital enters rural land through the authority of local chiefs. Thousands of families have been relocated, hence the grammar and agency of resistance to mining expansion is increasingly focused on claims over land and on corruption allegations against local chiefs who, armed with support from the state, tend to control mining revenues and have positioned themselves as gatekeepers for mining capital and champions of mining-led rural development (Manson 2013; Mnwana 2014, 2015; Mnwana and Capps 2015).

The detailed ethnographic research conducted on the platinum belt enables this chapter to detail some of the less reported forms of social differentiation that complicate rural resistance to mining and its forceful entry into communal land. I detail the findings based on two villages on the platinum belt: Lesetlheng in North West province and Ga-Sekhaolelo in Limpopo province. Common features make the two village communities quite suitable for exploring the evolving forms of resistance, particularly how resistance to mining-led dispossession connects to claims over land and new forms of differentiation at a local level. Although located hundreds of kilometres apart, in two different provinces, both villages are very close to major platinum mining operations; they have experienced significantly heightened resistance to mining expansions over the past few years, and resistance to mining intersects with claims over land.

LESETLHENG – CLAIMING WILGESPRUIT

One of the oldest villages in the Bakgatla area, Lesetlheng lies on the north-eastern foot-hills of the Pilanesberg Mountains. The village is one of the thirty-two that constitute the Bakgatla rational authority area in North West province, under the jurisdiction of the Moses Kotane Local Municipality. Currently *Kgosi* (chief) Nyalala Pilane is the ruling chief in the Bakgatla area amid prolonged resistance to his political leadership and con-trol over mining revenues. *Kgosi* Pilane has entered into numerous deals on behalf of the ordinary villagers in the Bakgatla area.

Lesetlheng is one of many villages in the Bakgatla area where most agricultural land is rapidly being fenced off for mining operations. On the north-western side this vil-lage is flanked by the mining operations of Pilanesberg Platinum Mines (PPM) and the Sedibelo Project – a Bakgatla-owned mining project. Lesetlheng has also become a mag-net for many outside migrant mineworkers seeking rental accommodation. The main road which connects this village to the mining operations offers easy access to transport for these migrants.

The PPM began digging its open pit around 2008. The Itereleng Bakgatla Mineral Resources (Pty) Limited (IBMR) Sedibelo Project began its development in 2007. The impact of these operations is already visible. Huge tracts of communal farming land have been fenced off. Villagers blame the chief and the mines for not consulting them before these projects were initiated. Some village groups also contest the mining contracts that *Kgosi* Pilane signs on behalf of the community. They claim that their forefathers bought the mineral-rich farms as private properties and they should never have become tribal land in the first place (Mnwana 2015). As a result, there is an ongoing land dispute which also involves the nearby farm Wilgespruit. The dispute over this platinum-rich land tends to unravel new forms of differentiation and community fracture.

The land claim

The farm Wilgespruit 631 (2JQ) is currently registered as a tribal property. The minister of rural development and land reform holds the title deed in trust for the Bakgatla-ba-Kgafela traditional community. This farm contains rich platinum group metal reserves. The mineral rights on this farm are held by IBMR, a Bakgatla-owned holding company controlled by *Kgosi* Pilane.

A group of Lesetlheng residents dispute the tribal ownership of Wilgespruit, claim-ing that their forefathers bought it. According to the claimants, the original buyers were constituted as a private syndicate from thirteen clans. All of them resided in Lesetlheng between 1916 and 1919 when the farm was bought. The segregationist colonial policy of that time compelled African group land-buyers in South Africa to register their purchase through the aegis of a chief. The state regarded such land as de jure 'tribal' properties and such purchases were transferred to the minister of native affairs who kept the title 'in trust' for the chief and his 'tribe'.

Wilgespruit was historically one of the most productive farms in the Bakgatla area. Some of the elders in Lesetlheng narrated how their families used to harvest countless bags of sorghum, maize, beans and many other crops. Literature also attests to this. Breutz (1953: 282), for instance, enumerates 221 bags of sorghum and 485 bags of maize that were harvested at Wilgespruit in 1949 alone. The harvest of sorghum at this farm far exceeded other farms in that year, and it produced the second largest harvest of maize.

However, when this study was conducted most of the agricultural land at Wilgespruit had been fenced off for mining operations. Families who still had cattle were using the remaining land for grazing. It was becoming increasingly difficult for Lesetlheng famers to visit their cattle posts as the entrance was often guarded by heavily armed private security officers. But there was physical evidence that this farm was once a piece of productive agricultural land. The small mud and corrugated iron structures where people used to live during the ploughing season were still there. It was also common to see rusty old ploughs and other farming implements lying around. Some of the former ploughing plots had small dams that various clans had dug to water their crops. Some of these dams were still there although most of them had dried up. In 2009, IBMR attempted to relocate the farmers on Wilgespruit but abandoned the plan when Lesetlheng residents resisted.

Dibeso and 'others'

The entry of mining economy has ushered in new forms of struggles in Lesetlheng. The occupation of Wilgespruit by the mine, and discontent, led in 2007 to the creation by land claimants of a village movement called Lesetlheng Land Committee (LLC). Its goal is to mobilise the villagers on issues relating to land, mining impact and revenues. The Lesetlheng claimants made this application in 2012 through the Department of Rural Development and Land Reform (DRDLR). A commissioner was appointed to investigate the application in terms of the Land Titles Adjustment Act, No 111 of 1993.

Since its formation in 2007, the LLC had always enjoyed a popular following in Lesetlheng. Like other formations in the village, the LLC was perceived to be representing the whole village. But things took an unexpected shift in 2012, when the Land Title Adjustment Application Commission began its investigation. The commissioner appointed to investigate their claim by the DRDLR requested the claimants' family trees. This required the claimants to validate their claims by demonstrating who the original buyer was in each family, and how they are related to members of the original land-buying syndicate. Sensitive issues started to surface. Some of the elders had always known that not every family that was ploughing on Wilgespruit was descended from the original buyers. The requirement for land claimants to produce family trees raised two contentious issues. First, the descendants of non-buyers were not going to submit family trees since their ancestors did not contribute to the farm's purchase. As such, they were excluded. This exclusion discouraged some of the village members who did not belong to the thirteen clans of buyers. Subsequently, the support for the LLC dwindled as many people decided not to attend land meetings because they felt left out of the Land Title Adjustment Application (LTAA).

The LTAA exposed divisions between the buyers and non-buyers. It also unravelled splits within the thirteen clans of the descendants of the land-buying syndicate. The questions of which families or households would submit claims on behalf of each clan, and who would submit a claim on behalf of each family in a clan, also proved contentious. The main issue was whether to include the families whose ancestors were not among the syndicate. This produced new group identities and new terms among the villagers. According to the Lesetlheng claimants, the actual families that bought Wilgespruit are called *dibeso*. A *sebeso* (singular for *dibeso*) is the main family in the *kgoro* (clan). One informant explained:

> *Kgoro* refers to a clan which is a group of households that mainly share the same surname and some identity. However, some clans expanded by allowing other families who either married or sought refuge to become members of their *kgoro*. Apparently, the expansion was due to either a strategy to strengthen the clan or out of pure humility and compassion. For example, the Matshego clan in Lesetlheng is made out of four surnames. Matshego is the *sebeso* (interview, Pretoria, 10 November 2013).

The clan itself had never been an egalitarian social unit. In Lesetlheng; for instance, it is said that some of the in-migrant families were often called *bagotsi-ba-mollo* (*bakgotsi*) – those who make fire for others. This term was applied to families who were adopted by clans of buyers. *Bakgotsi* denotes families of lower social status within a clan. The *bagotsi* were usually landless immigrants of distinct ethnic origins. The host clans would grant them ploughing land on Wilgespruit, some cattle, and equipment. In return, the *bagotsi* were required to provide labour. Their daily task was to wake up early every morning and make fires for the main families in the clan. *Bagotsi* also performed various other tasks, including helping with ploughing and looking after cattle.

The differentiated structure of clans faded over the years with the decline of subsistence agriculture. However, as a result of the new mining economy new forms of differentiation and exclusive group identities have emerged. For instance, some informants argued that the notion of *sebeso/dibeso* was recent. They said it had emerged as a response to the challenge of distinguishing between the descendants of the buyers and the non-buyers. Several elders in Lesetlheng could not tell when and how the notion of *dibeso* came into being.

The notion of *dibeso* underpins the tensions that have emerged among residents, especially around the rights to exclusive group access to platinum revenues. A village elder who was also an active member of the LLC offered the following explanation:

> [*Kgosi*] Nyalala has been calling meetings and telling people that we, the people of Lesetlheng, are claiming land which belongs to the thirty-two villages of Bakgatla.

> Look, people know that their forefathers never bought Modimo Mmalo [Wilgespruit]. They have never used that land. No other village has land that is divided according to clans. Our farm is divided according to the thirteen clans – those who bought it. These clans must get their share of mining revenues first and then a certain percentage will go to the Bakgatla tribal office. That percentage will be shared by the whole community (interview, Lesetlheng, 7 August 2013).

Other clan divisions surfaced over whether women should be allowed to submit claims during the application process. The majority of male elders felt that women were not eligible since, according to custom, women did not inherit land. An elderly man argued:

> It is the men who inherit the land. If there is some movable property like money, we share with the female siblings. But the land is shared among the males only (interview, Lesetlheng, 6 September 2013).

Because of this disagreement the LLC handed the responsibility over to individual clans to decide whether to include women. Eventually, most clans decided to include women, but a few women were still excluded by their clans' male elders. This exclusion mainly targeted three categories of women: those who joined the clan through marriage – *ngwetsi* – widows, and daughters or granddaughters of the original buyers who married into clans of non-buyers.

As the discussion below will demonstrate, resistance to platinum mining and dispossession in Limpopo displays similar hidden forms of social differentiation. Such a paradox became particularly evident in the context of massive relocation of families and vanishing rural livelihoods as Anglo American Platinum's (Amplats) operation continued to expand.

GA-SEKHAOLELO – RECLAIMING THEIR HOME

Ga-Sekhaolelo is located about thirty kilometres north of the town of Mokopane (formerly Potgietersrus) in Limpopo province within the jurisdiction of the Mogalakwena Local Municipality. It is one of forty-three villages in the Langa-Mapela traditional authority area under *Kgoshi* (chief) Kgabagare David Langa. Although they have a history of diverse ethnic origins, the majority of residents in the Mapela area are Sepedi speakers (Jackson 1981).

Ga-Sekhaolelo is one of the villages that has been relocated by Amplats's Mogalakwena Mine, which has operated in this area for decades, to make way for the expansion of its open cast activities. The Mogalakwena Mine is Amplats's most prized asset and the largest open pit mine in the world. Between 2007 and 2014, Amplats relocated 459 Ga-Sekhaolelo families from Mohlotlo (on the farm Overysel 815LR) to the farm Armoede 823LR; hence the new village is also called Ga-Sekhaolelo (Amplats 2014). This was part of massive relocations of villagers by the mine which saw approximately 1 000 families – more than 7 000 people – in different villages of the Mapela area being moved from their homes to neighbouring farms (Amplats 2014: 10).

Relocation and the problematic representation

In 2014 Amplats reported that it had spent almost R800 million on relocating Mapela residents since 1998 (when initial 'consultations' began) (Amplats 2014). At the time this study was conducted there were still about eleven families who had resisted relocation and were occupying their homes in Mohlotlo amid the mine dumps. Conditions for these families when we visited were difficult, with no ploughing fields, water sources, schools or animals. Strikingly, we found that some of the relocated people of Ga-Sekhaolelo in Armoede wanted to return to Mohlotlo.

The view from the mine – that its relocations are improving people's lives, which is why 'the great majority of people have voluntarily chosen to relocate' (Amplats 2008: 4) – is contradicted by our findings, which suggest that there is significant dis-content among the relocated people of Armoede. Discontent is rooted in unfulfilled promises by the mine, loss of ploughing fields, marginalisation of some social groups and lack of services.

During the first stage of the relocation process, the mine consulted the Mapela chief at the time (*Kgoshigadi* Atalia Thabantsi Langa – the predecessor of and mother to the current chief) who instructed the *mantona* (headmen) of the affected villages to over-see the formation of village relocation committees, the relocation steering committees (RSCs). The RSC for Ga-Sekhaolelo consisted of ten members. This committee reached an agreement with Amplats about relocation in October 2002. In 2003, the RSCs were reconstructed as nonprofit organisations ('section 21 companies') 'in order to be able to enter into legal contracts with Anglo Platinum as representative structures for the respec-tive villages' (Farrell et al. 2012: 198). Former members of RSCs, now 'directors' of these nonprofit section 21 companies, were paid monthly 'stipends' of between R4 000 and R6 000. (According to our respondents, Amplats facilitated the reconstitution of RSCs into section 21 companies. Amplats, they said, was paying a lawyer who negotiated on behalf of the relocating communities, and advised the communities to reconstitute RSCs into section 21s.)

Our findings also suggest that during relocation Amplats took little consideration of the social dynamics around notions of the household, property rights and the cultural and spiritual meanings attached to the land and the graves. This created new divisions on the level of the household as well as the community.

Compensation: 'homeowners' and others

At the level of the family, Amplats primarily dealt with the heads of households ('home-owners'). According to the mine:

> The head of each household signed an agreement in which the terms of his/her relo-cation were agreed together with the size and location of the house to which he/she and the family living in the present house would be relocated. Minutes of the meetings proving consultations are available. (Amplats 2008: 17).

The mine gave each head of household a file – a 'red or green file' – which detailed the specifics of the old and the new homesteads including an audit of trees, ploughing fields and other things to be compensated. This was part of the audits and agreements forged with individual homeowners and ensured that the sizes of the new houses were equal to those the relocated families had in Mohlotlo. The file also served as a means of identifica-tion for the head of household in negotiations with the mine (Amplats 2008: 19).

The mine's primary focus on the homeowners alone when distributing relocation triggered a negative reaction from other social categories and members of the family/household unit. Young people in Ga-Sekhaolelo who took part in this study stated that in March 2001, while relocation negotiations were still in progress, Chieftainess Langa and her traditional council, Amplats representatives and the local municipality decided that that headmen should stop issuing new residential land (plots) until the relocation process was over. This decision was taken on 17 March 2001. According to the minutes of this meeting that we obtained from *Ntona* Sekhaolelo and his village council (on 7 April 2015) new stands were to be issued at Armoede after relocation, and Amplats manage-ment promised to build toilets, provide water taps and erect fencing. Young people who had applied for residential stands had to wait for the relocation to be complete, with the hope of getting fenced plots with toilets and water taps. It is said that Amplats did not fulfil this promise (interview: *Ntona* Sekhaolelo, Ga-Sekhaolelo, 7 April 2015). Group interviews with young people in Ga-Sekhaolelo, and our observations, suggest that there is mounting anger among the youth towards the mine. Unemployment is among the main causes of this anger.

When asked to comment about the mine's local recruitment strategy *Kgoshi* Langa concurred:

> To a large extent the problem with this mine [Mogalakwena] is that it is mechanised. It is not labour intensive. People get employed on contracts but permanent jobs are few. For the mine to employ them [local people] they must have maths and science. So those who don't have maths and science feel that they are being marginalised. (interview, *Kgoshi* KD Langa, 10 June 2015).

At the household level, we also found women to be vulnerable to marginalisation during relocation. Customarily, married women had access to land rights through their husbands. Amplats channelled relocation compensation and other benefits to male household heads since men are the main holders of land rights. In cases where the husbands had passed away, their widows became recipients. However, when both parents had passed away the surviving female children would not be eligible to receive direct compensation or have the new house registered under their names unless there was no male sibling (interview, Ga-Sekhaolelo, 8 April 2015).

We also observed that in cases where two or more male siblings continued to live in their parents' homestead in Mohlotlo after their parents passed on, relocation displaced the siblings who, according to custom, are not entitled to inherit their parents' homestead. For instance, before relocation, Mr Hlongo,[5] a man in his late sixties, had stayed in his deceased parents' homestead with his family (wife and children), sharing with his younger brother and his family. During relocation, the mine gave the new home in Armoede to his younger brother since according to local custom the youngest male inherits the land and homestead of the deceased parents. Mr Hlongo and his family could not stay with his brother in the new home for two reasons. First, unlike the old homestead, the new house did not belong to his late parents – it was his younger brother's property. Second, unlike the old homestead which was traditionally built with separate small structures, the new house in Armoede is a modern structure with rooms inside it, not separate small structures. As such, it is not suitable to permanently accommodate more than one family as was the traditional homestead in Mohlotlo. Mr Hlongo and his family left Mohlotlo through mine relocations in 2007 without any compensation and went around the villages looking for a place to stay. They obtained a piece of land – a residential plot – in Ga-Chaba (a nearby village) through a local headman. Mr Hlongo's wife's family (also living in Ga-Chaba) helped them to build a shack on the new residential plot where they now live. They survive on a government old age grant and they also plant maize and some vegetables in their homestead garden.

Resistance to mining continues to intensify in the Mapela area. The loss of agricultural land and access to natural resources owing to the expansion of the Mogalakwena mine and its community relocation processes have triggered feelings of discontent, displacement and dispossession in the Mapela villages that have been relocated and those located close to the mining operations. There have been several episodes of similar community protests against the mine – either violently suppressed by the police or ending in short-term agreements between the community and the mine. In August 2015, a two-week intensive community protest against the mine left the chief's home burnt down, mine property vandalised and more than fifty villagers arrested. The controversial R175 million 'settlement' agreement entered into by *Kgoshi* Langa with Amplats in April 2015 on behalf of people in the Mapela area has triggered even more local tensions and divisions. Such new developments are quite intricate and, as such, cannot be discussed fully within the scope of this chapter.

DISCUSSION AND CONCLUSION

Scholars generally agree that private ownership in the form of individual titling cannot be regarded as an appropriate mechanism for strengthening African property rights and that the flexibility and negotiability of customary systems of tenure may still secure land rights of the poor community members (Peters 2004; Woodhouse 2003; Cousins 2007). However, in situations of increased competition over land and natural resources, there is evidence that the negotiability of resource rights under customary tenure may increase inequality, social differentiation and even privatisation and commodification of access and control over communal rights, since the customary systems of negotiation tend to be limited for some social categories (Peters 2004; Woodhouse 2003). The rapid loss of communal land through mining on the platinum belt epitomises this phenomenon, particularly in the villages of the Mapela and Bakgatla traditional authority areas. The cases of Lesetlheng and Ga-Sekhaolelo villages indicate that the continued weakness and ambiguity of land tenure rights of African families in the former homeland areas make it easy for mining capital to enter communal land and displace villagers through the power of local chiefs who are assumed to be custodians of communal property. Such an assumption – by capital and the state – is ahistorical and carries no precolonial precedent. In precolonial land tenure systems chiefs had limited control over communal property – in fact, the easy 'availability of land made it relatively easy for groups to move between chiefdoms' (Delius 2008: 15).

The character of resistance and discontent produced by the mining activities in the study communities underpin a serious flaw carried by the dominant 'communal' categorisation of land tenure rights in South Africa. In both villages resistance to mining is connected to claims over property rights – land. Such claims by ordinary villagers reject the authority of chiefs over property. The move by Lesetlheng residents to resist mining expansion by claiming ownership of the mineral-rich farm which was purchased by their predecessors is significant evidence of the multilayered historical character of African property rights. As such, the state's formal and legal interpretations of ownership over rural land often differ from the meaning attached to land by its African owners, occupiers and users. There is also strong evidence that precolonial land tenure in Africa was 'both communal and individual' in nature (Cousins 2007: 284). Rights of access were derived from membership in a group or allegiance or affiliation to a particular political authority – usually an authority of a traditional ruler (chief) (Berry 1989; Shipton and Goheen 1992; Cousins 2007).

In both communities studied, ethnographic material revealed the marginalisation of other social categories, particularly the youth and women. Paradoxically, such marginalisation occurs even within the processes of group claims to land rights. The findings point towards the less reported reality of a more complex rural social milieu. As these struggles have shown, mining-led dispossession has led not only to conflicts between the local people and the powerful mining capital but also to significant struggles among the ordinary rural people.

This results from the historical structure of customary land rights in Mapela and the way in which the mine interpreted those rights when distributing its relocation benefits. Amplats focused on, and mainly dealt with, the heads of households. The historical structure of customary land rights seems to have favoured the elders – who, according to our respondents, were mainly male household heads. As a result, adult household members who were not favoured by custom to hold land rights were marginalised and displaced when their families were relocated by the mine.

Since rights to communal property are complex and multilayered, the rapid loss of land rights because of mining produces new forms of dispossession and inequality. This can be called dispossession within dispossession. The cases of Lesetlheng and Ga-Sekhaolelo revealed that mining not only causes conflict between the rural poor and the state or local chiefs; it can also unravel social differences at even the most micro levels of rural society – clans and families. The practice of engagement and community representation by mining capital shows little understanding of the complexity of structure of rural society and the multilayered character of communal property rights. Not only does this finding reveal a significant lacuna in the understanding of South Africa's rural social milieu, it renders the post-apartheid minerals reform less fulfilling when held against its rhetorical promise of redressing apartheid injustices, including eliminating the legacy of social, political and economic exclusion of Africans in the former homeland areas.

This discussion has demonstrated new forms of resistance and social differentiation that are emerging on South Africa's platinum belt as rural citizens are reclaiming their property rights in the context of mining-led dispossession. The limited kinds of compensation that rural communities receive for their losses – mining revenues, new homesteads for relocated families and sporadic miniscule monetary compensation – tend to exacerbate local tensions and inequality as other social categories and groups at the community, clan and even family levels tend to be excluded. As a consequence, despite several policy developments the current modalities of platinum mining expansion, like its gold counterpart, is less likely to benefit the local communities, workers and other rural citizens in the impoverished areas where the mines draw their labour.

NOTES

1   Also called 'bantustans': ethnically defined semi-autonomous African 'states' that were created during apartheid for Africans/blacks in South Africa in order to exclude them economically, socially and politically. Homelands were dissolved in 1994.

2   This work was conducted under the SWOP Mining and Rural Transformation in Southern Africa (MARTISA) project, generously funded by the Human Rights and Governance Programme of the Ford Foundation. An earlier draft of this work was presented at the conference 'Africa Since Independence' held at the University of Ibadan, Oyo State, Nigeria, from 3–5 August 2016. The author's travel costs to this conference were generously funded by the Friedrich Ebert Stiftung South Africa.

3   The term 'indigenous' here is applied loosely to refer to local African ('black') people in rural South Africa. I am aware that the term is highly contentious in other parts of the world.
4   The Natives Land Act of 1913 and the Native Trust and Land Act of 1936.
5   Not his real name.

REFERENCES

Amanor, KS and Ubink, JM (2008) Contesting land and custom in Ghana: Introduction. In JM Ubink and KS Amanor (eds) *Contesting land and custom in Ghana*. Leiden: Leiden University Press.

Amplats (Anglo American Platinum) (2008) *The facts*. http://www.angloplatinum.co.za (accessed 9 April 2010).

Amplats (Anglo American Platinum) (2014) Motlhotlo village relocation Mogalakwena mine. In *IAIA symposium presentation Kruger National Park*. http://www.iaia.org/ (accessed 10 July 2015).

Amplats (Anglo American Platinum) (2015) *Mine profile: Mogalakwena*. http://www.angloamerican.com/media/our-stories/mine-profile-mogalakwena (accessed 1 August 2015).

Berry, S (1989) Social institutions and access to resources. *Africa* 59 (1), 41–55.

Berry, S (1993) *No condition is permanent: The social dynamics of agrarian change in Sub-Saharan Africa*. Madison: The University of Wisconsin Press.

Breutz, PL (1953) *The tribes of Rustenburg and the Pilanesberg districts*. Pretoria: Government Printer.

Chanock, M (1989) Neither customary nor legal: African customary law in an era of family law reform. *International Journal of Law, Policy and the Family*, 3 (1), 72–88.

Claassens, A (2008a) Customary law and zones of chiefly sovereignty: The impact of government policy on whose voices prevail in the making and changing of customary law. In A Claassens and B Cousins (eds) *Land, power and custom: Controversies generated by South Africa's Communal Land Rights Act*. Cape Town: UCT Press.

Claassens, A (2008b) Power, accountability and apartheid borders: The impact of recent laws on struggles over land rights. In A Claassens and B Cousins (eds) *Land, power and custom: Controversies generated by South Africa's Communal Land Rights Act*. Cape Town: UCT Press.

Claassens, A (2011) Resurgence of tribal levies: A double taxation for the rural poor. *South African Crime Quarterly*, 35, 11–16.

Cousins, B (2007) More than socially embedded: The distinctive character of 'communal tenure' regimes in South Africa and its implications for land policy. *Journal of Agrarian Change*, 7 (3), 281–315.

Cousins, B (2008) Characterising 'communal' tenure: Nested systems and flexible boundaries. In A Claassens and B Cousins (eds) *Land, power and custom: Controversies generated by South Africa's Communal Land Rights Act*. Cape Town: UCT Press.

Delius, P (2008) Contested terrain: Land rights and chiefly power in historical perspective. In A Claassens and B Cousins (eds) *Land, power and custom: Controversies generated by South Africa's Communal Land Rights Act*. Cape Town: UCT Press.

Deininger, K (2003) *Land policies for growth and poverty reduction*. A World Bank policy research report. Washington, Oxford: World Bank, Oxford University Press.

Farrell, LA, Hamann, R and Mackres, E (2012) A clash of cultures (and lawyers): Anglo Platinum and mine-affected communities in Limpopo Province, South Africa. *Resources Policy*, 37, 194–204.

Jackson, AO (1981) *The Ndebele of Langa*. Pretoria: Department of Co-operation and Development.

Mamdani, M (1996) *Citizen and subject: Contemporary Africa and the legacy of late colonialism*. Princeton: University Press.

Manson, A (2013) Mining and 'traditional communities' in South Africa's 'platinum belt': Contestations over land, leadership and assets in North-West Province c. 1996–2012. *Journal of Southern African Studies*, 39 (2), 409–423.

Mnwana, S (2014) Chief's justice? Mining, accountability and the law in the Bakgatla-ba-Kgafela traditional authority area, North West Province. *South African Crime Quarterly*, 49, 21–29.

Mnwana, S (2015) Mining and 'community' struggles on the platinum belt: A case of Sefikile village in the North West Province, South Africa. *The Extractive Industries and Society*, 2, 500–508.

Mnwana, S and Capps, G (2015) *'No chief ever bought a piece of land!' Struggles over property, community and mining in the Bakgatla-ba-Kgafela Traditional Authority Area, NorthWest Province*. South Africa Working Paper: 3. Johannesburg: Society, Work and Development Institute, University of the Witwatersrand.

NDP (2012) *National Development Plan 2030: Our future – make it work*. Pretoria: National Planning Commission, The Presidency.

Peters, PE (1984) Struggles over water, struggles over meaning: Cattle, water and the state in Botswana. *Africa*, 54 (3), 29–49.

Peters, PE (2004) Inequality and social conflict over land in Africa. *Journal of Agrarian Change*, 4 (3), 269–314.

Shipton, P and Goheen, M (1992) Understanding African land-holding: Power, wealth, and meaning. *Africa: Journal of the International African Institute* 62 (3), 307–325.

Stats SA (Statistics South Africa) (2014) *Poverty trends in South Africa. An examination of absolute poverty between 2006 and 2011*. Pretoria: Statistics South Africa.

Woodhouse, P (2003) African enclosures: A default mode of development. *World Development*, 31 (10), 1705–1720.

CHAPTER 14

Challenging environmental injustice and inequality in contemporary South Africa

Jacklyn Cock

———

Environmental injustice is an expression of deepening inequality and is widespread in post-apartheid South Africa but, paradoxically, there is no strong, mass-based environmental movement. Environmental injustice and inequality is evident in poor people's exposure to toxic pollution, and in the lack of access to critical resources, including nutritious food, clean water and affordable energy. This chapter suggests, however, that while there are formidable constraints, a unified, embryonic environmental justice movement *could possibly* be emerging from the way in which the current ecological crisis is driving new initiatives. These initiatives are: building popular power, promoting counter-narratives such 'food sovereignty' and 'energy democracy', developing new strategies including formal and informal alliances, a strategic use of the law, innovative tactics and the use of symbolic power with a strong normative dimension to dramatise both the causes and the consequences of the ecological crisis. Grassroots organisations are organising around concrete issues in the everyday experience of working people – especially rising food and energy prices. A growing number of these initiatives are drawing from the travelling and adaptive discourse of environmental justice which has the capacity to connect particularistic local struggles, generalise them and forge global alliances, particularly around one of the most destructive activities on the planet: coal mining.

THE TRAVELLING DISCOURSE OF ENVIRONMENTAL JUSTICE

The concept of environmental justice provides a radical alternative to the discourse of ecological modernisation which has been criticised for its reformism and over-emphasis on consensual politics (Warner 2010). '[T]he central argument of [ecological modernisation] is that industrial societies can be made sustainable with only modest adjustments and corrections' (Warner 2010: 553). Environmental justice also provides an alternative to traditional understandings of conservation, questioning the market's ability to bring about social or environmental sustainability, and represents a powerful challenge to the increasing commodification and financialisation of nature. The emphasis on class in the discourse of environmental justice also presents a challenge to the fashionable notion of 'the Anthropocene' as a new geological epoch in which nature is dominated by 'humanity' as a universalistic social category (Baskin 2015; Moore 2015). In this paradigm 'the Indian subsistence farmer [and] the African herder become part of one "humanity" with the inhabitants of the rich world, despite clearly being very differentially responsible for ecological devastation' (Baskin 2015: 16). The notion is not only class-blind but profoundly anti-democratic in promoting 'planetary managerialism and the rule of experts' (Baskin 2015: 13). The elitist nature of this approach is most dramatically evident in the Ecomodernist Manifesto (2015), which claims that technology can harness 'humankind's extraordinary power to create a good Anthropocene'. The document operates as a kind of tranquilliser, reassuring us that no fundamental change in the distribution of power and resources is necessary to address the inequalities which both produce and reflect the ecological crisis.

By contrast, the discourse of environmental justice is broad and inclusive. 'At the current moment, as an analytical and political term, it has come to subsume and absorb both environmental racism and environmental inequality as a master frame' (Sze and London 2008: 1347). Since its emergence in the USA in the 1970s, environmental justice has expanded both thematically and geographically to encompass factors additional to race associated with disproportionate environmental impacts such as class and gender. It is now a driver for organisations and movements all over the world incorporating a diversity of issues and analysis (Sze and London 2008; Schlosberg 2013). This involves 'a convergence of social movements, public policy and scholarship' (Sze and London 2008: 1332). However, 'the environmental justice movement has failed to gain the attention it deserves from social movement scholars' (Bond 2015: 17).

A mobile and adaptive discourse

The discourse of environmental justice originated in the USA in opposition to practices termed 'environmental racism' meaning the disproportionate effects of environmental pollution on racial minorities (Bullard 1993). It was radicalised in South Africa in a process of translation from the North to the global South. The linkage of notions of rights, justice, power and equality meant that the South African adaptation of the concept involved a commitment to radical, transformative change. Fusing equity with ecological sustainability, it is foundational to many current struggles which target the experience and the structural causes of environmental injustice.

The concept of environmental justice was first introduced in South Africa formally by a US sociologist speaking at a conference of environmental activists in 1992. The concept resonated with the experience of black South Africans. As one participant said, 'It was articulated as a black concept and a poor concept and it took root very well'. Furthermore, this intervention came at a charged political moment; the 'reversal' of environmental racism was understood as central to the process of democratisation, especially between 1990 and 1994.

The most dramatic outcome of the conference was the creation of the Environmental Justice Networking Forum (EJNF) (Cock 2012), which signalled a decisive break with the dominant, narrow, authoritarian conservationism dominant at the time. The EJNF described itself as a 'democratic network, a shared resource, a forum which seeks to advance the interrelatedness of social, economic, environmental and political issues to reverse and prevent environmental injustices affecting the poor and the working class'. It brought together hundreds of organisations ranging from community based organisa-tions (CBOs) to nongovernmental organisations (NGOs), from churches to trade unions. It took up grassroots issues such as the mercury poisoning of workers and communities, the toxic legacy of asbestos mining, illness as a result of working with poisonous sub-stances, the absence of basic services such as access to water and sanitation, and waste dumps situated next to townships. The EJNF also did high-profile policy work, playing a leading role in post-apartheid environmental policy formulation such as in the National Environmental Policy Process (CONNEP) which formulated South Africa's progressive 1998 National Environmental Management Act, a framework law that laid down the principles for further legislation, and also formulated section 24 of the new Constitution, the 'environmental justice right'. This work represented a challenge to the dominant nar-row understanding of environmentalism in the country at the time.

A RECONFIGURATION OF THE DISCOURSE OF ENVIRONMENTALISM

During both the colonial and the apartheid regimes environmentalism operated effec-tively as an authoritarian conservation strategy which was mainly concerned with the protection of threatened plants, animals and wilderness areas. This meant the neglect of urban, health, labour and development issues (Cock and Koch 1991). So, for many black South Africans dispossession was the other side of conservation as they were for-cibly removed to create national parks and 'protected areas' and in the process lost their land and livelihoods (Walker 2008). One example is that of the Makuleke people who were evicted (their huts burned and their crops destroyed) from the northern area of the Kruger National Park in 1962. While the new post-apartheid board of the South African

National Parks ensured that the Makuleke had their land restored to them, many claims of land dispossession by indigenous communities have still not been resolved. As Bond wrote, 'one of the striking aspects of restitution policy has been the disjuncture between the wide and unreflective public support for the idea of restitution and the messy, conflictful and unsatisfactory nature of implementation' (Bond 2015: 17).

Under apartheid the national parks reflected the culture and practices of white exclusivity and domination. Until the 1980s, in the Kruger National Park African visitors were only allowed accommodation at a camp with very rudimentary facilities. Since then the national parks have become more inclusive and the value of cultural diversity as well as biodiversity has been made explicit through the promotion of local tourism and the development of cultural heritage sites such as Thulamela, the walled stone remains of a vital fifteenth-century trading centre. Some progress has also been made in improving relations with neighbouring communities, but they continue to live in desperate poverty. Improvements in communication are largely due to environmental justice organisations, particularly the People and Parks Project of the Group for Environmental Monitoring demanding change from a 'fortress and fines' model of conservation in which neighbouring communities were perceived and treated as threats.

Fragments remain in post-apartheid South Africa of the linkage of environmentalism with conservation. The protection of biodiversity is often eclipsed by survivalist concerns with jobs and livelihoods. A workshop participant recently commented, 'White people must be mad to care so much about the poaching of rhinos when black children are going hungry.' However, the reconfigured discourse of environmentalism involves a stress on material conditions, particularly on survivalist concerns such as access to food, water and energy, the areas where inequality is most apparent. For example, many participants at the foundational workshop of the Vaal Environmental Justice Alliance (VEJA) in 2005 found the concept compelling for this reason. Some defined it very broadly, such as environmental justice meaning the creation of jobs, the total eradication of poverty, the equal distribution of wealth, ending discrimination due to illness and health protection. The majority of the young, black participants linked the concept to protecting livelihoods: for example, 'environmental justice to us means that natural resources need to be used in a way that will preserve them for generations to come. The environment must provide the resources to live. You can't tell a hungry person not to kill an animal, or a cold person not to cut down a tree and make a fire to warm himself. We must not destroy the environment which is our source of life.' Many expressed anger against corporations in the Vaal area who were concerned with profit at the expense of environmental and social justice and whose emissions were creating severe air and water pollution. Samson Mokoena, who is now the coordinator of VEJA, explained in an interview:

> For me with environmental justice you become yourself … you engage with real issues that the community is faced with every day, like having water in your tap. It's a powerful concept because it links all the issues. It shows how everything is connected.

Environmental injustice involves the externalisation of the costs of production by powerful corporations in the form of toxic pollution of the air and groundwater, as well as the enclosure or dispossession of natural resources such as land and water (Hallowes 2011). It continues in post-apartheid South Africa as inequality deepens, and at least 54 per cent of the population are classified as 'poor' (Stats SA 2014). Black South Africans continue to live on the most damaged land, in the most polluted neighbourhoods often adjoining mine dumps, waste sites or polluting industries, without adequate services of refuse removal, water, electricity and sanitation. In the province of Gauteng there are some 1.6 million people living on mine dumps that are contaminated with uranium and toxic heavy metals, including arsenic, aluminium, manganese and mercury. There are well documented health risks. Associated with exposure to high levels of uranium, for example, are 'kidney damage and disease, neurological problems and cancer' (Herrmannsen 2015: 3).

While there have been improvements in air quality legislation, especially in the Vaal Triangle, with legal limits set for pollutants such as sulphur dioxide and particulate matter, industries have been given a reprieve of up to five years to comply with air quality limits that came into effect in 2015. Health problems abound in mining-affected communities. 'An average of 42 tons of dust – both toxic and potentially radioactive – enters the air in the West Rand every day' (Herrmannsen 2015: 4). The community of South Durban is struggling to survive the highest rate of asthma in the world from exposure to toxic chemicals from oil refining.

Much of this toxic pollution is hidden and unseen: the millions of tonnes of carbon dioxide and other greenhouse gases that we emit each year are invisible; so too are the toxic chemicals in highly processed 'fast foods' that South Africans consume regularly, the pathogens in the water that irrigates our vegetables, the brine injected into chickens to increase their weight, the 4 billion litres of polluted water, mainly from dysfunctional sewerage plants, that are released into our dams and rivers every day (let alone the heavy metals, many of which are carcinogenic) are all unseen. Toxic pollution requires a process of social recognition.

However, a number of factors make this recognition difficult. Environmental risks are ubiquitous in industrial society. Pollutants are:

> … the stowaways of normal consumption. They travel on the wind and in the water. They can be in anything and everything, and along with the absolute necessities of life – air to breathe, food, clothing – they pass through all the otherwise strictly controlled and protected areas of modernity' (Beck 1992: 41).

Many of the threats – such as traces of toxic heavy metals in water – are only detectable and explicable through the application of specialised forms of scientific knowledge – and in addition there is a political invisibility in that the interests and power relations involved in much damage to the environment are obscure and hidden. This applies particularly to the intricate interconnections which constitute the 'minerals-energy complex' (Fine and

Rustomjee 1996), the system of accumulation which continues to dominate the South African economy and which involves protecting and promoting the political interests involved in extractivism.

ENVIRONMENTAL JUSTICE ORGANISATIONS AND STRUGGLES

Paradoxically, while environmental injustice persists, 'there is no clearly identifiable, relatively unified and broadly popular environmental movement in the country' (Death 2014: 1216). Instead, environmentalism is fractured and diverse. Death maintains that the explanation lies:

> … in the contrasting political opportunities for different elements within the environmental movement. More radical or confrontational movements are marginalised and harassed, whereas technical or expert groups are incorporated and often co-opted. This is a self-reinforcing dynamic which prevents the formation of a strong and coherent popular environment movement, as it reinforces perceptions of 'green' conservation organisations as elitist, pro-business, and detached from the concerns of the majority of the population (Death 2014: 1226).

Current environmental justice struggles involve a range of mobilising issues, although the most common demands and claims relate to 'rights' and health, a tendency related to the constitutional framing of the right in the post-apartheid era of all 'to live in an environment that is not harmful to health or wellbeing'. The overall focus on the concrete issues in everyday life flows from the recognition that it is the poor and the working class who are most burdened by environmental injury. Poor people are also the most vulnerable to the effects of climate change such as more extreme weather events, crop failures, rising food prices and water shortages.

NEW ORGANISATIONS

This is the context in which new environmental justice organisations are emerging such as the WoMin (a regional alliance of organisations and movements focused on extractivism from a feminist perspective), the Highveld Environmental Justice Network (made up of some twenty-five grassroots organisations) and Mining Affected Communities United in Action (Macua) which brings together over one hundred CBOs. While heavily criticised as 'tame' and 'reformist', the 2015 Alternative Mining Indaba brought together more than 150 activists from vibrant community organisations, and another hundred NGO workers, according to Matthews Hlabane of the newly formed Green Revolutionary Council. The recently founded South African Food Sovereignty campaign is gathering momentum and the new Centre for Environmental Rights is involved in exposing the lack of effective regulation and in teaching communities how to use the law to try and enforce compliance with environmental legislation. Established environmental justice organisations such as Earthlife Africa, the Benchmarks Foundation, Action Aid, Groundwork, Biowatch, VEJA, the Environmental Monitoring Group and the South Durban Community Environmental Alliance are consolidating the bridging of ecological and social justice. Overall, there is a strong emphasis on supporting the 'front line communities' most affected by extractivism, for example through exchange visits, direct legal assistance and information sharing meetings, such as the 'Push Back Coal' workshops hosted by Groundwork and the Society, Work and Development Institute. This goes some way to avoid the usual tension between NGOs and grassroots communities. For example, an Earthlife official said recently: 'We don't like to talk about capacity building because we ourselves learn a lot from these communities.'

One of the distinctive features of the new initiatives is a continental or regional focus. For example, WoMin is mobilising against extractivism on a continental scale. Recently it convened a gathering of activists from some twenty-four organisations in the Southern African region calling for building 'popular alliances against Big Coal' and a new form of development that 'recognises and supports the work of care and reproduction' (WoMin Declaration 24 January 2015). The WoMin African Gender and Extractives Alliance convened a regional gathering of more than sixty women activists in 2015 in Nigeria and resolved 'to unify our struggles through a women-led regional campaign for climate, energy, food and gender justice' (statement issued 29 October 2015). Other examples are the 'people's dialogues' of the Rural Women's Assembly which has a continental focus, as well as exchange visits between communities and countries.

These organisations are also developing innovative strategies ranging from activist schools, direct protest action such as the occupation of Eskom headquarters, people's assemblies for grassroot communities to 'speak out' on their experiences of hunger and drought, food sovereignty festivals and recipe books which celebrate poor women's resourcefulness. Another fairly new tactic is strategic litigation, for example by the Centre for Environmental Rights over the award of mining licences in protected areas. Unlike the dependence on legal expertise involving a displacement of collective mobilisation, these actions are empowering.

All these initiatives are developing new alliances, forms of power and new narratives such as of 'food sovereignty', 'transformational feminism', 'energy democracy' and variants of 'environmental justice'. They are part of a growing emphasis on moving beyond denunciation of the present order to formulate alternative social forms. For example, the current food regime in South Africa is marked by the coexistence of hunger (14 million people) and extravagant over-consumption and waste (a third of all food produced). It is also ecologically unsustainable in its dependence on fossil fuels. Many grassroots women are mobilising in new organisations or consolidating older organisations to challenge the present corporate dominance of the food system These groupings are building a 'counter power' based on how black, working-class women are the 'shock absorbers' of the climate crisis, experiencing most intensely the devastating impact of rising food prices, water scarcity and energy poverty. Agro-ecology is increasingly promoted as an alternative to industrial agriculture, based on local solutions using local inputs (local seeds, organic manure, mulching, natural pest management) which are labour absorbing and affordable. It is an element of 'food sovereignty' which is the foundational alternative concept to the existing food regime. This puts the needs of those who produce and consume food – rather than the interests of markets and corporations – at the centre of the food system. It challenges the present system of industrial agriculture and the weak and descriptive notion of food security which 'tells us nothing about who actually controls the whole food chain' (George 2010: 134).

Several organisations, such as the Southern Cape Land Campaign, are not only mobilising opposition to fracking but are also 'exploring alternatives which will foster energy democracy and transformative development while protecting the natural resources and people of the Karoo' (Black Thursday Southern Cape Land campaign statement, 13 July 2015). This emphasis on alternative forms of 'development' applies to diverse struggles, such as that of the peasants organised in the Environmental Justice Alliance 'Sustaining the Wild Coast' centred on the Amadiba Crisis Committee (ACC) in Xolobeni. Threatened by an Australian titanium mining company, they reject being described as 'poor' because their present livelihoods involve strong social networks and access to the natural resources needed for subsistence farming for 200 households (Bennie 2011).

Other organisations are promoting concrete post-carbon alternatives such as Earthlife's Sustainable Energy and Livelihoods Project which combines water harvesting, food sovereignty and clean energy through installing, maintaining and training women on the use of agro-ecology, biogas digesters and PVC solar power units. In Ivory Park, the Solidarity Economy Movement has established agro-ecological food gardens and a bakery which supplies nutritious bread at half the retail price. These initiatives are generating demands which either challenge or cannot easily be accommodated by neoliberal capitalism. However, many of these local groupings are facing increasing intimidation and threats of violence, ranging from beatings and the burning down of activists' homes to murder. The ACC, elected by the community in 2007 to represent them in their struggle against mining by the Australian mining company, Minerals Commodities Ltd, have experienced violent threats for years, including police shootings and raids in 2015. This pattern reached a peak when the chairperson of the ACC, Sikhosiphi Rhadebe, was brutally assassinated at his home on 22 March 2016. At the time, an official from the mining company commented, 'In my experience there is no development without blood.' Within a few hours, social media mobilised statements from 120 organisations condemning the murder. Activists from Somkhele and Fulani, who have engaged in nonviolent tactics of resistance to coal mining such as marches and blocking access roads, report intimidation, beatings and the burning of their houses. In many desperately poor communities, anti-mining activists are under tremendous social pressure, accused of being 'anti-development' and 'preventing job creation'. Rising poverty and unemployment means that such pressures will increase.

NEW COALITIONS AND ALLIANCES

One hopeful sign is that coalitions are forming across previous divisions, although it also must be acknowledged that many of these new coalitions are fragile, untested and dependent on donor money. Some of these new alliances or coalitions are between formerly antagonistic groupings, such as those concerned with conservation of threatened plants, animals and wilderness areas and those concerned with social needs. An example is the struggle against the proposed open cast Fuleni Coal mine stretching 3 550 hectares close to the border of Hluhluwe iMfolozi Park, one of Africa's oldest game reserves and central to rhino conservation, where local women have mobilised with the support of eight conservation organisations such as the Wildlife and Environment Society of Southern Africa and community groupings such as Macua, WoMin, and Groundwork and formed the iMfolozi Community and Wilderness Alliance. This organisation recently joined forces with the People Opposing Mining at Xolobeni on the Wild Coast in a protest outside the Durban offices of the Department of Mineral Resources. There are powerful forces involved in this struggle; interests in the coal mine have included Glencore and BHB Billiton, the world's largest commodity trader and mining house respectively. Resistance is focused not only on the ecological effects such as disturbances to wildlife, noise, seismic vibrations, dust, water and light pollution, but also on the destruction of the houses and livelihoods of the 16 000 people living in the path of the mine, the damage to eco-tourism as well as the lack of consultation and disregard for human rights. Their resistance has been strengthened by the disruption and experience of air pollution caused by the Somkhele coal mine to the neighbouring villagers. Not only was there no consultation with the community when the mine was established in 2006, but they have suffered loss of access to grazing land and water sources, as well as noise and air pollution. They have also received threats of violence, harassment and intimidation, while they focus on peaceful resistance such as marches, petitions and blocking access roads with rocks and burning tyres. At the same time, the community is divided. A member of the traditional council said the council had originally supported the mining after being convinced by the mining company Ibutho Coal that it would bring development to the community. 'The company had promised us that mining would come with development. Young people would be sent to universities to acquire mining skills' (cited in *The Mercury*, 27 April 2016).

Another example of disparate groupings uniting is the Save Mapungubwe Coalition which was formed to safeguard the Mapungubwe National Park, a World Heritage site, from an Australian-based mining company, Coal of Africa. The diverse coalition included environmental NGOs such as World Wildlife Fund (WWF) and the Endangered Wildlife Trust (EWT) as well as local people and land claimants. Such alliances are beginning to close (or, at least, to narrow) a historic gap. In the past, environmental initiatives involved a fault line which divided the 'movement' into two main streams: those organised around the discourse of conservation and those organised around the discourse of environmental justice. Another hopeful development is that new linkages exposing the false binary of 'jobs' versus 'environmental protection' are emerging between another set of distinct and often antagonistic groupings – labour and environmental justice activists. An example is the formal organisation established by the Congress of South African Trade Unions (Cosatu) consisting of representatives from all twenty-two affiliate unions and from key environmental organisations. Now defunct because of splits in Cosatu, this new grouping promoted their shared research into coal mining, chemicals and poultry farming for a five-year period. They engaged in a good deal of popular education and formulated policy positions around a 'just transition', fracking and the food crisis. Some cooperative relations remain intact; for example, Macua and the National Union of Metalworkers of South Africa (Numsa) jointly drew up a petition for the October 2015 anti-corruption march over dishonesty in the government's awarding of mining licences – although it is worrying that at the Workers' Summit of 20 April 2016, part of the process of launching a new labour federation, the summit declaration was ecologically blind. The emphasis was rightly on how 'workers face attacks on their living standards and job security'; the challenge to environmentalists is to persuade this new grouping that one source of these attacks is climate change.

Another example of unions and environmental organisations collaborating is the Climate Jobs Campaign which has collected 100 000 signatures in support of creating jobs to address the environmental crisis and the growing unemployment crisis. The campaign is driven by a coalition that started with forty labour and environmental organisations in 2011. Based on meticulous research, it has demonstrated that up to three million jobs are possible, reducing environmental damage and challenging capitalist ownership in favour of community-owned projects. It has been described by Sandra van Niekerk, the campaign's national coordinator, as 'one of the largest cross-sector collaborations in the country' (cited in Kings 2015: 4). It was endorsed by fifty-one African countries in the Abuja Declaration of 2016.

There has been collaboration in the form of joint protest marches and petitions between sections of the labour movement and environmentalists over energy issues. Energy poverty is widespread as electricity prices have risen dramatically in recent years. Numsa is strongly promoting the environmental justice notion of energy democracy as a building block towards an alternative future: it means 'the right of communities to have access to sufficient energy within ecological limits from appropriate sustainable sources for a dignified life' and involves 'resisting the agenda of the fossil fuels corporations and reclaiming the energy sector as part of 'the commons' (Cock 2015: 23). Social ownership of resources that are outside the market and democratically controlled is the potential of decentralised renewable energy with power and heat produced closer to the site of final use. The expansion of the present privatised renewable energy programme means that electricity could become totally unaffordable for the mass of South Africans. This programme has produced 6 300 MW since its inception in 2011 (Baker and Burton 2015: viii) but has created few of the jobs and skills locally that are desperately needed. As a Numsa official pointed out, 'Renewable energy at the service of capital accumulation could result in even harsher patterns of displacement and appropriation of land than those brought about by other forms of energy' (Abrahamsky 2012: 349).

Altogether, three very different sets of binaries which were blockages to the emergence of a strong environmental justice movement are dissolving – or at least loosening: first, at a political level the binary which opposes 'jobs' with 'environmental protection'; second, at an organisational level the binary between environmental justice and the conservation of nature which is associated with dispossession and exclusion; and third, epistemologically the binary which, according to Moore (2015), is rooted in the rise of capitalism itself, between 'nature' and 'society'. Many environmental activists are challenging the instrumental 'resource management' approach to nature and promoting a holistic, ecological view of people, animals and plants as forming a relational unity, an integral whole. This provides a strong contrast to the dualistic understanding of 'nature' and 'society' as separate entities with 'the human mission to extract rather than to conserve' (Berkes 2008: 265).

COAL AS A UNIFYING ISSUE IN A POTENTIAL MASS BASED ENVIRONMENTAL JUSTICE MOVEMENT

The link between environmental injustice and inequality is clearest in relation to food, energy and water. Coal has an impact on all three issues and could constitute a powerful ground for united action among the disparate groupings described above.

South Africa is the world's fifth largest producer of coal, which accounts for 92 per cent of our electricity, and the state is promoting the expansion of coal mining. Two new coal-fired power stations (among the largest in the world) are being built, and another eleven smaller ones are planned, as well as well as forty new coal mines, most of them in Mpumalanga on the most fertile land in the country. There were over 1 600 operating coal mines in 2014, the number having increased since 2004 when the Minerals and Petroleum Development Act (MPRDA) came into operation (DMR Annual Reports cited by Hermanus 2015: 6). Despite strong state policy on mine closure and rehabilitation, according to the Centre for Environmental Rights (CER) there are some 6 000 derelict and ownerless mines in the country which present vast environmental challenges such as acid mine drainage. The flow of acid mine drainage (polluted water from old mining areas, including coal) is having devastating consequences. Communities living close to the operative coal-fired power stations and open-pit working or abandoned mines, are dealing with mass removals and dispossession, loss of livelihoods, threats to food security, health problems associated with water and air pollution, damage to their homes from blasting, corruption in the awarding of mining licences and inadequate consultation (Groundwork 2014a, b; Hallowes and Munnik 2016). The CER has established that many existing coal mines have been operating for years without proper licences (including water licences). This is especially serious as South Africa is a water-scarce country and 83 per cent of our rivers are badly polluted. Kusile, the coal-fired power station currently under construction, will use 71 million litres of water a day (Groenewald 2012). The expansion of coal mining threatens food security. Almost half, 46 per cent, of

South Africa's high potential agricultural land is in the Mpumalanga Highveld, yet 61 per cent of the total land area of Mpumalanga is under mining and prospecting rights and rights applications (Davies 2014 cited by Hermanus 2015: 7). A report by the Bureau for Food and Agricultural Policy concluded that mining activities will mean a substantial loss of maize production and would have an impact on the availability and price of this staple food.

Opposition to coal is a theme in many of the environmental initiatives cited above, and is implicit in the counter-narratives of 'food sovereignty' and 'energy democracy'. Formal alliances in opposition to the wide range of negative effects of coal are growing. Opposition to the MPRDA provides a good example of growing environmental justice collaboration. A submission on how it would disadvantage affected communities was made to the Parliamentary Portfolio Committee on Mineral Resources by the CER, Groundwork, Earthlife, VEJA, the Environmental Monitoring Group and others. Much cooperation centres on challenging the eleven proposed privately owned coal-fired power stations, as well as trying to force compliance with environmental regulations by existing power stations and coal mines. The Life After Coal Campaign includes the CER, Earthlife Africa, Groundwork, Greenpeace Africa, 350Africa org. and the South African Faith Communities Environmental Institute. A coalition of eight civil society organisations (linking local communities and conservation groups) represented by CER has instituted legal action following the granting of a coal mining right to Atha-Africa Ventures inside the sensitive Mabola Protected Environment which was established to safeguard three rivers rising in the mountains of the area and is largely composed of wetlands and pans. The linking of principles of social justice with ecological sustainability in the discourse of environmental justice is providing the impetus for many of these struggles.

International linkages are strong in the climate justice movement. In different networks such as Climate Justice Now the theme of justice is stressed in both global and local terms: globally on how a wide range of activities have contributed to an ecological debt owed to countries in the global South, and locally on how it is the poor and the powerless who are bearing the brunt of climate change.

The political space for taking this normative emphasis further could be the notion of a 'just transition', which has both national and global resonance.

A 'JUST TRANSITION' FROM FOSSIL FUEL CAPITALISM

There is a widespread understanding of the need to change the current dependence on fossil fuels in South Africa, but there is no consensus on either the depth or the direction of such change. In one sense, then, the notion of a 'just transition' is an empty signifier with no agreement as to its meaning or content.

Two broad approaches to the notion of a 'just transition' exist within the labour movement: (i) a minimalist position that is primarily defensive, emphasising social protection, shallow, reformist change with green jobs, retraining and consultation; (ii) an alternative notion of a just transition involving transformative change and totally different forms of producing and consuming (Cock 2012).

This could be another false binary which fails to distinguish between the long-term and short-term interests of labour. While, as Klein (2014) powerfully demonstrates, addressing the climate crisis 'changes everything' and is in the long-term interests of labour, in the short term the immediate needs of vulnerable workers in extractive industries have to be met. This is particularly true in relation to increasing unemployment, casualisation, outsourcing and poverty, and implies that more attention needs to be paid to strategic rather than principled positions – in other words, to the modalities of a 'just transition'.

There are elements of both the defensive and transformative approaches in the Cosatu policy on climate change, which affirms that 'a just transition towards a low carbon and climate-resilient society is required' (Cosatu 2011). While this policy statement was endorsed by all affiliates at the time, strong differences have emerged between the National Union of Mineworkers (NUM) and Numsa, for example. NUM is increasingly defensive of the interests of some 90 000 coal miners, in the face of the threats of job losses from mine closures, falling coal prices (60 per cent since 2012), mechanisation, demands from environmental activists to 'keep the coal in the hole' and the divestment movement. Differences over models of economic growth also need to be addressed because while many environmental activists advocate 'deindustrialisation' and 'zero growth', labour prioritises economic growth for job creation. Furthermore, efforts to restore the 6 000 abandoned or ownerless mines in the country have been largely unsuccessful. The NUM favours 'clean coal' from expensive and untested technological innovations such as carbon capture and storage. Some scepticism has been expressed on the impact of labour. For example:

> While parts of organised labour provide a progressive voice on climate change, mitigation policy, environmental justice and a just transition, such statements do not appear to have any real impact given the realities of the carbon-intensity of many important union sectors' (Baker and Burton 2015: 10).

Not only the NUM but also the biggest transport union in the country, the South African Transport and Allied Workers Union (Satawu), have expressed concern about job losses affecting their members who are coal truck drivers. But the union has also contributed to the Million Climate Jobs Campaign. It is important not to underestimate the extent to which – in the current context – workers are desperate to maintain their jobs. Clearly, debate is needed on the modalities of a just transition led by labour. A just transition should be conceptualised in developmental terms and address questions of inequality, transparency and democracy. It must include 'issues such as access to energy for the poor, the role of labour and the social consequences of energy exploitation and infrastructure development, regardless of whether it is high or low carbon' (Baker and Burton 2015: 1)

The obstacles, however, are formidable, not only involving the divisions in the labour movement. Coal is South Africa's third largest export by value and the coal-dominated electricity sector is an important component of the minerals-energy complex which has historically relied on cheap coal and cheap labour. It 'encompasses critical links and networks of power between the financial sector, government, the private sector and parastatals such as the Industrial Development Corporation and Eskom (Baker and Burton 2015: 8). Four dominant companies have 'enormous collective bargaining power' (Nakhooda 2011: 21; cited by Baker and Burton 2015: 22). The state-owned monopoly utility, Eskom is 'the fulcrum on which the input of coal and output of cheap electricity turned with large mining houses providing coal at one end and receiving electricity for the extraction and refining of other commodities at the other' (Baker and Burton 2015: 14). A further difficulty is that the power of the minerals-energy complex is difficult to establish because of a lack of transparency and power struggles within the policy sphere (Baker and Burton 2015). At the same time, 'coalitions (such as the Chamber of Mines, the Energy Intensive Users Group and Busa) concerned with maintaining the status quo are well organised and have used the discourse of growth, employment and competitiveness to hinder the implementation of mitigation policy' (Baker and Burton 2015: 2).

Environmentally destructive developments are often justified in terms of job creation; 'challenges to mining are dismissed as anti-growth' (Davies 2014: 15). The invisibility of much toxic pollution is often aggravated by ignorance and confusion in affected communities. As is written of a contaminated community in Argentina, 'the culture of toxic uncertainty' is very debilitating (Auyero and Swistun 2009: 108) and is complicated by the widespread corporate practices of deceit and denial of responsibility for pollution (Markowitz and Rosner 2002).

Despite all these constraints, the concept of a just transition should be grounded in the notion of fundamental change towards social and economic justice. It needs to be democratised in a process of transparent and inclusive debate. Part of the challenge is to develop new forms of power, what Wainwright (2013) has called 'power as transformative capacity' to challenge the environmental injustice and inequality which are intrinsic to fossil fuel capitalism. Doing so involves developing the associational power of workers organised in trade unions as well as the symbolic power which draws its strength from making moral claims of 'right' and 'wrong'. It also involves stimulating the political imaginaries necessary to envisage alternative social forms such as energy democracy and food sovereignty.

CONCLUSION

An ecological transformation is required as part of a 'new liberation struggle' in South Africa. Driven by a strong environmental justice movement this would involve a just transition from the present fossil fuel regime that is moving us towards ecological collapse and catastrophe. The implication is that what Von Holdt and Webster (2006) conceptualised as a triple transition from democracy (economic liberalisation, political democracy and postcolonial transformation) requires a fourth dimension: an ecological transition to a society marked by the linkage of justice to sustainability.

This chapter has pointed to a set of initiatives which could potentially cohere into a unified, mass-based environmental justice movement to drive this ecological transition. It is an incipient possibility which may or may not materialise. While much of the collective action concerns inequalities in access to food, water and energy and the damaging impacts of coal, the agreement is largely around common principles and analysis, rather than on concrete strategy and tactics. The constraints include the power of social forces supporting the fossil fuel industry, increasing desperation among the unemployed for jobs which is linked to growing divisions in affected communities, as well as how much popular mobilisation is localised, episodic, discontinuous and focused on service delivery issues which are not framed as 'environmental issues'. But we have a historical model of unified environmental action in the EJNF and collectively all the current initiatives confronting different aspects of the ecological crisis are challenging inequality and demonstrating an alternative paradigm, a different relationship between human beings and between human beings and nature. All the emerging discourses of environmental justice, energy democracy, food sovereignty and transformative feminism are profoundly subversive of capitalist forms.

Many of the initiatives described are part of strong networks, local and global. All over the world the discourse of environmental justice is creating a form of 'epistemic solidarity', in forging alliances locally and globally between North and South, and in linking the principles of social justice and ecological sustainability. Many of the environmental justice struggles on the African continent are against the dispossession and toxic pollution involved in extractivism, so the South African case is not unique. This 'second scramble for Africa' involves the appropriation of Africa's profitable natural resources by powerful multinational corporations. Throughout the continent poor people are not passive victims of these processes. Instead, in this context of crisis, they are drawing from the travelling and adaptive discourse of environmental justice which has the capacity to connect particularistic, local struggles, generalise them and forge global alliances. The current unprecedented global concentration of corporate power calls for these forms of transnational solidarity.

REFERENCES

Abrahamsky, K (2012) Energy and social reproduction. *The Commoner*, 15, 337–350.
Auyero, J and Swistun, D (2009) *Flammable: Environmental suffering in an Argentine shantytown.* New York: Oxford University Press.
Baker, L and Burton, J (2015) *The political economy of decarbonisation: Exploring the dynamics of South Africa's electricity sector.* Cape Town: Energy Research Centre, University of Cape Town.
Baskin, J (2015) Paradigm dressed as epoch. *Environmental Values*, 24 (1), 1–29.
Beck, U (1992) *The risk society.* Oxford: Oxford University Press.

Bennie, A (2011) Questions for labour on land, livelihoods and jobs: A case study of the proposed mining at Xolobeni, Wild Coast. *South African Review of Sociology*, 42 (3), 41–59.

Berkes, F (2008) *Sacred ecology*. 2nd ed. New York: Routledge.

Bond, P (2015) Challenges for the climate justice movement. Unpublished paper.

Bullard, R (ed.) (1993) *Confronting environmental racism: Voices from the grassroots*. Cambridge, MA: South End Press.

Cock, J (2012) South African labour's response to climate change: The threat of green neo-liberal capitalism. In S Mosoetsa and M Williams (eds) *Labour in the global south: Challenges and alternatives for workers*. Geneva: ILO. pp 19–40.

Cock, J (2015) Moving towards an alternative eco-socialist order in South Africa. *At Issue Ezine*, 17 (5), 22–28.

Cock, J and Koch, E (1991) *Going green: People, politics and the environment*. Cape Town: Oxford University Press.

Cosatu (Congress of South African Trade Unions) (2011) *A just transition to a low-carbon and climate resilient economy*. Johannesburg: Cosatu.

Davies, T (2014) Environmental crisis in Mpumalanga: Why is nobody listening. Groundup.org.za, 15 September.

Death, C (2014) Environmental movements, climate change and consumption in South Africa. *Journal of Southern African Studies*, 40 (6), 1215–1234.

Ecomodernist Manifesto (2015) Unpublished Paper. www.ecomodernism.org.

Fine, B and Rustomjee, Z (1996) *The political economy of South Africa: From minerals energy complex to industrialization*. Boulder: Westview.

George, S (2010) *Whose crisis? Whose future?* Hoboken: Wiley.

Groenewald, Y (2012) *Coal's hidden water cost to South Africa*. Johannesburg: Greenpeace.

Groundwork (2014a) *Shell: Don't frack the Karoo*. Pietermaritzburg: Groundwork.

Groundwork (2014b) *Slow poison: Air pollution, public health and failing government*. Pietermaritzburg: Groundwork.

Hallowes, D (2011) *Toxic futures: South Africa in the crisis of energy, environment and capital*. Pietermaritzburg: UKZN Press.

Hallowes, D and Munnik, V (2016) *The destruction of the Highveld Part 1: Digging coal*. Pietermaritzburg: Groundwork.

Hermanus, M (2015) Impact of the minerals and petroleum resources development act on levels mining, land utility and people. Unpublished paper.

Herrmannsen, K (2015) Living in a toxic wasteland. *Daily Maverick*, 1 November.

Kings, S (2015) State ignores proposal to climate-proof SA and create jobs. *Mail & Guardian*, 24 September.

Klein, N (2014) *This changes everything: Capitalism versus the climate*. New York: Simon and Shuster.

Markowitz, D and Rosner, M (2002) *Deceit and denial*. Berkeley: University of California Press.

Moore, J (2015) *Capitalism in the web of life*. New York: Verso.

Schlosberg, D (2013) Theorising environmental justice: The expanding sphere of a discourse. *Environmental Politics*, 22 (1), 37–55.

Stats SA (Statistics South Africa) (2014) *Poverty trends in South Africa*. Pretoria: Stats SA.

Sze, J and London, J (2008) Environmental justice at the crossroads. *Sociology Compass*, 2 (4), 1331–1354.

Von Holdt, K and Webster, E (2006) *Organising on the periphery: New sources of power in the South African workplace*. Johannesburg: Sociology of Work Unit

Wainwright, H (2013) Transformative power: Political organisation in transition. *Socialist Register*, 49, 137–158.

Walker, C (2008) *Landmarked: Land claims and land restitution in South Africa*. Johannesburg: Jacana.

Warner, R (2010) Ecological modernisation theory: Towards a critical ecopolitics of change. *Environmental Politics*, 19 (4), 538–556.

CHAPTER 15

The geography of nuclear power, class and inequality

Jo-Ansie van Wyk

Democratic South Africa still grapples with one of the artefacts of apartheid – an apartheid geography that continues to be a spatial manifestation of race, class and inequality. This is particularly evident in the country's nuclear geographies where nuclear colonialism (a system whereby government and business target communities directly or indirectly to maintain the nuclear process) has been perpetuated by the democratic government since 1994 (Endres 2009: 39). The South African government, despite the ruling party's historically fierce opposition to nuclear energy (EMG and Western Cape ANC 1994), intends to perpetuate these geographies as well as to add new nuclear geographies such as at Bantamsklip and Thuyspunt.

Scant attention has been paid to the socio-economic impact on the local host communities in close proximity to these nuclear facilities (DEPP 2009). This atomic amnesia corresponds to the neglect, in the past, by scholars, the nuclear industry and the government to the communities close to a nuclear installation or a uranium mine. Typically, these communities are predominantly black as the legislation at the time of their construction prohibited nuclear installations within fifty kilometres of white communities. For the purpose of this chapter, three nuclear facilities – the Koeberg Nuclear Power Station (hereafter Koeberg) in the Western Cape; the facilities of the Nuclear Energy Corporation of South Africa (Necsa) (hereafter Pelindaba) at Pelindaba; and the National Radioactive Waste Disposal Facility (hereafter Vaalputs) at Vaalputs in the Northern

Figure 15.1: South Africa's nuclear geography

Nuclear sites in South Africa

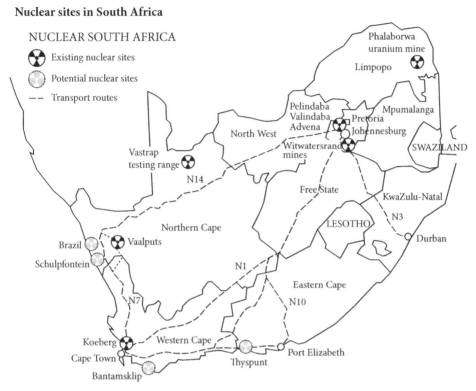

Source: Fig (2007).

Cape – illustrative of the country's nuclear geography, were selected for analytical purposes (see Figure 15.1 and Table 15.1). Each of the sites represents a specific aspect of the nuclear fuel cycle or nuclear energy complex in the country (see Table 15.1).

All of these facilities are part of South Africa's pre-1994 nuclear energy and weapons legacy. More pertinent to this study, these facilities represent instances of South Africa's nuclear geography. Other examples of this include, for example, the Vastrap Test Site in the Kalahari Desert (Von Wielligh and Von Wielligh-Steyn 2014); St Lucia where South Africa tested ballistic missiles in the early 1990s; Johannesburg and its surrounding areas as uranium naturally occurs with gold deposits here and has been reported to be an element in the city; and the Gauteng province's growing radioactive and acid mine water drainage problem.

The objective of this chapter is four-fold. First, it outlines and defines the concept of nuclear geography and its corollaries, environmental racism and justice, nuclear

Table 15.1: Selected South African nuclear geographies, ca. 2017

	Vaalputs (Northern Cape)	Koeberg (Western Cape)	Pelindaba (Northwest)
Origin	Portions of the farms Vaalputs (portions Garing, Geelpan) and Bokseputs (portion Stofkloof)	Farm Duynefontein	Farm Welgegund
Size (ha)	10 000	3 000	2 500
Date of acquisition	1983	1971	
Initial year of operation	1986	1984	1965
Facility	Radioactive waste disposal site	Nuclear power plant	Nuclear research facility, production of medical isotopes
Description of facility	Management and storage of low to intermediate level waste	Generated 1800MW electricity, contributes 5% to country's power generation	Safari-I nuclear reactor, historically site of nuclear weapons programme
Operator of facility	Necsa	Eskom	Necsa

Sources: Hambleton-Jones (1984); Eskom (2016).

community and nuclear economy. Second, the chapter explores the origins and the present state of South Africa's nuclear geography. Third, it focuses on nuclear geography as an aggravating factor in social inequality and class differences in the affected communities, and locations. Finally, the chapter situates nuclear geography in the country's future nuclear expansion plans.

NUCLEAR GEOGRAPHY, CLASS AND INEQUALITY

Nuclear geography is here defined as the spatial distribution of power, political processes and decisions related to nuclear energy, facilities, mines and infrastructure. The nuclear arms race of the Cold War had a spatial, or geographical, dimension: a race between the West and the East, or the East-West conflict. Nuclear weapons, for example, were tested and detonated in isolated and underdeveloped areas such as the Sahara Desert, various atolls in the Pacific, and in Siberia. A third manifestation of nuclear geography is the former Soviet Union's so-called closed cities, including *atomgrads* (atom cities), closed and secret cities around the country's nuclear installations and programmes – at its zenith, the Soviet Union had forty such cities in isolated areas whereas only ten exist in Russia today and remain under the purview of the Ministry of Defence, the state-owned nuclear agency (Rosatom) and the Russian Space Agency (Bacon 2014: 47). With the collapse of the Soviet Union, some of these closed cities relaxed entry requirements and overall poor governance resulted in illicit drug trade, unemployment, crime, nuclear trafficking and corruption (Shelley 2014: 299). A final manifestation is the position of American First Nations such as the Western Shoshone and the Southern Paiute in respect of the Yucca Mountain Nuclear Waste siting process, described as nuclear colonialism owing to their exclusion from the siting decision (Endres 2009: 39–60).

These examples highlight various general but sometimes overlapping dimensions – spatial (geographic and environmental), political, economic, scientific and technological, and societal – of nuclear geography. *Spatially* refers to a specific geographical location with a nuclear energy facility and infrastructure (nuclear power stations, nuclear weapons, radioactive waste facility) and uranium (mining). The *political* dimension of nuclear geography relates to the power relations between nuclear actors (states with nuclear weapons, business and government institutions), but also to the relations between these actors and the host community where these facilities and infrastructure have been established, or where uranium mining occurs.

Economically, the political dimension of nuclear geography relates to state-market-class relations (often-unequal relations) and tensions in relation to the particular location. The fourth dimension, *technology*, refers to the motivations for the development of and employment of nuclear energy in all its forms. The *societal* dimension refers to the social impact such as class contestation and the inequality of nuclear energy on host communities. Nuclear communities in these geographies share a number of characteristics such as isolation, exclusion, health issues and nuclear socio-economics. The last-named refers, inter alia, to employment levels, literacy rates, property prices, local economies, health, and access to and the distribution of resources.

Nuclear geography is a particular manifestation of power. Nuclear energy contributes to the status and prestige of the state, whereas nuclear host communities experience this spatial manifestation differently. Hierarchies of states, communities and people are created. One such hierarchy relates to class. Apart from the class division between nuclear weapons states and non-nuclear weapons states; among those in the nuclear industry; and between nuclear scientists and the public; nuclear geography also creates class divisions between the centre (of political authority, power and elites) and the periphery (host and other affected communities). These vertical and horizontal expressions of power inevitably result in class contestation and inequality in respect of access to, accumulation of, control over and the distribution of resources.

SOUTH AFRICA'S NUCLEAR GEOGRAPHY, CLASS AND INEQUALITY

This section analyses in detail the five dimensions of nuclear geography in South Africa cited above. For the remainder of this section I refer to the indicators of these dimensions:

Table 15.2: Dimensions and indicators of South Africa's nuclear geography

Dimension	Indicator
Spatial (geographic and environmental)	Isolation and remoteness of host communities Environmental degradation Impact on livelihoods
Political	Historical nuclear ambitions and grievances (international isolation and domestic opposition) Nuclear colonialism
Economic	Economic marginalisation Political economy
Science and technology	Political purpose Type of technology
Societal	Social marginalisation Powerlessness Culture of acceptance Captivity Expectations Landscapes of risk

Source: Adapted from Blowers (1999: 247).

South Africa's historical nuclear ambitions and grievances; isolation and remoteness of host communities; environmental degradation; socio-economic marginalisation; political economy; technological aspects; powerlessness; culture of acceptance; captivity; expectations; and landscapes of risk (see Table 15.2); each of which reinforces inequality and class distinction in the country.

History, the mineral-industrial complex and political ambitions

South Africa's nuclear geography is inextricably linked to its apartheid past as the country's domestic race-based policies resulted in domestic, regional and international opposition and isolation. South Africa's efforts to survive this proved to be the *raison d'être* of its nuclear energy ambitions and the development of nuclear facilities, creating nuclear geographies often characterised by further political and socio-economic accumulation and dispossession.

South Africa's nuclear geographies reflect the full nuclear fuel cycle from, for example, uranium mining and processing (Gold Reef in Gauteng); enrichment (Pelindaba); power generation (Koeberg); and radioactive waste disposal (Vaalputs). Given the secretive origins of the country's nuclear energy complex, communities next to these facilities were not always informed of their purpose. Moreover, nuclear energy always has radioactive waste that needs to be disposed of. Because of the longevity of radioactive waste, the siting of such a facility requires careful planning and should consider seismic stability, geology and host communities. In this instance, the siting of Vaalputs illustrates the link between nuclear geography, class and inequality.

Out of site, out of mind: Spatial and political remoteness and marginalisation

With Pelindaba (inaugurated by the then prime minister, Hendrik Verwoerd), operational since 1965 and the government's further nuclear energy and weapons ambitions, several studies for further feasibility were undertaken. In 1977, for example, the government appointed a specialist group to investigate nuclear energy matters. One of its recommendations was the location and acquisition of a suitable site for the storage of radioactive waste. This recommendation was accepted in 1978. Following a site selection project led by the Nuclear Development Corporation of South Africa (Nucor) (later the Atomic Energy Corporation (AEC) and today the Nuclear Energy Corporation of South Africa, (Necsa)), in February 1983 the government purchased three farms (see Table 15.1), collectively known as Vaalputs, to serve as its future radioactive waste disposal site (Hambleton-Jones 1984).

Besides their status as nuclear facilities, Vaalputs, Koeberg and Pelindaba share similar socio-economic 'backyards' – a contributing factor to inequality and class contestation in these locations. In all three cases, the backyards include farms, unique communities and examples of apartheid urban and rural development. In the case of Vaalputs, several Nama and coloured settlements are located close to the facility. The selection criteria for Vaalputs (which was one of three sites originally identified) included geology, rainfall and groundwater recharge, seismic hazard probability, mineral potential, agricultural production, population density, corrosion by groundwater, ecologically sensitive areas, surface and groundwater hydrology, growth potential and political boundaries. Nucor's comment on the local population near Vaalputs is significant:

> The nearest population centres within a 100 km radius of Vaalputs are Nababeep, Concordia, O'Kiep, Springbok, Kamieskroon, Garies and Kliprand, none of which has more than 8 500 inhabitants. The estimated population within that radius is about 15 000 people, concentrated mainly in the abovementioned towns. Within a radius of 25 km the estimated population is about fifty people (Hambleton-Jones 1984).

The report mentioned so-called white communities only and did not mention the local predominantly Nama and coloured communities and settlements closer than 25 km from the site. At the time, the AEC established an exclusive 50 km zone around white-run municipalities. However, there are indigenous Nama settlements less than 24 km from Vaalputs. Vaalputs's host communities form part of the Kamiesberg local municipality, which is about 10 000 ha in size and is the largest of the cases selected here. It is divided into four municipal wards and provides services to the villages and settlements of Kamassies, Rooifontein, Nourivier, Leliefontein, Paulshoek, Kamieskroon, Kharkams, Tweerivier, Koiingnaas, Hondeklipbaai, Soebatsfontein, Spoegrivier, Klipfontein, Garies, Lepelfontein and Kheis (Kamiesberg Municipality 2015: 43).

Just over two decades after 1983, a Necsa official admitted that the Vaalputs site was selected on a 'purely technical and scientific basis without involving the stakeholders', that the expropriation of the farms occurred 'without the consent of the [white] owners', and that the local communities in the vicinity of Vaalputs were also not consulted (Bredell 2005: 115) – instead, local communities were simply informed that a new nature reserve was to be established in the area (Greenpeace 2011: 19).

Vaalputs is geographically the country's most remote nuclear facility. Koeberg's backyard illustrates another kind of remoteness. Developed as a coloured-only working-class urban area outside the Cape Town city centre from 1977 until 1986, Atlantis is not only a prime example of apartheid urban planning and forced removals, but it is also in close proximity to Koeberg. Pelindaba's backyard includes Atteridgeville, which was established in 1939 as a blacks-only township west of Pretoria and 5 km from the Pelindaba complex. Like the other sites, the communities of Atteridgeville and others close to Pelindaba were also not consulted prior to the establishment of the nuclear complex. The geographical locations of the Vaalputs host communities, of Atlantis and of Atteridgeville correlate with the political remoteness and isolation, and the marginalisation of these host communities (Greenpeace 2011: 19).

Political economy and socio-economic impact

The geographical location of each of the selected sites has a significant socio-economic impact on host communities, contributing to class contestation and inequality. When Vaalputs's host communities were finally informed of the real purpose of the site, the government made significant socio-economic promises such as employment opportunities, schools and social services to these communities. A Necsa official observed:

> Promises made with regards to the upgrading and further development of local infrastructure and electricity supply to rural areas also did not realise as it was initially expected. The radioactive waste in the repository is further seen to affect the local image and potentially affecting the sale of local sheep farming products. Although the repository does contribute to the local economy in terms of direct purchasing of materials, supplies, vehicles, fuel, contracted services, etc., the impact of these contributions are negligible when compared to the real needs for growth in this area. All these aspects have from the onset aided in cultivating negative attitudes towards the

radioactive waste repository in the public arena as there seemed to have been no significant social or economic benefits for the communities hosting the repository (Bredell 2005: 115).

The statement also confirms the prevalence of a particular political economy, or 'economic stigma' (Greenberg 2009: 920) around these facilities. In South Africa, nuclear facilities are typically state-owned and -operated. Nuclear installations employ very few of the local population as the skills required often do not exist in these communities. In the case of Atlantis, for example, rather than providing employment opportunities at Koeberg, government-sponsored industries that were part of the country's military-industrial complex were established around the urban area with a 'ready-made' pool of labourers. Thus, very few nuclear-related skills – critical for the country wanting its new nuclear expansion plans to succeed – have been transferred to these communities.

Around Koeberg, class distinctions and inequality are further illustrated by property prices with that of Bloubergstrand and Melkbosstrand (predominantly owned by white middle-class people), for example, higher than those closer to Koeberg and in Atlantis and informal settlements such as De Noon. Similarly, property prices in so-called white areas such as Pecan Wood Estate, Schoemansville, Hartbeespoortdam, and Broederstroom around Pelindaba are also on average higher than those in, for example, Atteridgeville, Lanseria, Laudium, Diepsloot, and GaRankuwa – historically and predominantly Indian and black African, and thus residential areas that are less developed and receive poorer service delivery.

A further example of the political economy of these sites is the effect on agriculture. In the case of Vaalputs, host communities rely on subsistence farming in former so-called 'coloured reserves', now communal land. Commercial and subsistence farming also occur in Pelindaba's and Koeberg's hinterlands. Agricultural production in the Koeberg area includes predominantly grain, fruit, grapes and wine for the domestic and the international market (products intended for the latter of higher quality and organically grown). Koeberg's marine environment also has the reputation of a nuclear facility, which compromises the livelihood of traditional fishing communities. In the case of Pelindaba, agricultural production is compromised by the poor water quality of the Hartbeespoort Dam and the Crocodile River – a problem compounded by acid mine drainage and the drought of 2016.

A final example of the political economy of these sites is government's rationale for maintaining historical and initiating new nuclear geographies: namely the sector's contribution to the fiscus and economic development. According to the state-owned power utility and owner-operator of Koeberg, Eskom, Koeberg contributes significantly to the Western Cape economy. Besides employing more than 1 500 people, the facility spends more than R100 million on suppliers in the province and makes an annual direct investment of R300 million to the province's economy. In addition, Koeberg is one of the top three ratepayers in the city of Cape Town (Stott 2013).

Great expectations and acquiescence

One theme emerging from nuclear host communities are that their original expectations (socio-economic development and investment) were not met. According to a resident of Nourivier, a settlement close to Vaalputs:

> They [government officials] made various promises to the community. They said they were going to build a high school. In the end, we learnt it would be a nuclear waste dump. All the communities surrounding Vaalputs were misled. We weren't truthfully informed from the start (Greenpeace 2011: 19).

In an effort to improve the relations between itself and the Vaalputs communities, Necsa established a trust fund for the Vaalputs communities in the 1990s, which raised further expectations of large social investment. Necsa did invest in health and education programmes as well as unspecified social programmes. In 1996, the Vaalputs Community Forum (VCF) was established and consisted of Necsa officials, local farmers, and members of the trust representing the local communities. The VCF achieved some successes albeit in non-nuclear matters such as vermin control, maintenance of fences and infrastructure. More importantly, the VCF enabled communication between Necsa and the affected communities.

In 2004, the government formalised, regulated public forums on nuclear installations, and established so-called public safety information forums (PSIFs) for nuclear sites (Bredell 2005: 118). However, the dire need of these communities, poor coordination and Necsa's financial state contributed to expectations not fulfilled, resulting in negative attitudes towards Necsa (Bredell 2005: 115). A similar view was expressed during public hearings on nuclear energy in 2007 when the representatives of the community of Komaggas close to Vaalputs stated that 'many promises were made which were not fulfilled', also indicating that the relationship between government and the host community 'was not harmonious' (Namaqualand Stakeholders 2007).

In the case of Vaalputs, community members' expectations of social investment were more prevalent than their interest in the site's safe operations; a preference predominant for some years (Necsa 2012, 2013a, 2013b, 2013c). The Kamiesberg Municipality area has a Gini coefficient of 0.56; thus significant inequality in terms of wealth distribution (Kamiesberg Municipality 2015: 43). In fact, a Necsa official indicated that safety 'should again' be the 'primary focus' of the Vaalputs PSIF (Necsa 2012).

Lower expectations of social investment than those of the Vaalputs host communities seem to be the case of Pelindaba and Koeberg. According to Eskom, Koeberg makes substantial social investments in the communities around it. For example, since 2012 it has contributed to the development of the Atlantis Incubator Project to stimulate small businesses; contributed to public awareness at schools; invested in frail care; and adopted a farm school as well as a school close to De Noon (an informal settlement in Koeberg's backyard) (Stott 2013).

Technology and scientific authority

That nuclear geography and the geography of scientific authority have been linked is due to the spatial aspects of nuclear scientific and technological practices (Kirsch 2000: 180). Examples of this link include the use of scientific data to justify and support specific decisions; the scientific control of nuclear sites; the uneven distribution of and access to scientific information; and the power relations between scientists and a nuclear host community (Kirsch 2000: 180). In the case of Vaalputs, scientific conclusions determined the siting and decision-making (Hambleton-Jones 1984). Both the Vaalputs (Necsa 2012, 2013a, 2013b, 2013c) and Koeberg (Earthlife Africa 2007) host communities have complained about the highly technical nature of the information presented to them at PSIF meetings. An Atlantis representative, for example, observed that 'Eskom needed to pitch the "tone" of the meetings correctly', indicating that presentations 'were highly technical in nature' (Earthlife Africa 2007). A review of the Koeberg PSIF minutes from 2011 until 2015 reveal the level of sophistication of the meetings which were focused on safety and emergency preparedness, technical, urban developments, and the impact of Fukushima (Eskom 2016). A similar review of the minutes of the Pelindaba PSIF meetings from 2010 to 2015 (NNR 2016) produced the same results. However, the minutes of the Vaalputs PSIF indicate a greater degree of nuclear trauma of the host community where seemingly more and accessible information and social investment is required (Necsa 2012, 2013a, 2013b, 2013c).

The authority awarded to science was also questioned by the Namakwalandse Aksiegroep vir Omgewingsgeregtigheid (Namaqualand Action Group for Environmental Justice). In their submission to Parliament, their spokesperson, Andy Pienaar, observed:

> The technocrats of all stripes urge us to trust them and not stifle the advancement of science. Eskom go as far as to argue that the containment of nuclear waste is a problem solved. Leave it to the experts, they argue. One Eskom representative even complemented the Namaqua Community and said they have reason to be proud of the 'Mercedes-Benz of a facility in waste disposal at Vaalputs'. Our community decline that sort of compliment. As a community of faith, rooted in the absolute presence of God, we know it is impossible to put our trust in science and the assurances of men. We urge all the stakeholders not to belittle the moral imperatives and set themselves up as God (Namakwalandse Aksiegroep vir Omgewingsgeregtigheid 2007).

The reference to the status of Vaalputs is typical of nuclear sacrifice zones and so-called 'nuclear technoaesthetics' (Masco 2006: v) where public officials often inform communities in these zones that they should be proud of the facility and that any sacrifice they make is for the national and common good. The strong focus on science rather than on other issues has also been evident at the PSIF meetings. Given their expectation for community development, one Vaalputs PSIF member requested Necsa to clarify what kind of educational assistance was offered to the community. Necsa (2013a) confirmed that it 'only awards bursaries' to scientists and engineers. Scientific evidence is also often used to justify the use and safety of nuclear energy. Recently, Tina Joemat-Petersson, as minister of energy, observed that her department was planning to 'demystify nuclear at the candidate sites' identified for government's nuclear expansion plans (DOE 2016a) and that South Africans 'should be proud of the country's renewable energy success story' (DOE 2016b).

Landscapes of risk

Communities in these nuclear sacrifice zones find themselves in landscapes of risk. Table 15.3 outlines some of the socio-economic indicators of the selected nuclear geographies. Nationally, rural households earn less (R47 000 per annum) than urban households (R118 500 per annum), which affects the socio-economic status and class of rural communities. Besides this, female-headed households tend to earn less than male-headed households. Table 15.3 confirms this situation in the case of Vaalputs in comparison to the Koeberg and Pelindaba host communities. Urban nuclear host communities fare much better, but are still below national averages. Nationally, the Gini coefficient is 0.65; 0.55 for black Africans; 0.53 for coloureds (0.56 for the Vaalputs community); and 0.42 for whites (Stats SA 2014: 35, 41, 46, 56; Kamiesberg Municipality 2015: 42).

Apart from the socio-economic risks of these host communities, questions have also been raised about their physical health. The health of workers at nuclear facilities and that of the populations of surrounding communities have for decades been shrouded in secrecy. Former employees of Pelindaba and Vaalputs have complained about their health with little government response and compensation (Fig 2009: 69–77). Both Necsa (Bredell 2005: 116–7) and Eskom, as state-owned entities, have refuted claims of radiation exposure to former employees of both Vaalputs and Pelindaba (PMG 2007). Further claims of radiation exposure were made by independent investigations by individuals (De Waal and Pienaar 2014), and civil society organisations such as Earthlife Africa (2007), Greenpeace (2011) and the Pelindaba Working Group (2007). By 2011, at least 500 former Pelindaba employees have sought compensation for radiation exposure (Greenpeace 2011: 20). In response, Necsa (2011) explained to the Vaalputs PSIF that since 2005 several investigations were conducted; that medical records were studied; and that no incidents have occurred and no records existed to confirm that employees at Vaalputs were exposed to radiation.[1]

However, in 2012, the National Nuclear Regulator (NNR) (2012) suspended all activities associated with the receipt of radioactive waste packages at Vaalputs owing to the facility's non-compliance in respect of permitted surface doses. In some instances, employees decided to keep quiet because they feared the termination of their employment (Greenpeace 2011: 19). Questions have been raised about the management of Necsa, which may affect these facilities and host communities. In 2015, Necsa failed to produce an annual report and its financial affairs have been questioned; resulting in a dressing-down of the corporation by the Parliamentary Portfolio Committee on Energy

Table 15.3: Socio-economic indicators of selected nuclear host communities

Economic indicators

	Vaalputs (Kamiesberg Municipality)	Koeberg (Atlantis)	Pelindaba (Atteridgeville)
Income (% earning less than ZAR 80 000 p.a.)	75	60	50
Dependency ratio (%)	57.9	46.1	39.6
Formal dwellings (%)	95.6	84.5	92.6
Education (% of population with Matric)	6.8	29.1	38.6
Settlement (% urban or rural)	100 Rural	100 Urban	100 Urban
Unemployment (%)	38.8	26.5	30

Social indicators

	Vaalputs (Kamiesberg Municipality)	Koeberg (Atlantis)	Pelindaba (Atteridgeville)
Population	10 187	67 491	64 425
Population density (persons/km²)	1	2 340	6 550
Race	85.6% Coloured	85% Coloured	99.1% Black
Working age (15–64) (% of population)	63.3	68.5	72
Female-headed households	40.9	39.2	42.9
Youth unemployment rate (%)	40.4	31.9	31.6

Source: Stats SA (2011).

(Times Live 2015). Similarly, Vaalputs' safety records are mixed. The NNR has in several instances not awarded an operating licence because of noncompliance at the site. In 1996, for example, the NNR recorded fifty-five violations of the site's licence and closed it until Necsa complied (Fig 2010: 24).

A further aspect of the notion of landscapes of risk relates to the environmental impact of nuclear energy and, thus, matters of environmental justice. Leakages from some of the packages transported from Koeberg to Vaalputs have been reported, and complaints about the poor state of the road to the Vaalputs facility that host communities use, as well as the outsourced company that transports the radioactive waste to Vaalputs (Grootboom 2015). Some reports have referred to genetic mutations of plants and animals in close proximity to these installations (Pelindaba Working Group 2007). This chapter has already mentioned that the hinterlands of each of the selected cases rely on agriculture for their livelihoods. Despite annual investigations into the water quality of Vaalputs host communities (Necsa 2013a), residents remain cautious of the quality of their water, which is drawn from aquifers (Greenpeace 2011: 19–20).

Some concerns (see Gould 2009: 88–121) have also been expressed that South Africa's nuclear past was not raised at the Truth and Reconciliation Commission (TRC). In fact, the TRC tended predominantly to political matters, and not to the socio-economic and environmental issues that emerged regarding the country's nuclear past and related political decisions (TRC 2002).

CONCLUSION

No space is neutral. This is particularly the case in South Africa, where apartheid was based on a racial and spatial division of society. Scant attention has been paid to the class contestations and equity in respect of South Africa's nuclear host communities. Typically, spatially, politically and socio-economically isolated, these host communities were not consulted when sites were originally selected. This lack of public consultation; poor social investment by state-owned nuclear entities; and no compensation continue in the post-apartheid regime. Official neglect of host communities and individuals working at these sites has become the norm; a norm perpetuated by most in the South African population.

Contemporary South Africa has had some contestation about large-scale government projects and their siting; as indicated by the siting of the Square Kilometre Array (SKA) project as well as government's intention to explore shale gas in the Karoo. These issues, as well as the country's nuclear geographies, call for 'spatial equity' (Lidskog 2005: 191). The large-scale government projects add to the triple exposure of these host communities to socio-political vulnerabilities: political alienation and scientific domination; radiation exposure; *and* spatial isolation with environmental degradation. This contributes to host communities' sense of powerlessness. Although PSIFs exist, communities maintain that they have little influence over decisions – evident in meagre public consultation on the country's nuclear expansion programme and existing facilities.

Post-apartheid, the 'ongoing generation of inequality' (Hart 2013: 158, 233) persists. This chapter has focused on the five dimensions of South Africa's nuclear geography and deduced that host communities have remained neglected in democratic South Africa, and – once the new saga for the new sites emerges – will remain neglected, perpetuating apartheid-era nuclear geography and inequality. This corresponds with the so-called distant decay function where opposition to nuclear facilities is less the further away a site is (Aldrich 2013: 269) – which has been evident in the absence of communities (such as Hondeklipbaai and Spoegrivier) furthest away from Vaalputs (Necsa 2013a, 2013b, 2013c).

These indicators of nuclear geography and its link with class contestation and inequality is further evident in government's response to nuclear host communities. The South African government (past and present) has employed four instruments – coercion, hard social control, incentives, and soft social control – in response to these communities (Aldrick 2008: 56). Coercion is evident in the historical selection of sites where private land was expropriated without consultation with the future host communities. These communities experienced apartheid geography based on white privilege. Hard social control remains evident in the poor levels of public consultation with host communities – and thus further inequality in terms of access to information and the decision-making process. Typically, government sets the agenda and host communities respond to it. The third instrument, incentives, is evident in the offering and promising of rewards such as employment, social investment and infrastructure development. Finally, soft social control aims to change host communities' preferences in respect of nuclear facilities by the actual provision of education, social investment, resources and opportunities.

NOTE

1   According to the minutes, Necsa (2011) explains 'dat daar verskeie ondersoeke sedert 2005 gedoen is, mediese rekords na gegaan is, bevindinge was voorgehou aan die betrokke rolspelers, en dat die stelling ongrondig is siende dat daar geen insident of rekords bestaan wat dit kan bevestig nie.'

REFERENCES

Aldrich, D (2013) A normal accident or a sea-change? Nuclear host communities respond to the 3/11 disaster. *Japanese Journal of Political Science*, 14 (2), 261–276.
Aldrick, D (2008) *Site fights: Divisive facilities and civil society in Japan and West*. New York: Cornell University Press.
Bacon, E (2014) *Contemporary Russia*. 3rd ed. London: Palgrave Macmillan.
Blowers, A (1999) Nuclear waste and landscapes of risk. *Landscape Research*, 24 (3), 241–264.
Bredell, PJ (2005) Public involvement in the establishment and operation of the low and intermediate level waste repository at Vaalputs in South Africa. In International Atomic Energy Agency (IAEA) (2007) *Low and intermediate level waste repositories: Socio-economic aspects and public involvement*. Proceedings of a workshop held in Vienna, 9–11 November 2005. IAEA-TECDOC-1553. Vienna: IAEA. pp. 114–120.

DEPP (Department of Engineering and Public Policy) (2009) *Nuclear power and communities.* Pittsburgh: Carnegie Mellon University. http://www.andrew.cmu.edu/user/mk08/Nuclear%20 Power%20and%20Communities%20Final%20Report.pdf (accessed 15 June 2016).

De Waal, M and Pienaar, J (2014) Apartheid's nuclear shame. *Ground Up.* 27 June. http://www.groundup. org.za/article/apartheide28099s-nuclear-shame_1938/ (accessed 9 June 2016).

DOE (2016a) *Briefing to the Portfolio Committee on Energy. 2nd and 3rd quarters performance reports 2016/17 FY.* 19 April. http://pmg-assets.s3-website-eu-west-1.amazonaws.com/160419quarter2. pdf (accessed 17 June 2016).

DOE (2016b) *Energy for the nation.* https://www.energy.gov.za (accessed 17 June 2016).

Earthlife Africa (2007) *Submission by Atlantis community representative.* Submission to the Portfolio Committee on Environmental Affairs and Tourism Public Hearings on Nuclear Energy in South Africa. Parliament. 20 June. https://pmg.org.za/committee-meeting/9013/ (accessed 9 June 2016).

EMG (Environmental Monitoring Group) and Western Cape ANC (African National Congress) Science and Technology Group (1994) The nuclear debate. In *Proceedings of the conference on nuclear policy for a democratic South Africa, Cape Town,* 11–13 February. Cape Town: EMG.

Endres, D (2009) The rhetoric of nuclear colonialism: Rhetorical exclusion of American Indian arguments in the Yucca Mountain Nuclear Waste siting decision. *Communication and Critical/Cultural Studies,* 6 (1), 39–60.

Eskom (2016) *Public safety information forum.* http://www.eskom.co.za/Whatweredoing/Electricity Generation/KoebergNuclearPowerStation/MoreAboutNuclearSafety/Pages/Public_Safety_ Information_Forum_PSIF_Information.aspx (accessed 13 June 2016).

Fig, D (2007) *Why the nuclear industry is not good for our people.* Presentation to Portfolio Committee on Environment and Tourism. 20 June. https://pmg.org.za/committee-meeting/9013/ (accessed 14 August 2017).

Fig, D (2009) In the dark: Seeking information about South Africa's nuclear energy programme. In K Allen (ed.) *Paper wars: Access to information in South Africa.* Johannesburg: Wits University Press.

Fig, D (2010) *Nuclear energy rethink? The rise and demise of South Africa's pebble bed modular reactor.* Institute of Security Studies (ISS) Paper 210. Pretoria: ISS. http://www.issafrica.org (accessed 9 June 2016).

Gould, C (2009) The nuclear weapons history project. In K Allen (ed.) *Paper wars: Access to information in South Africa.* Johannesburg: Wits University Press.

Greenberg, M (2009) How much do people who live near major nuclear facilities worry about those facilities? Analysis of national and site-specific data. *Journal of Environmental Planning and Management,* 57 (7), 919–937.

Greenpeace (2011) *The true cost of nuclear power in South Africa.* http://www.greenpeace.org/africa/ global/africa/publications/the%20true%20cost%20of%20nuclear%20power%20in%20sa-screen. pdf (accessed 15 June 2016).

Grootboom, GA (2015) *Questions to the minister of transport.* 6 November. https://pmg.org.za/commit-tee-question/1590/ (accessed 20 June 2016).

Hambleton-Jones, BB (1984) *Summary of investigations carried out prior to 19 October 1984 regarding the location of the Vaalputs radioactive waste disposal site for the burial of intermediate and low-level waste.* Pretoria: Nuclear Development Corporation of South Africa (Pty) Limited (NUCOR). http://www.iaea.org/inis/collection/NCLCollectionStore/_Public/16/041/16041729.pdf?r=1 (accessed 15 June 2016).

Hart, G (2013) *Rethinking the South African crisis: Nationalism, populism, hegemony.* Pietermaritzburg: UKZN Press.

Kamiesberg Municipality (2015) *Reviewed integrated development plan 2015/6.* 26 May. http://nc.spisys. gov.za (accessed 9 June 2016).

Kirsch, S (2000) Peaceful nuclear explosions and the geography of scientific authority. *Professional Geographer*, 52 (2), 179–192.

Lidskog, R (2005) Siting conflicts – democratic perspectives and political implications. *Journal of Risk Research*, 8 (3), 187–206.

Masco, J (2006) *The nuclear borderlands. The Manhattan Project and post-Cold War New Mexico.* Princeton: Princeton University Press.

Namakwalandse Aksiegroep vir Omgewingsgeregtigheid (2007) *Letter to the chairperson of the Portfolio Committee on Environmental Affairs and Tourism Republic Hearings on Nuclear Energy in South Africa on 20 June 2007.* 14 June. http://pmg-assets.s3-website-eu-west-1.amazonaws.com/docs/2007/070620pienaar.htm (accessed 10 June 2016).

Namaqualand Stakeholders (2007) *Submission to the Portfolio Committee on Environmental Affairs and Tourism Public Hearings on Nuclear Energy in South Africa.* Parliament. 20 June. https://pmg.org.za/committee-meeting/9013/ (accessed 9 June 2016).

Necsa (Nuclear Energy Corporation of South Africa) (2011) *Notule van die Vaalputs PSIF.* 2 September. http://www.nnr.co.za/public-information/public-safety-information-forums/(accessed 10 June 2016).

Necsa (Nuclear Energy Corporation of South Africa) (2012) *Notule van die Vaalputs PSIF.* 31 October. http://www.nnr.co.za/public-information/public-safety-information-forums/ (accessed 10 June 2016).

Necsa (Nuclear Energy Corporation of South Africa) (2013) *Minutes of Vaalputs PSIF.* VLP-MIN-13/036. 10 September. http://www.nnr.co.za/public-information/public-safety-information-forums/ (accessed 10 June 2016).

Necsa (Nuclear Energy Corporation of South Africa) (2013b) *Minutes of Vaalputs PSIF.* VLP-MIN-13/050. 21 November. http://www.nnr.co.za/public-information/public-safety-information-forums/ (accessed 10 June 2016).

Necsa (Nuclear Energy Corporation of South Africa) (2013c) *Notule van die Vaalputs PSIF.* 28 February. http://www.nnr.co.za/public-information/public-safety-information-forums/ (accessed 10 June 2016).

NNR (National Nuclear Regulator) (2012) *The National Nuclear Regulator (NNR) suspends activities associated with the receipt of radioactive waste packages by the National Radioactive Waste Repository in the Northern Cape – Vaalputs.* Media release. LB/35/5/54/0/08. 19 April. http://www.nnr.co.za/wp-content/uploads/2012/05/NNR%20Suspends%20Radioactive%20Waste%20Repository%20-%20Vaalputs.pdf (accessed 13 June 2016).

NNR (National Nuclear Regulator) (2016) *Public safety information forums.* http://www.nnr.co.za/public-information/public-safety-information-forums/ (accessed 13 June 2016).

Pelindaba Working Group (2007) *Copy of oral submission presented to Environment and Tourism Portfolio Committee Public Hearings on Nuclear Energy.* 20 June. https://pmg.org.za/committee-meeting/9013/ (accessed 9 June 2016).

PMG (Parliamentary Monitoring Group) (2007) *Minutes of Environment and Tourism Portfolio Committee Public Hearings on Nuclear Energy.* 20 June. https://pmg.org.za/committee-meeting/9013/ (accessed 9 June 2016).

Shelley, L (2014) *Dirty entanglements: Corruption, crime, and terrorism.* Cambridge: Cambridge University Press.

Stats SA (Statistics South Africa) (2011) *Census 2011.* http://www.statssa.gov.za (accessed 15 June 2016).

Stats SA (Statistics South Africa) (2014) *Poverty trends in South Africa: An examination of absolute poverty between 2006 and 2011.* Report No. 03-10-06. http://www.statssa.gov.za/publications/Report-03-10-06/Report-03-10-06March2014.pdf (accessed 17 June 2016).

Stott, AK (2013) The current status of nuclear energy in South Africa. In *Presentation to the South African National Energy Association (SANEA)*. 19 June. http://www.sanea.org.za/CalendarOfEvents/2013/SANEALecturesCT/Jun19/TonyStott-Eskom.pdf (accessed 10 June 2016).

Times Live (2015) *Necsa given the boot*, 16 October. http://www.timeslive.co.za/thetimes/2015/10/16/Necsa-given-the-boot (accessed 20 June 2016).

TRC (Truth and Reconciliation Commission) (2002) *Final report. Volume 1–7*. http://www.justice.gov.za/trc/report/ (accessed 20 June 2016).

Von Wielligh, N and Von Wielligh-Steyn, L (2014) *Die bom: Suid-Afrika se kernwapenprogram*. Pretoria: Litera.

Contributors

Jacqui Ala is senior lecturer in International Relations at the University of the Witwatersrand, Johannesburg.

Stephanie Allais is the director of the Centre for Researching Education and Labour, University of the Witwatersrand, Johannesburg.

Doreen Atkinson is a research associate in Development Studies at the Nelson Mandela Metropolitan University, Port Elizabeth.

David Black is Lester B Pearson professor of International Development Studies in the Department of Political Science at Dalhousie University, Canada.

Sarah Bracking holds a Department of Science and Technology and National Research Foundation funded South Africa Research Chair Initiative (SARChI) in Applied Poverty Reduction Assessment at the University of KwaZulu-Natal, Durban.

Jacklyn Cock is an emeritus professor in Sociology at the University of the Witwatersrand, Johannesburg.

Daryl Glaser is an associate professor in Political Studies at the University of the Witwatersrand, Johannesburg.

Gilad Isaacs is a lecturer in the School of Economic and Business Sciences at the University of the Witwatersrand, Johannesburg.

Samuel Kariuki is an associate professor in Sociology at the University of the Witwatersrand, Johannesburg.

Neva Makgetla is a senior economist in Trade and Industrial Policy Strategies in the Presidency, Pretoria.

Rasigan Maharajh is professor extraordinary at the Centre for Research on Evaluation, Science and Technology at Stellenbosch University, and chief director of the Institute for Economic Research on Innovation at Tshwane University of Technology, Pretoria.

Enver Motala is a researcher at the Nelson Mandela Institute for Rural Education and Development at the University of Fort Hare, Alice.

Sonwabile Mnwana is a senior researcher at the Society, Work and Development Programme (SWOP) at the University of the Witwatersrand, Johannesburg.

Jana Mudronova is doing her PhD in Development Studies at the University of the Witwatersrand, Johannesburg.

David Neves is a senior researcher at the Institute for Poverty, Land and Agrarian Studies at the University of the Western Cape, Cape Town.

Samuel Oloruntoba is a senior lecturer in International Political Economy at the Thabo Mbeki Leadership Institute, University of South Africa, Pretoria.

Devan Pillay is an associate professor in Sociology at the University of the Witwatersrand, Johannesburg.

Roger Southall is an emeritus professor in Sociology at the University of the Witwatersrand, Johannesburg.

Salim Vally is an associate professor in Education at the University of Johannesburg and director of the Centre for Education Rights and Transformation.

Jo-Ansie van Wyk is a professor in International Politics at the University of South Africa, Pretoria.

Index

Printed and bound by CPI Group (UK) Ltd, Croydon, CR0 4YY

16/04/2025

14658447-0001